Teaching and Learning
Elementary Social Studies

Ninth Edition

Teaching and Learning Elementary Social Studies

Arthur K. Ellis

Seattle Pacific University

Boston • Columbus • Indianapolis • New York • San Francisco • Upper Saddle River
Amsterdam • Cape Town • Dubai • London • Madrid • Milan • Munich • Paris • Montreal • Toronto
Delhi • Mexico City • Sao Paulo • Sydney • Hong Kong • Seoul • Singapore • Taipei • Tokyo

Acquisitions Editor: Kelly Villella Canton
Series Editorial Assistant: Annalea Manalili
Vice President, Director of Marketing: Quinn Perkson
Senior Marketing Manager: Darcy Betts
Production Editor: Cynthia Parsons
Editorial Production Service: TexTech International
Manufacturing Buyer: Megan Cochran
Electronic Composition: TexTech International
Interior Design: TexTech International
Photo Researcher: Annie Pickert
Cover Designer: Elena Sidorova

Library of Congress Cataloging-in-Publication Data

Ellis, Arthur K.
  Teaching and learning elementary social studies / Arthur K. Ellis. —9th ed.
    p. cm.
  ISBN-13: 978-0-13-703949-4
  ISBN-10: 0-13-703949-2
  1. Social sciences—Study and teaching (Elementary).   I. Title.
  LB1584.E39 2010
  372.83'044—dc22

                                          2010001270

10 9 8 7 6 5 4 3 2 1

www.pearsonhighered.com

ISBN 10: 0-13-703949-2
ISBN 13: 978-0-13-703949-4

Brief Contents

Table of Contents

Chapter 3 *Social Studies and Diversity in America   50*

Chapter 4 *Setting and Achieving Social Studies Standards   68*

Chapter **5** *Three Ways to Center the Social
Studies Curriculum: The Learner,
Society, and Knowledge 100*

Chapter **6** *Planning for Social Studies Teaching
and Learning 118*

Chapter **7** *Successful Strategies for Social
Studies Teaching and Learning   150*

Chapter 8 *Assessing Social Studies Learning* 196

Chapter 9 *Inquiry, Discovery, and Problem Solving: Children as Researchers* 224

Chapter 10 *Social Studies and the Integrated Curriculum* 252

Chapter 11 *Exploring Our Geographic World* 274

Chapter 12 *Making History Come Alive* 314

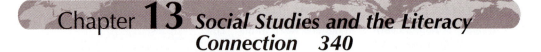

Chapter **13** *Social Studies and the Literacy Connection   340*

Chapter **14** *Epilogue: Keys to Where We've Been...   360*

Preface

Life nourishes.
Environment shapes.
Influences complete.
— Lao Tzu

Welcome to the ninth edition of *Teaching and Learning Elementary Social Studies.* This book is about children and how they learn, specifically how they learn to become citizens, scholars, and self-realized persons. The central themes of social studies are citizenship and civic responsibility, time and space, individuals and groups, culture and cultural diversity, how people make a living, and what it means to be human in its many manifestations. This book attempts to combine how children learn best with what they should be learning in the social studies curriculum.

Childhood is a time of wonder, of beginnings, and a time to be celebrated; the Japanese proverb teaches us that "it is like the springtime to be a child." Graham Greene noted in his book, *The Power and the Glory,* that "there is always one moment in childhood when the door opens and lets the future in." For some children, that moment comes earlier than for others, but when it happens, childhood is over; a person moves on to the next phase. I recall a conversation I had with a first-grader named Jon. He told me he had never heard of social studies but that he was interested in elves. Did I know where any elves lived? Yes, of course. What a reminder of the wonders and joy of childhood. I suppose in time he will grow up and stop believing in elves, but I hope not.

You and I have chosen careers that focus on childhood and childhood learning. It is an honorable thing. How fortunate we are! The children we teach represent at once the past, present, and future. They are the inheritors of our great and noble traditions. We accept them as they are and for who they are, and we cherish the deepest hopes for their happiness and fulfillment in an uncharted future. I will attempt to illustrate in the pages that follow ways to involve children in school and community life; projects and activities that are at once enjoyable and meaningful; good literature in the form of biographies, histories, and historical fiction; individual and collaborative learning; study of maps and globes; how people make their living; and what it means to be good citizens and lifelong learners.

This is a book about the nature of teaching and learning. I want this book to honor your dream of school life as a happy time, a time filled with joy and wonder. You are among the most fortunate of people: Your role is to help shape young lives. You prepare children for citizenship, self-realization, scholarship, and even eventually for their own careers. If this book serves its purpose, you will find it to be helpful in making your own learning environment one of inquiry, discovery, construction, collaboration, and civility. Children learn what they live; their experiences shape who they are and who they will become day by day. As John Dewey once noted, the *quality* of the experience is everything.

The contents of this book have changed somewhat over time, but the philosophy preserves the same simple idea I started out with some years ago, one that the Councils of the Iroquois Nation expressed far better than I could with my poor words: Children deserve the maximum amount of respect. I am convinced that the wisdom present in that thought represents the best place to begin. Children are capable, they want to learn, and they care about other people. You have to believe this to be a good teacher. And believing it, you begin to act on it. And where leadership is positive, harmony and endeavor will follow. We need to challenge children academically, nurture them emotionally, work with them socially, and watch in wonder as they grow in all three ways.

New to This Edition

Much like a gardener who cares about his or her flowers and trees, I've done some pruning, trimming parts of the previous edition of this book that I thought could be improved and cutting out portions that I thought had outlived their usefulness. Also, I've done some new planting in this edition. You'll find new material on the social studies standards and new attention to the knowledge base, that is, what children should know. The many additional lessons and activities that appear throughout this new edition are linked directly to the standards. You will find insights from the work of such theorists as Jerome Bruner, Jean Piaget, and Lev Vygotsky, much of it presaged by the contributions of John Dewey. Each has contributed much to constructivst thought and the emergence of the idea of children as constructors of knowledge.

Other areas of the social studies curriculum receiving new or improved attention in this edition include the idea of children as researchers, interdisciplinary teaching and learning, connections to literature, and citizenship education. Much that is new is included in the chapters on teaching/learning strategies, children as makers and readers of maps, and the continued quest for literacy, with new material on electronic literacy using the myriad sources of the Internet. And I've given major new focus to the important area of character education, moral development, and service learning. As always, I have attempted to invite the reader into the conversation through the use of questions, activities, and opportunities to reflect on ideas. I hope you will find the book to be both theoretical and practical in the spirit of the idea that good theories should yield good practice.

I assume full responsibility for any shortcomings, errors, or feats of omission found in these pages. The strengths of this book, such as they are, owe much to the contributions of my many friends and colleagues who are committed to excellence in childhood learning.

Let the wise listen and add to their learning.
—Proverbs

Introduction

As a book continues on through succeeding editions, it is a challenge to keep the best of what made the book successful while adding fresh material to give the reader new insights. This is so because any book is constrained by size. After all, I want you to be able to carry it!

I hope the philosophy of this text remains clear: This is a book about teaching and learning social studies *with* children, not *to* them. As John Dewey taught, classrooms improve when the teacher becomes a learner and the learners become teachers. To help you achieve this admirable goal, I've woven seven recurring themes into the chapters. They are as follows:

1. *Integration.* Just as a society is best when it is truly integrated, so are classrooms and schools. Integration begins with people. Subject matter will follow. Children come to school seeing a world connected. They are connected to their families, friends, and neighbors. Connection is meaningful; it is the opposite of alienation. As your classroom becomes integrated, it will make sense to integrate subject matter. Social studies (note the word *social*) is the single best connecting centerpiece of the curriculum. History, geography, economics, and the other social sciences are merely the beginning point. Music, art, drama, science, mathematics, language, and physical education are natural realms of connection and integration with social studies. The irony is that children are ahead of adults in sensing connections. They are your best allies in the quest.

2. *Citizenship.* Children need to experience democracy in a diverse society. School is the proving ground of that experience. Our nation is increasingly pluralistic. Our world is a fascinating place of similarities and differences to be discovered, understood, and appreciated. Young people need to learn, day by day, the rights and responsibilities of citizenship, civil behavior, and concern for others. Social studies offers splendid opportunities in tolerance, respect, awareness of self in the context of others, and all that it means to be a citizen of the classroom, school, community, nation, and the world beyond. Resolving conflicts, team building, making decisions, playing and working together, and creating community are fundamental aspects of civic education. Of all the subjects in the curriculum, only social studies focuses directly on democracy and citizenship.

3. *Inquiry and discovery.* Young people are curious by nature. They ask questions, they want to know how things work and why things are the way they are. Each day in the life of a child is a day of discovery. Children are on a quest to organize, adapt to, and

become part of the world around them. Good teachers understand the readiness of young learners to observe, record, classify, estimate, compare, and hypothesize. These are the tools of the explorer. This is how concepts, skills, and values develop in spiral-like fashion as students inquire at increasing depths of sophistication on their journey through school.

4. *Interest.* The Doctrine of Interest was first proposed in the first century by Roman educator Quintilian, who suggested that children should be encouraged to pursue their *interests* in learning. In the twentieth century, philosopher Alfred North Whitehead wrote in his essay, *Aims of Education,* "there can be no mental development without interest." Interest and passion for learning are the keys. But what if children express no interest in certain things you and I think are important for them to learn? I have attempted to show you that you can have it both ways. The noble goal of self-realization implies that children should learn what they want to learn, but you can lead them to *want* to learn matters of educational significance by *creating* interest. We know children prefer activity over passivity, involvement over boredom, friendship over isolation, and opportunity over coercion. This can be achieved, and my task is to work with you to make social studies special.

5. *Creative expression.* Emerging brain science research supports what insightful teachers have always known: Childhood is a time of great creativity. Elizabeth Lawrence wrote, "There is a garden in every childhood." We know that nature is at its creative best in gardens when flowers bloom, trees blossom, and the earth renews itself. Childhood is a time of artistry, philosophy, and big ideas. Children love to draw, sing, dance, play, and make things. In fact, children are our best teachers when it comes to seeing the relationship between constructivism and constructionism. This books supports creative expression through activities, lessons, and suggestions for creating a world of exploration based on multiple intelligences, varying styles, developmentally appropriate experiences, and practical hands-on learning.

6. *Reflection.* The English philosopher and scientist Francis Bacon wrote that *experience, mind, and meaning* are the road to deeper learning. Your students will have experiences in inquiry, creativity, collaboration, projects, and other activities. But experiences, no matter how enjoyable, are enhanced when we process them through the mind, thinking about them. This is how we reach meaning. The process is known as *reflection.* A reflective classroom is one where students are given voice, given time to think and talk and write and draw about what they are learning. You will find a number of reflective strategies imbedded in this book. They are practical, easy to use, and helpful as students take responsibility for their learning.

7. *Community.* The Greek word *paideia* is translated approximately as "learning from the culture." Your classroom is a place to begin, but building community means reaching out beyond the confines of classroom and school. The local community is readily available, and it is filled with rich resources including museums, libraries, parks, galleries, and interesting people of all ages. The world beyond is available through the Internet, film, newspapers, and other means of reaching out to a global society. Your classroom is your base, and the wonderful things that happen there are the launching pad for exploring the world beyond.

You teach children born in the twenty-first century. Many of them will live well into the twenty-second century. How do we best prepare them for life in an uncharted future? You will work with them on the front end of their life journey. You have the honor and privilege of being there at the beginning. The role you play is crucial in shaping their young lives. As you model the themes just set forth, you put things in motion. Your students look to you for guidance, and they are watching you as a model of behavior. Each act of kindness, civility, and support on your part reverberates through the present into the future. Your ability to inspire young learners to become citizens, scholars, and self-realized human beings will make so much difference. You really do have a wonderful job!

> *In all your teaching, show integrity.*
> —Paul the Apostle

About the Author

Arthur Ellis is Professor of Education and Director of the Center for Global Curriculum Studies at Seattle Pacific University. Before that, he was Professor of Education at the University of Minnesota. Dr. Ellis taught elementary and middle school in Oregon and Washington before completing his doctorate at the University of Oregon. He holds honorary doctorates from the University of the Russian Academy of Education and is a corresponding professor at three universities in Russia. He also works closely with the College of Education and the Department of Philosophy at Zhejiang University in China. Several of his books have been translated into Russian, Chinese, and Korean versions. One of his most recent publications was a study of service learning published by the Japanese Research Institute of Higher Education.

Teaching and Learning
Elementary Social Studies

Social Studies
Definitions and Rationale

 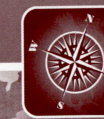  

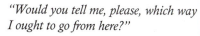

"Would you tell me, please, which way I ought to go from here?"

"That depends a good deal on where you want to get to," said the Cat.

"I don't much care where—," said Alice.

"Then it doesn't matter which way you go," said the Cat.

"—so long as I get somewhere," Alice added as an explanation.

"Oh, you're sure to do that," said the Cat, "if you only walk long enough."

—Lewis Carroll, *Alice's Adventures in Wonderland* (1865)

As we begin our journey, let's take a moment to look at the journeys of two characters from children's fiction: Alice in *Alice's Adventures in Wonderland* and Dorothy in *The Wonderful Wizard of Oz*. Each met a rather bizarre set of folks as she tried to find her way—Alice out of Wonderland and Dorothy to the Emerald City. Their experiences were different, to be sure. Poor Alice had no clear goal and kept asking for directions from highly unreliable characters. Dorothy knew where she was headed and had only to follow the Yellow Brick Road, but she had to avoid the obstacles put in her path to get there. Alice was in a state of perpetual uncertainty; Dorothy knew all along exactly what needed to be done.

We might say that Alice was working her way through a maze, while Dorothy had a map. Alexander Pope, an English writer and philosopher, once observed that learning should be a map, not a maze. A well-taught social studies curriculum is just that: a map that helps make sense of the human experience.

*S*ocial studies is the study of human beings. Specifically, social studies focuses on human activities in the past, present, and emerging future. It is the study of other people, places, and events across time and space. At the same time, it is direct life experience in what it means to be a citizen, a participant, and a self-realized individual. In other words, you don't just *learn* social studies as a school subject; you *take part* in it. In that sense, social studies demands of teachers and students a deeper level of knowledge. It demands knowledge lived, not just information studied.

The skills and ideas learned in social studies should be put to direct and practical use in the form of classroom and school governance, of realizing one's unique potential, of growing awareness of others and concern for their welfare, and for free and full participation in the group. Abraham Lincoln's well-chosen phrase "of the people, by the people, and for the people" goes to the very heart of an uplifting social studies experience. My task in this book is to facilitate your journey, not to give you easy answers but to challenge you and your students to rise to the occasion of making social studies eminently rewarding, enjoyable, and worthwhile.

Although the term *social studies* was coined in the second decade of the twentieth century, it was not until 1993 that a final version or official definition was ratified by the National Council for the Social Studies (NCSS). Of course, there was no hurry; but, on the other hand, it's nice to know what this area of the curriculum is officially all about. Just imagine: You may have gone through some of your school years studying an area of the school curriculum that had not been officially defined. Horrors! So, at long last, here it is:

> *Social studies* is the integrated study of the social sciences and humanities to promote civic competence. Within the school program, social studies provides coordinated, systematic study drawing upon such disciplines as anthropology, archaeology, economics, geography, history, law, philosophy, political science, psychology, religion, and sociology, as well as appropriate content from the humanities, mathematics, and natural sciences. The primary purpose of social studies is to help young people develop the ability to make informed and reasoned decisions for the public good as citizens of a culturally diverse, democratic society in an interdependent world.

Certain elements of this definition are particularly appealing. Notice the commitment to integrated studies. This makes good sense when the subject matter is people. Notice also the emphasis on civic duty, the public good, and the individual as decision maker, as well as the attention paid to democracy, cultural diversity, and interdependence. In my opinion, this is good and noble rhetoric. Any teacher who takes these ideas seriously will no doubt do worthwhile things with children. My only reservation with this definition, although perhaps it's implied, is the lack of a statement about the personal fulfillment of the individual. I firmly believe that social studies can do much to help a child along the road to self-realization, through the soaring vision found in biographies, the arts, and music; through the great mysteries unlocked for a child who discovers the world of maps, stories, and histories; and, most of all, in the wonderful realm of group activities, projects, and shared experience.

Nevertheless, the official definition of social studies represents a useful point of departure, a place from which to begin the journey. After all, it wouldn't be social studies in a democracy if we all agreed on every aspect of this wonderful area of the curriculum. But more and more, the curriculum is governed by standards set by associations such as the NCSS, state departments of education, and even the federal government through

Keys to an Exemplary Social Studies Program

An exemplary social studies program should involve social studies teachers and curriculum that engage students according to the following criteria:

The Teacher

- Demonstrates both scholarship and expertise in the curriculum
- Participates in all aspects of the development of the curriculum, including setting goals and objectives, implementation, evaluation, and revision
- Uses sound instructional theory and practice

The Curriculum

- Is guided by thoughtfully selected as well as clearly stated and defined goals and objectives
- Is based on sound scholarship from the content areas relative to the social studies
- Sets high expectations for students and uses a variety of systematic and valid measures to assess student performance
- Relates appropriately to the age, maturity, interests, and needs of the students for whom it is designed

- Incorporates effective instructional strategies and techniques that engage students directly and actively in the learning process both in and out of the classroom
- Provides valid evidence that the outcome of the program is consistent with the stated goals and objectives
- Is consistent with the 10 thematic strands identified by NCSS Curriculum Standards for Social Studies (see Figure 3.1 on page 54)

The Students

- Critically examine significant content, issues, and events from a variety of perspectives
- Participate actively in their school community and world
- Engage in focused systematic observations and comprehensive decisions
- Understand democratic principles and participate in the democratic process

Source: Adapted from criteria outlined by the National Council for the Social Studies Curriculum Awards, available at *www.ncss.org/awards/curriculum.html.*

laws such as the No Child Left Behind Act. Take a few moments to study the Keys to an Exemplary Social Studies Program, based on NCSS standards. We will spend the course of this book attempting to bring these ideas to life.

The Excitement and Wonder of the Quest

Please join me in an adventure. It will take us on a journey in celebration of childhood. There is a beautiful Japanese proverb that says it is like the springtime to be a child. I think it is also like the springtime to be a teacher. It is a joyous, spontaneous, nurturing calling. To see children grow in their sense of wonder and their love of learning, and to think that you can play a part makes teaching a privilege and a joy. Friedrich Froebel, a great educator who invented the kindergarten, understood this well. He called it that because he thought a school should be like a garden of children. It is a shining golden metaphor.

Our travels through this book take us into the land of social studies. There are other realms, to be sure, each one important. But for now, we will map and chart that subject in the curriculum that is devoted to the study of human beings. We both know why you decided to become a teacher. It is because you believe in the possible. It is because you genuinely like people. It is because you love to learn. These assets you possess serve you well. And what could be more interesting than to take children into the land of learning about others who have lived before us (history), who live in different parts of the world (geography), who make a living in different ways (economics), who look at the world differently (sociology and anthropology), and who want the best for society now and in the future (civics)?

I'd like to take just a few moments to think with you about what a privilege it is to teach social studies to young people. Your own experience in social studies, your memories, may be mixed. I say that because it happens to be so often the case. People talk about the drudgery of having to memorize names and dates and places. You can turn that around by following one simple idea: *Knowledge is action*. When you and your students engage in construction, drama, art, music, community involvement, service to others, and team building, a classroom is transformed. Among the most gratifying comments a teacher can hear are: Can we keep working on this? Do we have to put our stuff away now? Please, just a few more minutes.

The social studies textbook your students have is a tool, one of many. Don't let it take over the life space of the curriculum. The textbook provides a certain structure of scope and sequence, but please remember that it is one of many tools in your tool kit. To the extent that your classroom and the spaces and places beyond become places of active learning, you will have understood the wonder of childhood. The educational philosopher John Dewey wrote long ago that children have four natural instincts that they bring to school. They are:

1. *Young people love to talk.* Your classroom should be a place of conversation. Language and intellect co-develop. They support one another. As students work together on projects, they will talk about what they are doing. This is powerful learning.
2. *Young people love to construct.* Kids understood constructivism long before it became the rage in educational psychology. They learn by building things, by using their hands in connection with head and heart. Your classroom needs to become a construction zone.
3. *Young people love to inquire.* Children bring the gift of curiosity to school. Our task as teachers is to enhance, not dampen, that instinct. Social studies is about people. Learning about different people involves families, communities, food, clothing, shelter, traditions, habits, aspirations, and play.
4. *Young people love to express themselves.* Each child is an individual who is in the process of becoming who they are, a process of self-discovery, an adventure in life. One of the happiest tasks of a teacher is to get to know his or her students as individuals, to support their interests, their talents, and their dreams. Every child is talented if only we will recognize that.

The poet William Wordsworth, reflecting on childhood, wrote of the "glory and the freshness of a dream." The best teachers of children are those who are able to make dreams reality.

Finding Your Way

Please accept this invitation to join me in an adventure. I hope it will be one of discovery, wonder, curiosity, and excitement. As your guide, my task is to make our travels into the world of social studies worthwhile. Your time is valuable, so I thank you in advance for accompanying me. I have made a map of our travels to make it easier to find our way. The map is this book. A map is a tool, and a tool is only as good as the person who uses it. If you will think of this book as a resource that can enhance your own abilities, skills, and imagination, then I think our journey will be quite a success. Let's get started.

This adventure actually began with your decision to become a teacher. Our journey together through these chapters is one part of that larger voyage. I think I know why you chose teaching. My guess is that teaching chose you. You have a dream. You want to make a difference in children's lives. You like people. You like working and playing with others. I'm happy to have you as a companion.

Social studies is the study of people: It is where the dream comes true. Social studies is the story of human beings, past, present, and future. In social studies, we teach and learn with children the lessons derived from a study of the past. We teach and learn with them how to live in the present. And we prepare young people as best we can to live purposeful lives in the future. By working and playing together, we learn the strengths of diversity as well as the common bonds of our shared humanity that make us, finally, one.

In Chapter 1, we chart our course. It is sunrise on a golden morning as we journey forth. Are you ready? The Chinese proverb tells us "a journey of a thousand miles begins with a single step." Let's get started.

A Rationale for Social Studies Education

From time to time, someone will question the validity of social studies as an elementary school subject. Some critics would prefer to see social studies replaced with history, geography, and perhaps civics as separate subjects. At another extreme are those who feel that social studies ought to be combined with science and taught as environmental studies.

The first group argues that social studies is a watered-down form of several subjects brought together under the umbrella of "people-related" topics and that history and geography, in particular, suffer as a result. These critics point to the widespread historical and geographic illiteracy among today's students. The second group complains that it is unrealistic to expect elementary teachers (especially at the primary level) to have to prepare lessons in both social studies and science when there is so much reading, language, spelling, math, and so forth that must be covered. If social studies and science were combined, they argue, the teacher would have more time in the day and would probably do a better job of teaching the combined subject.

Both of these criticisms of social studies are reasonable, and they ought to be considered fairly. I agree with futurist Alvin Toffler's point that *every* subject in the school curriculum ought to be continually reexamined and not taken for granted. It is, there-fore, healthy to question the appropriateness of social studies or any other subject.

Some elementary school teachers teach social studies each day with great earnest-ness; and some teachers, feeling considerable pressure to produce results in other areas, say they work social studies in when and where they can. So it goes. Of course, social studies has been around as a school subject for some time (since about 1918), so it does have the force of tradition behind it. Therefore, the search for a rationale may lead teachers initially to say: Why wouldn't we have social studies? We've always had it! After all, social studies is largely an adapted, interdisciplinary form of two subjects, his-tory and geography, that have been considered important for centuries.

Our search for a rationale begins with the premise that a number of unique char-acteristics of social studies must be identified—things that only social studies can do for young learners. Social studies supports at least five critical areas of learning (see Figure 1.1), listed here in no particular order:

- *Citizenship: Social studies provides a forum for children to learn about and practice democ-racy.* From ancient Athens, to the English Magna Carta, to the councils of the Iroquois nation, to the Constitution of the United States, to Martin Luther King Jr.'s "I Have a Dream" speech, the idea of participatory government and freedom for the individual represents one of humankind's noblest achievements. Surprisingly few people in the

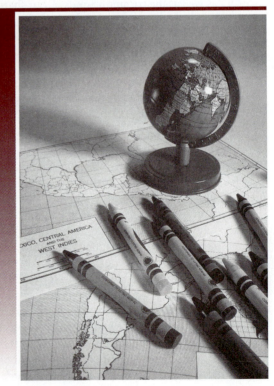

The goals of social studies encompass a wide range of knowledge, skills, and values.

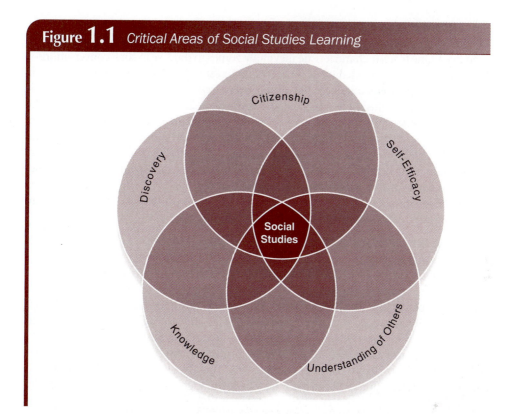

Figure 1.1 *Critical Areas of Social Studies Learning*

world today have the opportunity to live in democratic societies. This precious heritage of Americans is, as Thomas Jefferson said, "renewed with each succeeding generation." The rights and responsibilities of adults living in a democratic society include freedom of speech, worship, assembly, the press, and so on. You have the privilege—and mandate—to set those rights and responsibilities in motion through stories, activities, discussions, and projects with the children you teach.

• *Discovery: Social studies is designed to help children explain their world.* Jean Piaget wrote that the two most important tasks of childhood are organization and adaptation. By *organization,* he basically meant the ability to understand and classify things with respect to how they work. For example, a child's initial insights into the U.S. economic system or to the location of continents on the world map represent examples of organization. *Adaptation* refers to the process of accommodating oneself to one's environment. A child who enters school has already adapted considerably to the environment through speech, dress, rules at home, and so forth, but school is designed to expand such adaptation greatly through formal learning processes. These processes are intellectual, social, emotional, and physical. A good social studies program provides insights to one's history, culture, and landscape—in short, to the world and how it works. Jerome Bruner wrote that most of what happens appears as chaos to children because they don't understand how things work. An effective teacher replaces chaos with understanding.

- *Self-concept: Social studies can help children along the road to positive self-development.* People who reflect on their school days often speak about teachers who really affected their lives. One teacher characteristic inevitably comes to the fore in such conversations— something like: "She [He] showed a personal interest in me." The research literature in effective teaching frequently uses the term *pervasive caring* as an important characteristic of good teachers. Thus, both anecdote and research bear testimony to the teacher who cares. Because social studies is the area of the curriculum dedicated to the study of human beings, it lends itself quite naturally to the care and nurturing of the individual child. After all, you would not want to be accused of spending time teaching children about community helpers, economic systems, other cultures, and so on without first tending to the needs of the children in your own classroom. Unless the lives of the children you come in contact with daily are touched by you in a positive way, they will be hard pressed to learn anything meaningful about the lives of others.

- *Knowledge: Social studies should help children acquire a foundational understanding of history, geography, biography, and the social sciences.* It is difficult to say exactly how much knowledge of history or of the other disciplines children ought to acquire in their elementary school years. The sources of children's knowledge are several, and school alone will not account for their knowledge of the world. Indeed, teachers carry far too heavy a burden when they assume responsibility for *all* learning that children achieve. The best access to knowledge is found in listening and speaking, reading and writing, and observing and recording. You will need to give serious consideration to how you will build the knowledge base most effectively. But clearly, you are the one who is responsible for teaching children the basics of history, geography, and citizenship.

- *Understanding of others: Social studies ought to promote in children a genuine sense of the social fabric.* Children come to school from increasingly smaller families. The one-parent, one-child family is not uncommon. Opportunities for give and take within the family structure are lessened not only because there are fewer family members but also because people within a family spend less time interacting with each other in task-related activities (chores, etc.) than they used to. But the social needs and potential of human beings remain constant. The question is: What will you do to promote a sense of others in your classroom? From the day they enter school, children need to be supported and guided in their attempts to cooperate, share, and contribute. A sense of others includes respect for and tolerance of the child at the adjoining desk, an openness to alternative points of view, a willingness to take part in group efforts, and an expanding view of the community as not merely something the child is a part of but as something he or she can make better through participation in it. Cooperative learning ideas introduced over the past few decades offer virtually unlimited possibilities for you to develop the social fabric with your social studies program as its centerpiece.

Social Studies Curriculum Patterns

Let's come back to the idea of social studies as the study of human beings. First, social studies is the only curriculum subject with people as its subject matter. People are often considered in language arts and science, but in social studies, people remain the constant focus. Social studies deals directly with the basic needs of human beings: food, clothing, shelter, belonging, security, and dreams. Everyone, everywhere, throughout history has had these needs, but it takes a good teacher to help students understand and recognize these needs in themselves and in others. For a snapshot of a typical K–6 social studies curriculum, see Figure 1.2.

Social studies, like other subjects of the elementary school curriculum, is designed to be taught in increments, or in a developmental sequence. This means that instruction proceeds from the simple to the complex, from the familiar to the remote, from the known to the unknown. Thus, kindergarten and first-grade students spend much social studies time studying self-awareness and families because these two topics have a sense of relevance and immediacy to young children. In time, the horizons widen to neighborhoods, communities, cities, regions, the nation, and the Western and Eastern hemispheres. Such a progression from self to the world in the study of people is known as the *widening horizons* or *expanding environments curriculum*.

Integrated with the idea of widening horizons is a second thought. Called the *spiral curriculum,* it is designed to enhance such key factors as reinforcement of knowledge and ideas, concept and skill development, and transfer of learning. Thus, even though self-awareness and family studies are found in the early primary years, they are not abandoned as topics of later study. They are too important to set aside. Instead, the spiral curriculum calls for introducing concepts and skills at simple levels, to be pursued at deeper levels of sophistication each time they are revisited. Therefore, sixth-graders ought to be capable of conducting relatively sophisticated neighborhood studies if the concept of a neighborhood has been sequentially reinforced in a variety of settings over the years.

The other facet of the spiral curriculum that needs to be developed is the early introduction of topics that experts once thought were beyond young children. Through television, young children are aware of elections, space travel, unemployment, and global conflicts. It would be folly to ignore these national and global events; they can, at the very least, be treated impressionistically.

Thus, the widening horizons and spiral curricula work in concert. Let's take a look at each idea in greater detail.

Widening Horizons

The widening horizons philosophy states that the study of human beings should begin with examples from the local environment. Thus, first-graders might find themselves learning about the family and the neighborhood. Certainly, these are two aspects of humanity that are within the realm of the daily experience of young learners. Each day, they interact with family members. They walk or ride through neighborhoods on the way to school, and they play there during their free time. Thus, when thoughts about families and neighborhoods are presented in the classroom, students can relate them to their own life experiences.

After a study of the family and the neighborhood, students expand their horizons to the community, the city, the state, the region, the United States, and finally the wider world. Each new area of study is an outgrowth of those that preceded it. In moving from the close and familiar examples of people to those farther away and more remote in terms of experience, students are following what seems to be a logical progression.

Figure 1.2 *Outline of Social Studies Content*

Kindergarten

Tools for learning about the world:
maps, photos, globe

The *individual* and others

Living in a family

Going to school

Changes in seasons, animals,
people

Need for food, clothing, shelter

Need for rules

Different places to live

Grade 1

Tools for learning about the world:
maps and photos

The individual and the family

Needs of families:
Food
Clothes
Shelter

Families in neighborhoods

Living in the United States

Grade 2

Tools for learning about the world:
maps, photos, graphs

Setting for *communities:*
the earth, North America,
the United States

Large and small communities
made up of neighborhoods

Community services

Different kinds of work in
communities

Rules in communities

Communities long ago in our
country

Celebrating holidays in
communities

Grade 3

Tools for learning about the
world: maps, photos, graphs,
time lines, diagrams, tables

How to study a particular community

Representative communities in the
United States:
Cities, towns, and suburbs
Farms and ranches
Fishing communities

Need for rules

Communication

Grade 4

Tools for learning about the
world: maps, photos, time lines,
diagrams, tables

Forest regions in Washington state,
Hawaii, Puerto Rico, Russia,
Amazon Basins

Desert regions in southwestern
United States, Africa, Arabian
Peninsula

Plains regions in central and
coastal United States, China,
Kenya, Australia

Mountain regions in Colorado,
West Virginia, Switzerland

Interdependence of regions

Materials for learning about
one's own state

Grade 5

Tools for learning about the
world: maps, graphs, photos,
time lines, diagrams, tables

Ways of learning about the past

Chronological history of the
United States

An overview of the geography of
the United States

Geography of:
New England states
Middle Atlantic states
Southeast states
South Central states
North Central states
Mountain West states
Pacific states

History and geography of
Canada and Latin America

Grade 6

Tools for learning about the
world: maps, photos, graphs,
time lines, diagrams, tables

Beginnings of Western
Civilization:
Mesopotamia and Ancient
Egypt
Ancient Greece
Ancient Rome and the
Roman Empire

Geography and history of:
Western Europe
Eastern Europe and Russia
Middle East and North Africa
Africa south of the Sahara
South Asia, East Asia, and
Australia

Source: Adapted from *The World and Its People* (Glenview, IL: Silver Burdett).

Notice the relationship between the specific curriculum topics illustrated in Figure 1.2 and the widening horizons graphic shown in Figure 1.3.

Even though it remains essentially intact as the dominant curricular pattern for elementary social studies, the widening horizons approach has its detractors. In a simpler era, when travel and television were less influential for some and nonexistent for others, perhaps it was reasonable to expect children to learn more gradually about worldwide events. But much has changed since the widening horizons curriculum was proposed half a century ago. Further, not one shred of empirical evidence has ever been produced to substantiate its structure. Obviously, it is difficult for very young children to understand events that occur in remote corners of the globe or that occurred centuries ago. But we know that they are indeed interested in other peoples and other times and that there is much they can understand through stories, film, and play. The other side of this issue is that older children ought to study families and neighborhoods. Those are not exclusively topics for primary school children to study. If they were, sociologists, geographers, and historians wouldn't study them.

Spiral Curriculum

Perhaps the most intriguing new curricular approach to social studies is the spiral curriculum. The basic idea of the spiral curriculum is that within each discipline of the social sciences there exists a basic structure, composed of concepts and processes, that can be adapted for use in the teaching of elementary social studies. Proponents of this point of view suggest that the social sciences contain the fundamental ideas (concepts) and procedures (processes) a learner needs to become an independent problem solver.

The presentation of ideas from social science to young learners can be accomplished in a number of ways, including 50-minute lectures each day, but why would any teacher want to do that? The key to the spiral curriculum is to identify and teach real social science concepts in a developmentally appropriate way. Thus, children are recognized and respected as *young* learners who need active experience in order to build

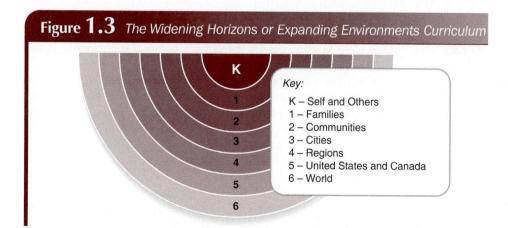

Figure 1.3 *The Widening Horizons or Expanding Environments Curriculum*

Key:
K – Self and Others
1 – Families
2 – Communities
3 – Cities
4 – Regions
5 – United States and Canada
6 – World

Two young geographers compare the Eastern and Western regions of the United States.

up their *schema,* or knowledge base, yet meaningful content is not sacrificed. Therefore, you can expect that I will keep reminding you of terms such as *experience, activities,* and *inquiry.* The concepts you will teach remain essentially the same from kindergarten to sixth grade. That is how the spiral works. Teachers and students keep revisiting the same important ideas at increasingly sophisticated levels over time. This makes it easier for a school faculty to work together to articulate the curriculum. Of course, the content is different each year, but the ideas or concepts are the same. Chapter 9 is important in this regard because it introduces and explains these key concepts.

Here is a brief example of how the spiral curriculum works (see Figure 1.4). Perhaps you wish to teach children the historical concept of the *oral tradition,* which is the handing down of life activities and patterns through the spoken word (stories, reminiscences, and so on). It is an important source of knowledge of the past, especially knowledge of everyday life patterns. A primary teacher might introduce the concept by asking children if they know stories about their parents' or grandparents' childhoods. The teacher then shares a family story or two that was told (and perhaps retold) to him or her, working a little geography into the story, showing where incidents took place (perhaps in another state). Later that day, as the children prepare to go home, the teacher hands out a letter for parents, which asks them to share a story from their childhood with their child. When the children

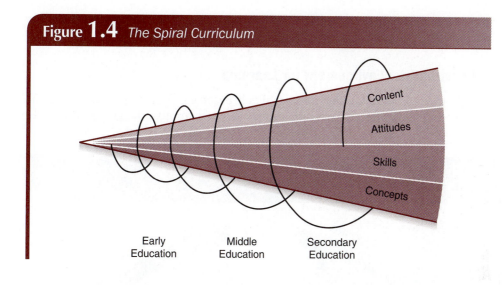

Figure 1.4 *The Spiral Curriculum*

Content

Attitudes

Skills

Concepts

Early
Education

Middle
Education

Secondary
Education

return to school, the teacher asks them to discuss and draw pictures about something from their parents' childhood stories. The teacher takes time to explain the idea of traditions, relating this experience to larger, shared traditions such as Thanksgiving, as well as stories about famous people from history. After the stories are collected and illustrated, the class prepares to compile them into a history book. The teacher introduces the rich oral traditions of certain Native American tribes and other groups that depended more on the spoken than the written word.

Now all of this is rather simple and introductory, which is exactly the right idea. This teacher has done a good job of setting the stage for the concept of the oral tradition to emerge. As students progress through the year and through the grades beyond, the concept is revisited time and again in different contexts. It is compared and contrasted with the written tradition and other ways of preserving the past. Students become historians who investigate and re-create the past through stories handed down. They write plays, put on pageants, listen to storytellers and guest speakers, read the work of other historians, and build the concept deeper and deeper. Philosopher Jean-Jacques Rousseau wrote more than two centuries ago, "Teachers, teach less, and teach it well." This is the essence of the spiral approach to the curriculum: to identify a few key concepts and to teach them well with depth.

The Environment for Social Studies Learning

For effective social studies learning to take place, the environment must be conducive to free and open inquiry. The chemistry or mix of basic ingredients is something that will be examined later, but for now, here is a brief look at several aspects of a supportive social studies learning environment: a constructivist environment for learning, productive and reflective thinking, and provisions for differences in learners. Many states provide guidelines or frameworks for what and how students should learn. See, for example, the California Framework in Figure 1.5.

A Constructivist Environment for Learning

Most teachers would agree that students should become increasingly self-sufficient and less dependent on direct supervision as they progress through the grades. Curiously,

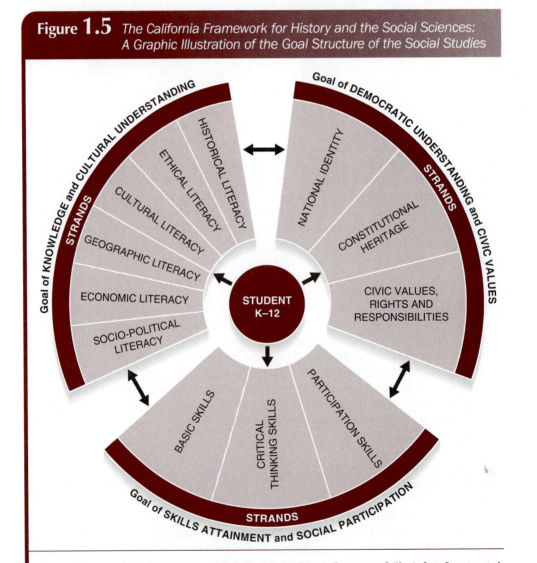

Figure 1.5 *The California Framework for History and the Social Sciences: A Graphic Illustration of the Goal Structure of the Social Studies*

Source: The History–Social Science Framework for California Public Schools (Sacramento: California State Department of Education, 1998, 2009).

however, it is not uncommon to find that precisely the opposite occurs. A certain type of teacher—the teacher whose presence dominates the classroom, who passes judgment on every pupil response, who always decides who will or will not be called on, who asks questions that have "right" and "wrong" answers, and who reduces the students' concept of learning to paper and pencil, read and recite, listen and give back—causes students to become directly dependent on her or him, not on their own latent powers.

Eventually, students construct their own knowledge. Teachers must make a conscious attempt to help students become confident in their own abilities by assuming less directive postures and by seeing themselves in the role of facilitators of learning, not dispensers of information. A teacher must be open to the students' views even when those views fail to coincide with the teacher's own. A teacher must ensure that students acquire the skills necessary to survive and prosper as inquirers.

The following goals are directed toward the creation of a constructivist environment:

- To recognize that human beings actively construct knowledge and that they should not be viewed merely as passive receivers
- To teach a research methodology that enables children to look for information to answer questions they have raised, and to use the conceptual framework developed in the course (e.g., to apply the concept of system to new areas)
- To help youngsters develop the ability to use firsthand sources—both the materials provided and the materials they gather in their communities—as evidence from which to develop hypotheses and draw conclusions
- To conduct classroom discussions in which youngsters learn to listen to others as well as to express their own views
- To legitimize the search—that is, to give sanction and support to open-ended discussions for which definitive answers to many questions are *not* found
- To encourage children to reflect on their own experiences
- To create a new role for the teacher, in which he or she becomes a resource rather than an answer giver
- To utilize people in the community as resources

A social studies classroom should be a challenging, exploratory environment. It should be a place of excitement and energy, of movement and collaboration. It should be physically, socially, and intellectually attractive to children. Ideally, a child walking by your classroom will feel a genuine desire to come in.

Asking *questions* is at the heart of the matter:

Can you sketch a map of your room at home?
How is *longitude* different from *latitude*?
Why do people around the world live in such different kinds of homes?
In what ways have you grown this year?
What does it mean to be a good citizen?
How is learning together different from learning alone?

"Butterfly and Flower" by six-year-old child.

What did you learn about history today?

Could you teach someone at home something you learned today?

What causes conflict between people?

How can our class use creative ways to teach the rest of the school about safety issues on the playground?

How much television do I watch? How else do I spend my time? How else could I spend my time?

Good questions lead to exploration, research, discovery, and activity. As the year progresses, you should see growth and development in your students' ability to ask and answer important questions. They need to learn the difference between a *memory question* (What is the capital of Argentina?) and an *exploratory question* (What do you think should be done to improve our environment?). Questions and problems ranging from the lowest to the highest levels of thinking are important—and the key is balance.

An active learning environment provides the greatest opportunities for reflective thinking by children. Children's play, construction, games, drawing, music, reading,

"Still Life with Flowers and Vase" by seven-year-old child.

writing, acting, and movement take on great meaning when the children are asked to reflect on them, to discuss purpose, learning, enjoyment, and growth. It is one thing to build a colonial village and quite another to reflect on people's lives then and now. But building the village is crucial because it gives a concrete, experiential point of reference for reflection.

Provisions for Learner Differences

Every teaching situation involving two or more students contains a number of learner differences; these may be intellectual, experiential, social, emotional, preferential, or developmental. To provide for these differences while presenting a cohesive program is one of the great challenges of teaching social studies—or any other subject, for that matter. Even if a teacher had diagnostic instruments available for determining which particular learning situation would suit which particular student(s) at which particular time, there would be no way to guarantee delivery of the many possible alternatives. The more reasonable course of action, given present possibilities, is to become acquainted with each student as a person with unique needs, interests, and learning styles rather than as a potential reservoir of information, and to provide for a variety of different learning styles.

For example, for a primary class studying the Japanese family, typical alternative activities might include viewing a film on family life in Japan, inviting a Japanese person to visit the classroom, preparing and eating food similar to that eaten by people in Japan, role-playing various roles in the Japanese family, putting together a photo-mural of life in Japan from magazine pictures, listening to the teacher read about various tasks performed in a Japanese household, writing letters to children in a Japanese school, and making charts on differences and similarities between our lives and those of the Japanese. Although this type of planning certainly does not provide for every type of individual difference, it does provide the variety necessary to ensure that a number of basic skills are developed while different interests are taken into account.

The Roles of the Teacher

As a school subject in the context of the school day, social studies is one of a number of subjects you teach. It therefore must compete for your energy and time on your schedule with reading, mathematics, science, and language. You are, of course, expected to teach all these subjects well.

Following are 12 roles of the social studies teacher. They span the range of expectations held for you as measures of competence. How competent are you? Your skills as a social studies teacher can hardly be viewed apart from your competencies as a teacher in general. But social studies is fundamental as a school subject because of its commitment to the fulfilled person, the informed citizen, and the contributing individual. To the extent that these ideals become reality for your students, they will improve their performance throughout the entire curriculum. Check yourself against these 12 roles as you reflect on your performance as a teacher of elementary social studies. Each role is explained in greater detail in various portions of this book.

   1. *Use a variety of teaching strategies.* Variety accomplishes at least two things. First, it makes learning more enjoyable because it resists the boredom of a set, highly predictable routine. Second, it increases your chances of reaching the wide range of learning styles found in every classroom. Think for a moment of the possibilities: small-group discussion, whole-class discussion, committee work, drama, construction, drawing, films, speakers, silent reading, problem solving, and so on.

   2. *Build bridges to other subjects.* Social studies is inherently interdisciplinary. It is possible to make logical and useful connections between social studies and almost any other subject. Cultural areas such as art and music, skill areas such as reading and math, and inquiry areas such as science are all natural subjects for integration with social studies. When you build these bridges, you achieve a natural reinforcement of subject matter, you make learning seem more real, and you present students with many opportunities to experience learning transfer.

   3. *Teach to the real world.* Applications ought to be built into every lesson. The best applications tie school learning into the real world. The subject matter of social studies is people, so you should be able to apply ideas about individuals and groups of any size to the real world of your students.

   4. *Emphasize hands-on experiences.* Most children of elementary age are in stages of intuitive and concrete learning. Such direct, active experiences as making things, investigating, and play can form the basis for learning more remote and abstract ideas.

A good teacher cares deeply about children's freedom, interests, belongingness, and dreams.

5. *Keep the focus on people.* Human beings are the subject matter of social studies. Sometimes those people live far away or existed long ago. Do not forget that you have a group of human beings in your classroom. Provide time for sharing, for cooperating, for expressing feelings, and for caring about each other. Research shows a steady decline in students' concepts of themselves as learners as they progress through the school years. Resolve to turn that around.

6. *Gather materials.* It's true that a good social studies teacher is a scrounge. You need to be on the alert for copies of used *National Geographic,* old maps, books, pictures, construction materials, games, and any other materials you can beg, borrow, or purchase reasonably. When your friends know it is for a worthy cause, they may be able to help.

7. *Encourage reflective thinking.* The value of experience increases to the extent that children reflect on it. They need to talk about, plan, assess, and thoughtfully consider the conceptual, moral, and social aspects of the time you and they spend together learning. Are the children learning ideas? Are the experiences purposeful and socially redeeming? Are lives being improved?

8. *Teach values.* Integrity, trust, cooperation, respect, and dignity can be modeled, talked about, and expected in your classroom. Do not shy away from these basic values. Instead, take every opportunity to explore them with your students.

9. *Give students freedom.* It is a curious fact that freedom is encouraged and expected in our Western societies, but we give little of it to the students in our schools. Where will they learn to use freedom in a responsible way? Give your students a certain amount of free time, perhaps on one day a week, just to see what they will do with it. If you have developed a rich environment and modeled learning well, they will use it productively.

10. *Create a sense of place.* If your students must spend six hours a day in your room, make it a challenging, attractive place to be. Do not overlook the value of displays, bulletin boards, interest centers, game tables, reading corners, and privacy areas. It does not take much to make a place magic for a young child.

11. *Promote success.* Many of your children will have an almost desperate need to experience success. Some will view themselves as largely unsuccessful. For a few children, you may need to scale down the amount and difficulty of the work. For others, you may have to intensify the complexity of the work. All people need to experience success or they tend to give up, become apathetic, and cease to learn.

12. *Reward excellence.* If you seriously consider these roles, you will have some amazing outcomes in social studies. Do not let the fine work of your students go unnoticed. Inform them of their progress. Let parents know how well their children are doing. Display your students' work in the hallway or media center. Promote a sense of public recognition and appreciation for excellence.

Summary

Social studies is the study of human beings. The purpose of social studies in the elementary school curriculum is to introduce children to the world of people. Your task as a teacher of social studies is to make this world come alive. You need to share with children the excitement and creativity that are generated by inquiry, projects, cooperative efforts, integration of the arts, and other imaginative strategies. It isn't easy. It takes much thought and energy to move away from a worksheet-centered, read-around-the-room, emotionless approach to this subject.

The challenge of this first chapter has been to open up to you the world of possibilities inherent in the social studies curriculum. Think of yourself as an explorer on the edge of a great adventure as you approach this complex, intriguing subject. As you catch a glimpse of the vision of what social studies can become in the hands of a caring teacher, you are on the threshold of limitless possibilities.

This introductory chapter makes the following points:

1. *Social studies is the study of human beings.* The purpose of social studies in elementary and middle schools is to introduce students to the excitement of learning about a world of different cultures and people over time and across space.

2. *Citizenship is a cornerstone of social studies teaching and learning.* The students you teach are citizens of their classroom, their community, their country, and our world. Citizenship should come alive in your classroom and school. You can make this happen.

3. *The social sciences are the foundation of social studies.* History, geography, economics, psychology, anthropology, sociology, and political science all contribute content, skills, and values to student learning.

4. *The social studies curriculum is a meaningful combination of the* widening horizons *approach and the* spiral curriculum. The *widening horizons* is the approach in which student learning proceeds from the here and now to the far away and long ago, and the *spiral curriculum* asks teachers to visit and revisit important concepts and themes at increasing levels of sophistication. The two curriculum patterns are integrated through activities, inquiry and discovery, constructivist learning, and collaboration.

5. *Social studies can, and ought to be, the centerpiece for integrating your curriculum*. Social studies naturally connects to literacy, numeracy, science, and the arts.

6. *The National Council for the Social Studies (NCSS) is the official professional organization in this area of the curriculum*. NCSS has established standards for K–12 teaching and learning.

Explorations

Reflect On . . .

1. Compare a recently published elementary social studies textbook with one at the same level that was published a few years ago. Make your own inferences about the changes that have taken place in the social studies curriculum. What might be some reasons for these changes?

2. Try to imagine a classroom where social studies was being taught really well. What would it look like? What would it feel like? How would you describe the teacher's behavior? In what kinds of activities and experiences would the students be involved?

In the Field

3. Talk to elementary school children about what they are doing in social studies. Try to piece together the scope and sequence of the social studies curriculum from their perspective. How much do you think these students understand about how their social studies program is organized? About its goals?

4. Interview an elementary school teacher who has taught for five or more years. Ask what changes have occurred in the curriculum. What does he or she see as the most important reasons for these changes?

For Your Portfolio

5. Review several new social studies programs. (You can do this online through publishers' catalogues.) Analyze the content of each program to see which one best suits your perspective. If you are currently teaching, see what it would take to get that program implemented in your classroom.

Continuing the Journey: Suggested Readings

Barton, K., & Levstik, L. (2005). *Doing History: Investigating with Children in Elementary and Middle Schools* (3rd ed.). Mahwah, NJ: Lawrence Erlbaum.

Bolen, J. (2000). "Taking Students Seriously." *Social Studies and the Young Learner, 11*(1), 6–8.

Good advice for relating to students in meaningful ways. The journal itself is an essential resource for the elementary social studies teacher.

Boyd, C. D., & Berkin, C. (2005). *Social Studies Plus! A Hands-on Approach*. Columbus, OH: Scott Foresman.

Burstein, J. (2009). "Do as I Say *and* Do: Using the Professor-in-Residence Model for Teaching Social Studies Methods." *The Social Studies, 100*(3), 121–127.

An article that explores modeling by a methods professor who teaches preservice teachers in an actual Classroom (sixth-grade) setting.

Duncan, J., & Lockwood, M. (2008). *Learning Through Play*. New York: Continuum.

Levstik, L., & Tyson, C. (Eds.). (2008). *Handbook of Research in Social Studies Education*. New York: Routledge.

Libresco, A. (2008). "Teachers Who Shaped Our Lives." *Social Studies and the Young Learner, 21*(1), 8–10.

Inspiring article about what really matters in teaching students.

Marzano, R., & Brown, J. (2009). *Handbook for the Art and Science of Teaching.* Washington, DC: ASCD.

Very helpful guide to research-based teaching and learning. A must for your professional library.

National Council for the Social Studies. (2002). *National Standards for Social Studies Teachers.* Silver Spring, MD: Author.

National Task Force for Social Studies. (2008). *Expectations of Excellence: Curriculum Standards for Social Studies* [Draft]. Waldorf, MD: National Council for the Social Studies.

Ponder, S., & Lewis-Ferrell, G. (2009). "The Butterfly Effect of Citizenship Education." *The Social Studies,* 100 (3), 129–135.

Good focus on growth and development as well as outcomes for an important social studies concept, that of citizenship education. Article uses stages of butterfly as metaphor.

www.creativeteachingsite.com (n.d.). *Website offers many useful ideas for involving students actively and meaningfully.*

www.internet4classrooms.com/social.htm (n.d.). *Website provides activities and links to a wealth of social studies ideas for elementary and middle school. Ret. aug 2009*

Wiggins, G., & McTighe, J. (2007). *Schooling by Design.* Alexandria, VA: Association for Supervision and Curriculum Development.

Websites

U.S. Department of Education. *Federal Resources for Educational Excellence.* (August, 2009). *www.free.ed. gov/index.cfm*

National Council for the Social Studies. *www. socialstudies.org/* (August, 2009).

The National Board for Professional Teaching Standards Improves Teaching and Student Learning. *www.nbpts.org/* (August, 2009).

"Concept to Classroom is an online series of FREE, award-winning professional development work-shops covering important and timely topics in education. The workshops are intended for teachers, administrators, librarians, or anyone interested in education—and there's no technical expertise required. They are self-paced, so you can explore them on your own time and go back as often as you like; you can take all of the workshops, or just one" *www.thirteen.org/edonline/*

Related NCSS Standards and Principles of Powerful Social Studies

Curriculum Standards

Definition of social studies according to NCSS:

"The National Council for the Social Studies, the largest professional association for social studies educators in the world, defines social studies as:
  "the integrated study of the social sciences and humanities to promote civic competence.

Within the school program, social studies provides coordinated, systematic study drawing upon such disciplines as anthropology, archaeology, economics, geography, history, law, philosophy, political science, psychology, religion, and sociology, as well as appropriate content from the humanities, mathematics, and natural sciences. The primary purpose of social studies is to help young people make informed and reasoned decisions for the public good as citizens of a culturally diverse, democratic society in an interdependent world" (p. 6).

Purpose of social studies according to NCSS:

"The purpose of social studies is the promotion of civic competence—the knowledge, intellectual processes, and dispositions required of students to be active and engaged participants in groups and public life. Although civic competence is not the only responsibility of social studies nor is it exclusive to the field, it is more central to social studies than any other subject area in the schools. By making civic competence a central aim, NCSS long has recognized the importance of educating students who are committed to the ideas and values of democracy. Civic competence requires the ability to use knowledge about one's community, nation, and world, apply inquiry processes, and employ skills of data collection and analysis, collaboration, decision-making, and problem-solving. Young people who are knowledgeable, skillful, and committed to democracy are necessary to sustaining and improving our democratic way of life, and participating as members of a global community.

"The civic mission of social studies demands the inclusion of all students addressing cultural, linguistic and learning diversity including differences based on race, ethnicity, language, religion, gender, sexual orientation, exceptional learning needs, and other educationally and personally significant characteristics of learners. Diversity among learners embodies the democratic goal of embracing pluralism to make social studies classrooms laboratories of democracy.

"In democratic classrooms and nations, understanding civic issues—such as health care, immigration, and foreign policy—involves several disciplines. How social studies marshals the disciplines to this civic task takes various forms. It can be taught in one class, often designated "social studies," that integrates two or more disciplines. On the other hand, it can be taught as

separate discipline-based classes (e.g., history, geography). These standards are intended to be useful whatever the organization or instructional approach (for example a problem-solving approach, an approach centered on controversial issues, a discipline based approach, or some combination of approaches). These decisions are best made at the local level. To this end, the standards provide a framework for effective social studies within various curricular perspectives" (pp. 6–7).

Organization of curriculum according to NCSS Themes:

"The Ten Themes are organizing strands for the social studies program. The ten themes are:

   I. Culture
  II. Time, Continuity, and Change
 III. People, Places, and Environments
  IV. Individual Development and Identity
   V. Individuals, Groups, and Institutions
  VI. Power, Authority, and Governance
 VII. Production, Distribution, and Consumption
VIII. Science, Technology, and Society
  IX. Global Connections
   X. Civic Ideals and Practices

"The themes represent strands that should thread through a social studies program, pre K through grade 12 as appropriate at each level. While at some grades and courses, some themes will be more dominant than others, all themes are highly interrelated. To understand culture, for example, students need to understand time, continuity, and change; the relationship among people, places, and environments; and civic ideals and practices. To understand power, authority, and governance, students need to understand the relationship among culture; people, places, and environments; and individuals, groups, and institutions. As an illustration, history is not confined to Theme II. Similarly, geography draws from more than Theme III.

"The thematic strands draw from all of the social science disciplines and other related disciplines and fields of study to provide a framework for social studies curriculum design. The themes provide a basis from which social studies educators will more fully develop their program by consulting detailed content in the standards developed for history, geography, civics, economics, psychology, and other fields. Thus, the NCSS social studies curriculum standards serve as the organizing basis for the social studies program and content and other standards provide additional detail for the curriculum design" (p. 8).

Source: National Task Force for Social Studies. (2008). *Expectations of Excellence: Curriculum Standards for Social Studies* [Draft]. Silver Spring, MD: National Council for the Social Studies. The Council's website is www.socialstudies.org

Teacher Standards

"The pedagogical standards itemized below focus on teacher knowledge, competence, and dispositions beyond the subject matter that is the focus of the Subject Matter Standards. They are intended to assure that social studies teachers possess the general pedagogical knowledge, capabilities, and dispositions needed to create the kinds of learning experiences and classroom and school environments that are envisioned by recent reform movements and validated by research. As such, these standards favor learner-centered, meaningful, integrative, value-based, challenging, and active instruction. They see teachers as instructional decision-makers, members of school-based learning communities, and members of the larger community of stakeholders who can help support the learning of students" (pp. 51–52).

"1. Learning and Development

Social studies teachers should possess the knowledge, capabilities, and dispositions to provide learning opportunities at the appropriate school levels that support learners☐ intellectual, social, and personal development.

"2. Differences in Learning Styles

Social studies teachers should possess the knowledge, capabilities, and dispositions to create at the appropriate school levels learning experiences that fit the different approaches to learning of diverse learners.

"3. Critical Thinking, Problem Solving, and Performance Skills

Social studies teachers should possess the knowledge, capabilities, and dispositions to use at the appropriate school levels a variety of instructional strategies to encourage student development of critical thinking, problem solving, and performance skills.

"4. Active Learning and Motivation

Social studies teachers should possess the knowledge, capabilities, and dispositions to create at the appropriate school levels learning environments that encourage social interaction, active engagement in learning, and self-motivation.

"5. Inquiry, Collaboration, and Supportive Classroom Interaction

Social studies teachers should possess the knowledge, capabilities, and dispositions to use at the appropriate school levels verbal, nonverbal, and media communication techniques that foster active inquiry, collaboration, and supportive interaction in the classroom.

"6. Planning Instruction

Social studies teachers should possess the knowledge, capabilities, and dispositions to plan instruction for the appropriate school levels based on understanding of subject matter, students, the community, and curriculum goals.

"7. Assessment

Social studies teachers should possess the knowledge, capabilities, and dispositions to use formal and informal assessment strategies at the appropriate school

levels to evaluate and ensure the continuous intellectual, social, and physical development of learners. They should be able to assess student learning using various assessment formats, including performance assessment, fixed response, open-ended questioning, and portfolio strategies.

"8. Reflection and Professional Growth

Social studies teachers should possess the knowledge, capabilities, and dispositions to develop as reflective practitioners and continuous learners.

"9. Professional Leadership

Social studies teachers should possess the knowledge, capabilities, and dispositions to foster cross-subject matter collaboration and other positive relationships with school colleagues, and positive associations with parents and others in the larger community to support student learning and well-being."

Source: National Council for the Social Studies. (2002). *National Standards for Social Studies Teachers.* Silver Spring, MD: Author. The Council's website is www.socialstudies.org

Chapter 2

Children in a Democracy

Teaching and Learning Responsible Citizenship

Keys to This Chapter

- What is the Citizen's Role in American Democracy?
- Active Citizenship
- Service Learning as Citizenship
- The Meaning of Citizenship: A Global Perspective

"No one is born a good citizen; no nation is born a democracy. Rather, both are processes that continue to evolve over a lifetime. Young people must be included from birth. A society that cuts off from its youth severs its lifeline."

—Kofi Annan,
    Nobel Peace Prize Recipient and
    Seventh Secretary-General
    of the United Nations.

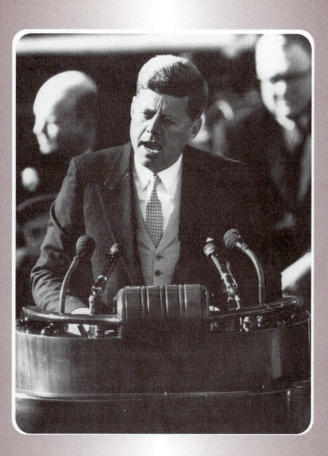

In his inaugural address, President John F. Kennedy said that "the torch has been passed to a new generation, born in this century. . . ." President Kennedy's reference was to a new generation of citizens, born in the twentieth century. Our challenge is to pass the torch of excellence to yet another new generation of citizens, born in the twenty-first century.

This lovely metaphor, the passing of the torch, hearkens back to the Olympic games of ancient Greece when each runner would pass the Olympic flame on to another until finally it reached the stadium where the games were held. The tradition continues to this day. It is worth noting that Athens was the site of the world's first democracy. Citizenship is an idea born in ancient Greece.

If we are going to help children learn to be citizens, we would do well to begin with a definition of the term itself. To be a citizen is to hold a position of rights and responsibilities in society. In a democratic society such as ours, citizens are the rulers. The government belongs to the people. In his famous

Gettysburg Address, Abraham Lincoln spoke of a government "of the people, by the people, for the people." This beautiful phrase defines the role of the citizen in lyric poetry.

Let's miniaturize this idea of citizenship for a moment. Of course, we know that citizens of the United States exercise their rights and responsibilities on a large scale given the size of our country. But if we think of your classroom as a miniature of society, we can make the idea of citizenship a developmentally appropriate experience. If you think of yourself and your students as citizens of your classroom and school, then you have made a good beginning.

Keep in mind the old saying that children learn what they live. They are shaped by their experiences. So, to teach and learn citizenship with children, we must create a democratic society for them to live in. I know some teachers have had success in treating the kids in their room as citizens rather than as students. It may sound like a mere name change, but it can bring about a powerful shift in perception of everyone's role.

The quantum leap involved in making a classroom a miniature democracy is in fact quite a jump. The children you work with will be expected to be self-governing. This means major responsibilities for each child. This means major rights for each child. This means the creation of an atmosphere of cooperation, civility, and discipline. This means team building, working and playing together, an atmosphere of support for each other, and a commitment to individual and collective interests.

The class meetings, the shared decision making, the team work and projects, the informal discussions, and the civil society that you create in your classroom will be the foundation. As students become citizens of the classroom, you will set the stage for the next step, that is, learning the history and traditions of citizenship. This is the academic knowledge that you and your "fellow citizens" will apply as your classroom becomes a civil society. School and community service projects will follow as students begin to understand that citizenship involves reaching out to others, participating in the public square, and respecting the rights of their fellow human beings.

When John Dewey wrote that knowledge comes to life in activity, he literally was saying that textbook information without application and testing in the crucible of experience is dead knowledge. In the sense of his quote, your classroom becomes an experiment in democracy! You and your students are testing each day the ideas of rights and responsibilities, freedom and duty, and civility and collaboration.

Effective citizenship education has been a major concern of educators in the United States throughout our nation's history. Much of what occurs in schools each day, including the teaching of the three R's, can be interpreted as preparation of our citizens. President James Madison underscored the importance of citizenship education when he stated, "A people who mean to be their own governors must arm themselves with the power which knowledge gives." And the philosopher scientist Herbert Spencer restated so well the importance of citizenship education when he wrote "the need to function as effective citizens calls for familiar school subjects: history, civics, economics, and politics. *These subjects should stress practical application.*" (italics added)

What Is the Citizen's Role in American Democracy?

It is always useful to approach teaching and learning as problem solving. Don't worry if you can't answer the question just posed now or if you and your students can't solve it completely, even in a year's time. It takes a lifetime of learning to be a good citizen. Your job is to get children started in the right direction.

Figure 2.1 identifies the roles of a citizen according to the *National Standards for Teaching Citizenship and Civics,* developed by the Center for Civic Education. Note the spiraling effect of a single important question throughout the K–12 curriculum. The question remains the same throughout the entire school experience, but the response deepens with each grade level. The contexts change. The experiences take on greater sophistication as students move from elementary to middle to senior high school.

Young children learn about individual responsibility by helping to make classroom rules and learning to follow them. They also learn that people must take responsibility for their actions. These early experiences serve as the foundation for increasingly sophisticated experiences throughout the succeeding school years.

Citizenship Is Participating in Society

At its best, a school is a community of learners. This implies that the children and teachers, administrators, and support staff who go there will find themselves in a communal setting. A true community is a relational place where people work together, play together, and share their thoughts, feelings, and dreams. School is a socially contrived environment. This means that society has determined that academic learning should take place in social settings.

The term *public school* originally meant that students learned in each other's company rather than privately from a tutor. In the first century A.D., Roman orator Quintilian advocated public schools over private instruction because, he argued, in public settings, children have the benefit of friendships, examples, and associations. In other words, Quintilian felt that the school environment would make children better Roman citizens. Like Plato before him, Quintilian thought that group play was especially productive for children. Games, activities, and free play put children in situations in which moral issues, differences of opinion, camaraderie, sharing, and give-and-take inevitably arise.

In more recent times, such theorists as Jean Piaget and Lev Vygotsky have addressed the idea of *social knowledge*. Social knowledge arises from shared group experience. When children and teachers play and work together on projects, activities, and other aspects of school life, they become bonded through their commonly held knowledge and collective memory. This leads to a sense of community, a sense of belonging—the beginning of citizenship. Just how this happens is captured by Don Rowe (1992), who writes:

> Schools are highly complex communities [with] value systems linked to their purpose and role, power structures, and rules enforced by a justice system. The "citizens" (or "subjects") of school communities can exhibit widely differing degrees of loyalty to the

Figure 2.1 *Standards for Teaching Citizenship and Civics: The Roles of the Citizen*

K–4	5–8	9–12
What Are the Roles of the Citizen in American Democracy?	**What Are the Roles of the Citizen in American Democracy?**	**What Are the Roles of the Citizen in American Democracy?**
The meaning of citizenship	The meaning of citizenship	The meaning of citizenship in the United States
Becoming a citizen	Becoming a citizen	Becoming a citizen
Rights of individuals	Personal rights	Personal rights
Responsibilities of individuals	Political rights	Political rights
Dispositions that enhance citizen effectiveness and promote the healthy functioning of American democracy	Economic rights	Economic rights
Forms of participation	Scope and limits of rights	Relationships among personal, political, and economic rights
Political leadership and public service	Personal responsibilities	Scope and limits of rights
Selecting leaders	Civic responsibilities	Personal responsibilities
	Dispositions that enhance citizen effectiveness and promote the healthy functioning of American constitutional democracy	Civic responsibilities
	Participation in civic and political life and the attainment of individual and public goals	Dispositions that lead the citizen to be an independent member of society
	The difference between political and social participation	Dispositions that foster respect for individual worth and human dignity
	Forms of political participation	Dispositions that incline the citizen to public affairs
	Political leadership and public service	Dispositions that facilitate thoughtful and effective participation in public affairs
	Knowledge and participation	The relationship between politics and the attainment of individual and public goals
		The difference between political and social participation
		Forms of political participation
		Political leadership and careers in public service
		Knowledge and participation

Source: Adapted from *National Standard for Civics and Government* (Calabasas, CA: Center for Civic Education, 1997, 2008).

Two young Americans display their "good citizenship" awards.

community. Pupils who feel disregarded by a school (or at odds with its aims) will have little reason to feel a sense of obligation to uphold its values or rules (p. 160).

The power of the school's social system to make a child feel part of things (or alienated) is enormous. Therefore, the social studies teacher's role is crucial. You must take seriously the social aspects of the school curriculum. How a child feels about being included or excluded will go a long way toward determining his or her lifelong view of the value of participating in society.

Oh, the responsibilities of an elementary teacher are never ending! But it's worth it, because you have the opportunity to do such important work. Just imagine: Your job is about improving people's lives. What could be more significant?

Citizenship Is Serving the Community

To be a citizen means many things. We are citizens of the world, citizens of our country, citizens of our state or province, citizens of our school and classroom, and citizens of our family. One of the arenas of citizenship that children need to experience is citizenship in the local community. The community affords opportunities for participation at many levels; children can be helpful citizens by picking up litter, planting trees, helping elderly people, and undertaking service-learning projects.

One group of primary school children studied a crosswalk near their school with the idea of making it safer. Their work was very important because it probably prevented injuries or loss of life. A class of middle school children were successful in having chlorofluorocarbon-containing styrofoam cups removed from the school district's purchasing list. A third-grade class studied their school's playground equipment and were successful in having dangerous equipment replaced. An intermediate-level class decided to "adopt" a retirement home near their school; they were successful in making ties and friendships between themselves and the elderly. As Martin Luther King Jr. once said, "Everyone can be great, because everyone can serve."

> **Figure 2.2** *Practical Ways to Teach and Learn Citizenship with Children*
>
> *Involve your students with the establishment of classroom rules.* Keep the rules simple and few. Make sure that the class thoroughly discusses the rules and that they are "published" for all to see.
>
> *Create a number of classroom jobs that need to be performed.* Give everyone numerous chances to serve over the course of the year. Remember that Martin Luther King Jr. once observed that everyone can be great because everyone can serve.
>
> *Hold regular classroom elections to positions of responsibility.* Discuss the significance of roles of president, vice president, secretary, and so on with the students.
>
> *Hold regular classroom meetings to discuss issues, problems, and opportunities that arise at school.* Give the students as much responsibility as possible for conducting the meetings.
>
> *Create, with your students' input, service opportunities that are schoolwide.* Give your students opportunities to help make the school a better place.
>
> *Create service opportunities in the community.* Service learning is a wonderful way to grow as a participating citizen. Service learning can include a wide range of possibilities such as cleaning up around the school or working with a nearby retirement home.
>
> *Invite people from the community to visit your classroom,* including civic officials, fire, police, and government workers, volunteers who have made a difference, and other role models.
>
> *Take time to discuss the meaning of important documents and symbols* with the class, for example, the words to the flag salute; the meaning of the U.S. motto, *e pluribus unum;* the words to the "Star Spangled Banner"; and the symbolism of the U.S. and state flags.
>
> *Involve the press.* Ask reporters from local newspapers and radio and television stations to visit your class. They can speak to the responsibility of the press in a free society.

WHAT ARE THE KEY CONCEPTS OF CITIZENSHIP EDUCATION?   There are many key concepts relating to effective citizenship education. The following are only a few: patriotism, government, participation, caring, rights and responsibilities, and rules and laws. (Figure 2.4 illustrates the relationships between a citizen's rights and responsibilities.)

Active Citizenship

Americans live in the world's oldest constitutional democracy. The U.S. Constitution was drafted and ratified in the period from 1787–1789, well before far older European nations began their march toward democracy and citizenship. And today, more than two centuries later, the Declaration of Independence and the American Revolution still serve as reminders that free institutions and individual freedoms are precious achievements. The road to freedom has not always been an easy one for many Americans. In 1863, black Americans were finally set free from the tyranny of slavery, and in 1918, women were at long last allowed to vote.

Believe me, teaching citizenship education to young children is one of the most important contributions you can make as a teacher. The children you teach will assume positions of leadership and responsibility well into the twenty-first century. More and more of them will have been born in this century, which means they will set the course

Figure 2.3   *A Child's Essay on Citizenship*

What is a good citizen?
I think a good citizen is a person who does what he or she is asked to do and obeys the rules. Another thing a good citizen does is when he or she is nice to one another and helps someone out if somebody is hurt or needs help with schoolwork. That's what I think a good citizen is.

Lauren Griffin
Mr. Johnson's class Grade 5

Figure 2.4   *Citizen's Rights and Responsibilities*

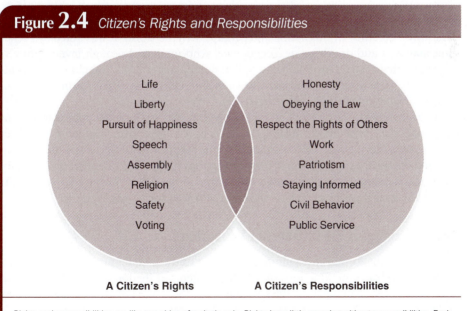

A Citizen's Rights	A Citizen's Responsibilities
Life	Honesty
Liberty	Obeying the Law
Pursuit of Happiness	Respect the Rights of Others
Speech	Work
Assembly	Patriotism
Religion	Staying Informed
Safety	Civil Behavior
Voting	Public Service

Rights and responsibilities are like two sides of a single coin. Rights have little meaning without responsibilities. Each gives meaning to the other.

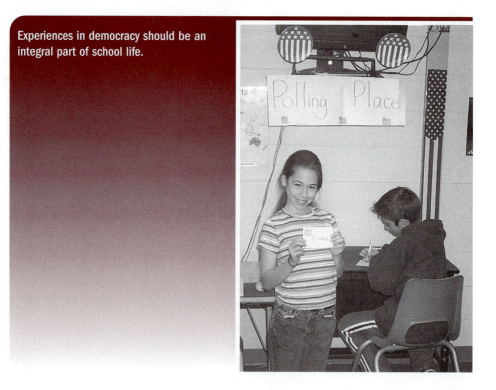

Experiences in democracy should be an integral part of school life.

for the twenty-second century. The trust and responsibility placed in your hands is one of destiny—certainly of this nation and perhaps even the world. It was noted by French statesman and author Alexis de Tocqueville, who made a thorough investigation of American life in the nineteenth century, that democracy is not a "machine that would go of itself." It is your task and mine to keep democracy alive by inspiring the young toward meaningful participatory citizenship.

Citizenship education at its best takes place at two separate but related levels that we can call the *formal* and the *informal*. Each is necessary, and each supports the other. *Formal citizenship education* involves the academic study of history, civics, literature, the arts, and other subjects. *Informal citizenship education* is experiential, often involving the life of the classroom, the playground, the community, and the home. The high art of teaching weaves the formal and the informal into a seamless whole.

Formal Strategies for Citizenship Education

As just noted, the formal curriculum involves the study of civics and government. Students need to learn the functions of political systems at the local, state, and national levels. They need to understand the relationship of the United States to other countries, many of which have quite different systems of governance.

Following is a sampling of specific strategies that can be used at the elementary level, each of which takes into account developmentally appropriate practice:

- Students should learn that in most cases, elections decide who will govern. They should know the basic responsibilities of their mayor and city council, their governor and state legislature, and their president and Congress. Every city and town has a charter; obtain a copy for your class to study.
- Students should learn that certain officials are appointed to office. This includes many officials who serve in the judicial branch of government, including the U.S. Supreme Court. A letter written by your class to a member of the judiciary is sure to bring a response.
- Students should become acquainted with the meanings of such documents of liberty as the Magna Carta, the Declaration of Independence, and the Constitution. Many children have never even been taught the meaning of the flag salute, even though they may go through the ritual daily.
- Students need to understand the rights and duties of citizens in a democracy. Reviewing the Bill of Rights is a good place to start. Your class can author its own Bill of Rights and Responsibilities.
- Share the newspaper with your students. Every day, it contains articles about local, state, and national government; international affairs; and other issues of moral, social, and political significance.
- Students need to become familiar with the lives and contributions of outstanding citizens. No child should leave elementary school without formal knowledge of the work of Martin Luther King Jr., George Washington, Abraham Lincoln, and others who sacrificed much to make all Americans' lives better.

Informal Strategies for Citizenship Education

Formal citizenship education initiates the process by exposing children to ideas, but ideas take hold best when they are related to direct experience. That's the role of informal teaching and learning, and it's especially crucial at the elementary level. Experience is the key. As stated throughout this book, children learn what they live.

Here are some sample informal strategies:

- *Create opportunities for service learning at all levels, K–12.* All children need to become involved in community projects, and community members need to become involved in the life of the school. Your task is to determine and arrange age-appropriate opportunities for your students to serve.
- *Make your classroom and school miniature democracies.* The essence of democracy is citizens' engagement in decision making and conflict resolution, in working with others, in taking responsibility, and in practicing self-governance. Holding class meetings, participating in school assemblies, and helping to make rules of conduct give students the practice they need to become responsible citizens.

- *Be sure your students have opportunities to work with others beyond the classroom.* Older students can pair with younger students for tutorial purposes, and volunteers from the community can be invited to work with students in school.
- *Connect the classroom to the home.* Assign topics for students to discuss with their families.
- *Take advantage of the opportunities to reflect on the social/moral life of school.* Issues related to fairness, sharing, cooperation, bullying, cheating, fighting, and the like occur quite naturally in classrooms and schools. They provide opportunities for reflection and action by students.
- *Create a civil society.* Manners are close to morality. Children need to experience a polite, concerned, and compassionate environment in the classroom. How they are treated there will be mirrored in how they treat others. Respect builds respect. Tolerance creates tolerance.

Teaching Citizenship

Citizenship education is clearly to be a central focus of the social studies. Whether it should continue to be was asked many times in the twentieth century. This question has recently gained renewed emphasis. Current societal problems, a stress on back to basics, and an increased concern for patriotism and global education have all worked to renew interest in citizenship education. The National Council for the Social Studies has defined outcomes for citizenship education (see Figure 2.5). Researchers and writers in the area of citizenship education also have given us a clear picture of how schools can contribute to the goal of producing good citizens. They point to such factors as school and classroom climate, teaching practices, student experiences, and the content and materials taught and learned.

John Dewey's dream of school as a miniature democracy represents a school and classroom ideal. In fact, there are a number of ways in which a school *cannot* be a democracy, but it can be a place where certain democratic values can be lived and learned. For example, you can allow your students to participate in decisions that affect school and classroom life. It is easy for adults to overlook how meaningful it is for a child to choose among alternative possibilities in carrying out an assignment. Students can and should be encouraged to make classroom rules. They should have class government with elected officers. They should take responsibility for helping to decorate and keep the room orderly.

Beyond these matters, a more subtle issue of class climate emerges. It has to do with how open your classroom is. According to Angell's (1991) review of the research, an *open classroom* is characterized by democratic leadership behaviors, positive teacher verbal behaviors, respect for students, peer interaction, open discussion, student participation, and cooperation. Interestingly, another factor related to openness is the use by students of source materials other than textbooks. According to researcher Torney-Purta (1983), allowing students to express their opinions freely is the most positive contribution a teacher can make toward the acquisition of democratic values.

Teachers who are committed to citizenship education realize that good citizenship is an active role, and therefore the classroom must be a place dedicated to active

---

Figure 2.5 *NCSS Expectations for Civic Education*

Social studies programs should include experiences that provide for the study of *the ideals, principles, and practices of citizenship in a democratic republic,* so that the learner can:

Early Grades

a. identify key ideals of the United States' democratic republican form of government, such as individual human dignity, liberty, justice, equality, and the rule of law, and discuss their application in specific situations;
b. identify examples of rights and responsibilities of citizens;
c. locate, access, organize, and apply information about an issue of public concern from multiple points of view;
d. identify and practice selected forms of civic discussion and participation consistent with the ideals of citizens in a democratic republic;
e. explain actions citizens can take to influence public policy decisions;
f. recognize that a variety of formal and informal actors influence and shape public policy;
g. examine the influence of public opinion on personal decision-making and government policy on public issues;
h. explain how public policies and citizen behaviors may or may nor reflect the stated ideals of a democratic republican form of government;
i. describe how public policies are used to address issues of public concern;
j. recognize and interpret how the "common good" can be strengthened through various forms of citizen action.

Middle Grades

a. examine the origins and continuing influence of key ideals of the democratic republican form of government, such as individual human dignity, liberty, justice, equality, and the rule of law;
b. identify and interpret sources and examples of the rights and responsibilities of citizens;
c. locate, access, analyze, organize, and apply information about selected public issues—recognizing and explaining multiple points of view;
d. practice forms of civic discussion and participation consistent with the ideals of citizens in a democratic republic;
e. explain and analyze various forms of citizen action that influence public policy decisions;
f. identify and explain the roles of formal and informal political actors in influencing and shaping public policy and decision-making;
g. analyze the influence of diverse forms of public opinion on the development of public policy and decision-making;
h. analyze the effectiveness of selected public policies and citizen behaviors in realizing the stated ideals of a democratic republican form of government;
i. explain the relationship between policy statements and action plans used to address issues of public concern;
j. examine strategies designed to strengthen the "common good," which consider a range of options for citizen action.

Source: Expectations of Excellence: Curriculum Standards for Social Studies (p. 44), Bulletin 89, Fall 1994, 2009, Washington, DC: NCSS. © National Council for the Social Studies. Reprinted by permission.

Keys to Effective Citizenship Education

The Carnegie Corporation and the Center for Information and Research on Civic Learning and Engagement (2003) commissioned a group of more than 50 distinguished scholars and practitioners to summarize the evidence in support of civic education in K–12 school settings. The group cited these six research-based recommendations for effective programs:

- *Study a wide range of topics*. Students perform better on tests of civic skills and knowledge if they have studied a range of relevant subjects, such as the Constitution, U.S. history, the structure of government and elections, and the legal system.
- *Use interactive lessons*. Students who participate in active debates related to current issues have greater interest in politics, improved critical-thinking and communication skills, and are more likely to say they will vote and volunteer as adults.
- *Include service learning*. Service learning provides students with applications of what they learn. Service learning can be more effective at installing civic skills and values

among students than volunteer work that's not connected to the school curriculum.
- *Encourage student participation in school governance*. Research suggests that giving students more opportunities to help manage their own classrooms and schools builds civic skills and attitudes.
- *Encourage extracurricular participation*. Long-term studies show that students who participate in extracurricular activities remain more civically engaged than those who do not.
- *Consider using simulations*. Evidence indicates that simulations of voting, trials, legislative deliberations, and diplomacy can lead to students becoming more interested in and informed about politics and government.

Of course, these research findings need to be applied in developmentally appropriate ways for children to benefit from them. But notice that the common thread running throughout the findings is that classrooms and schools that practice democracy, active learning, and engagement in the community are making a difference.

learning. A great deal of support has already been given to active learning for other pedagogical reasons, so this only strengthens the case. Passively learning facts about citizenship will not do. Children must experience active learning in order to practice doing what involved citizens do. Nothing does this better than group projects that involve teamwork, decisions, investigation, and production.

A number of learning strategies are recommended to facilitate citizenship education, many of which are discussed in other chapters in this book. Those strategies include practice in class discussion, the use of open-ended and higher-level questions by teachers, research by children using sources other than textbooks, writing projects (including letter writing), cooperative group projects, brainstorming, role-play, simulations, field trips and on-site investigations, observation, class meetings, class and school government, community service projects, and interaction with guest speakers. Of particular importance is the much needed component of reflective thinking. The strategies enumerated in this paragraph have much deeper implications for learning and for application to life experiences when students are given ample opportunity to discuss, reflect, seek meaning, and employ a range of metacognitive techniques.

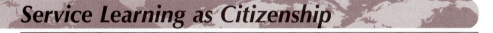

Service Learning as Citizenship

One of the most practical, experiential ways for young people to learn about citizenship and civic duty is through service learning. When done properly, service learning combines academic learning with community service. It provides a wonderful link between knowledge and action. John Dewey wrote time and again that knowledge comes to life in action. Without activity, knowledge is inert. Aristotle reminds us that in order to understand something, we must *do* the thing we are trying to understand. As you can see, this is an old idea.

Community service learning projects deserve additional mention here because they truly are at the heart of what it means to be a participating citizen in one's classroom, school, and community. Several aspects of service learning need to be taken into account in order to maximize the potential of different projects.

1. *Community service projects should address real needs.* There is no need to contrive projects when every school, every community has real needs for improvement. Environmental concerns are found everywhere. Cleaning up a stream, a pond, even a vacant lot; improving a park or a school playground; making a crosswalk near the school safer—the list goes on. Involvement with a nearby retirement home has the potential to bring joy to lives and to give students fulfillment in getting to know an older generation. My experience with such projects always leaves me wondering who gains more, the elderly folks or the kids. Working with the local library, museum, historical society, garden club, and other community agencies invariably draws students into history, geography, culture, and other aspects of community life.

2. *Community service projects should culminate in performance.* By performance, I mean a pageant, a fair, a celebration, a dinner, a play, public displays, readings, or some means of providing a tangible, real-world outcome to the efforts you and your students have made to make the world a better place. Far too many school experiences are merely bookish and have no outcome other than the test on Friday. This is the real world; participate in it.

3. *Community service projects should be connected to academic learning.* It is one thing to clean up a stream. That in itself is worthwhile. But it is value added when your students read about ecology, learn from experts, and connect their practical work to mathematics, science, art, literature, geography, and history. The academic connection is crucial.

4. *Community service projects should involve reflective thinking.* As projects are carried out, it is important to hold discussions and opportunities for students to express themselves and to think about what they are learning. A few minutes of reflective thinking and assessment each day will go a long way toward deepening students' perspectives on what it means to be a citizen. Following is an example of a child's reflection on her visit to a nearby retirement home:

> When our class went there first I didn't know what to think. The people were old and it smelled funny. But everyone was nice they were happy when we gave them the pictures. My friend Helen put my picture of my dog on her wall. His name is Tykey. Now she asks me about Tykey and I told her he took some meat off the table when my mom went outside. The we started laffing. Helen is happy to see me I love her. Some of the people ded there to. Mrs. Lowe talked to us about it.

Following—from the National Youth Leadership Council (*www.nylc.org,* retrieved June 22, 2009)—are concrete examples of service learning carried out by elementary school students. I list them here to give you ideas about where you might begin.

The National Council for the Social Studies (see Figure 2.7) has identified a number of recommendations for early- and middle-grade students to become involved in global citizenship. Today students are able to exchange ideas and information with students around the world. A fourth-grade class in California exchanges weather data each day with a class in New Zealand. Sixth-graders in Florida exchange local histories with a class in Scotland. A first-grade class in Michigan exchanges art work with a class in Russia.

Cooking Club

Kindergarten through Grade 6 and Special Education

Subjects: Reading, Math, and Communication

Special needs students chose nondisabled peer buddies to assist them in mastering the skills necessary to shop for groceries and prepare a nutritious meal. The special education students began by practicing their ability to read labels and recipes, along with the math skills to make change for food purchases. As a group, they chose an ethnic theme and searched for appropriate recipes. They planned the meal, made a grocery list, and purchased the ingredients. The students prepared the food and served it at a multicultural celebration, where visitors from a local senior center were guests of honor.

In the process, students began to rely on each other, instead of adults, for assistance with making decisions. Through ethnic foods and customs, the students shared their knowledge of other cultures with the guests. The special education students increased their reading, math, and communication skills, and improved their ability to develop peer relationships with nondisabled students. The nondisabled students increased their awareness and acceptance of students with disabilities.

Family Bookworks

Grade 2

Subject: Reading and Art

In partnership with a local book center, students created books recording family stories and traditions. Artists trained the teachers in bookmaking, allowing them to guide their students through the process. Each student wrote a personal narrative. The families then joined their children at the book center, where they constructed and decorated the books together. The books were displayed publicly at a local department store. The second graders also read their books to the kindergarten students, and hosted an event where the stories were read for all of the families. At the end of the school year, students were given the option of donating their books to the second grade library.

This project also had a number of related activities: Families were invited to the school to participate in a folklore event with a local storyteller. At the event, the families wrote and designed books of their favorite folktales from their cultural and ethnic backgrounds, and shared their work at the end of the day. A paper artist also worked with students to help them create and design their own symbol of peace using handmade paper. The symbols were then assembled into a beautiful hanging mosaic at a peace prize festival and the school's peace site dedication.

Quilt-Makers Project

Kindergarten

Subjects: Math, Reading, and Art

It all began as an introduction to the letter "Q": Quilt-related literature, both fiction and nonfiction, was read to the kindergarteners to give them the historical and cultural backgrounds on the origins of quilts. They reflected on how quilts relate to family traditions, and discussed the emotional and physical comfort a quilt can provide.

The children then took their love of quilting one-step further, creating a quilt to comfort a baby residing in a nearby shelter. The students used their imaginations and artistry to create quilt squares. When the quilt squares were completed and stitched together, each child took the quilt home for a night. Parents and children wrote and drew their thoughts and impressions in a journal that accompanied the quilt. The process culminated when the baby and mother visited the classroom and received the quilt.

The Honduras Project

Grades 1 through 3

Subjects: Math, Reading, Spanish, Art, and Geography

After learning that schools in Honduras lacked books, elementary students launched The Honduras Project. They wrote letters in Spanish to their peers in Honduras, raised money, and charted the progress of their fundraising. The students raised $1,000, which they used to provide books for the Honduran students. Through the process, they enhanced their skills in math, reading, Spanish, art, geography, and design.

Figure 2.6 *Preamble to the United Nations Charter*

UNITED NATIONS HIGH COMMISSIONER FOR HUMAN RIGHTS

Charter of the United Nations

Preamble

We the Peoples of the United Nations Determined

to save succeeding generations from the scourge of war, which twice in our lifetime has brought untold sorrow to mankind, and

to reaffirm faith in fundamental human rights, in the dignity and worth of the human person, in the equal rights of men and women and of nations large and small, and

to establish conditions under which justice and respect for the obligations arising from treaties and other sources of international law can be maintained, and

to promote social progress and better standards of life in larger freedom,

And for These Ends

to practice tolerance and live together in peace with one another as good neighbors, and

to unite our strength to maintain international peace and security, and

to ensure, by the acceptance of principles and the institution of methods, that armed force shall not be used, save in the common interest, and

to employ international machinery for the promotion of the economic and social advancement of all peoples,

Have Resolved to Combine Our Efforts to Accomplish These Aims

Accordingly, our respective Governments, through representatives assembled in the city of San Francisco, who have exhibited their full powers found to be in good and due form, have agreed to the present Charter of the United Nations and do hereby establish an international organization to be known as the United Nations.

The Meaning of Citizenship: A Global Perspective

The ancient Greek philosopher Diogenes made a reputation by carrying a lantern through the nighttime city streets searching for an honest man. Apparently, this was not an easy quest in the city of Athens in his day. When asked what country he was from, Diogenes' famous reply is said to have been, "I am a citizen of the world!" And Socrates himself proclaimed, "I am a citizen, not of Athens or Greece, but of the world." So, you can see that the idea of global citizenship is hardly a new one.

No one can reasonably deny that the twenty-first century world is interdependent. The insight expressed in chaos theory that when a butterfly flaps its wings in Beijing, the effects are felt in the Caribbean is a reminder that what affects one affects all. Satellite

---

Figure 2.7 NCSS Standards for Global Education

Social studies programs should include experiences that provide for the study of *global connections and interdependence*, so that the learner can:

Early Grades

a. explore ways that language, art, music, belief systems, and other cultural elements may facilitate global understanding or lead to misunderstanding
b. give examples of conflict, cooperation, and interdependence among individuals, groups, and nations;
c. examine the effects of changing technologies on the global community;
d. explore causes, consequences, and possible solutions to persistent, contemporary, and emerging global issues, such as pollution and endangered species;
e. examine the relationships and tensions between personal wants and needs and various global concerns, such as use of imported oil, land use, and environmental protection;
f. investigate concerns, issues, standards, and conflicts related to universal human rights, such as the treatment of children, religious groups, and effects of war.

Middle Grades

a. describe instances in which language, art, music, belief systems, and other cultural elements can facilitate global understanding or cause misunderstanding;
b. analyze examples of conflict, cooperation, and interdependence among groups, societies, and nations;
c. describe and analyze the effects of changing technologies on the global community;
d. explore the causes, consequences, and possible solutions to persistent, contemporary, and emerging global issues, such as health, security, resource allocation, economic development, and environmental quality;
e. describe and explain the relationships and tensions between national sovereignty and global interests, in such matters as territory, natural resources, trade, use of technology, and welfare of people;
f. demonstrate understanding of concerns, standards, issues, and conflicts related to universal human rights;
g. identify and describe the roles of international and multinational organizations.

Source: Expectations of Excellence: Curriculum Standards for Social Studies (p. 45), Bulletin 89, Fall 1994, 2009. Washington, DC: NCSS. © National Council for the Social Studies. Reprinted by permission.

Figure 2.8 *The Statue of Liberty Drawing of a Lithuanian Child Involved in Exchanging Letters with American Students*

Figure 2.8 *The Statue of Liberty Drawing of a Lithuanian Child Involved in Exchanging Letters with American Students*

telemetry, television, and the Internet have created the global village predicted half a century ago by Marshall McCluhan. Corporations are multinational. The oceans and the atmosphere belong to us all. A treasure such as the Amazon Rainforest may be located in Brazil, but what happens to ecology of that region has worldwide consequences.

Children today are connected to the world. A generation ago, pen pals wrote to each other using "snail mail." Today they correspond instantly through the various avenues of the Internet. News is instantaneous. I remember talking to an elderly woman who told me that when her great grandmother was a child living in Oregon, the family received the news of Abraham Lincoln's assassination several days after it happened. Today we know immediately about earthquakes, volcanic eruptions, and other events taking place around the globe.

Now more than ever our children must learn to live together peacefully. Overarching organizations such as the United Nations struggle to bring collaboration to global efforts. Volunteer organizations such as Doctors without Borders make heroic efforts to bring healing to suffering people in war-torn countries. The World Health Organization does its best to combat epidemics and pandemics. The Charter of the United Nations, written in 1948 (see Figure 2.6), seems even more relevant today than ever before.

WHAT IS GLOBAL EDUCATION?   It is a way of viewing the world. Simply stated, global education is a systematic effort to communicate the awareness that the planet Earth and the people who live on it are increasingly *interdependent*—that is, we are all citizens of the world as well as of our respective nations. It is a way of viewing and thinking about the world that is quite different from traditional models.

Summary

A child is a citizen of the family, classroom, school, community, state, country, and the world. Inevitably, our citizenship takes place within diverse and pluralistic environments. The abiding concepts of rights and responsibilities are found within this framework. The classroom and the school offer wonderful possibilities for participation, cooperation, team building, and esprit de corps. These are the building blocks of citizenship education.

Citizenship education is a part of every school activity, but it is especially central to the social studies experience. Elementary social studies stresses its importance at each grade level. Students learn the ideas of citizenship best when they are given the opportunities to experience it in the classroom, the school, and the community.

A classroom should be a miniature community, democratic in structure and experience, in which students participate actively and reflectively in decision-making processes and where they learn what it truly means to work and play together. As they mature, their horizons continue to expand and their sense of rights and responsibility deepens.

The young people of today will be those who govern tomorrow. This is how democracy works. In a nation of laws and democratic traditions, each new generation assumes the rights and responsibilities passed on to them by their elders. To be a citizen of a democracy is a rare and precious privilege. Even though the idea of the citizen can be traced back to ancient Greece, it is remarkable to think that most of the people living in the world today, in the twenty-first century, do not hold the rights and privileges of democratic citizenship.

Children learn what they live. They are shaped by their experiences. To the extent that your classroom is a place of democracy, your students experience citizenship. The projects you and your students engage in, the service you and they perform for others, the willingness with which you model shared decision making, openness to everyone's ideas, and the opportunities you give your students to express themselves freely and responsibly are the measures that will count.

Citizenship education is a cornerstone of the social studies curriculum. As you pass the torch to the children you teach, you do honor and justice to your profession by making your classroom and school a shining light of freedom, opportunity, duty, and service.

Here is a closing thought for your consideration: Philosopher Mortimer Adler has written that only in a democracy can a person be considered a citizen. In an autocracy, a person is not a citizen but a subject. Without freedom and the duties attendant to freedom, there is no citizenship in its deeper meaning.

With that thought in mind, I challenge you to make your classroom a place of opportunity rather than one of restraint. I challenge you to make your classroom a place where children are truly citizens.

Explorations

Reflect On . . .

1. Voting is considered both the right and the responsibility of a citizen, yet less than 50 percent of U.S. citizens typically vote in elections. Why do you think this percentage is so low?
2. What are the key differences between primary-grade and intermediate-grade experiences in citizenship education? What are the key similarities?

In the Field

3. What examples of community service-learning activities have you seen in the classrooms you have visited? How might you make these activities even more focused on citizenship?

4. Describe at least three activities you have observed in schools that taught lessons about citizenship. These don't have to be planned activities but can be the results of spontaneous interactions in the classroom, on the playground, or in the lunchroom.

For Your Portfolio

5. Research citizenship education on the Web. Find at least three sample lessons on citizenship that are interactive and stress participation as an active citizen. Print these out and include them in your portfolio.

Continuing the Journey: Suggested Readings

Biesta, G., Lawy, R., & Kelly, N. (2009). "Understanding Young People's Citizenship Learning in Everyday Life." *Education, Citizenship and Social Justice, iv* (4), 5–24.

How young people in a democracy learn citizenship through ordinary day-to-day events is the key idea of this insightful article.

Cheney, L. (2008). *We the People: The Story of Our Constitution.* New York: Simon & Schuster.

This children's book provides valuable insight into the idea of citizenship as it was conceived by the founders of the United States.

Covey, S. (2008). *The 7 Habits of Happy Kids.* New York: Simon & Schuster.

The author suggests concrete ways to nurture young people in order for them to achieve levels of happiness and belonging in life. These habits are essential attributes of citizens in a democracy.

Ellis, A. (2010). *Teaching, Learning, & Assessment Together: The Reflective Classroom.* Larchmont, NY: Eye on Education, Inc.

One of the goals of education stressed in this book is to deepen and enrich the social and moral fabric of school life through participation and sense of others.

Glover, R., & O'Donnel, B. (2003). "Understanding Human Rights: The Development of Perspective Taking and Empathy." *Social Studies and the Young Learner, 15* (3), 15–18.

Ideas for helping children understand and appreciate the fundamental rights of all human beings.

Hadaway, N., & McKenna, M. (2007). *Breaking Boundaries with Global Literature: Celebrating Diversity in*

K–12 Classrooms. Newark, DE: International Reading Association.

In this volume, teachers will find stories for guiding students toward an understanding of global awareness and constructive activism.

Laughlin, M. A., & Hartoonian, H. M. (1999). *Succeed with the Standards in Your Social Studies Classroom.* Portland, ME: J Weston Walch Publishing.

This book gives practical steps for integrating standards into everyday social studies teaching and learning.

Learn and Serve: America's National Service Learning Clearinghouse. (2009). *K–12 Service-Learning Project Planning Toolkit.* Scotts Valley, CA: RMC Research Corporation. *www.servicelearning.org*

This organization provides practical help to teachers and students who want to become involved in community life through service projects. It is an excellent way to teach citizenship through direct experience.

Maxim, G. W. (2005). *Dynamic Social Studies for Constructivist Classrooms* (8th ed.). Columbus, OH: Pearson Prentice Hall.

Constructivist learning theory encompasses an important set of current teaching and learning principles. Use this volume to incorporate these principles into your regular classroom practice.

National Council for the Social Studies. (2007). *Service- Learning: An Essential Component of Citizenship Education.* Washington, DC: NCSS Board of Directors. *www.socialstudies.org/positions/servicelearning*

NCSS emphasizes civic responsibility and academic learning through meaningful service. Integration of academic skills and knowledge with active involvement in the community is highlighted.

National Council for the Social Studies. (n.d.). *www.socialstudies.org/* (April, 2009).

National Task Force for Social Studies. (1994). *Expectations of Excellence: Curriculum Standards for Social Studies.* Waldorf, MD: National Council for the Social Studies.

This book outlines the 10 themes of social studies along with their standards. This volume also emphasizes the importance of using social studies to teach students democratic values.

National Task Force for Social Studies. (2006). *National Standards for Social Studies Teachers.* Waldorf, MD: National Council for the Social Studies.

This document describes and explains social studies subject matter standards including which knowledge, capabilities, and attitudes students should develop through social studies learning. Moreover, this document describes pedagogical standards for effective social studies teaching.

Nelson, P. (2005). "Preparing Students for Citizenship: Literature and Primary Documents." *Social Studies and the Young Learner, 17*(3), 21–29.

The study of original source materials by young citizen historians.

Rizzo, M., & Brown, J. (2006). *Building Character through Community Service: Strategies to Implement the Missing Element in Education.* Lanham, MD: Rowman & Littlefield Education.

This is a practical book filled with service learning materials including sample letters, worksheets, and step-by-step instructions.

Rubin, B., & Giarelli, J. (2007). *Civic Education for Diverse Citizens in Global Times: Rethinking Theory and Practice.* Lawrence Erlbaum Associates.

This book explores four themes of civic education including diversity, global context, practicing civic education, and integration of historical understanding.

U.S. Department of Education. (n.d.). *Federal Resources for Educational Excellence. www.free.ed.gov/index.cfm* (April, 2009).

This Website includes more than 1,500 federally supported teaching and learning resources. This is an excellent place to locate new and useful resources for planning social studies lessons.

Walsh, J. A., & Sattes, B. D. (2004). *Quality Questioning: Research-Based Practice to Engage Every Learner.* Thousand Oaks, CA: Corwin Press.

At the heart of social studies learning is the process of questioning and discussing. This book provides insights about these important classroom practices.

Wenmik, S. (2004). "Reporting on the Process of Legislation: A Civics Webquest." *Social Studies and the Young Learner, 17*(1), 11–14.

Insights to how legislation originates in a democracy and how it becomes law.

Social Studies and Diversity in America

Working with children is the easiest part of education for democracy, because children are still undefeated and have no stake in being prejudiced.
    —Margaret Halsey

NOVUM AMSTERODAMUM

From its very beginnings, our society has been pluralistic. By the middle to late seventeenth century, New Amsterdam, now known as New York City, was a place of great diversity. In addition to the Dutch, English, German, and Scandinavian residents, it also was populated by Africans, Huguenots, Jews, and Indians. Many of the Africans were in fact free people nearly 200 years before the Civil War. (*Sources:* "Ethnicity in 17th Century English America," in R. Baylor (ed.), 2003. *Race and Ethnicity in America.* (New York: Columbia University Press.)

As you can see, diversity is not new in our land. However, the young citizens whom you teach or will teach represent an increasingly diverse society. The United States has historically been a nation of immigrants; only Indians, or Native Americans, can lay claim to being indigenous inhabitants of this land. In a sense, the nation is an ongoing experiment, constantly testing whether peoples of wide-ranging cultural, ethnic, and religious backgrounds can live together in harmony. Today the premise of this experiment is being tested even more rigorously than in the past. Minorities are becoming majorities, and divisions between peoples appear wider and deeper than ever.

As the United States grows culturally more diverse, the need for developmentally appropriate education designed to help children understand, tolerate, and appreciate cultural differences becomes increasingly critical. One of your tasks as a

social studies teacher is to create conditions in your classroom that lead to greater understanding, increased tolerance, and a deepened sense of appreciation toward others.

The life of an elementary teacher is challenging, difficult, and complex. On some days, you will wish you had done certain things differently. On the worst days, teaching may hardly seem worthwhile and you may wonder whether you've chosen the right career. But on the good days, those doubts will fade away. There is probably no other profession that brings with it so many rewards. The rewards of teaching come in many forms. And often, the rewards are unexpected. The great investigator of childhood growth and development, Jean Piaget, once noted that all genuine learning is spontaneous. It happens in the moment. The rewards of joy, accomplishment, sharing, persistence, teamwork, and a job well done seem to happen along the way.

Teaching social studies is one way to ensure that these rewards will come your way. Why is this so? Social studies is learning about human activity, and the best way to learn about human activity is to make sure that every child you teach feels that he or she is truly part of the daily life of the classroom. In other words, experience is the best teacher. If the experience is one that is positive, uplifting, respectful, and sensitive, then children will feel included. And this is where cultural sensitivity begins: with *inclusion*. Each child must be included. There is no room for exclusion.

Think of yourself as the conductor of a fine symphony orchestra. This is a useful metaphor for the role of the teacher. You are the leader of a talented group of individuals whose success depends on their ability to work together. The members of the orchestra *must* work together—in concert, to be exact. To be *in concert* means to be in harmony. Here is the key to a fine orchestra: In order to produce beautiful music, the orchestra must be a collection of very different musicians playing very different instruments dedicated to producing the same piece of music together. Each instrument (percussion, brass, woodwinds, and strings) has its certain beauty when played alone, but when all the instruments are played together, something much greater happens. In other words, diversity in harmony produces the best effect.

Just as diversity strengthens an orchestra, diversity has the potential to make your classroom a better place to work and play. Each child is needed because in the best social studies classrooms, teamwork is a daily occurrence. It is obvious that different instruments are needed in order to complete the requirements of a symphony performance. Notice that I said the different instruments are *needed,* not just *tolerated.* This is the transformation achieved by great teachers. Every child feels *needed.* When a child tells a parent, "I need to go to school today because we're working together on our project" (or words to that effect), we have a glimpse of a teacher who has transformed the culture of the classroom from passive to active, from one of restriction to one of opportunity, from one where attendance is required to one where children desire to be there.

Diversity in the United States and in the Classroom

American society has always been diverse, even in the earliest days of settlement. That our society has become and will continue to become more pluralistic and diverse is obvious in any number of ways, from the numbers reflected in the official U.S. government census to the proliferation of ethnic cuisine in regional restaurants to the multitude of languages heard on the streets of any large city. The evidence is all around us. A child hanging onto a parent's hand at the local grocery store will see shelves stocked with products from all over the world, representing a range of ethnicities (Hispanic, Thai, Caribbean, South Asian, Chinese—an endless array!) that probably would not have been there even a decade ago. Clothing, architecture, films, television, music—all reflect the growing diversity of this nation.

It is one thing, however, for a society to be diverse and another for it to provide equal opportunity for all its members. Public education has long been seen as a venue for "melting" the various ethnicities together. In the nineteenth century, educational leaders such as Horace Mann, often considered the "father" of American public education, led the way for schools to offer daily opportunities for children to work and play together across economic, religious, and social barriers. Mann was convinced that a democratic society could survive and prosper only if it were truly integrated. Thus, one major purpose of schooling was born: to become a crucible of democracy. It was a noble dream, one that today places schools and teachers in a more strategic role than Mann might ever have imagined.

As a teacher, you are a major player in this great democratic experiment. The National Council for the Social Studies (NCSS, 1994) says that "social studies teachers should possess the knowledge, capabilities, and dispositions to organize and provide instruction at the appropriate school level for the study of culture and cultural diversity" (p. 18). And the NCSS is clear about its expectations for learners, for teachers, and for classrooms (see Figure 3.1).

But when a single classroom may include students from eight or ten different ethnic or cultural backgrounds, students whose first language is not English, and students with a variety of disabilities, what does it mean to be able to "provide instruction at the appropriate school level"? In the past, children from minority backgrounds, second-language English speakers, children with disabilities, and children from lower socioeconomic backgrounds were often relegated to second-class citizenship in the classroom. In the second half of the twentieth century, great strides were made toward achieving equality and inclusion. But there is a long distance still to go.

A wide range of thought and activity can exist within the framework of rules, norms of behavior, and law. This fact leads to two values you will definitely want to emphasize in teaching social studies to children: (1) diversity and differences and (2) respect for individual rights. Rosa Parks was a true pioneer of the twentieth century Civil Rights movement. Her courage stands as a testament to the positive effects one individual can have in a democratic society (see Figure 3.2). Democratic societies, such as those in the United States and Canada, place great value on the uniqueness of the individual and on personal freedom to pursue a path of self-determination in life. In a democracy, differences must not only be tolerated, but they must also be respected. Any truly democratic society is diverse in any number of ways.

Children need to learn through your teaching and your example that a genuine emphasis on the rights of individuals means accepting the rights of those who may be different from oneself. This lesson seems obvious, but nowhere should these primary values be more evident than in your classroom. The children you teach will vary greatly,

Figure 3.1 *NCSS Standards*

1.1 Culture and Cultural Diversity. Candidates in social studies should possess the knowledge, capabilities, and dispositions to organize and provide instruction at the appropriate school level for the study of culture and cultural diversity.

1.2 Time, Continuity, and Change. Candidates in social studies should possess the knowledge, capabilities, and dispositions to organize and provide instruction at the appropriate school level for the study of time, continuity, and change.

1.3 People, Places, and Environment. Candidates in social studies should possess the knowledge, capabilities, and dispositions to organize and provide instruction at the appropriate school level for the study of people, places, and environment.

1.4 Individual Development and Identity. Candidates in social studies should possess the knowledge, capabilities, and dispositions to organize and provide instruction at the appropriate school level for the study of individual development and identity.

1.5 Individuals, Groups, and Institutions. Candidates in social studies should possess the knowledge, capabilities, and dispositions to organize and provide instruction at the appropriate school level for the study of individuals, groups, and institutions.

1.6 Power, Authority, and Governance. Candidates in social studies should possess the knowledge, capabilities, and dispositions to organize and provide instruction at the appropriate school level for the study of power, authority, and governance.

1.7 Production, Distribution, and Consumption. Candidates in social studies should possess the knowledge, capabilities, and dispositions to organize and provide instruction at the appropriate school level for the study of production, distribution, and consumption of goods and services.

1.8 Science, Technology, and Society. Candidates in social studies should possess the knowledge, capabilities, and dispositions to organize and provide instruction at the appropriate school level for the study of science, technology, and society.

1.9 Global Connections. Candidates in social studies should possess the knowledge, capabilities, and dispositions to organize and provide instruction at the appropriate school level for the study of global connections and interdependence.

1.10 Civic Ideals and Practices. Candidates in social studies should possess the knowledge, capabilities, and dispositions to organize and provide instruction at the appropriate school level for the study of civic ideals and practices.

Source: © National Council for the Social Studies, 1994, 2009. Reprinted by permission.

perhaps with respect to race/ethnicity, religion, socioeconomic status, intelligence, motivation, and self-concept. You will have diversity within your classroom because classrooms are microcosms of society. To what extent will you tolerate, appreciate, and celebrate these differences? Will you show as much respect for the poor child as you show for the well-to-do child? Will you be as tolerant toward the slow learner as you are toward the student who catches on quickly to everything you assign? Will the child whose behavior is often less than socially desirable be welcome in your classroom, or will that child have to find compassion elsewhere? These are the real issues you must resolve every day of your teaching career.

Figure 3.2 *Rosa Parks: A Person of Dignity and Courage*

Rosa Parks died in October of 2005 at the age of 92. She died in Detroit, where she had lived for some years. She was an old woman, and it is quite possible that many young people living today do not even know who she was or what she did a half century ago that was so remarkable. What she did that took so much courage and determination has become commonplace in today's world. She took a seat on a city bus on her way home from work.

Rosa Parks lived in Montgomery, Alabama, for much of her life, and it was in that city more than 50 years ago that she performed a simple act of courage that helped change the world. On her way home from work she took a seat in a section of a city bus reserved for white people. The rule of the day in that city and throughout much of the American South was that white people sat in one section and colored people sat in an area reserved for them in the back of the bus.

When a white male passenger asked—or told—her to move, she refused. This act of defiance made headlines. By sitting where she did not "belong" she had broken the rules, violated the established norm of behavior, and otherwise made of herself a nuisance. The police were called to arrest her. This action proved to be the catalyst for the more than year-long Montgomery Bus Boycott, a watershed in the annals of American civil liberties.

What Rosa Parks did was at once outrageous and reasonable. It was outrageous because it was against the law. It was reasonable because she acted in defiance of a bad law, one that simply had to change.

Rosa Parks was in many ways an ordinary person. She gave no famous speeches, wrote no best-selling books, ran for no political office. She is best remembered today as a person who merely wanted to be treated equally, with dignity and respect. In that sense, Rosa Parks takes her place as a citizen of the United States who truly understood what it means to be a citizen.

The Melting Pot

The Melting Pot is the name of a play written by Israel Zangwill and performed on Broadway in 1908. The play, based on Shakespeare's *Romeo and Juliet,* is about two young immigrants to America, each of different ethnicity. Their love for each other overcomes long-standing prejudices, hatreds, and suspicions of other cultures. The play's theme was that God was using America as a "crucible" to melt the many ethnic groups of Europe into one "metal" called "Americans." Zangwill used the idea of different metals melted in a pot to form one metal.

Today, other metaphors are sometimes used, for example, the United State as a "tossed salad." What is your opinion of the "melting pot" and "tossed salad" metaphors? Can you think of another metaphor that you feel describes the United States as a nation of many peoples? The official motto of the United States is *e pluribus unum,* Latin for "one out of many."

Israel Zangwill

The Role of Social Studies Education in Promoting Pluralism and Diversity

Social studies plays a dual role in promoting diversity and pluralism. First, the classroom climate must be one of respect, dignity, caring, and support for every child. This expectation is or should be true about every aspect of the school day and is not unique to the social studies. Second (and this role *is* unique to social studies education), social studies is the study of the contributions, traditions, and world views of people from all backgrounds, cultures, races/ethnicities, language groups, and religions. In other words, social studies is the study of humankind.

One specific goal of social studies education is to create awareness of and appreciation for others. We study ancient civilizations not merely to build up the information needed to pass tests but to gain an understanding of the human adventure over time. We

Children in costume celebrate the Chinese New Year. Such experiences bring cultural understanding to life.

study other cultures in order to discover that there are many ways in which to organize families, communities, and whole societies. There is no room for condescension: We do not think in terms of *inferior* and *superior* or even *strange* and *familiar*. We simply seek to understand the differences. This is part of the long-term process of helping children to grow into reflective, caring citizens.

Cultural Sensitivity in Social Studies Curricula

Banks and Banks (2009) define four levels of curriculum that represent how diversity content is typically taught in the social studies classroom. Their model is hierarchical, thus offering a map to teachers who truly wish to teach meaningful content while ensuring balance and fairness toward different points of view, particularly on sensitive issues. In this sense, the model represents growth and development on the part of the teacher. The four levels that Banks and Banks define include the following:

1. *The contributions approach.* At this level, students are exposed to information that generally lacks a conceptual frame. Holidays, special occasions, food, and famous people are emphasized without providing a larger context. Typically, the textbook sets the course of the curriculum.

2. *The additive approach.* Here, the basic structure of the curriculum still does not change; it remains textbook coverage. However, the teacher adds a conceptual framework and thematic teaching that set the various holidays and personalities within a larger context of social struggle. Cultures outside the mainstream—Native American, African, East Asian, and so on—may be featured.

3. *The transformational approach.* At this level, teachers begin to introduce fundamental change into the curricular structure. Students are encouraged to examine ideas, events,

Students participate in a lively debate over school uniforms. Such experiences allow young people to learn to deal with different opinions in a civil manner.

and issues from divergent perspectives. Christopher Columbus's voyage to the New World, for example, may be seen not simply from the European standpoint as a great step forward but also as a dangerous intrusion from a Native American one. Similarly, a study of the westward expansion may look at this movement from both the pioneer and Native American perspectives. Concepts such as *conflict* and *tolerance* are studied reflectively.

4. *The social action approach.* This level represents a fundamental change from "learning about" to making decisions, conducting investigations, and engaging in social action. It is a problem-solving, reflective thinking approach to the social studies curriculum in which students are supported in their efforts to make a difference in the world. Knowledge and skills become tools for change rather than serving as ends in themselves. See, for example, how Canadian students were successful in removing Styrofoam containers from the British Columbia Ferry System.

The Banks and Banks (2009) model is intended to provide a means for teachers (and schools) to examine the level of cultural sensitivity in their social studies programs. But it is also a useful way of thinking about teaching and learning in general. Although you may be constrained by district, state, or even federal standards and guidelines from implementing the curriculum of your choice, I encourage you to study the Banks model carefully as you prepare lessons, units, and ongoing experiences for the children you teach.

Child's drawing honoring the character of the great leader, Chief Joseph.

A PORTRAIT OF CHIEF JOSEPH

Creating a Culturally Responsive Learning Environment

All of us desire to create classroom environments where children feel welcome, engaged, and appreciated for who they are. This is especially so in the case of social studies, because in social studies, the subject matter and the experience are ideally one. We don't just study citizenship, we engage in it. We don't just tell children about tolerance, we practice it together. The gap between what we teach and what we live must be closed if social studies is to come to life in any meaningful way. But how does this happen in day-to-day practical classroom life?

Hamilton (2000, 2004) offers a number of insights designed to promote a *culturally responsive learning environment*. Her ideas are simple yet profound. Put into practice, they have the potential to create a truly democratic community in miniature. The classroom becomes a place where diversity is seen as positive and where pluralism is celebrated along the way. Specifically, Hamilton identifies five practices that involve such important concepts as interest, relevance, collaboration, meaning, community, trust, and openness. These concepts come to life as they are actually lived by students who are then challenged to reflect on the quality of their experience.

Hamilton's (2000, 2004) ideas work at a variety of levels of growth and development, but I have attempted to capture and expand on them here with an emphasis on the elementary level social studies experience:

- *Coursework based on human needs and childhood interest.* When students feel their basic needs of safety, belonging, and curiosity are being met, they are ready for the challenges of ideas that are relevant to their lives, challenges that are developmentally appropriate and of interest.

- *Teaching as a collaboration with learners.* This involves nurturing students to believe in their own ideas and to express them in an accepting, caring environment. It also involves a search for meaning in what is being taught and learned, raising issues of honesty, value, and worth. The image of a great coach comes to mind—a coach who cares about young people, who holds them to standards, and who wants the best for the individuals and the team.

- *A community of learners who share and work together in a spirit of collaboration.* John Dewey thought an elementary classroom was at its best when it was a miniature community in which democracy, in the full sense of the term, came to life. Integration of subject matter is a wonderful thing, but integration of people who care and share is even more profound.

- *The development of a classroom environment that is blame free and based on trust and transformation.* I have seen such classrooms, and they are a beauty to behold. Such classrooms are overwhelmingly positive, polite, trusting places. Not only do the individuals in them grow and prosper, but so does the group. This kind of environment seems to blossom more readily where there is esprit de corps, where projects are being carried out, and where real-world applications are being made.

- *The development of classrooms where students are treated equally and invited to address behaviors and policies that are prejudicial.* In such a classroom, communication is real and fairness and justice are not abstract concepts but part of the expectations of daily life. Few teachers practice prejudicial behaviors consciously, and few teachers encourage such behaviors on the part of their students. Rather, such unfortunate behaviors more often arise when conscious attempts to ensure fairness and justice are not routinely part of the discussion of daily life. What is the key to this? The key is to adhere faithfully to the first four ideas found in this list.

Cultural Sensitivity: The Teacher as Learner

What can the teacher do to create a more culturally sensitive classroom climate? How does the social studies teacher contribute to the growth and development of future citizens, who will take their places in an increasingly pluralistic society? How do you as a teacher encourage your students to view diversity as positive?

These are not easy questions, and much is at stake in their answers. The very survival of our democracy depends on the attitudes that our children take into the future. If they are willing to embrace and even celebrate a society where all members are equal, where all members are treated with respect, and where each has an equal opportunity to succeed, then and only then is there hope for our success as a nation and a people. In a day when so much is demanded of teachers in terms of the development of student skills and knowledge and when that development is evaluated frequently by state and federally mandated tests, let us not lose sight of the fact that attitudes are equally important.

Here is an opportunity for you to assess your own attitudes and potential to succeed in a classroom environment where diversity is found. Research (Diller & Moule, 2005; Haberman, 1996) has shown that certain traits are related to success in teaching, especially success in teaching diverse student populations. Take a moment to respond to the statements in Figure 3.3 about teacher characteristics. For each statement, consider certain priorities in social studies teaching and respond "Yes," "No," or "Not sure." After you have done so, continue reading to examine the research results related to success in working with diverse student groups.

Did you answer "Yes" to most or all of the survey questions? "Yes" answers demonstrate cultural sensitivity. Research studies have shown that the qualities represented in these questions are shared by effective teachers in diverse, pluralistic school environments. No matter how you may have answered the questions, however, there is always room for improvement in your work with children. The best teachers are lifelong learners filled with the desire to be the best they can possibly be. Take the time to discuss the questions in this survey with your colleagues. They are far from trivial.

Haberman (1996) reports that the characteristics illustrated in the statements in the survey in Figure 3.3 are most likely to enhance cross-cultural teaching and learning. Diller and Moule (2005) identify four key teacher traits that are likely to enhance the successful interaction of teachers and culturally diverse students: care, dialogue, passionate pursuit, and openness to learning. What do these characteristics mean to you? To me, they identify a teacher who truly cares about each student; who creates an environment where everyone is encouraged to speak and to listen politely and thoughtfully when

---

Figure 3.3 *A Survey of Teacher Characteristics*

1. I believe the social studies teacher is responsible for engaging all students in purposeful learning experiences.   YES   NO   NOT SURE

2. I believe it is important for the social studies teacher to try to establish meaningful rapport with all students.   YES   NO   NOT SURE

3. I believe it is important for the social studies teacher to place emphasis on nurturing and coaching children to learn, supporting their curiosity and creative expression.   YES   NO   NOT SURE

4. I believe that children with difficult home lives deserve teachers who are willing to persist and offer emotional and academic support even when it appears difficult to do so.   YES   NO   NOT SURE

5. I believe it is important for the teacher to place greater emphasis on children's efforts at school rather than on their seeming academic ability.   YES   NO   NOT SURE

6. I believe it is important for teachers to reflect on and learn from their own mistakes.   YES   NO   NOT SURE

Source: M. Haberman, "Selecting and Preparing Culturally Competent Seachere for Urban Schools," in *Handbook of Research on Teacher Education* (2nd ed.), ed. J. Sikula, T. Buttery, & E. Guyon, (New York: Macmillan, 1996).

---

others speak; who brings energy, joy, and a sense of wonder to activities and experiences; and who is a model of lifelong learning.

One of the joys of teaching is found in the experience of humility. Some teachers discover this sooner than others. No matter how much you know or think you know, you can always be taught by your students. Teaching and learning are truly reciprocal. Sometimes it is difficult to know who is teaching whom—whether the teacher is teaching the students or the students the teacher. John Dewey (1916) acknowledged this many years ago when he wrote that the best classroom is one where the teacher becomes a learner and the learners become teachers.

During my own third year of teaching, I found myself in a new school and district, one quite different, in many ways, from the one in which I had spent my first two years. During the first week, I disciplined a child for some misbehavior that I no longer remember. I always tried to speak privately later in the day to any child I had disciplined; it seemed then, as it does now, a reasonable thing to try to talk privately after feelings had subsided. When I asked the child, whose name was John, if he wanted to talk about the incident, he told me that he felt I was picking on him because of his race. I was completely surprised. It hadn't occurred to me that race might have played a role in my actions. But I realized that John may have seen the incident differently. We had different perspectives on the same event. It was the beginning of the year, and we knew very little about each other.

I realized that John's interpretation of our interaction may have reflected his own experience, which had taught him to feel that way. By calling that to my attention, he was teaching me. If we consider John's misbehavior as a miniature historical event, isn't it reasonable to assume that more than one perspective exists? Just as eyewitnesses saw the Battle of Lexington differently, so John and I saw our interaction differently.

John was polite and expressed himself clearly. We got to know each other better as a result of our conversation. I realized that I needed to earn his trust—that he was not going to simply hand it to me because I was an adult authority figure. In fact, my role as an adult and authority may have made me harder to trust than a peer. This was the beginning of a wonderful teacher–student relationship, for which I take very little credit. John's own civility and patience made this interaction more congenial than some (and I do not mean to suggest that because he was polite, he deserved to be heard, whereas a student who responded more belligerently would be less worthy of concern). Our task is to take students as they come to us and to treat them with dignity and honor, even in the most difficult situations. So the next time you sit down to plan a lesson, don't overlook the possibility that you might be planning a learning experience for yourself as well as for your students.

Preparing Children for a Diverse World

The challenge of preparing children to take their places as citizens in a pluralistic society never ends. It is a journey more than a destination. One of the key principles of the UNESCO Earth Charter reads, "Honor and support the young people of our communities, enabling them to fulfill their essential role in creating sustainable societies." When we are called on (in the same document) to "eliminate discrimination in all its forms, such as that based on race, color, gender, sexual orientation, religion, language, and national, ethnic, or social origin," we begin to realize the enormity of the task. But as the old cliché goes, "No one said teaching was ever going to be easy."

Two ideas are worth bearing in mind as you prepare your students to be thoughtful citizens. The first has to do with the day-to-day social and moral fabric of school life. The children you teach are there to learn from you, in all the ways that such a trust implies. Children's learning process begins with or is founded on how they are treated routinely, every day, day in and day out. It is often the little incident that makes the difference: the casual exchange, the small smile, the encouraging remark, the cheerful hello. Your students are watching you and learning from your actions. No doubt in your reading methods class, you have learned that the more often your students see you read, the more they will value reading. In the same way, your students will notice how you treat them and how you treat others. They will look to you for guidance, reassurance, fairness, and leadership in its many manifestations. Remember always that children live what they learn and learn what they live. Your attitudes and behaviors will be contagious. Kindness, firmness, openness, caring, nurturing, and curiosity will spread through a classroom; they cannot be stopped. In the religion and philosophies of India, this is known as *karma*.

The second idea to keep in mind in preparing your students to become thoughtful, participant citizens in a diverse world is related to both the child and the curriculum. The social studies curriculum is about more than simply *covering* a course of study that represents a typical scope and sequence. It is also about *uncovering* and *recovering*. What do I mean? Simply this: The act of discovery consists of uncovering previously

Our American society is pluralistic and culturally rich.

unknown knowledge and ideas. Childhood is a time of discovery, and discovery at its best involves uncovering new ideas and recovering early knowledge.

The child who learns that Columbus sailed to the New World and opened two continents to European settlement and conquest also needs to learn that the native peoples of those continents probably viewed that historical event from the perspective of being overrun and oppressed. Likewise, the child who learns about the freedom and opportunity sought by early settlers in this country needs to learn that while many achieved this American dream, many others did not. We can only discover what we can uncover. And at some point, children discover that history is often recorded and published by those who were empowered in any given historical situation—by those who held the upper hand. In their journey of discovery, they need your help in uncovering the sometimes hidden evidence of diverse perspectives.

Beyond that, children discover that neither naïveté nor cynicism has much to offer. The conceptual secrets to be discovered are balance, openness, and reason. The human experience is filled with hope and wonder, just as it is filled with deceit and despair. Wisdom, that undervalued commodity in our world today, comes slowly, incrementally. Poet T. S. Eliot wrote of the hierarchy of information, knowledge, and wisdom. Our knowledge is only as good as our information. What knowledge is of most worth? Moreover, our adventure toward wisdom depends greatly on what we already know. Somewhere along the way on the journey from information to wisdom, we begin to put knowledge together into meaningful structures called *concepts*. It doesn't happen overnight. The quality of our knowledge and ultimately our wisdom becomes a product of the quality of our experience. This is the joy, the high moral ground, of teaching and learning with children. Use their time and yours well, and great things will happen.

Summary

Few issues are more vital to the preservation and improvement of a democratic society than the issue of respect for differences. The United States has been a nation of diversity since its founding. Even in colonial times, American society was probably the most diverse in the world. Diversity enriches a nation and its people. Democracy demands multiple perspectives in order to remain dynamic. The genius of the American nation is not that it is simply a homogeneous racial or ethnic enclave, rooted in traditions that cannot be changed, but that it is a nation dedicated to equality, opportunity, and freedom for all its peoples, regardless of their heritage. This has caused us to be a forward-looking nation, one that embraces pluralism and celebrates diversity.

One of the privileges of being an elementary teacher is that you are entrusted by the public to nurture young lives. I can imagine no greater honor. But with trust and honor come duty and obligation. The young citizens who come to your classroom each day are watching you, imitating you, and seeing in you what it means to be a responsible, caring adult. As you model respect, dignity, trust, and hope in their presence, you send them a powerful message of right and proper conduct in a civil society. In social studies, children will learn the history, geography, and civics of their country and of other countries. This is necessary, valuable, and appropriate. But the lessons learned will have little meaning if they are not lived by you and your students.

As you create conditions for community, tolerance, freedom, and opportunity in your classroom, you sow the seeds of a democratic, civil society that will bloom for years to come. Never underestimate your influence. As Henry Adams wrote, "A teacher affects eternity."

Explorations

Reflect On . . .

1. What do you consider to be the most important qualifications for a teacher who works with children of different cultural and racial/ethnic backgrounds? Why? What might a prospective teacher do to ensure that he or she will enter the classroom with those qualifications intact?

2. Social studies is the only curricular area that has human beings as its subject matter. Given the pressing educational issues related to diversity, what are the implications of this for the way your students study history, geography, civics, and the other social studies disciplines?

In the Field

3. Visit a local elementary school (or the one in which you are teaching), and select a unit or chapter from the social studies textbook that is in use at any level that interests you. Look for evidence of sensitivity to race/ethnicity, age, gender, and so on. What grade would you give this material for cultural sensitivity? Why? At what level of the Bankses' hierarchy does the material seem to fit?

4. Consider your own heritage. Create a family tree that identifies your ancestors and notes where they came from. In what ways do you think your own heritage has affected you? What do you perceive as the benefits and limitations that your heritage provides you as a teacher? If any of your relatives are teachers, ask them how they feel their heritage has affected their teaching, if at all.

For Your Portfolio

5. Plan a learning experience for an extended activity called "What Is an American? Who Is an American?" Create an interdisciplinary experience that includes the visual arts, music, and drama, along with civics, history, geography, and the other social sciences.

Continuing the Journey: Suggested Readings

Banks, J. A., et al. (2005). *Democracy and Diversity: Principles and Concepts for Education in a Global World.* Retrieved June 7, 2009, from *http://education.washington.edu/cme/DemDiv.pdf*

Campbell, W. J., Baikaloff, N., & Power, C. (2008). *Towards a Global Community.* New York: Springer.

Cochran-Smith, M., Feiman-Nemser, S., & McIntyre, D. J., eds. (2008). *Handbook of Research on Teacher Education* (3rd ed.). New York: Routledge.

Cole, R. (2008). *Educating Everybody's Children.* Alexandria, VA: Association for Supervision and Curriculum Development.

Danker, A. C. (2003). "Multicultural Social Studies: The Local History Connection," *Social Studies, 94*(3), 111–117.

Practical ways to acknowledge diversity in the local community.

Danker, A. C. (2005). *Multicultural Social Studies.* New York: Teachers College Press.

Delgado-Gaitan, C. (2006). *Building Culturally Responsive Classrooms.* Thousand Oaks, CA: Corwin Press.

Diller, J., & Moule, J. (2005). *Cultural Competence: A Primer for Educators.* Belmont, CA: Wadsworth.

This book serves as a useful introduction for teachers who wish to increase their own sensitivity to multicultural issues.

Ellermeyer, D., & Chick, K. (2003). *Multicultural American History: Through Children's Literature.* Minneapolis, MN: Greenwood.

A cornucopia of good reading that connects U.S. history to literature for young people.

Gillan, M. M., & Gillan, J. (1999). *Growing Up Ethnic in America.* New York: Penguin Books.

A sensitive portrayal of a minority perspective.

Grant, C., & Sleeter, C. (2007). *Doing Multicultural Education for Achievement and Equity.* New York: Routledge.

Haberman, M. (1996). "Selecting and Preparing Culturally Competent Teachers for Urban Schools." In J. Sikula, T. Buttery, & E. Guyon, eds. *Handbook of Research on Teacher Education* (2nd ed.). New York: Macmillan.

A research-based analysis of findings and implications that all teachers need to know.

Hamilton, M. H. (2000). "Creating a Culturally Responsive Learning Environment for African American Students." In M. Magolda, ed., *Teaching to Promote Intellectual and Personal Maturity: Incorporating Students' Worldviews and Identities into the Learning Process.* San Francisco: Jossey-Bass, pp. 45–54.

A kid's view of history with regard to treatment of minorities.

Hamilton, M. H. (2004). *Meeting the Needs of African American Women: New Directions for Student Services.* San Francisco: Jossey-Bass.

This book provides useful insights to complex issues. Hamilton provides clarity and direction applicable to a variety of situations at different levels

Knowles, E., Knowles, L., & Smith, M. (2007). *Understanding Diversity Through Novels and Picture Books.* Santa Barbara, CA: Libraries Unlimited.

McCall, A. L. (2002). "That's not Fair! Fourth Graders' Responses to Multicultural State history," *Social Studies, 93*(2): 85–91.

The ideas found here are practical and profound. This is an excellent beginning reference for any teacher who values sensitivity to others.

Scott, C., Gargan, A., & Zakierski, M. (1997). *Managing Diversity-Based Conflicts Among Children.* Bloomington, IN: Phi Delta Kappa Educational Foundation.

Ideas and techniques for conflict resolution with children in pluralistic settings.

Shrestha, L. B. (2006). *The Changing Demographic Profile of the United States.* Washington DC: Congressional Research Service.

Wheat, B., & Robinson Kapavik, R. (2005). "The Civil Rights Movement: A Humanities Rainbow," *Social Studies and the Young Learner, 17*(1), 15–16.

This article will help teachers of elementary-age students communicate positive ideas of diversity and pluralism.

Websites

National Association for Multicultural Education: Advocates for Educational Equity and Social Justice. *www.nameorg.org/*

The Center helps build relationships across differences to create a more inclusive and equitable community. In addition, The Center celebrates and teaches

diversity in order to foster conversation and respect among cultures. *www.diversityed.org/*

The Global Classroom Connection exists to bring classrooms across the world together to develop cross-cultural understanding. *www.classroom-connection.org/*

Related NCSS Standards and Principles of Powerful Social Studies

Curriculum Standards

The civic mission of social studies demands the inclusion of all students addressing cultural, linguistic and learning diversity including differences based on race, ethnicity, language, religion, gender, sexual orientation, exceptional learning needs, and other educationally and personally significant characteristics of learners. Diversity among learners embodies the democratic goal of embracing pluralism to make making social studies classrooms laboratories of democracy (p. 6–7).

Generally:
Theme I. Culture
Social studies curriculum should include experiences that provide for the study of culture and cultural diversity.

Human beings create, learn, and adapt to culture. Culture helps people to understand themselves as both individuals and members of various groups. Human cultures exhibit both similarities and differences. All, for example, have systems of belief, knowledge, values, and traditions. Each is also unique. In a multicultural democratic society, students need to understand multiple perspectives that derive from different cultural vantage points. This understanding allows them to relate to people in this and other nations.

For early grades:
Theme I: Culture
Social studies program should include experiences that provide for the study of culture and cultural diversity.

Purposes:

The learner will understand how human beings create, learn, and adapt to culture. They will understand how multiple perspectives derive from different cultural vantage points in order to better relate to and interact with people in this and other nations. This information will help learners make informed decisions in an increasingly interconnected world.

Source: Excerpted from National Task Force for Social Studies. *Expectations of Excellence: Curriculum Standards for Social Studies* (Washington, DC: National Council for the Social Studies, 2008) [Draft].

Teacher Standards

2. Differences in Learning Styles

Social studies teachers should possess the knowledge, capabilities, and dispositions to create at the appropriate school levels learning experiences that fit the different approaches to learning of diverse learners (p. 1).

Teacher Expectations
Teachers of social studies at all school levels should provide developmentally appropriate experiences as they guide learners in the study of culture and cultural diversity to assist learners to understand and apply the concept of culture as an integrated whole that governs the functions and interactions of language, literature, arts, traditions, beliefs, values, and behavior patterns;

- guide learners as they predict how experiences may be interpreted by people from diverse cultural perspectives and frames of reference;
- enable learners to assess the importance of cultural unity and diversity within and across groups;
- have learners interpret patterns of behavior as reflecting values and attitudes, which contribute

to or pose obstacles to cross-cultural understanding. P. ?

Source: Excerpted from National Council for the Social Studies. *National Standards for Social Studies Teachers* (Silver Spring, MD: Author, 2002, revised 2006). The Council's website is www.socialstudies.org

---

SAMPLE LESSON 3.1   Diversity: Comparing Cultures

AGE LEVEL: Primary or Intermediate

NCSS STANDARD: THEME I: CULTURE.

Social studies programs should include experiences that provide for the study of culture and cultural diversity.

KNOWLEDGE: Explore and describe similarities and differences in the ways different social groups meet similar needs and concerns

KEY IDEA: All cultures share some characteristics.

INSTRUCTIONAL OBJECTIVE: Students will compare their own culture with the culture of another group and identify similarities and differences with regard to food, shelter, language, religion, art, and beliefs.

SET: Locate and share an image from a culture that is unfamiliar to your students. Discuss the image so that students identify at least one characteristic that the image has in common with their own culture. For example, showing a picture of Salish Native Americans traversing waterways of the Pacific Northwest in a canoe might remind students of the time they rode in a boat or went fishing.

INSTRUCTION: The day before you begin this lesson, go to your school librarian and ask for help finding children's books that discuss different cultures. Look for short books with pictures. Be sure that the books you choose are appropriate for the age and reading level of your students. Your librarian can help you in this area. Gather enough books, with a few extras,

so that you can use them for small group work. Choose one of these books to share with the class. After reading the book with students, discuss cultural aspects that the book portrayed. When applicable, organize your discussion around these topics: food, shelter, language, religion, art, and beliefs. Conclude the discussion by having students identify similarities and differences between the book that you read and their own culture.

REFLECTION/ASSESSMENT: Organize students into groups of three or four. Distribute the books that you gathered from your school's library. Have students take turns reading the book to each other. Younger children can show the pictures to one another. Distribute one large piece of paper to each group, have students write or illustrate about the culture that the book depicted. Again, this work can be organized around the following concepts: food, shelter, language, religion, art, and beliefs. As groups finish their work, have them identify one similarity and one difference between their own culture and the culture that they learned about from their library book.

CLOSURE/ENRICHMENT: Have each group of students share their findings. As groups share, make a record of the similarities and differences that students mention on the board in the form of a t-chart. Complete the lesson with a discussion about what all people seem to have in common according to your chart.

Chapter 4

Setting and Achieving Social Studies Standards

Keys to This Chapter

- The Nature of Knowledge
- Content Standards and Performance Standards
- The National Council for the Social Studies as a Guide to the Knowledge Base
- What Children Should Know and Be Able to Do
- The Structure of the Social Science Disciplines as Fundamental Knowledge

Any time you sincerely want to make a change, the first thing you must do is to raise your standards.

     —Anthony Robbins

The nicest thing about standards is that there are so many to choose from.

     —Andres Tannenbaum

The central question of this chapter—What should elementary students know and be able to do?—is not an easy question to answer, and discussing it raises a considerable amount of controversy. We can begin our quest with the content, concepts, and methods of elementary social studies. They are derived primarily from history, geography, and the social sciences. Social studies is both integrative and broad in scope by its very nature. After all, when the subject matter is human beings and their interaction with the environment, then we have a wide-ranging course of study. This is both a strength and weakness of this area of the curriculum. It is a strength because human behavior takes so many forms over time and place that we are never at a loss for interesting material. The weakness may be that there is so much to learn that it seems, at times, overwhelming. Children are all too easily overwhelmed by names, dates, facts, and so on. The secret is to bring meaning to knowledge. Good teachers have always known that.

"Knowledge is of two kinds. We know a subject ourselves, or we know where we can find information upon it."
              —Samuel Johnson

You can see from the 1775 Samuel Johnson quote (by the way, he wrote the first dictionary of the English language) that there is an age-old perception of the differences people have in mind when they speak about knowledge.

In a nutshell, the argument is over whether knowledge is strictly content, strictly process, or, as Dr. Johnson suggests, both. A recurring issue in teaching and learning social studies is that of what and how much children should know about history, geography, and the social sciences. It is easy to find critical commentaries regarding how little today's students know, especially compared to students of generations past. Similarly, it is not particularly difficult to find commentaries arguing that the amount of content knowledge someone has is insignificant. This argument holds that the important thing is that people have process skills that enable them to locate and use knowledge when needed. Each of these arguments contains a certain measure of truth and a good dose of exaggeration.

Actually, the content versus process debate will probably never be completely solved, simply because it hinges so much on opinion and philosophy of teaching and learning. Let me illustrate the point by asking you to examine the two accompanying boxes: Keys to Progressive and Essentialist Education. They present the basic arguments from the progressive (process orientation) and essentialist (basic skills and knowledge) points of view, respectively. Take a moment to consider each and whether you favor one perspective more than the other or whether perhaps you see certain advantages in each.

Content Standards and Performance Standards

The standards movement began in education in the 1980s in the wake of the *Nation at Risk* (1983) report, which lamented the perceived academic shortcomings of U.S. schools. The first standards were developed in mathematics, and soon other areas of the curriculum began to follow suit. By the mid-1990s, social studies had standards in place. A great deal has been written about social studies standards. Because social studies is an umbrella for a number of disciplines, including history, geography, and the social sciences, it has been a monumental undertaking to complete the work of developing standards in all these areas. The word *standards* means many things to many people. However, a useful place to begin an examination of social studies standards is to explore the differences between *content* standards and *performance* standards.

Content standards are the facts, information, knowledge, understandings, and values that students are reasonably expected to acquire at the completion of various checkpoints on their way through school, typically at the end of certain grade levels. The issue is what students should know. So, for example, if we agree that students should know that a market exists whenever buyers and sellers exchange goods and services, then we have established a content standard. This represents a content standard in economics. If we agree that students should be able to explain how the three branches of the federal government provide checks and balances on one another, we have established a content standard in civics.

Performance standards, on the other hand, are statements that serve as indicators of evidence that students can make applications of knowledge and skills. Performance standards typically spell out certain measurable levels of proficiency, or what a student must do to demonstrate an ability. The issue is what students are able to do. An example from geography might be the ability to construct from memory a map of the world showing the locations of significant landforms, bodies of water, and political divisions. An example from anthropology could be a student's ability to show how the diffusion of ideas learned at school affects her or his life at home.

Given the day-to-day realities of school life, the separation of content and performance standards is not so clear, nor should it be. In the best learning experiences, knowing and doing are inseparable. Aristotle wrote that if you want to learn something, the best way is to do it. This wise insight informs us that knowledge without application is inert.

The Nature of Knowledge

Who was the first president of the United States? Who is the woman whose profile has recently appeared on a U.S. coin? How many time zones does the United States have? Which state is bordered by more states than any other? What were the principal causes of the Civil War?

Keys to Progressive Education — *Process*

- Learning how to learn is at the heart of the matter. Students need to learn how to deal with unknown outcomes and challenges. In this sense, knowledge is seen as dynamic and ever changing rather than as static.
- Subject matter does not represent an end in itself; rather, it provides the raw material for learning and is relevant when it can be put to use. Textbooks, lectures, and formal examinations are considered artificial; true learning takes place when real problems of living are engaged and subject matter is used as a tool or instrument for learning.
- Experience is the key to productive learning. Learning should be active, exploratory, and socially engaged. A school should be a miniature democracy, a community where citizenship is learned through experience.
- Learner interest is significant. Human beings learn best when they have the opportunity to study those things that interest them most.
- Project learning is productive because of its practical, problem-solving, creative, social, and open-ended attributes.
- Real-world connections provide a sense of relevance and enable students to feel that they are taking part in public life.
- Reflective thinking should accompany active learning to provide a sense of purpose, balance, and assessment.
- The *process* of education should take precedence over the *product*. Learning represents continuous growth and is a complex enterprise.

Table 4.1 *Social Studies Standard Articulated by Grade Level—Strand 3: Civics/Government*

Concept 4: Rights, Responsibilities, and Roles of Citizenship

The rights, responsibilities and practices of United States citizenship are founded in the Constitution and the nation's history.

Kindergarten	Grade 1	Grade 2	Grade 3	Grade 4
PO 1. Identify examples of responsible citizenship in the school setting and in stories about the past and present.	**PO 1.** Identify examples of responsible citizenship in the school setting and in stories about the past and present.	**PO 1.** Discuss examples of responsible citizenship in the school setting and in stories about the past and present.	**PO 1.** Describe the rights and responsibilities of citizenship: a. good sportsmanship b. participation and cooperation c. rules and consequences d. voting	**PO 1.** Discuss ways an individual can contribute to a school or community.
PO 2. Recognize the rights and responsibilities of citizenship: a. elements of fair play, good sportsmanship, and the idea of treating others the way you want to be treated b. importance of participation and cooperation in a classroom and community c. why there are rules and the consequences for violating them d. responsibility of voting (every vote counts)	**PO 2.** Describe the rights and responsibilities of citizenship: a. elements of fair play, good sportsmanship, and the idea of treating others the way you want to be treated b. importance of participation and cooperation in a classroom and community c. why there are rules and the consequences for violating them d. responsibility of voting (every vote counts)	**PO 2.** Describe the rights and responsibilities of citizenship: a. elements of fair play, good sportsmanship, and the idea of treating others the way you want to be treated b. importance of participation and cooperation in a classroom and community c. why we have rules and the consequences for violating them d. responsibility of voting	**PO 2.** Describe the importance of students contributing to a community (e.g., service projects, cooperating, volunteering).	**PO 2.** Identify traits of character (e.g., responsibility, respect, perseverance, loyalty, integrity, involvement, justice and tolerance) that are important to the preservation and improvement of democracy.

Grade 5	Grade 6	Grade 7	Grade 8
PO 2. Describe the character traits (i.e., respect, responsibility, fairness, involvement) that are important to the preservation and improvement of constitutional democracy in the United States.	**PO 2.** Discuss the character traits (i.e., respect, responsibility, fairness, involvement) that are important to the preservation and improvement of constitutional democracy in the United States. Connect with: Strand 2 Concept 5	**PO 2.** Discuss the character traits (e.g., respect, responsibility, fairness, involvement) that are important to the preservation and improvement of constitutional democracy in the United States.	**PO 2.** Discuss the character traits (e.g., respect, responsibility, fairness, involvement) that are important to the preservation and improvement of constitutional democracy in the United States.
PO 3. Describe the importance of citizens being actively involved in the democratic process (e.g., voting, student government, involvement in political decision making, analyzing issues, petitioning public officials).	**PO 3.** Describe the importance of citizens being actively involved in the democratic process (e.g., voting, student government, involvement in political decision making, analyzing issues, petitioning public officials). Connect with: Strand 2 Concept 5	**PO 3.** Describe the importance of citizens being actively involved in the democratic process (i.e., voting, student government, involvement in political decision making, analyzing issues, petitioning public officials).	**PO 3.** Describe the importance of citizens being actively involved in the democratic process (i.e., voting, student government, involvement in political decision making, analyzing issues, petitioning public officials).
		PO 4. Explain the obligations and responsibilities of citizenship: a. upholding the Constitution b. obeying the law c. paying taxes d. registering for selective service e. jury duty	**PO 4.** Explain the obligations and responsibilities of citizenship: a. upholding the Constitution b. obeying the law c. paying taxes d. registering for selective service e. jury duty
		PO 5. Describe the impact of Constitutional Amendments	**PO 5.** Describe the impact that the following had on rights for individuals

Source: Retrieved from World Wide Web Nov. 2009 *www.ade.state.az.us/standards/sstudies/articulated.* Approval 9.26.05. Updated 5.22.06. This table contains selected Performance Objectives from the Arizona Social Studies Standard Articulated By Grade Level. To see the complete listing of Performance Objectives for Strand 3:Civics/ Government Concept 4, go to: http://www.ade.state.az.us/standards/sstudies/articulated

Perhaps you think I'm trying to draw you into a game of Trivial Pursuit. No, on the contrary, I'm merely bringing up an issue that has become one of paramount debate in recent years—that of what and how much children ought to know as a result of their experiences with elementary social studies. At the heart of this matter is the process/product controversy, the essence of which is whether greater emphasis should be placed on *how* to learn or *what* to learn. Everyone agrees that both are important, but the argument is focused more on where the appropriate balance lies than on anything else.

Keys to Essentialist Education —*Content*

- The true purpose of education is intellectual and academic, not social and emotional.
- Education should be rigorous and demanding. The teacher's role is that of scholar who challenges students to reach higher levels of academic achievement.
- Academically talented students should especially be challenged because they represent the nation's future talent pool in a meritocratic society.
- The core disciplines, such as history and geography, should represent the essence of the curriculum. Activities in peer relations, life adjustment, and so on should be downplayed.
- Standards are necessary, as are standardized tests of achievement. Standards help teachers and students focus on essential knowledge and skills.
- Educational fads—such as learning styles, self-esteem curricula, and so on—are distractions from the real issue, which is to provide each student with the basic skills and knowledge necessary to achieve in life.
- Traditional forms—including textbooks, examinations, grades, graded schools, standards for promotion, and the like—are of proven worth and should be maintained.

What do you think about this? Perhaps your opinion is influenced by your own experience with social studies during your school years. Maybe you were the type of person who enjoyed learning the names of rivers and mountains, about the way people made a living in distant lands, or about life in ancient times. Maybe you weren't. Take a moment to write briefly your own recollections of social studies, especially how you felt about it.

ALL BOOK - BORED TO DEATH

Whether your memories were positive, negative, or mixed is no doubt influenced by (1) your attitude toward the subject matter itself, (2) the kinds of experiences you had in learning the subject matter, and (3) who taught you. In most cases, the subject matter itself is the least important of the three considerations. One person may remember studying Latin America and how boring it was. Another person may remember studying Latin America and how much fun it was when the class got to fix a Latin American meal and how kind and enthusiastic the teacher was about things. Elements such as these tend to interact and influence how a person feels, not just about social studies but also about school learning in general.

Each of us has a certain amount of portable knowledge of history, geography, and the like. This knowledge belongs to us, and we carry it around with us inside our heads. It is committed to memory. Of course, memory fits into two categories: long term and short term. Some things we seem to remember all our lives, and other things, well, we just hope we can remember them for the big test! But whatever we know, we had to *acquire* the knowledge because we weren't simply born with it.

Knowledge Received

There are three ways that people know what they know. The first way, and the most common, is *knowledge received*. People receive knowledge from many sources: lecture, explanation, story, sermon, song, textbook, film, and so on. The point is that the knowledge first belongs to someone else, and it is then transmitted to another through some medium. This is essentially a passive view of knowledge acquisition. That, however, can be misleading because the level of a person's motivation will determine his or her level of involvement. Perhaps you can recall being told a story when you were a child and your own imagination was participating actively along with the storyteller. Knowledge received implies that experts are at the source and novices who need to know something are on the receiving end. The expert may be a lecturer, the author of a textbook, a gifted storyteller, or whatever, but the point is that the relationship between the expert and the learner is unequal. Another point worth considering about knowledge received is that it is secondhand knowledge. The learner generally trusts the accuracy of the authority because the learner is dependent on the expert source of information.

Most of your knowledge and mine is knowledge received. We didn't create it, and we probably had no way to verify it; rather, we tend to trust its accuracy. For example, you may know some things about life in ancient Greece or colonial America. It is likely that you received that knowledge from some source or perhaps a number of sources. It is important for a teacher to convey to students that no text on any subject is entirely accurate. There is no such thing as complete accuracy; only degrees of accuracy are found.

Knowledge Discovered

A second way people know what they know is *knowledge discovered*. This means of knowing is quite different from knowledge received. The implication of knowledge discovered is that some thing, event, circumstance, or whatever exists that you do not

Students learn about colonial life from an expert reenactor during a field trip.

know about; however, by applying yourself, you can find out. In a nutshell, the difference between these first two forms is as simple as the difference between being told by someone else and finding out for yourself.

In essence, this changes the learning equation fundamentally. The center of gravity shifts to the learner. The teacher, or other expert source, becomes a facilitator. This puts the teacher in an extremely important role because he or she must arrange the environment for learning in such a way as to be challenging, motivating, and filled with possibilities. Discovery learning assumes that students will investigate, experiment, use trial and error, and reach conclusions for themselves. Thus, in their quest for knowledge, students become historians, geographers, and so on.

The teacher who involves students in knowledge discovered must create a rich environment, know when to ask questions, know when to lend support and cues, and, most difficult of all, know when not to intervene. All this raises teaching to a higher art form.

Knowledge Constructed

The third way people know what they know is *knowledge constructed*. Here, there is no assumption of the prior existence of certain knowledge; that is, being told or even finding out will not work at this level. At a simple level, imagine an empty lot with little on it. You decide to build a house there. You change things as a result of your effort. Now knowledge of a house in that part of town is common—others know about it, too. Knowledge constructed implies the building of new structures, the writing of new stories or accounts, the reassembling of existing knowledge into new forms, and so on. **Creativity and originality** are keys to knowledge constructed, although the creativity may exist within an already developed pattern. Projects, plays, building, and drawings are examples of knowledge constructed.

Knowledge of this third kind also exists as a social construction. Children working together will talk about what they are doing. They will make decisions, have agreements and disagreements, organize themselves, socialize, reflect, and find themselves linked to something greater than that which exists when people work alone. Thus, a far more subtle kind of knowledge emerges. It is a knowledge of friendship, collaboration, and teamwork. This kind of knowledge must be experienced in order for it to be real. To deny this kind of knowledge to children in the name of teaching social studies would be ironic, to say the very least.

Russian psychologist Lev Vygotsky noted the importance of language and thought as dependent on each other for their development. When children work together on a project, a mural, a play, or a construction activity, they will have the opportunity to express their ideas and feelings during the process. They are engaged in constructing knowledge as they talk and listen to each other. The importance of this can hardly be underestimated. When people express themselves verbally in connection with their involvement in an activity, they have the possibility to reach higher levels of consciousness about what they are doing. They can reflect, decide, evaluate, and employ a range of metacognitive strategies that are not available to the person working alone.

In summary, it is fair to say that all three ways of knowing are strategic and complementary. People simply cannot discover or create everything they need to know, so received knowledge plays a vital role in human development. On the other hand, knowledge received must be balanced with knowledge discovered and constructed. The wise teacher understands the relationship among all three and uses all three. When President Thomas Jefferson sent Lewis and Clark on their three-year expedition to the West of North America, he chose them because they were well read and had received knowledge from multiple sources over the years. He also chose them because he knew they were discoverers, and, indeed, they discovered many plants, animals, rivers, mountain passes, and so on along the way. But Jefferson also knew these expedition leaders would construct new knowledge of the West as a result of their experiences. Their maps, charts, and descriptions created new knowledge of a landscape known well perhaps to certain Native Americans but hardly at all to European Americans. Today their journal accounts are considered to be one of the great epic stories of the nineteenth century.

A gifted teacher is aware that the well-known journeys of discovery found in text and film are qualitatively no different from the journeys of discovery that her or his students are involved in as they learn about their world and construct both personal and collective meanings of it. The key is balance. All three ways of knowing are necessary, and each complements the others.

The National Council for the Social Studies as a Guide to the Knowledge Base

The past decade has seen the development of national standards in all the major areas of school curriculum. The standards for social studies were completed under the aegis of the National Council for the Social Studies (NCSS) in 1994 and were revisited and slightly revised in 2009. The standards serve as a general framework for the knowledge and experiential basis of social studies. The purpose of the standards is not, as some have feared, to create a national curriculum. Rather, the intent is to establish a sense of direction and a goal structure.

The NCSS notes that the standards should support three intended outcomes. Let's take a look at each of these.

First, the standards should serve as a framework for K–12 social studies program design through the use of 10 thematic strands. As illustrated in Figure 4.1, 10 thematic strands represent broad categories of teaching and learning and are meant to provide only the most general sense of coverage. However, they convey the essence of the spiral curriculum concept of visiting and revisiting a few key ideas from kindergarten through twelfth grade.

The 10 key strands from the NCSS standards represent powerful ideas about human behavior. As you examine them carefully, you will see that they are concept statements from history, geography, and the social sciences. They are a logical place for you to begin thinking about the spiral curriculum and its potential to build a schema for young learners. These ideas need to be emphasized and reemphasized each year at increasing levels of sophistication. The standards are, in fact, the cornerstone of the social studies goal structure. As you plan lessons, units, and experiences, you should seriously consider them. I would go so far as to say that every social studies experience should relate to one or more of the strands. The point that must be underscored, however, is that the ideas need to be taught and learned in developmentally appropriate ways.

Second, the NCSS standards serve as a guide for curriculum decision making by providing performance expectations regarding knowledge, processes, and attitudes essential for all students. At one level, decisions about what textbooks to adopt, which materials to use, and so on should focus on the knowledge, processes, and attitudes exemplified in the 10 concept statements. The hope is that commercial textbook companies and experimental projects alike will take the standards into account so that a measure of commonality will emerge. This is not to say that every program should look alike, especially in a day of site-based decision making. Rather, the point is that educators can begin to address these fundamental questions: (1) What knowledge of history, geography, and social science should children possess? (2) What skills of critical thinking and problem solving should children attain? (3) What values of citizenship and self-fulfillment are basic to positive growth and development for children in a democratic society?

Third, the NCSS standards should provide examples of classroom practice to guide teachers in designing instruction to help students meet performance expectations. As you design lessons and units, you will want to take into account the performance

Figure 4.1 *NCSS Standards: Ten Key Strands*

I. Culture

Human beings create, learn, and adapt culture. Human cultures are dynamic systems of beliefs, values, and traditions that exhibit both commonalities and differences. Understanding culture helps us understand ourselves and others.

II. Time, Continuity, and Change

Human beings seek to understand their historic roots and to locate themselves in time. Such understanding involves knowing what things were like in the past and how things change and develop—allowing us to develop historic perspective and answer important questions about our current condition.

III. People, Places, and Environment

Technological advancements have insured that students are aware of the world beyond their personal locations. As students study content related to this theme, they create their spatial views and geographic perspectives of the world; social, cultural, economic, and civic demands mean that students will need such knowledge, skills, and understandings to make informed and critical decisions about the relationship between human beings and their environment.

IV. Individual Development and Identity

Personal identity is shaped by one's culture, by groups and by institutional influences. Examination of various forms of human behavior enhances understanding of the relationships between social norms and emerging personal identities, the social processes which influence identity formation, and the ethical principles underlying individual action.

V. Individuals, Groups, and Institutions

Institutions exert enormous influence over us. Institutions are organizational embodiments to further the core social values of those who comprise them. It is important for students to know how institutions are formed, what controls and influences them, how they control and influence individuals and culture, and how institutions can be maintained or changed.

VI. Power, Authority, and Governance

Understanding of the historic development of structures of power, authority, and governance and their evolving functions in contemporary society is essential for the emergence of civic competence.

VII. Production, Distribution, and Consumption

Decisions about exchange, trade, and economic policy and well-being are global in scope and the role of government in policy making varies over time and from place to place. The systematic study of an interdependent world economy and the role of technology in economic decision making is essential.

VIII. Science, Technology, and Society

Technology is as old as the first crude tool invented by prehistoric humans, and modern life as we know it would be impossible without technology and the science which supports it. Todays technology forms the basis for some of our most difficult social choices.

IX. Global Connections

The realities of global interdependence require understanding of the increasingly important and diverse global connections among world societies before there can be analysis leading to the development of possible solutions to persisting and emerging global issues.

X. Civic Ideals and Practices

All people have a stake in examining civic ideals and practices across time, in diverse societies, as well as in determining how to close the gap between present practices and the ideals upon which our democratic republic is based. An understanding of civic ideals and practices of citizenship is critical to full participation in society.

Source: National Council for the Social Studies, *Expectations of Excellence: Curriculum Standards for Social Studies,* (Washington, DC: Author, 1994). © National Council for the Social Studies. Reprinted by permission.

expectations implied in the strands. In order to give you a clearer idea of this, Figures 4.2 and 4.3 illustrate at the primary and middle grades, respectively, *performance expectations* (i.e., what should students know and be able to do as a result) and *classroom examples* showing how teachers can bring the NCSS standards to life.

Figure 4.2 *Standard VII: Production, Distribution, and Consumption—Primary Grades*

Social studies programs should include experiences that provide for the study of *how people organize for the production, distribution, and consumption of goods and services,* so that the learner can:

Performance Expectations

a. give examples that show how scarcity and choice govern our economic decisions;

b. distinguish between needs and wants;

c. identify examples of private and public goods and services;

d. give examples of the various institutions that make up economic systems such as families, workers, banks, labor unions, government agencies, small businesses, and large corporations;

e. describe how we depend upon workers with specialized jobs and the ways in which they contribute to the production and exchange of goods and services;

f. describe the influence of incentives, values, traditions, and habits on economic decisions;

g. explain and demonstrate the role of money in everyday life;

h. describe the relationship of price to supply and demand;

i. use economic concepts such as supply, demand, and price to help explain events in the community and nation;

j. apply knowledge of economic concepts in developing a response to a current local economic issue, such as how to reduce the flow of trash into a rapidly filling landfill.

Focus on the Classroom: Standards into Practice

Performance Expectations: e, i

At the beginning of a unit on economic specialization in production, Mark Moran's early primary class is divided into two teams of cookie makers. Both teams make gingerbread cookies. One team works as an assembly line, each person having a special job—rolling out the dough, cutting the basic shape, making the almond mouth, locating raisin buttons, etc. The second team works as individuals, each person creating his or her own gingerbread cookies. Both teams have the same supplies to work with.

After they have finished baking their cookies, the students examine the cookies and identify the advantages and disadvantages of each method of producing cookies. Ideas that emerge relate to division of labor, pride, creativity, independence, specialization, and quality control.

Students subsequently prepare summaries in writing about how they produced their cookies. Moran evaluates the quality of the student writing by determining how accurate the students are in detailing the production process and the extent to which evidence of key concepts is present.

In the weeks that follow this lesson, students examine other situations involving assembly line production, including a field trip to a local plant where pickup trucks are assembled.

Source: National Council for the Social Studies, *Expectations of Excellence: Curriculum Standards for Social Studies* (Washington, DC: Author, 1994), p. 69. © National Council for the Social Studies. Reprinted by permission.

Figure 4.3 *Standard I: Culture—Middle Grades*

Social studies programs should include experiences that provide for the study of *culture and cultural diversity,* so that the learner can:

Performance Expectations

a. compare similarities and differences in the ways groups, societies, and cultures meet human needs and concerns;

b. explain how information and experiences may be interpreted by people from diverse cultural perspectives and frames of reference;

c. explain and give examples of how language, literature, the arts, architecture, other artifacts, traditions, beliefs, values, and behaviors contribute to the development and transmission of culture;

d. explain why individuals and groups respond differently to their physical and social environments and/or changes to them on the basis of shared assumptions, values, and beliefs;

e. articulate the implications of cultural diversity, as well as cohesion, within and across groups.

Focus on the Classroom: Standards into Practice

Performance Expectations: a, c, d, e

The fifth grade students in Rose Sudmeier's class are sharing the stories behind their names in small groups. In constructing a "native culture" in their classroom, they have studied the place/environment, including descriptions, vocabulary development, visual presentations, and survival in the environment. This process led to a look at the people living in that place. They are now talking about naming traditions in general and how they came to be named.

The class researches the tools, food, and other survival necessities that would be needed in their place. They then begin to discuss what the people might do at night when it was dark or during the day when work was done and how traditions, such as the naming tradition, might be passed on. At this point, Sudmeier brings in her colleague, Dave Trowbridge, and his geography class from the high school, which has been studying traditions, storytelling, art, and music of the Northwest Coastal Indian tribes.

The high school students visit the fifth grade class on two different days, showing the elementary students how to do basic dance steps and how to make dancing masks. They also tell them stories of various legends and play musical tapes. The fifth graders continue their study for another three days on their own. The high school students plan a return visit for the end of the week, when they also invite the fifth graders to be their guests in a potlatch. At the potlatch, the high schoolers entertain the fifth graders with stories and then have them join them in dances and use the masks they had shown them how to make. In keeping with the potlatch tradition, the guests receive small gifts from the high school students at the end.

As an evaluation tool, Sudmeier has the children keep journals in which they write about their culture, traditions they started, poetry they wrote about their environment, and reflections on their participation in the various activities. She looks for the journals to be thoughtfully written, expressing positive views, accurate in the information presented, creative, and reflective.

Source: National Council for the Social Studies, *Expectations of Excellence: Curriculum Standards for Social Studies* (Washington, DC: Author, 1994), p. 79. © National Council for the Social Studies. Reprinted by permission.

Key Strands as Powerful Ideas

The 10 key strands from the NCSS standards (Figure 4.1) represent powerful ideas about human behavior. As you examine them carefully, you will see that they are concept statements from history, geography, and the social sciences. They are a logical place for you to begin thinking about the spiral curriculum and its potential to build a schema for young learners. These ideas need to be emphasized and reemphasized each year at increasing levels of sophistication. They are in fact the cornerstone of the social studies goal structure. As you plan lessons, units, and experiences, you should seriously consider them. I would go so far as to say that every social studies experience should relate to one or more of the strands. The point that must be underscored, however, is that the ideas need to be taught and learned in developmentally appropriate ways.

The key strands also serve as guides for curriculum decision making. At one level, decisions about what textbooks to adopt, which materials to use, and so on should focus on the knowledge, processes, and attitudes exemplified in the concept statements of the strands. The hope is that commercial textbook companies and experimental projects alike will consider the strands so that a measure of commonality will emerge. This is not to say that every program should look alike, especially in a day of site-based decision making. Rather, the point is that we can begin to address these fundamental questions: (1) What knowledge of history, geography, and social science should children possess? (2) What skills of critical thinking and problem solving should children attain? (3) What values of citizenship and self-fulfillment are basic to positive growth and development for children in a democratic society?

The third use of the strands is that they can serve as a guide to classroom practice. As you design lessons and units, you will want to consider the performance expectations implied in the strands. To have a clearer idea of this, refer to Figure 4.2 on page 80, and Figure 4.3 on page 81. These figures illustrate, at primary and intermediate levels, *performance expectations* (that is, what should students know and be able to do as a result) and *classroom examples* showing how teachers can bring them to life.

What Children Should Know and Be Able to Do

The sheer amount of information and knowledge that exists in today's world is so overwhelming that it seems an impossible task to decide exactly what students of certain grades and ages should know. But compared to the world of the future, this is nothing. As difficult as it is to calculate the growth of knowledge, it appears that the knowledge base doubles every six months or so. Much of what we "know" today will be wrong or obsolete in the near future. Many of today's skills will be consigned to the dustbin of history tomorrow. Imagine trying to keep up with events in history. Each day adds another chapter. A year or so ago, elementary age students were still learning that our solar system has nine planets. Now astronomers tell us that there are eight. Poor Pluto has been demoted from planet to large rock.

It is not easy for teachers to keep up with changing events and with the many avenues of information that are available. Libraries still exist and probably always will, but the

Internet—a dream only a few decades ago—exists today. Virtual libraries on the Internet give teachers and students access to information sources that are far more plentiful than even the best library could hold. Just imagine—a little more than a century ago, a main requirement for teaching a particular grade was to have completed at least one grade above it. So, if you had finished eighth grade, you could teach seventh or lower. Now teachers are expected to have completed a baccalaureate degree or more to be eligible to teach in elementary school.

Rather than give up, let's explore some thoughts on what you and your students should know and be able to do. The first thing to do is relax; neither you nor I can know everything, so we must be selective. This translates into the oft-heard phrase, "less is more." Depth is more significant than breadth. The coverage mentality does not work for at least two reasons: (1) There is too much to cover and (2) the knowledge gained is superficial and goes in one ear and out the other.

A second thought is that "learning how to learn" serves people well as knowledge grows exponentially. Learning how to learn is as much about a person's attitude as anything else. To the extent that you model your own curiosity, your discoveries, your reading, and your involvement in civic life, you are teaching kids that learning is an active ongoing process that lasts a lifetime.

A third point is one made convincingly by the psychologist Jerome Bruner that learners need to focus on the *structure* of knowledge rather than merely on content. This means an emphasis on discovery, inquiry, collaboration, sharing, service learning, lots of reading and writing, and other active forms of learning, not merely what, but how and why as well. Bruner's ideas on the structure of knowledge focus primarily on *methods* or *processes* used in social science and on *concepts* or *key ideas* from the social science disciplines. See Figures 4.2 and 4.3 for examples of key concepts (ideas) and processes (methods) used in the social sciences. Be sure that they are built in as integral components of your social studies curriculum.

As the study of human beings and their interactions, social studies offers many opportunities for acquiring the kind of knowledge of human behavior that will benefit your students even in an unknown future. We could call these qualities *life skills*. Four such life skills have been identified in social science research, particularly in the work of David McClelland at Harvard (Ellis, 2010). Among those qualities are team building, adaptability, and self-regulation. How do students acquire such knowledge? There is no other way than modeling and practice.

Team building happens as students work and play together under the guidance of a teacher who values collaboration, group projects, games, drama, and other experiences that bring children together. Such opportunities make social and moral growth possible as students learn in an atmosphere where fairness, sharing, civility, and support for each other are part of the fabric of school life. Team efforts allow students to experience something they could never experience alone. To be a part of something, a class play, a mural project, or a historical investigation in the community, to name a few examples, opens the door to what are known as *transcendent experiences*. It is difficult to explain transcendent experiences to people who have never had them, but the best I can do is to say that something happens when you become part of a larger effort; you become part of a team doing something special. It has been said by more than one psychologist that young people who do not have them will invariably find engaging in group work and team building difficult and unrewarding.

Adaptability and resilience are skills that will always be necessary. No matter how much new knowledge is created, no matter how much things change, human beings who are able to adapt to circumstances will be more successful than those who are not. One way to give students practice in adaptability is to vary the learning situations in which they find themselves. Also needed are experiences in initiative taking. This means a classroom in which students are not merely following directions. Classrooms need to be places of freedom and opportunity as opposed to places of restraint and coercion. This does not equate to chaos. Your classroom should be a place where there is order based on a few simple rules while allowing mobility and creativity. The best social systems (think of your classroom as a social system) are those that are securely anchored at the base by a few simple and clear rules while allowing maximum flexibility at the top so that students are free to be creative and experience adaptability as a daily occurrence.

Self-regulation includes goal setting, self-discipline, organization, and a desire to contribute. These qualities can be learned "on the job" so to speak, that is, at school. This parallels the thought that employers in the future will seek flexible people capable of learning on the job. The work of psychologist Albert Bandura in self-efficacy indicates that modeling behaviors by important adults (you) are crucial, especially in the growth and development of the young. High expectations of best efforts, a well-organized friendly atmosphere, support and concern for students, clear rules that your students have helped you put in place and are enforced, feedback on work completed, and a sense of community are all essential to the development of self-regulation by students. Finally, a word about goal setting. You and your class need both group and individual goals. When a fifth-grade teacher challenged her students on the first day of school in early September to read 1,000 books by early June, she set forth an exciting goal for the whole class, including herself. They made it! We know that high achievers have goals, but in your class everyone needs goals.

I have included this information because knowledge and activity go hand in hand, and unless children are engaged in activities that encourage the development of self-regulation, team building, and adaptability, the knowledge will go in one ear and out the other. This is knowledge in the form of life skills. Now we turn to knowledge of the social science disciplines in the form of their structures of concepts and processes.

The Structure of the Social Science Disciplines as Fundamental Knowledge

The social science disciplines of anthropology, economics, geography, history, sociology, and political science form the foundation of the social studies curriculum, particularly with regard to content. The social sciences are those areas of scholarly inquiry that focus in a systematic way on the study of human behavior. Each of the disciplines brings a uniquely different perspective to the ways that human beings interact with each other and with the environment in general.

A background in the social sciences is vital, because one task you face as a social studies teacher is to make the social sciences meaningful to young learners. Social studies and social science are not the same thing. *Social studies* is the adaptation of the scholarly disciplines through experiential learning that is developmentally appropriate to school students. Therefore, social studies is more than simplified social science. It is above all a course in the curriculum in which children learn citizenship, self-realization, and necessary social skills in addition to learning about the world far and near, long ago, and the present. The *social sciences* give structure to student learning in the form of key concepts and important methods of inquiry.

Anthropology

WHAT IS ANTHROPOLOGY? Anthropology has been characterized as the study of culture or the scientific study of human beings. The American Anthropological Association (2009) defines *anthropology* as "the study of humankind, from its beginnings millions of years ago to the present day." The central organizing concept of anthropology is culture. Its methods are comparative, that is, we study other cultures and compare their ways of life to our own and to one another. Anthropologists study cultures of the South Sea islands, rural folk societies around the world, and educational institutions such as your own classroom and school, just to name a few examples. Studies of food, clothing, and shelter as well as rituals, customs, and traditions are important to the anthropologist.

WHAT DO ANTHROPOLOGISTS DO? Anthropologists study cultures. They develop case histories of various tribal and ethnic groups, as well as descriptive accounts of the mores and patterns of different groups. Their data sources include the writings of previous investigators, plus artifacts, informants, and eyewitness accounts. Because their concern is with the concept of culture, anthropologists are generally interested in developing a total, interrelated picture of a society rather than in dealing exclusively with its economic patterns, power structure, or any other facet of that society's existence. In this respect, anthropology has been termed an *integrative science*.

Anthropologists investigate cultures using one or more of the following methods:

1. *Indirect observation.* Anthropologists pursuing indirect observation use maps, census data, the writings of previous investigators, the examination of artifacts, and interviews with informants. Indirect observation is useful for developing historical accounts of cultures and validating information obtained by other methods.
2. *Direct observation.* Anthropologists using direct observation spend time with their subjects, observing them and taking notes as they go about the business of living their lives. This method uses such tools as the camera, tape recorder, and field notebook.
3. *Participant observation.* Participant observation also depends on the investigator spending time with subjects. However, participant observers make an attempt to join their group and thereby become as inconspicuous as possible. The participant investigator often attempts to learn the language and customs of a group in order to gain some degree of acceptance. This approach was used rather effectively by an investigator who actually married the chief of a tribal group during the course of her work in Indonesia.

SELECTED ANTHROPOLOGICAL CONCEPTS   Certain terms and ideas can help define the conceptual structure of anthropology.*

- *Acculturation.* The changes resulting when two cultures make contact with one another (e.g., the changes in European and Native American societies following the voyages of Columbus).
- *Artifacts.* Objects produced by human beings, as opposed to natural objects. Artifacts provide clues to a group's values, economic system, technological orientation, and so forth.
- *Culture.* The personality or way of life of a group of human beings; the particular set of characteristics that unify a group and make it distinguishable from other groups. The attributes of culture include language, technology, religion, food, clothing, shelter, traditions, and ideas.
- *Diffusion.* The flow of ideas, traits, and tools from one culture to another. Racial characteristics, for example, are diffused as one culture marries into and mingles with another.
- *Enculturation.* Those learning experiences a person has as a result of his or her culture. The home and school are agents of enculturation.
- *Innovation.* The introduction of new ideas, traits, and tools into a culture as a result of invention, discovery, or diffusion.
- *Personality.* Traits, behaviors, and habits a person acquires as a result of membership in and interaction with a particular culture.
- *Role.* The status of a member of a particular culture and the resulting behavior exhibited by or expected of that person in a given situation.
- *Traditions.* Customs and beliefs of a culture that are transmitted from one generation to succeeding generations.

Keys to Anthropology

- All people have universal cultural traits, including the following:

  Language
  Technology
  Social organization
  Political organization
  Moral and legal sanctions
  Religion or philosophy
  Creative activities—art, music, dance . . .
  Ways of resolving differences

  Methods of protection
  Leisure activities
  Methods of education or enculturation

- All elements of culture, whether explicit or implicit, are integrated.
- A change in one aspect of culture influences the total pattern of culture.
- Cultural change may occur by diffusion, invention, and innovation.

---

*Selected social science concepts appearing throughout this chapter are adapted from *Selected Learner Outcomes for Social Studies* (St. Paul, MN: Minnesota State Department of Education, 1986).

Economics

WHAT IS ECONOMICS? According to the American Economic Association (2009), *economics* is the study of how people choose to use resources. Resource(s) is a key concept in economics. Resources are represented by land, labor, and capital and include such things as time, capability, and interest that people have in them. For example, oil was not typically seen as a valuable resource (in fact, it was a nuisance when it bubbled up in farm fields) until the industrial revolution. Now it is one of the world's most sought-after resources. This illustrates another concept of economics, that is, supply and demand. Demand worldwide for oil is tremendous, and the supply is limited.

Economists study the habits of producers and consumers. When consumers demand a certain trend in fashions, for example, producers will make more of a product. When demand lessens, stores will sell a product for less. In modern societies, people use money in the forms of cash, checks, and credit cards to purchase goods and services. In other societies, people barter, that is, trade goods and services.

When people realize they have limited time, money, and other resources, they make choices about what they can buy or do. These choices represent opportunity costs. If, for example, a child has a dollar to spend, she or he might decide to buy a candy bar or save the money for some purpose. The decision to buy the candy bar means a decision not to use the money in other ways, which represents the opportunity cost of buying the candy bar. A family that decides to choose between taking a camping trip or using their time and money for something else is faced with the opportunity cost of the camping trip.

Governments also make economic decisions. Taxes are an example of one way in which a government raises money, which then may be distributed for roads, education, or many other expenditures. Governments also provide services, such as those offered by police, fire, hospitals, and so on. *Microeconomics* is the study of how individuals make decisions, while *macroeconomics* is the study of larger-scale decision making at the levels of corporations and governments. Economics is the only social science that is recognized for eligibility for the Nobel Prize.

WHAT DO ECONOMISTS DO? Economists analyze the use of various resources. Their analyses are designed to deal with the problems arising due to the scarcity of material and technical resources. Such analyses result in recommendations regarding the kinds of choices that ought to be made in order to optimize the production and consumption of goods and services. Choices must be made among alternatives, whether those choices involve buying a bracelet versus going to a movie, going to Disney World versus paneling the family room, or spending government money for foreign aid versus spending it for domestic vocational education. Economists attempt to clarify and define objectives for persons, families, and nations in order to make them better able to understand the consequences of various uses of resources. Maher (1969) provides a simple example of an economic analysis of a situation:

> The land in a pea patch together with the farmer's labor, his shovel, his hoe, and some seed are *resources*. (Sunshine and rain are resources too, but the farmer has little control over them nor does he pay to use them.) Next, the *production* process includes plowing, planting, weeding, and harvesting the peas. The *output,* of course, is the peas—if everything

has gone well. But a bushel of peas is not the end of the whole activity. Rather, the satisfaction of hunger is the objective. For this satisfaction to take place, another process intervenes, namely, the process of *consumption*. When the peas are consumed, the *objective* is satisfied. (p. 1)

The economist is faced with analytical questions regarding the allocation of resources. This abiding problem of deciding how best to use resources faces all types of economic systems: barter, capitalist, communist, socialist, and so forth. Calderwood and associates (1970) illustrate the analytical questions facing the economist:

1. How shall the economy use (allocate) its productive resources to supply the wants of its people? In commonsense terms, *what* shall be produced and *how*?
2. How fast shall the economy grow, and how shall it obtain reasonably stable growth, avoiding both depression and inflation? In other words, *how much* shall be produced in total, and how many resources shall be devoted to increasing future capacity rather than to producing goods for current consumption?
3. How shall the economy distribute money incomes, and through them the goods and services it produces, to the individual members and groups in society? For whom shall the goods be produced?

SELECTED ECONOMIC CONCEPTS   These are the basic concepts that underlie the field of economics.

- *Allocation of goods and services.*   *Goods* are materials produced for consumption, and s*ervices* are skills or abilities sold to consumers. Different methods can be used to allocate goods and services. People acting individually and collectively through government must choose which methods to use to allocate goods and services. Related concepts include *supply* and *demand*.
- *Consumer.* A person or group that uses goods and services.
- *Corporation.* A company in which people invest money and share profits and losses.
- *Cost/benefit ratio.* Effective decision making in economics requires comparing the cost of doing something with the benefit derived from the same action. Most choices involve doing a little more or a little less; few choices are all or nothing.
- *Division of labor.* Assigning specific tasks to workers so each does a part of a total job.
- *Gain from trade.* Voluntary exchange occurs only when all participants expect to gain. *Trade* refers to the exchange of goods, services, and money that occurs among individuals or organizations within a nation, individuals or organizations in different nations, or between nations themselves. Related concepts include *exports, imports, barter,* and *tariffs.*
- *Incentives.* People respond predictably to positive and negative incentives, or rewards and punishments.
- *Producer.* The person or company that manufactures or creates a product.
- *Profit.* The net income derived from the sale of goods and services.
- *Scarcity.* Productive resources are limited; therefore, people cannot always have all the goods and services they want. Instead, they must choose some things and give up others.

- *Supply and demand.* *Supply* is the amount of goods and services available for consumption; *demand* is the need for and ability to purchase goods and services. The balance between these two forces at any give time influences prices and ultimately the stability of an economy.

Keys to Economics

- The individual plays three roles in economic life: worker, consumer, and citizen.
- The general social/political/economic environment affects the individual's economic opportunities and well-being.

- An individual's economic choices and behaviors may affect the system as a whole.
- The market system is the basic institutional arrangement through which production and distribution of goods and services are determined in a free economy.

Geography

WHAT IS GEOGRAPHY? Geography is a highly integrative discipline that addresses human activity in all aspects. Physical geography involves the study of landforms and water forms. Economic geography is the study of how people use their time and resources to make a living. Cultural geography attempts to explain why different cultures living in similar conditions have divergent life styles. The Association of American Geographers (2009) defines *geography* as the science of place and space. At a micro level, we could pose the geographic question of the places and spaces you occupy in a given day. This, of course, could be mapped. Maps are integral to geography. A map is actually a spatial essay, designed to convey certain information about space and place.

In more recent times, geographers have focused on the uses people make of the environment, which leads naturally to studies of ecology and environmental protection. Geographers study climate patterns and change, use of forest and agricultural lands, effects of human activity on lakes and streams, and the biodiversity of areas of the world, for example, the Amazon Rainforest.

Geography is a dynamic science. That is, it is more than memorizing states and capitals and so forth. Austin is the capital of Texas, and Harrisburg is the capital of Pennsylvania, but geographers attempt to explain *why* cities are located where they are and why they perform certain functions. Presently, geographers are studying internal migration in China, said to be the largest movement of people across the landscape in human history. This migration is economic, cultural, and political all at once, reminding us that geography is integrative as a discipline.

Geographers are keenly interested in the effects that the landscape has on human activity and the effects that human activity has on the landscape. Thus, climate and landforms limit what people can do in a given area while people can change a landscape from rich to poor through deforestation, pollution, and so on. People also can restore environments through careful nurturing of the lands and waters.

WHAT DO GEOGRAPHERS DO? Geographers develop descriptions of regions or places and investigate special topics involving spatial interactions. The two major types of inquiry that geographers pursue involve regions of the world, such as the Amazon Rainforest in South America and the Pacific Northwest of the United States, and special topics, such as migration patterns and urban settlement.

Geographic methods include analyzing existing maps; developing new maps (see Figure 4.4), graphs, and charts; interpreting aerial and other photographs; using statistical techniques to analyze data; and developing descriptions of places or phenomena.

SELECTED GEOGRAPHIC CONCEPTS These selected terms and ideas help form the conceptual structure of geography.

- *Areal association.* The relationship of phenomena on the earth's surface to one another, such as the relationship among soil, climate, and vegetation in a particular place.
- *Central place.* The focal point of a region. The central place of a region contains the specializations and services necessary to the function of that region. For example, Omaha, Nebraska, serves as a central place for the surrounding cattle country of that region.
- *Region.* An area on the earth's surface that has common properties—such as topography, climate, and soils—and that is bound together by a common focus in a particular central place. For example, the region of the Pacific Southwest has its focus in Phoenix, Arizona.
- *Situation.* The location of a place in relation to other places and the degree to which those other places are accessible. Thus, the situation of a particular place may change with the building of a railroad or with new developments in air transportation. A city such as Seattle, Washington, is in a more favorable trade situation now than it was 30 years ago. Its specific location on the earth's surface is unchanged, but the development of more efficient transportation systems makes it more accessible to Japanese as well as East Coast markets.
- *Spatial interaction.* The functional relationship between and among phenomena in a particular place. For example, textiles may be manufactured where cotton, water sources, a population of workers, and transportation networks for shipping are all available.

Keys to Geography

- Location of people and economic activities are influenced by external factors and internal value choices.
- Environmental conditions place restrictions on cultural choices.
- Nature and culture are interlocking components of the ecosystem.
- Movement of cultures from subsistent economies and self-sufficient communities toward surplus-oriented, interdependent cultures means an increased technology, trade, migration, and communication network.
- Highly specialized and specifically adapted livelihood forms have limited potential for cultural change. (Nomadic pastoralism and hunting societies are becoming extinct.)

Figure 4.4 *A Child's Perspective: Map of Shelton View Elementary School*

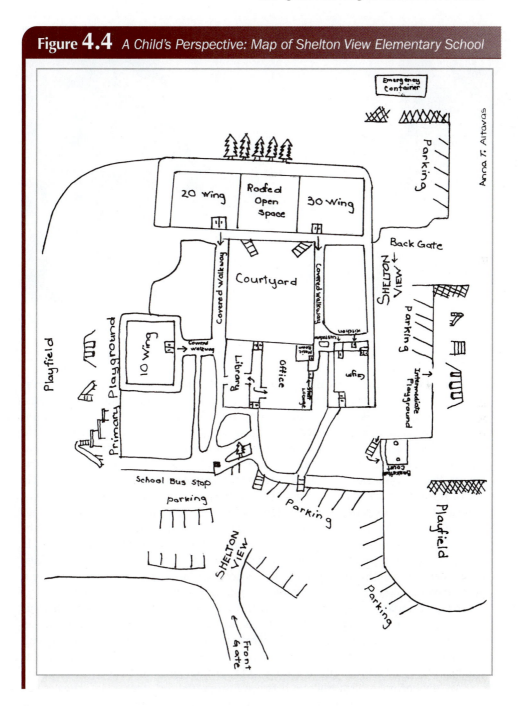

A young geographer puts the finishing touches on her map of the school grounds.

History

WHAT IS HISTORY?   *History* can be defined as the discipline that studies chronological records of events using analytical methods in an attempt to explain their causes. Chronos was the Greek god of time, and time is the key concept of history. As a discipline, history is far more dedicated to narrative, storytelling records of events than are the other social sciences. In fact, some authorities do not consider history to be a social science because its methods are so very different from those of the economist or sociologist. Because historians investigate events that have already taken place, their task is one of reconstruction and meaning-making of the past. Historiography, or the writing of history, did not exist in present-day form before the eighteenth century. Storytelling, religion, philosophy, literature, poetry, art, and music were considered more significant ways of bringing the past into the consciousness of those living in the present. This is not to say that history was left untold in ancient times; it merely took other forms. Thus, our modern sense of history as "accurate" is not the same as past histories that were a mixture of actual events with myths and legends and stories.

Today historians attempt to piece together the record of the past with as much accuracy as surviving records permit. But the challenge to the historian is that much has been lost over time. Of course, we are indebted to the ancient storytellers, but unraveling their facts from their fancies is not easy. The Bible is one example. It is a combination of history, literature, moral teachings, and spiritual guide to life.

An obvious point of distinction between history and the other social sciences lies in its primary focus on the past. This is a concern that plays only a supportive role in the other social science disciplines. History does share with the other social sciences the function of seeking explanations of human interactions as they are exemplified by individuals and institutions, groups, and situations through processes of inquiry. Collingwood (1946) lists four characteristics of history:

1. that it is scientific, or begins by knowing something and tells what it knows.
2. that it is humanistic, or asks questions about things done at determinate times in the past.
3. that it is rational, or bases the answers it gives on grounds, namely, appeal to evidence.
4. that it is self-revelatory, or exists in order to tell man what man is by telling him what man has done. (p. 18)

WHAT DO HISTORIANS DO?   Historians pose questions about human interaction in current and past events, seek appropriate sources of data, and attempt to develop explanations and inferences to answer those questions. Krug (1967) writes that "a historian starts his inquiry basically with three questions: 'What happened? How did it happen? Why did it happen?'" (p. 5) Such questions could, for example, serve as a guide to historical inquiry into the clashes between the executive and legislative branches of government during the Watergate inquiry.

Historians seek sources of data in a variety of places: museums, libraries, repositories, attics, archives, film depositories, and, of course, the field, where they may search for and use documents and other artifacts. Historical data consist of letters, paintings, photographs, films, charters, compacts, census tracts, financial records, household utensils, weaponry, statuaries, literature, people—there is an endless and ever-growing supply of sources. Unfortunately, historians have less control over the situations they investigate than psychologists, for example. As a result, the data sources that are preserved and located often seem to be available on a random basis. Historians work with sources they can locate, which means that priceless sources of data are often irretrievably lost or destroyed.

Keys to History

- Change has been a universal characteristic of all human societies.
- A knowledge of the past is necessary to understand present and future events.
- No historical events have resulted from a single cause.

- The leadership of certain individuals has had a profound influence on the course of history.
- Interpretations of the past are constantly changing as new data and trends result in altered perspectives.

Sociology

WHAT IS SOCIOLOGY?   The American Sociological Association (2009) defines *sociology* as "the study of social life, social change, and the social causes of human behavior." Sociologists study groups, norms of behavior, organizations, and entire societies. They are particularly interested in the ways in which people interact with each other in given settings. For example, a sociologist who chose to study your classroom as a micro society would be interested in student-to-student interaction and might compare it to the amount of teacher-to-student interaction as well as the time your students spend sitting in their seats working alone compared with the time they spend in group work.

The scope of sociology is very broad and encompasses nearly all aspects of human endeavor. Sociologists study religions, sports, hospitals, and schools. They study crime, work, play, leisure pursuits, clubs and other organizations, corporate culture, and just about anything you can think of in which human activity is present. Sociology is so all encompassing that it has become one of the most commonly sought fields of study by university students. Poverty, gender, race, ethnicity, social class, geriatrics, youth, and middle age crises are all objects of study by sociologists.

Sociologists give us descriptions of society, but they also search for meaning in terms of trends, changes, innovations, and traditions. In the famous Supreme Court case *Brown vs. the Board of Education* in 1954, sociological testimony was given in an attempt by the Court to determine the effects of segregated schools on students, teachers, families, and society at large. Sociologists use survey instruments and other opinion-gathering techniques such as interviews and direct observation.

WHAT DO SOCIOLOGISTS DO?   Sociologists spend their time studying groups. They ask analytical questions about groups and group behavior that can be answered through data gathering. The sociologist gathers data through means similar to those employed by the anthropologist: direct observation, indirect observation, interviews, and examination of the writings of other social scientists. In addition, sociological research has made extensive use of the questionnaire as a data-gathering instrument. Like other social scientists, the sociologist poses researchable questions, hypothesizes, selects appropriate sources of data, gathers and processes the data, and makes inferences or statements about the data.

SELECTED SOCIOLOGICAL CONCEPTS   Here are a few selected terms and basic ideas from sociology.

- *Integrated group.* A group in which members interact and communicate with one another and in which positions of dominance and hierarchy are established—such as a family, club, or classroom.
- *Nonintegrated group.* A group in which members are basically interchangeable with one another and in which lines of communication and interaction are not clearly established. A group of people waiting in line for the theater or a group of people shopping in a store are examples.
- *Norms.* Generalizable (to most members of any given group) patterns of behavior. Norms may be found in clothes, food, and shelter, for example.
- *Socialization.* Those things that happen to an individual as a result of his or her contacts with society and the influences that society has on the life of that individual.
- *Values.* Those beliefs that people internalize and act on as a result of their group experiences—for example, success, punctuality, generosity, and frugality.

Keys to Sociology

- Norms define the boundaries of social interaction.
- Differentiation of social roles is based on sex, age, kinship, and occupation.
- Complex, technological societies tend toward greater stratification.
- Social interaction involves cooperation, conflict, assimilation, and accommodation.

- Each society develops institutions to aid the socialization of its members.
- Socialization is the process by which the individual becomes a functioning member of society.
- Human survival depends on living in groups.

Political Science

WHAT IS POLITICAL SCIENCE?   The American Political Science Association (2009) defines *political science* as "the study of governments, public policies and political processes, systems, and political behavior." Obviously, politics are at the center of this branch of the social sciences. Political scientists are interested in *forms* of government, for example, democracy, republic, autocracy, and dictatorship. Political science is closely related to the fields of governance and law—local, national, and international. Political scientists analyze legislative, executive, and judicial systems at different levels of government.

Political science places emphasis on systems, which means that the political sphere is an interrelated, dynamic set of interactions among people and the power that they exercise or that is exercised on them. As you can see, there is great overlap among the social sciences, which is a good argument for social studies as an integrated subject for school students. For example, both sociology and political science involve the study of power. However, while the sociologist might study the power structure of street gangs, the political scientist would be more interested in the power of political or military leaders. Hybrid disciplines such as geopolitics involve both geography and political science. International relations, while a pursuit of the political scientist, is also a subject that attracts historians.

WHAT DO POLITICAL SCIENTISTS DO?   Political scientists attempt to determine the existence of and analyze the relationships among the people and institutions that make up political systems. Senn offers two methods by which political scientists derive explanations for human behavior in political systems: explanations by purpose or intention and probability explanations. A statement of the basic premises of these two methods is excerpted here from Senn's (1971) book *Social Science and Its Methods:*

> *Explanation by purpose or intention.* This method explains in terms of aims, plans, goals, or intentions. Whenever human beings are studied, the social scientist must take into account the fact that they have wills and change their future.
>
> Social scientists know that whenever human behavior must be explained, either in terms of the individual or in terms of groups, the plans, intentions, and goals of individuals themselves must be taken into account. We call this explanation by purpose.

Explanation by purpose is commonly used in two situations. First, a social scientist may ask a person what his purposes or intentions are or were when the purpose of the action the social scientist is attempting to explain is not clear. . . . Secondly, this kind of explanation is sought when the social scientist is ignorant of the connections between the actions of the group and the goals of the individual.

Probabilistic explanation. Probabilistic explanations occur when a social scientist says, "If a country is attacked, it is likely that it will defend itself." . . . Probabilistic explanations use terms of probability, not certainty, and the degree to which the premises follow is sometimes called the degree of confidence, and is sometimes given as a percentage.

Example: three out of four first voters select a candidate from the same party supported by their parents. . . . Therefore, we can conclude that the chances are three out of four that John (a first-time voter) will vote Democratic as his parents did. (pp. 145–154)

Political scientists are interested in more than the mere description of human behavior in response to political systems. Although they may attempt to develop an accurate description of human behavior—for example, voting patterns in an off-year election—such a description may serve as a prelude to the development of explanations of the purposes or intentions of voters in voting the way they did. This information could well be translated into a prediction of how voters, given certain profiles, might vote in future elections.

SELECTED POLITICAL SCIENCE CONCEPTS   Here are a few selected terms and basic ideas from political science (Easton, 1966, p. 5).

- *Authority.* The binding powers held by persons and/or laws over other persons. In a democracy, persons in a position of authority are either elected or appointed by elected officials and are therefore ultimately responsible to the people.
- *Government.* The officials, laws, and institutions that are responsible for maintaining social control and functions in a society.
- *Power.* Influence held by individuals or groups over others. Persons holding power in a democratic society are bound by existing laws and the right of voters to recall such laws. Within these constraints, persons holding positions of power may determine the behavior of others. For example, Congress exercised its constitutional power in passing legislation reducing highway speed limits to 55 miles per hour and more recently raising them to 65 miles per hour and higher. The executive branch exercises power by enforcing such a law.
- *Political system.* The set of interactions among persons, institutions, processes, and traditions by which a society is governed, or "a set of interactions, abstracted from the totality of social behavior, through which valued things are authoritatively allocated for a society."

Summary

Anthropology, economics, geography, history, sociology, and political science all involve the study of human beings. Therefore, all these areas are, by definition, included in social studies. This chapter described the structure of each of these social sciences and highlighted terms and key ideas from each. The key ideas listed with each discipline in this chapter make good concept statements on which to develop lessons, activities, and even units of instruction. Go back and skim them, and you will see what I mean.

Of course, when you select a key idea, you must do two things: (1) attach it to some appropriate content and (2) develop it by using an activity appropriate to certain age levels.

Explorations

Reflect On . . .

1. Make a list of differences between social studies and social science. Make a list of similarities between social studies and social science. Which list is longer? Why?
2. Think about the concept of change. Identify an example of change for each of the social science disciplines.

In the Field

3. Examine an elementary social studies textbook series. Try to determine which social science disciplines are stressed at each level.

4. "Geography and history should receive far more emphasis in elementary studies than the other social sciences." Do you agree or disagree with that statement? Why or why not? Talk to an elementary school teacher and ask the same question.

For Your Portfolio

5. Use one of the key ideas listed in this chapter and develop a lesson based on it.

Continuing the Journey: Suggested Readings

Checkley, K. (2007). *The Essentials of Social Studies, Grades K–8.* Alexandria, VA: Association for Supervision and Curriculum Development.

Ellis, A. (2010). *Teaching, Learning, & Assessment Together: The Reflective Classroom.* Larchmont, NY: Eye on Education, Inc.

Lare, G. (2006). *Social Studies Activities Book.* Lanham, MD: Rowan and Littlefield.

Leuenberger, C. (2007). *Data-Collection Mini-Books: Science, Math, and Social Studies.* New York: Scholastic.

List, H. (2008). *Dialogue, Discussion, and Debate: Social Studies.* Portland, ME: Walch Education.

Richardson, W. (2008). *Blogs, Wikis, Podcasts, and Other Powerful Web Tools for Classrooms.* Thousand Oaks, CA: Corwin.

Thombs, M., Gillis, M., & Canestrari, A. (2008) *Using Webquests in the Social Studies.* Thousand Oaks, CA: Corwin.

Thornton, S. J. (2004). *Teaching Social Studies That Matters: Curriculum for Active Learning.* New York: Teachers College Press.

Whitley, P., & Goodwin, S. (2007). *99 Jumpstarts for Kids' Social Studies Reports.* Westport, CT: Greenwood.

Websites

NCSS. *www.socialstudies.org/*

NCSS standards summarized. *www.education-world. com/standards/national/soc_sci/index.shtml*

Social studies standards from the state of California to compare to those of NCSS.
http://score.rims.kl2.ca.us/standards/

Related NCSS Standards and Principles of Powerful Social Studies

Curriculum Standards

NCSS themes and their social science counterparts follow. In addition, an example of the NCSS knowledge standard that accompanies the theme for early grades is included.

Anthropology/Theme I: Culture

Knowledge—the learner will understand:

- that "culture" refers to the behaviors, beliefs, values, traditions, institutions, and ways of living together of a group of people
- concepts such as: similarities, differences, values, cohesion, and diversity
- how cultural beliefs and behaviors allow human groups to solve the problems of daily living and how these may change in response to changing needs and concerns
- how individuals learn the elements of their culture through interactions with other members of the culture group
- how people from different cultures develop different values and ways of interpreting experience

History/Theme II: Time, Continuity, and Change

Knowledge—the learner will understand:

- that we can learn our personal past and the past of our community, nation, and world by means of stories, biographies, interviews, and sources such as documents, letters, photographs, artifacts, etc
- key concepts such as past, present, future, similarity, difference, and change
- key people, events, and places associated with the history of the community, nation, and world
- key symbols and traditions that are carried from the past into the present by diverse cultures in the United States and world

Geography/Theme III: People, Places, and Environments

Knowledge—the learner will understand:

- core concepts such as: location, physical and human characteristics of school, community, state, and region and the interactions of people in these places with the environment
- relationships among various community, state, and regional patterns of geographic phenomena, such as availability of land and water or places people live
- physical changes in community, state and region, such as seasons, climate and weather, plants, and animals
- factors that contribute to similarities and differences among peoples of school, community, state, and region including ethnicity, language, and religious beliefs

Sociology/V. Individual, Groups, and Institutions

Knowledge—the learner will understand:

- characteristics that distinguish individuals
- that individuals, groups, and institutions share some common elements but also have unique characteristics
- the impact of families, schools, religious organizations, government agencies, financial institutions, and civic groups on their lives

Political Science/Theme VI: Power, Authority, & Governance

Knowledge—the learner will understand:

- fundamental ideas which are the foundation of American constitutional democracy: Constitution, the rule of law, separation of powers, checks and balances, minority rights, separation of church and state
- fundamental American values: the common good, liberty, justice, equality, individual dignity

- the basic elements of governments in the U.S.: executive, legislative, and judicial authority
- the ways in which governments meet the needs and wants of citizens

Economics/VII. Production, Distribution, and Consumption

Knowledge—the learner will understand:

- how people and nations deal with scarcity of resources
- what they gain and give up when they make a decision
- how incentives affect people's behavior
- various organizations that help them achieve their individual goals (banks, labor unions)
- and be able to discuss the characteristics of entrepreneurs in a market economy
- the goods produced in the market and goods produced by the government; and
- the characteristics and functions of money

Source: National Task Force for Social Studies. Draft 2008. *Expectations of Excellence: Curriculum Standards for Social Studies* (Silver Spring, MD: National Council for the Social Studies, 2008.) The Council's website is www.socialstudies.org

Teacher Standards

What teachers should be able do with regard to disciplinary standards according to NCSS; these are a bit repetitive—there is more information regarding each should you want it.

History

Teachers who are licensed to teach history should possess the knowledge, capabilities, and dispositions to organize and provide instruction at the appropriate school level for the study of history.

Geography

Teachers who are licensed to teach geography at all school levels should possess the knowledge, capabilities, and dispositions to organize and provide instruction at the appropriate school level for the study of geography.

Civics and Government

Teachers who are licensed to teach civics and/or government at all school levels should possess the knowledge, capabilities, and dispositions to organize and provide instruction at the appropriate school level for the study of civics and government.

Economics

Teachers who are licensed to teach economics at all school levels should possess the knowledge, capabilities, and dispositions to organize and provide instruction at the appropriate school level for the study of economics.

Psychology

Teachers who are licensed to teach psychology at all school levels should possess the knowledge, capabilities, and dispositions to organize and provide instruction at the appropriate school level for the study of psychology.

Source: National Council for the Social Studies. *National Standards for Social Studies Teachers.* (Silver Spring, MD: Author, 2002). The Council's website is www.socialstudies.org

Three Ways to Center the Social Studies Curriculum

The Learner, Society, and Knowledge

Keys to This Chapter

- The Learner-Centered Approach
- The Society-Centered Approach
- The Knowledge-Centered Approach

"If facts are the seeds that later produce knowledge and wisdom, then the emotions and the impressions of the senses are the fertile soil in which the seeds must grow."
—Rachel Carson

Teaching is as much art as it is science. When it comes to social studies, good teachers will have different priorities. In other words, there is no one "right" way to organize a classroom to achieve the goals of citizenship, academic knowledge, and personal fulfillment. In this chapter, I will introduce you to three perspectives. They are:

- The learner-centered approach
- The society-centered approach
- The knowledge-centered approach

Each of these perspectives has its strengths. As you read about each, try to think of your own strengths and interests. The best teachers are often those who are the most excited about what they do. Therefore, you should play to your strengths. You may find that you like certain aspects of each approach. If this is the case, then you will want to achieve a balanced blend of the three.

Grab your coat and notebook, and come with me. We're going to visit some classrooms! Let's go find out what teachers have to say about how they teach elementary social studies. I've found three teachers with very different points of view about social studies. Aren't you glad we don't all think the same way about things? These teachers have thought a lot about social studies, and I believe you'll find each one of them interesting. The teachers and their names portrayed in this chapter are in fact composites of teachers from the many classrooms I visited.

Let me tell you a little about the teachers' approaches before we join them in their classrooms. The first, LeeAnn, is a learner-centered teacher. Her primary concerns are with the self-development and self-realization of each individual student. One of the hallmarks of the learner-centered approach is freedom of choice for the individual child. The needs of the student, play, and reflection are fundamental properties of the learner-centered curriculum. In such a classroom, you would expect to find students engaged in exploratory behavior, in individualized projects, and in activities such as games and other play-centered approaches to learning. The teacher assumes a low profile in which he or she organizes, facilitates, and participates in learning. Little whole-class instruction and little traditional seat work are found in learner-centered classrooms.

Our second teacher, Sasha, is a proponent of a society-centered classroom. His primary concern is directed toward the development of involved, participating citizens. Citizenship is the key concept of the society-centered approach. The society-centered teacher focuses on the use of democratic principles both in the classroom and in the involvement of the students in the community at large. In addition, the society-centered teacher focuses on the group and tries to build up its esprit de corps. Cooperative learning and other group-oriented strategies are hallmarks of the society-centered approach.

Emma, our third teacher, takes a knowledge-centered approach. As a knowledge-centered teacher, her primary focus is on the academic arena. A knowledge-centered social studies teacher is committed to ensuring that his or her students learn the course of study, whether it is U.S. history, geography, or something else. A good knowledge-centered teacher uses a variety of instructional strategies ranging from inquiry to seat work, but the focus is always on the course of study. It is common in such classrooms to find students doing basically the same assignments, although allowance is often made for differences in ability and interest. The most common manifestation of the knowledge-centered curriculum is the textbook; but, again, a good teacher utilizes a variety of sources. Of the three approaches, this one lends itself most closely to such traditional structures as lesson plans, tests, and structured activities.

As you read about and think about these teachers, consider your own developing ideas about social studies. For example, which of the three teachers is most like you with respect to philosophy? Do you disagree fundamentally with any of the teachers? Even though most of us tend to be eclectic in our approaches, we do have our priorities. How would you order the three approaches in terms of your priorities? It might be helpful to discuss these teacher profiles with several interested persons. Try to probe the strengths and weaknesses of each approach; this will enable you to clarify your own thoughts about social studies. Figures 5.1 through 5.3, interspersed throughout the chapter, provide visual explanations of the three curriculum approaches.

The Learner-Centered Approach

LeeAnn teaches fourth grade at Jackson School, an old brick building built in the 1920s and recently remodeled. The school and its asphalt playground occupy a square block in a city neighborhood called Richmond Heights, an area that has undergone considerable transition over the years. Some of the children who attend Jackson School live in the neighborhood. Others are bused in from points around the city. The ethnic composition of the school is African American, Hispanic, and Anglo. LeeAnn, a tall, attractive woman in her mid-30s, has taught at Jackson for eight years. Her hair is graying. She says, "The kids caused that. But then my daddy's hair was white from as far back as I can remember, so maybe that has something to do with it, too."

It is four o'clock on a winter Tuesday afternoon. Already it is growing dark outside. The students are long gone for the day, and LeeAnn is in a corner of the room placing chess pieces on a chessboard. The chessboard sits on a table underneath which are stacks of games, maybe a dozen or more. On the wall beside the table is a sign that says in construction paper letters, "Cooperate, Compete, but Always Play Fair." On the table with the chessboard are several books and booklets about the game of chess.

"This is our Game Center," says LeeAnn with a smile. "I suppose, year in and year out, it's my most popular center. But all the centers are popular because of a gradual process of natural selection: I dropped the ones students didn't like. This is a permanent center—it stays up all year. I introduce new games from time to time. Sometimes the kids will bring a game. Tomorrow I'm introducing chess. It's a surprise. You know, I never even knew how to play chess until about a year ago. Now I'm not too bad." (She laughs.)

"I'm always telling the kids that we've got to keep on learning, all our lives. So every year I try to learn at least five new things. It's a stretch, but that's my goal. I tell the kids about the things I'm learning, and they tell me about the things they're learning. As a result of my goal, I've got so many hobbies that I can't keep up with them. I've learned mountain climbing, car repair, roller-skating, watercolor painting, all in the last several years. Then I teach what I learn to the kids. They love it. I read on the bus, 30 minutes in the morning and 30 minutes in the afternoon. Right now I'm reading *Pride and Prejudice* by Jane Austen—you know, one of those books everyone was supposed to have read back in high school. I saw it on PBS and thought I ought to read the book. Look at the books in the Reading Center." (She points across the room.) "I use book lists to make sure the kids can choose from great literature, at their level—but you'd be surprised what their level is.

"Tomorrow's going to be fun. I can't wait to see their faces when I introduce them to chess. There are some kids in this room who will become great chess players. I just know it. We'll form a chess club, maybe have a tournament. Of course, I'll have to scrounge some more chess sets, but we have a good principal here. He'll get us some."

LeeAnn's classroom is an exploratory environment. She uses an interest-center approach. "Right now I have seven centers up. It's a little crowded. As you can see, this isn't the biggest classroom in the world. But with 31 kids, you've got to have alternatives."

The room itself presents an intriguing conception of space. LeeAnn has used tables, bookshelves, dividers, rugs, and other devices to create illusions of place and space, nooks and crannies, actually in much the same way that zoological architects create horizons of space for zoo animals to keep them from becoming neurotic over their confinement. (I do not intend to imply that there are strong parallels between children and animals, but schools, like zoos, can be somewhat confining.)

"Some of the centers change from time to time, but the Game Center, the Library, the Media Corner, the Shop, the Theater, the Fine Arts Center, and the Numbers Game are actually pretty permanent. You learn what the kids need and what they like. I guess I'm a learner-centered teacher, but not in the laissez-faire sense. You can't do just anything you want in this room. You have to show evidence that you are learning. For most of the kids that isn't too hard to do, but every now and then you will get someone who just has a hard time functioning in a relatively open, nondirective environment. To me, that's a challenge. I want that child to learn self-direction and self-reliance. He'll need it in life. So when I get someone like that, I start him out with quite a bit of structure, and usually he gets the idea after a while."

I ask LeeAnn if this type of teaching isn't a lot of work. "Yes," she says with a reflective pause. "But at least it's interesting work, and it's worthwhile. Parents tell me that they want their children in my room, especially the ones who have already had a child in here. I do a lot of one-to-one listening and counseling with the kids. The centers make that possible. You don't need an appointment to see me because I'm available. A lot of the talks I have with kids are related to academics. Right now some kids are working at the Shop, making a mural on the history and development of transportation. The plan is that the mural will stretch all the way around the room. Well, I've got to talk with those kids in order to help them come up with a plan. They know they have to do some reading and research to make their mural worthwhile. Then they

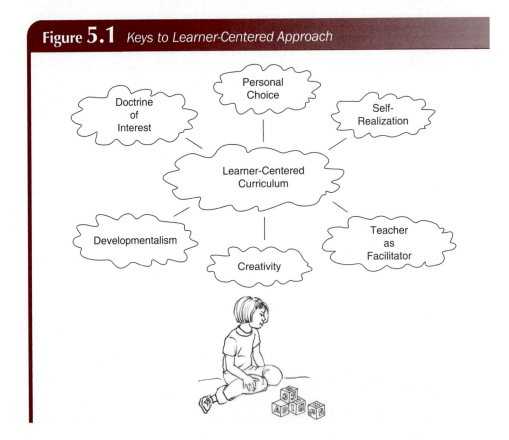

Figure 5.1 *Keys to Learner-Centered Approach*

want to put together models of boats, cars, covered wagons, planes, and so on. We'll discuss their project from start to finish.

"Of course, you end up talking with kids about personal problems, and some of those make you hurt inside. But we try to solve them, even if it means referral, which it sometimes does. I have to say—before I started using this approach, I didn't know my own students. Now I know them, and I want to make a difference in their lives.

"So, yes, it's a lot of work. But I was working just as hard before. Now, I feel like I'm working smart, not just working hard, as they say. I don't spend much time disciplining the kids. They learn self-discipline in this kind of environment. So I have more time to help someone with a math problem or with a moral dilemma. Actually, I do a lot more listening and counseling than I used to do. I don't claim to be a counselor, but I've taken some graduate courses in that area and have done quite a bit of reading, which has really helped. You see, this place basically runs itself, and most of my work is low profile, behind the scenes: getting materials ready, contacting the librarian, that kind of stuff. So I can spend a lot of time with the kids. We talk about everything. You've got to earn their trust, and some of them, many of them, have never trusted anybody. Some of them just want a hug sometimes, and they know I'll give them a big one.

"Oh, we have our problems. Last week, one of the kids took some money out of another student's desk. The only reason we know he did it was because he told another kid about it, and that kid told me. The whole thing left me depressed. We got the money back before it could be spent. Some of these kids are so poor, but that's not a good reason to steal." It is quiet for a moment. The only sound in the room is that made by a gerbil digging in some shavings in its cage beside us. Then LeeAnn says, "Let me show you the centers.

"This is the Game Center here. The idea is to give the kids an opportunity to socialize, learn to follow rules, take turns, win and lose, cooperate and compete. I think a lot of language development takes place at this center because of the give-and-take nature of games. The students feel good about learning games and becoming skilled at playing them. That's why chess is going to be so exciting. One of the things I try to encourage is creativity or inventiveness. Here, look at this." (She holds up a homemade game board and a small box that contains dice, cards, and game pieces. The game board is a map of the western states of the United States.)

"This is a board game called 'Pioneers' that several kids and I developed. It has some of the typical board game elements such as probability and decision making. We tried to make it authentic. Here's an example." (She reaches into another box and pulls out several booklets.) "These are excerpts from good books on pioneer life and the Westward Movement. Oh, boy, the kids did so much research and reading on the topic. One girl read 17 books on pioneers. She put together a prepared talk and has gone to quite a few rooms in the building to present it. She has a pioneer dress and bonnet she wears when she makes her presentation. We even videotaped it. That's her in the picture." (She points to a bulletin board covered with photographs of the students.)

LeeAnn walks over to the next center. For the first time I notice how small the room is. "This is the Fine Arts Center. It's always busy. We feature a different artistic medium from time to time so the kids can experience how one medium might differ from another. The kids paint with watercolors and oils, sketch, sculpt, do weaving, stitchery, crafts, and so on. You usually have to sign up in advance to work here, but the system seems to work.

"Over here is the Library. We have a collection of several hundred books, mostly donations, discards, and book club bonus books. The kids manage the Library. Being a room librarian is an honor and a real responsibility. Our school librarian is very helpful in training the kids. The magazines we have are all donated to us. The kids read them, but they also cut out pictures for displays and research."

We walk around the room and tour the other centers. Mostly, they are squeezed into corners or alongside a wall. The Media Corner has a television set with a DVD player as well as several notebook computers. "As you can imagine," says LeeAnn, "they love the DVD player. But it's not here just for entertainment. They watch National Geographic specials, science and literature videos, and so on. The central office, downtown, has a huge supply of good DVDs. It's a great teaching tool.

"I guess the Shop is my favorite center. You begin to see how smart some kids are who maybe don't excel in traditional academic ways. This is a colonial village under construction. It's one of those towns you get in a stiff paper book, and you cut and glue to put it together. After the students are finished putting it together, they'll prepare a narrative presentation to take to different classrooms."

LeeAnn points to a large box filled with electrical appliances: clocks, radios, an electric mixer, and more. "I don't know anything about that stuff. I need to learn. The kids mostly like to take the appliances apart. There is a man who does a great job of explaining how they work, and I had him come in last year. I have him booked again this March.

"The Theater is a center where the kids can do role-play, work with puppets, put on plays, make movies, and so on. There are several puppet shows they have done. They like dressing up in costumes and playing the parts of historical characters. We videotape some of the things they do and play it back. They enjoy watching themselves, and I think they learn from that.

"Well, those are our centers. Oh, that's the Numbers Game, over there, but you're mainly interested in social studies. The subjects run together here. Most of what we do is pretty interdisciplinary. It varies, but usually I plan about three hours a day for center time. Some things you have to do don't lend themselves to centers, so I use the rest of the day for them. I try to encourage the kids to use different centers, but it's not good to just jump around from one to another just to say you used them. Most of the center work takes the students into quite a bit of depth in whatever they're doing."

The Society-Centered Approach

Sasha is a young, energetic fellow with bushy hair and a smile that comes easily and often. He appears to be in a constant state of motion. Sasha teaches a combination third/fourth-grade class at Sunnyside Elementary School. The school is located in a lower middle-class suburb of a large city. Years ago, the area was considered a long trolley ride from the downtown urban center. Now, the trolleys are gone, and a second ring of more affluent suburbs lies beyond in what used to be the rural countryside. Many of the students' parents are employed at a nearby electronics firm. The ethnic composition of the school is predominantly White. There is a small but growing population of Southeast Asian students at the school, both Vietnamese and Hmong.

Sasha began teaching at Sunnyside School three years ago. Before that, he had taught at another elementary school in the same district. He takes a society-centered approach to social studies and tries to adapt the district's third- and fourth-grade social studies curricula to what he views as the pressing needs of society.

"This town is sandwiched in between the city and the growing area west of here. It's a little run down compared to what it used to be. I grew up around here, so I can remember it from earlier times. These kids I teach are pretty young, so I think a lot of people underestimate their abilities. But actually, they're capable of just about anything if you give them some support. It is sad, this business of the dumbing down of textbooks, or whatever you call it. Man, are the books stupid! I don't use our social studies texts at all. I wish we didn't even have them. I do try to follow the basic guidelines from the district and the state. But that's one thing I like about third and fourth. The curriculum is cities and regions. That gives you a lot of ground to cover!

"I really believe that a classroom should be a miniature democracy. I think John Dewey said that. And social studies gives me the focus for practicing democracy with these kids. Citizenship is the key."

I ask him how. "Well, for instance, what good does it do these kids—they're what, eight, nine years old—what good does it do them to read from a textbook about cities and regions? Most of them won't understand what they read, and even if they did, it doesn't mean much. They can learn a lot more about cities and communities and regions by getting involved. I mean, this is a city, after all! And we're right in the midst of a growing, important region of the country.

"I try to operate my social studies program at two levels. One level is the classroom and the school. The other level is the community itself, the real world. They're both important. I think student council is important. It's a good chance for kids to become involved in representative government. And I love school assemblies. There's something great about seeing several hundred kids in the gym for a schoolwide meeting with the principal up there in front. Talk about a sense of community. A school is a community, or at least it should be. I know this one qualifies. And it's their community, I mean the kids'. That's how I feel about our classroom, too. I want them to run this classroom using democratic principles. That means elections, rules, decisions, priorities, whatever. I don't make any rules. They make them all, and it works. All I do is approve the rules the class comes up with.

"We have a class meeting every Friday from 1 to 2 o'clock. The class reviews the week—you know, how things went. Everyone speaks up. We use a quality circles approach where we go right around the circle listening to each child. That way, every individual is heard from, not just the talkers and not just the fourth-graders.

"Sometimes we take on community or school projects. I think that's the best way to learn about how communities really work. I mean, at any level, there really are three branches of government, so you might as well have experience with those branches instead of just reading about them to pass a test. We've had the mayor here. We've been to City Hall on business. We try, as a class, to solve real problems. Some of the problems are confined to the school, and some take us out into the community, the real world.

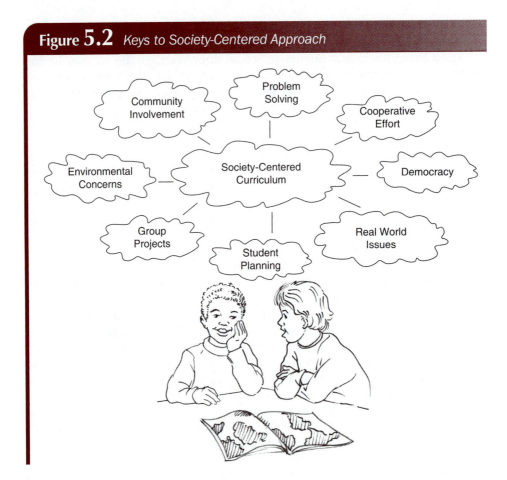

Figure 5.2 *Keys to Society-Centered Approach*

"You know, I read an article for a class I took. The article was called 'The Project Method,' and it was written back in 1918 by William Kilpatrick. Kilpatrick worked with John Dewey at Columbia University. Anyway, the idea of the article was to get the whole class involved in 'wholehearted purposeful activity,' as Kilpatrick called it. There are different kinds of projects, like putting on a school pageant or saving some wetlands. I mean, they really vary in scope. My class put on a pageant last year about the history of the community and our school. We did oral histories, took photographs, put up a temporary museum in the cafeteria, of all places. Man, it was fun. Quite a few old-timers took part. One guy, Mr. Stendal—he was 80-some-odd years old—had emigrated from Norway with his parents when he was just a young boy. But he could remember the voyage on the ship, and coming out to this part of the country from New York by railroad. We traced this area back to Native American times, before White settlement. Did you know that the Native Americans around here were quite advanced and highly civilized? We could learn a lot from them. There are ceremonial mounds not far from here. The class put together a large book and a media kit that is pretty impressive. We presented the book to the historical society, and they have it on display for visitors to look at. Projects like that make a better community.

"The class also did a little 20-page booklet on the history of the community We sold over 300 of them at $1.00 apiece. We used the money to pay a local artist to paint a beautiful picture of our school and the school grounds. The picture is in the front hallway of the school where everyone can see it and enjoy it.

"Another project we have done this year is to begin the planning and construction of an arboretum on the school grounds. The arboretum is in the painting, even though at the time the picture was painted, it didn't yet exist. You know—an artist's conception. I hope the real one is that beautiful. I guess we're lucky to have fairly large school grounds for an elementary school. Anyway, we got permission to turn the northeast corner of the grounds into an arboretum. Believe it or not, we had to go clear to the school-board level for permission. But that was good because the class got to present the proposal to the board. In fact, we had to present it twice. The first time, we were turned down. They said our plan was not complete enough, and they were right. The kids learned from that. So did I. The best community action has to be well planned.

"We got as many books as we could on parks and arboretums. Those kids had to read like crazy. I was right there reading with them because I didn't really know that much myself. Then we had three different guest speakers in to talk with the class. We had the owner of a plant nursery. He was great. In fact, he's going to furnish most of the plants to get us started. If people only knew how much businesses want to help the schools. We had a Japanese gardener in. He talked about beauty, serenity, and harmony in the care and development of a garden. It was incredible! Then we also had a landscape architect in from the University Arboretum. She reviewed all the sketches the kids had submitted and offered constructive criticism.

"Making models was fun. Everyone made one out of clay, dirt, twigs, evergreen limbs, craft sticks, and so on. We sent letters all over the country asking for advice and insight. We've been in the newspapers a couple of times over this project. That triggered some offers of help, including a free gazebo, which of course we will accept. The dedication of the project is set for Arbor Day this spring. It'll take about two more years to really complete the project, and then the maintenance will go on, but we are planning with minimal maintenance in mind.

"Oh, I almost forgot to tell you. We use cooperative learning groups, and that has helped me to structure activities more productively. The kids know how to work together for the good of everyone. They capitalize on each others' strengths and abilities and interests. Some of these projects are pretty big, and we really do need everyone to make them go. See our motto up there on the wall? 'WE CAN MAKE A DIFFERENCE.' Underline the word we. We're in this together. This room is a community."

I ask Sasha if his society-centered approach keeps the students from learning history and geography. "That question comes up from time to time. But listen, these little kids know about Teddy Roosevelt, Gifford Pinchot, the Sierra Club, Henry David Thoreau, John James Audubon, our National Park system, and why we have it. They learn about conservation firsthand, but they research it, too, to learn the history. And that's true in other areas of history and geography. They know about climate patterns and vegetation. They can tell you why some plants are suited to this ecosystem and some are not. But, most of all, they know about our democratic system and how it works. We don't shortchange content. But I do teach it in the context of problem solving.

"I'm an activist, and my social studies curriculum is about getting involved, caring about the community, helping to leave the world a little better than we found it. Maybe that sounds kind of trite or even self-serving to some people, but I believe social studies is something you do, not just something you learn from a textbook. I want these kids to believe in themselves and in America. And America is about families, and responsibilities, and freedom, and caring about others. Boy, you'd think I was running for office or something."

The Knowledge-Centered Approach

Emma teaches fifth grade at Whittier Elementary School. The school is located in an urban setting, and the socioeconomic mix of the surrounding neighborhood is varied. She is in her 12th year of teaching and has been at Whittier for seven years. She works closely with two other fifth-grade teachers, Freda and Kenji. They plan together, and they have carved up the teaching territory so that Emma teaches three periods of social studies while Freda does English and Kenji does math.

As you enter Emma's classroom, as I did on a sunny afternoon in early spring, you get an immediate sense of history. Along the wall above the chalk tray on two sides of the room are pictures, in chronological order, of the presidents of the United States. On a third wall are pictures of other famous Americans, such as Benjamin Franklin, Martin Luther King, Jr., Thomas Edison, and Eleanor Roosevelt.

In addition to the pictures, the walls of Emma's classroom are covered with maps of all sizes and kinds, copies of the Declaration of Independence and the Constitution, and other historical and geographic memorabilia. An area of several square feet of wall space is devoted to student-made maps, drawings, and essays. The only uncovered areas of the room are the floor and ceiling; even the windows are partially covered with students' traced maps. The impression is that of a cluttered gallery, the sort of interesting place that you'd like to poke around in for a while.

Emma projects an initial seriousness that quickly gives way to a shy, warm sense of humor and good-heartedness. "I try to create a sense of history," she says with obvious understatement. "That's why there's so much stuff up in here. There are three of us who teach fifth grade, and I teach all the social studies, which is mainly U.S. history and geography. Freda teaches all the English, and Kenji teaches math. We teach our own science, reading, art, and so on. One thing I like about this arrangement is the team planning. When we get together, we share what we're each trying to do with the specialized subject we teach. That keeps us all involved to a certain extent, and allows us to occasionally do some interdisciplinary teaching.

"My goal in social studies is to develop in students a love of the history and geography of the United States. I do everything I can to make it appealing. We use the textbook as a kind of common reference and as a guide to the course of study, but I don't depend on it too heavily. If you want depth, you have to go way beyond the text. It just skims the surface."

I ask her what she means by that. "Well, for example, look at this." She gets up and brings a textbook over to where we are sitting. She flips through the pages until she finds the passage on Columbus. "I guess this is reasonably okay from a factual standpoint. But it isn't conceptual. It doesn't capture the spirit of what he did. I mean, he opened up two whole continents to European settlement. That's amazing. No one else in history ever did that or ever will. And those were wild times. The kids need to sense the excitement of that period of history.

"Every student read at least one book on explorers during our unit on exploration. Our wonderful librarian does a great job, but sometimes I'm afraid we're going to wear her out. We had wonderful reports, artwork, construction-type projects, displays, drama, and other things. You know, Columbus, Magellan, and others were able to venture out across the open sea because a type of ship called the caravel was developed. It had a completely different hull and structure. It was a real technological breakthrough. I wonder how many children ever made the connection between the rapid advance of technology in Europe during the fifteenth century and all these voyages of discovery. Anyway, we made caravels and other kinds of ships out of balsa wood and tested their seaworthiness in a water tank. The kids got interested in developing new hull designs, so I let them experiment. We read excerpts from Columbus' log from a book I got from the library. Then I gave an assignment where everyone became an explorer and kept a log of their discoveries for two weeks. Also, each student chose two explorers from different periods of history and compared their discoveries. One student did a comparison of Anna Freud and Balboa. Can you imagine that? It was a great report. I love to see 10-year-old kids making connections like that.

"One thing I do is a 10-point quiz every Thursday. The students know it's coming, and it keeps them on their toes. It only takes a few minutes, and everyone keeps his or her own record. We use the honor system, and it basically works. Of course, it helps to read and discuss great stories where honor and trust are illustrated. That inspires the kids to raise the moral level of their own lives.

"Also, everyone has to turn in a one- or two-page essay every week. The essay must be on the content we are studying at the time. The essay is turned in first to Freda, and she grades it and makes suggestions about style, syntax, or whatever. Then it is turned in to me, and I grade it for the content.

"We have a Project Fair in the spring, and everyone enters a project. It's required. The projects must have social studies content, and they must incorporate English, which isn't too hard, and math, which can be a stretch. Also, we encourage the students to use music, art, drama, et cetera as part of their project, so they turn out to be pretty interdisciplinary. The projects are wonderful. The project is a major part of the quarter grade in social studies. On Project Night, when the parents come to see all 90-odd projects on display in the gym, it's pretty exciting. We don't judge the projects in any competitive way. In fact, everyone gets a blue ribbon. The reason we can do that is I personally won't okay a project for display unless I believe it represents the child's best effort. Every child is capable of excellence, but not necessarily in the same way. You should come back on May 23rd—that's Project Night. I guarantee you'll see 91 excellent projects because that's how many kids we have." (She laughs.)

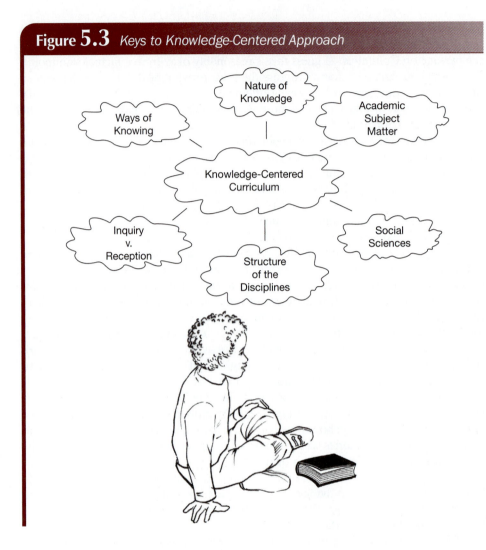

Figure 5.3 *Keys to Knowledge-Centered Approach*

"I love history, and I do volunteer work with the state historical society, and as a result, so do the kids. They become historians and geographers. We have contributed quite a bit of backyard history, especially tapes of old-timers, to the archives of the historical society. There's a nursing home near here, and the kids get extra credit for interviewing the residents. Some good friendships have come out of that, and some good history, too."

I ask Emma how she overcomes the negative attitudes that students so often have toward social studies. "Yes, that is a problem," she admits. "I don't know, for someone like me who loves history and geography to expect everyone else to love it is a little nearsighted. But all the new ideas about learning styles and different ways of knowing really help. I read parts of Howard Gardner's book on multiple intelligences, and that made quite an impression on me. There's way too much paper-and-pencil stuff and "read around the room" in social studies. Some kids are gifted when it comes to working with their hands, and some are talented at drama and art. I find that they all like to read if you give them something they can read that is worthwhile. And I have better readers tape portions of books or read to another student. Peer teaching really works—don't let anyone ever tell you it doesn't. Books, films, tapes, projects, plays, construction, artwork, music—that's my curriculum. That and the world outside. There has to be involvement: intellectual, social, and emotional involvement. I hate to say it, but the worst way to learn history is to read around the room from a social studies textbook, even though I guess some teachers do it. Personally, I'd fall asleep. Did you ever read around the room when you were a kid? Everybody is losing their place in the book for a bunch of different reasons.

"I want my students to be literate about our country. But I want them to enjoy it, because that's the only way they'll continue to learn on their own. Nobody ever got excited about a worksheet. If a child really believes that knowing history and geography is worthwhile, then you won't be able to stop her from continuing to learn.

"A couple of things I forgot to mention that you might be interested in: One is the Cultural Literacy Exam that I started last year. Are you familiar with the book *Cultural Literacy* by Hirsch?" (I nod.) "Well, I've developed a test of cultural literacy from some of the concepts and terms listed in the index of the book. I've tried not to make it just a test of unrelated facts and dates. I don't teach that way, so I don't like to test that way. I try to emphasize connection, not facts in isolation. Any way, it's quite a challenge for the students.

"The other thing is the Geography Club. I started it three years ago when we were asked to make proposals for teaching innovative courses for summer school in the district. Our principal gave me the idea. Now it goes during the school year, too. We meet once a month. The kids are assigned pen pals in other countries, and they exchange climate data, maps, photographs, recipes, anything related to geography or culture. The club does 'research,' too, like mapping neighborhoods. And, of course, we take field trips. Last summer we took an aerial field trip furnished by pilots from a flying club at a small airport near here.

"I guess you could call me a knowledge-centered teacher. I do think students need to learn ideas and information at school. I try to stress inquiry and involvement. And I try to make the learning meaningful and conceptual. I don't think every student needs to learn exactly the same thing in exactly the same way. I use a pretty straightforward unit approach starting with the Native Americans, the European background, and the voyages of exploration right on through the Civil War where our curriculum ends. But I try to connect the past to the present, and I try to connect the students' lives to the outside world."

Reflections

My purpose in bringing you with me to visit these three teachers was to give us the opportunity to listen to people who have thought a lot about what they do and who are able to speak reflectively about their practices. Even though they spoke to different emphases, these teachers have much in common. Each of them promotes active learning, projects, interdisciplinary themes, hands-on learning, cooperative efforts, reading and writing, and making connections. Each of them also cares deeply about children and about her or his work as a professional. Additionally, each has that valuable commodity called enthusiasm. Still, as we listened to them, it was also obvious that there were some subtle differences.

LeeAnn speaks convincingly about the importance of personal goal setting by children. She is clearly a developmentalist who, herself, is a lifelong learner, a goal she has for her students. She talks about hobbies and personal interests, about making learning fun, about personal morality and responsibility, about her role as teacher/counselor, and about creating a developmental exploratory environment. LeeAnn draws on day-to-day experience at school and in the children's lives to examine moral issues and to build up a sense of character. She also discusses at great length her organizational strategy of interest centers and explains how the centers approach makes it possible for her to really get to know the kids because it enables her to spend more time with individuals. So, we have an intelligent, caring professional whose reflective thought and teaching activity focus first and foremost on self-realization, a key to the learner-centered approach to curriculum.

Sasha speaks thoughtfully and persuasively about his role in building citizens. He wants his students actively involved in school and community. He discusses democracy and the importance of involving kids in experiences in democracy. Governing processes came up in his discussion in several forms: student government, city government, and school board. Sasha involves his students in the active use of power in their environment. Students make and live with the rules in his class. He speaks of class meetings, assemblies, city hall; in effect, he's preparing his students to be participants in their government. Community resources, both human and material, are important aspects of his teaching. Note that Sasha teaches subjects not as ends in themselves but as means to activist ends, such as building an arboretum, producing a booklet, and learning about who settled there and when.

Emma makes it abundantly clear that academic knowledge is important. She mentions subjects by name (e.g., history and geography); she talks about quizzes and grades; she refers to a number of historical allusions in her talk; she dwells on the importance of reading, writing, grammar, and mathematics; she uses literature to make moral points to the class; and she talks about her own love of history and geography. Emma brings up the issue of cultural literacy and her own role in creating a Cultural Literacy Exam, a clearly knowledge-centered piece of work. She discusses the connections she tries to develop between facts and information on the one hand and knowledge and concepts on the other. Obviously, she uses a wide range of strategies in order to make effective learners out of her students. She also searches actively for ways to make learning meaningful to the lives of her students, now and in the future.

Now that you have read the three teacher profiles, you are in a position to do some reflective thinking about the three approaches they represent. Identify what you think are the salient characteristics of each approach. Probably the best way for you to begin this task is with some brainstorming. List as many descriptive words or phrases as you can about each teacher's approach to the social studies curriculum:

LeeAnn   *Sasha*   *Emma*

A second step in the analysis is to identify three or four things you like about each approach. Focus on the positive attributes that you notice about learner-centered, society-centered, and knowledge-centered approaches in the profiles:

Positive attributes of the learner-centered approach:

_____

Positive attributes of the society-centered approach:

_____

Positive attributes of the knowledge-centered approach:

_____

The final step in this analysis is for you to synthesize all of this. You can do that by writing a brief statement of your own philosophy in which you describe your tendencies toward one or more of the three points of view.

My philosophy of social studies:

_____

Summary

There are three contrasting conceptions of the social studies curriculum's center: the learner-centered curriculum, the society-centered curriculum, and the knowledge-centered curriculum. Each has its proponents and merits. In the learner-centered approach to social studies, the role of teacher and of student is one of active personal engagement. The search is for personal meaning in learning. The goal is the self-realized individual. In the society-centered approach, the role of teacher and student is that of the actively participating citizen. Teamwork and cooperation are the hallmarks of society centering. The goal is to take part in society and to make a difference. In the knowledge-centered curriculum, the role of teacher and student is that of fellow inquirer. Knowledge is not just information or the accumulation of facts but insight into ideas and values. The goal is to develop individuals who want to learn and who prize the written word.

Explorations

1. Talk to several elementary school children. Ask them to describe the kinds of social studies activities they would like to do. Then make inferences about whether their descriptions are learner centered, society centered, or knowledge centered.

2. Thumb through the pages of an elementary social studies textbook. Try to find evidence of the three approaches to centering the curriculum.

3. Form a group with two other people who have read this chapter for a role-play activity. Draw straws to determine who will be the learner-centered

teacher, the society-centered teacher, and the knowledge-centered teacher, and plan the outline of a social studies unit on "Life in Colonial America."

4. Observe a primary-level social studies lesson. How would you describe what you saw from the perspective of this chapter? Repeat the activity at the intermediate level.

5. Try some role-play. Have a partner ask you about your social studies teaching. Keep it hypothetical, and just imagine yourself as a really dedicated social studies teacher. What will you say?

Continuing the Journey: Suggested Readings

Bruner, J. (1996). *The Culture of Education.* Cambridge, MA: Harvard University Press.

Crawford, G. (2007). *Brain-Based Teaching with Adolescent Learning in Mind.* Thousand Oaks, CA: Corwin.

Dederichs, P. H., Miller, C., Hellwege, K. H., & Olsen, J. L. (2008). *Games: Purpose and Potential in Education.* New York: Springer.

Dixon-Krauss, L. (1996). *Vygotsky in the Classroom.* New York: Longman.

Ellis, A. K. (2004). *Exemplars of Curriculum Theory.* Larchmont, NY: Eye on Education.

Hale, M., & City, A. (2006). *The Teacher's Guide to Leading Student-Centered Discussion.* Thousand Oaks, CA: Corwin.

Hirsch, E. D., Jr. (2006). *The Knowledge Deficit.* Boston: Houghton Mifflin.

Johnson, D. (2008). *Education for a Caring Society: Classroom Relationships and Moral Action.* New York: Teachers College Press.

Kohn, A. (2004). *What Does It Mean to Be Well Educated?* New York: Beacon Press.

McInerney, D., Dowson, M., & Van Etten, S. (2006). *Effective Schools.* Scottsdale, AZ: Information Age Publishing.

Murdoch, K., & Wilson, J. (2008). *Creating a Learner-Centered Primary Classroom.* Oxford, England: Routledge.

Riggs, E., Gholar, C., & Morgan, R. (2008). *Strategies That Promote Student Engagement.* Thousand Oaks, CA: Corwin.

Rose-Duckworth, R., Ramer, K., & Ritchart, R. (2008). *Fostering Learner Independence.* Thousand Oaks, CA: Corwin.

Sejnost, R., & Thiese, S. (2006). *Reading and Writing Across Content Areas.* Thousand Oaks, CA: Corwin.

Websites

Edutopia.org is an in-depth and interactive resource for core teaching strategies such as project learning, technology integration, and integrated studies. *www.edutopia.org*

"The Cooperative Learning Center is a Research and Training Center focusing on how students should interact with each other as they learn and the skills needed to interact effectively." *www.co-operation.org/*

"Dedicated to excellence and fairness in early education, the Core Knowledge Foundation is an independent, non-profit, non-partisan organization founded in 1986 by E. D. Hirsch, Jr., professor emeritus at the University of Virginia and author of many acclaimed books including *Cultural Literacy: What Every American Needs to Know* and *The Schools We Need and Why We Don't Have Them.*" *http://coreknowledge.org*

"Free resources for teaching civics and U.S. government." *www.c-spanclassroom.org/*

Related NCSS Standards and Principles of Powerful Social Studies

Teacher Standards

II. Pedagogical Standards

The pedagogical standards itemized below focus on teacher knowledge, competence, and dispositions beyond the subject matter that is the focus of the Subject Matter Standards above. They are intended to assure that social studies teachers possess the general pedagogical knowledge, capabilities, and dispositions needed to create the kinds of learning experiences and classroom and school environments that are envisioned by recent reform movements and validated by research. As such, these standards favor learner-centered, meaningful, integrative, value-based, challenging, and active instruction. They see teachers as instructional decision-makers, members of school-based learning communities, and members of the larger community of stakeholders who can help support the learning of students," (p. 50).

1. Learning and Development

Social studies teachers should possess the knowledge, capabilities, and dispositions to provide learning opportunities at the appropriate school levels that support learners' intellectual, social, and personal development.

2. Differences in Learning Styles

Social studies teachers should possess the knowledge, capabilities, and dispositions to create at the appropriate school

levels learning experiences that fit the different approaches to learning of diverse learners.

3. Critical Thinking, Problem Solving, and Performance Skills

Social studies teachers should possess the knowledge, capabilities, and dispositions to use at the appropriate school levels a variety of instructional strategies to encourage student development of critical thinking, problem solving, and performance skills.

4. Active Learning and Motivation

Social studies teachers should possess the knowledge, capabilities, and dispositions to create at the appropriate school levels learning environments that encourage social interaction, active engagement in learning, and self-motivation.

5. Inquiry, Collaboration, and Supportive Classroom Interaction

Social studies teachers should possess the knowledge, capabilities, and dispositions to use at the appropriate school levels verbal, nonverbal, and media communication" (p. 50).

Source: Excerpted from National Council for the Social Studies. *National Standards for Social Studies Teachers* (Silver Spring, MD: Author, 2002). The Council's website is www.socialstudies.org

Planning for Social Studies Teaching and Learning

Keys to This Chapter

- Teachers as Decision Makers
- Planning for Long-Range Goals
- Planning Lessons and Activities
- Teaching Concepts
- Teaching Skills
- Teaching Values
- Planning and Developing Units

When planning for a year, plant rice. When planning for a decade, plant trees. When planning for life, educate children.
        —Chinese proverb

A lot has been written and said about the value of planning over the years. We know, for example, that higher achieving students typically have goals and plans while lower achievers, sadly, do not. We know from the scriptural accounts that it was not raining when Noah built the Ark. He was definitely planning ahead. The author and activist Gloria Steinem once wrote that "dreaming is a form of planning." It's a beautiful thought, to have dreams.

The Roman poet Horace gave sage advice when he wrote in the first century B.C., "mix a little foolishness with your serious plans; it's lovely to be silly at the right moment." This is wonderful advice to teachers. Even the most serious social studies plan could benefit from a little humor. A classroom should be a place of joy, opportunity, and freedom to learn.

I suspect that Horace is also telling us that timing is everything when he uses the phrase *the right moment.* Three centuries before Horace, Greek philosopher Plato made it clear that the work of childhood is play. We should keep this in mind, as well. After all, we're helping to build lifelong memories and attitudes, so why not make them good ones?

A plan represents an organized way of thinking about the future. The future is unknown, but we still make plans because by doing so, we can at least have something to say about the future. The alternative is not appealing: To let the future merely happen is to place ourselves at the mercy of events. We know that one of the attributes of higher-achieving students is that they make plans for both the near and distant future. Likewise, an attribute of effective teachers is that they

plan carefully and flexibly, always building in variety and choice for their students. A good plan not only guides your actions, but it also allows you to reflect on what you did against some standard. A good plan exists in the future, present, and past in that it is at once a forecast, an experience, and a retrospective. A plan is speculative when it is drawn up, in motion when it is implemented, and history after it happens.

A plan for learning is therefore an enabling device that does three things:

1. Helps you think about what needs to be accomplished and why
2. Guides you and your students through experiences in much the same way a map guides a traveler
3. Provides a frame of reference for deciding to what extent the experience was meaningful

Careful planning empowers you. It makes you a true professional. Careful planning helps distinguish the teachers who do it from those who, content with mediocrity, merely make their way through textbooks with no strategic vision, occasionally hitting on a good activity here and there. That's not teaching; that's monitoring.

Teachers as Decision Makers

Teachers need to make several basic decisions as they plan for instruction. Those decisions relate to content, activities of the teacher, and activities of the learner.

First of all, you must make decisions about the content of your social studies program. I recommend a developmental approach to the teaching of content. This means that your instruction should proceed from what students already know and are able to do toward knowledge and skills beyond their present understanding. Thus, you will want to sequence your instruction from simple to complex. Facts can lead to concepts, which can in turn lead to generalizations. This progression happens, however, only if you are willing to make the connections. The same thing is true in the teaching of skills. Simple skills, such as measuring distance, can lead to more complex skills, such as accurately estimating distance and size.

Decision making about content also has another dimension. Suppose two fifth-grade teachers are each assigned to teach about the United States as the central focus of the social studies curriculum. One teacher might give more emphasis to history; the other might choose to emphasize geography. One might spend more time on the colonial era, concentrating on the family; the other might spend more time emphasizing settlement patterns in the New World. The point is that teachers have a great deal of autonomy within a prescribed curriculum, especially in social studies (as opposed to mathematics), where little agreement exists on what constitutes minimal content coverage of people, places, and events.

The second area in which you will make instructional decisions concerns the activities of the learners. What will your students actually do during social studies? Will they read? Orally? Silently? What will they read? Textbooks? Biographies? Original documents? Will they engage in discussion? If so, with whom? Will you lead the discussion,

A teacher in Japanese costume models role-play while teaching her students, creating a powerful effect.

or will students discuss ideas in small groups? Will your students be expected to listen as you lecture to them? Will they take notes? Will you have your students observe, do surveys, make maps, and draw pictures? Will they construct villages, put on plays, and tape news programs? Will they work individually? Cooperatively? Whatever your students do in social studies will be the result of the decisions you have made. One thing is certain: How students spend their time will have a great effect on both their attitudes and their achievements in social studies.

You will also make instructional decisions about your own conduct, or the activities of the teacher. As you plan for your behavior in the instructional process, keep in mind these principles of learning: motivation, retention, and transfer.

Motivation

Motivation is a powerful tool in the learning process. Consider yourself, for example: How motivated are you to be the best teacher possible? It's probably true that the level of your motivation will dictate the extent to which you succeed, assuming, of course, that you possess the basic abilities.

Here is something to keep in mind regarding motivation: A student's most powerful motivation to learn a school subject comes from his or her prior success in that subject. In other words, "Nothing succeeds like success." Successful experiences are those in which students feel a sense of involvement, mastery, enjoyment, and challenge. The question for you is: How can I make sure that my students succeed?

Retention

How well do you remember what you hear, see, and experience? The ability to recall information and events is retention at its simplest level. At a higher level, retention means how well you are able to use what you have learned. The key to memory and application is the learner's level of involvement in the learning process. I once worked for the National Science Foundation developing problem-solving units and training teachers to use the units in elementary classrooms. We discovered that the teachers behaved in their own classrooms essentially as we did when we taught them. If we lectured to them, they lectured to their students. If we got them actively involved, they involved their students. The old saying "I hear and I forget; I see and I remember; I do and I understand" comes to mind.

Few of us retain all or even very much of what we learn. Our memories are less than perfect, and we may not have fully understood what we were taught in the first place. As a teacher, your responsibility is to attempt to maximize students' *retention* of key ideas, skills, and values. Facts, names, dates, and places taught as items of specific knowledge are short-term memory items, at best. Long-term retention comes from active involvement in the learning process and emphasis on connections among ideas.

Transfer of Learning

The ability to transfer learning is the ability to take what we have learned in one situation and use it in another situation. Obviously, specific facts taught without any meaningful context have little potential for transfer. Such skills as observing, recording, and communicating, however, have unlimited transfer value. Concepts also transfer well. The child who internalizes such concepts as *supply and demand, cause and effect,* and *interdependence* has learned ideas that will apply in a variety of situations, now and in the future. Learning experiences should use facts and information as *tools* for thinking, rather than as ends in themselves. When this occurs, the potential for transfer greatly increases.

You also can promote the transfer of learning by making connections between and among the subjects you teach. Challenge yourself, for example, to use ideas from mathematics in social studies. If your students are learning to make graphs in math, give them the opportunity to graph such social science data as high and low temperature readings for a week. If your students are learning to write letters in language arts, have them send real letters to cities around the country, asking for information about climate,

CURRENT EVENTS
Focus on Planning

Whatever decisions you make about your instructional approach, I urge you to make current events and news reporting an integral part of your social studies curriculum. Encourage your students to be aware of the news, to learn to distinguish the superficial from the significant, and, in the inquiry spirit of this book, to become reporters themselves.

commerce, recreation, and agriculture. If your students are learning about perspective and shading in art, apply these concepts to student-constructed maps.

Planning for Long-Range Goals

The decisions you make about content, your students' activities, and your activities will be reflected in your planning for classroom activities. Generally, when you think of planning, daily lesson plans come to mind. Planning is so much more than that, however. Planning encompasses long-range goals as well as short-term objectives.

It is useful to think of the chunks of instruction for which you are responsible. In a global sense, you are responsible for the entire year. This is your largest chunk. Full-year planning is, by its very nature, quite general. For example, you will want to come up with four or five long-range goals for the year. Such goals might include "Developing a miniature democracy in my classroom," "Imparting a knowledge of the geography of the United States," or "Being committed to enhancing the self-concept of each child."

Long-range goals are not written in instructional terms, nor are they meant to be achieved quickly. The advantage to developing long-range goals is that they give you a sense of structure, a sort of intellectual scaffold from which to view learning in a meaningful, long-term perspective. You should know what your long-range goals are, and you should share them with your students. By discussing them from time to time, you and your class will be able to make reflective judgments about how well you are progressing. A useful frame of reference for thinking about long-range goals for your social studies program is to consider your students' academic needs, their social development, and their personal fulfillment. By including your students in planning, you will begin to get a far better sense of who they really are. The Keys to Developing a Successful Unit will be useful as you plan units for your own classroom.

Keys to Developing a Successful Unit

- Choose a suitable topic—for example, "Colonial Life," "Inventions and Discoveries," "Space and Place," "A Renaissance Fair," "The Age of Exploration," "Pioneer Life and Times," "Hopi Culture," "Japanese Families," or "A Better Community."
- Spend time reading about and researching the topic. Announce the topic to the class, and tell them to find out what they can in order to prepare for a planning meeting.
- Bring the class together for a discussion of the possibilities. Involve the students in planning.

- Collect resource materials (e.g., books, magazines, Websites), and establish centers or focal points of learning.
- Develop and distribute a list of types of activities related to the topic. The types should include (a) academic, (b) construction, and (c) social. The expectations should be for each student to show evidence of reading, writing, drawing, building, teaching, and performance.
- Develop strategies for involving the home. It is crucial that parents take part in some meaningful way.

- Meet with students to establish their personal goals and responsibilities.
- Meet with the whole class daily for times of sharing and team building.
- Encourage freedom, responsibility, creativity, and teamwork.
- Allow time for reflection. Ask: What are we learning?
- Involve resource people (e.g., librarians, artists, authors, scientists, professionals, workers, parents, service groups, retired people).

- Ensure that student work is presented, published, displayed, performed, and otherwise shared beyond the classroom.
- Plan assessment strategies that will show evidence of academic, personal, social, and citizenship growth. Include students in the assessment process, and expect them to assume responsibility for much of the assessment.
- Celebrate the experience in some meaningful way—for example, a party, a performance, or a similar activity.

Planning Lessons and Activities

Every lesson plan can be analyzed using two distinct criteria: mechanics and substance. Let's look at each individually.

Mechanics

To analyze the *mechanics,* think of placing a sort of template over the lesson that represents the procedures one reasonably ought to follow to obtain measurable, effective results. Generally, these procedures are thought of as steps, although there is no need to follow them slavishly in linear fashion. The steps come principally from the ideas about learning developed in the psychological literature, which include needing to establish purpose and key ideas, motivating students to learn, providing continuity in the learning process, and supporting concept development, transfer of learning, and reflective thinking.

A typical lesson includes six basic components, which are generally thought of as steps in lesson development: key idea, instructional objective, motivation (an anticipatory "set" or introduction), activity, assessment, and reflection or closure. Let's look at these individually.

1. *Key idea.* The key idea is the social science concept or generalization you want the students to learn. It represents the single most important thought or idea of the lesson. (See Chapter 3 for sample of key ideas from each of the social sciences.) For example, a key idea from history is "Our interpretations of the past change as new information is discovered." The key idea is the centerpiece of the lesson. Without it, you merely have an activity. With it, you have something special: an idea about human behavior.

2. *Instructional objective.* The instructional objective is the portion of the lesson plan that establishes its intent and proposed outcome. It is the means of operationalizing the lesson's key idea. The instructional objective must be clearly stated. It should tell what the students will do (e.g., discuss, list, classify, draw) under what conditions (e.g., small-group work, independent study). Students also need to know the intended purpose of the lesson. What should they know, feel, or be able to do as a result of the lesson?

3. *Motivation.* This stage is known variously as the *anticipatory set* or the *lesson introduction.* At this point of the lesson, you want to arouse students' attention, capture their imagination, or indicate how today's lesson is connected to yesterday's lesson. You are putting the activity into context and making it meaningful to your students. Motivation is a crucial issue early in the lesson because at this stage, you create the appropriate mental set and accompanying desire to learn. You can use any number of ways to motivate your students. You can try to make the lesson interesting or appealing, you can try to convince your students of the lesson's importance, or you can decide to use such extrinsic motivators as grades or special favors. In most cases, an interesting introduction designed to gain the students' attention will be sufficient.

4. *Activity.* This step represents the major teaching/learning focus of the lesson. At stake is the ratio of teacher activity to student activity: the behaviors of the teacher and students, the management of the activity and materials, the explanations and information offered by the teacher, the tasks given to the students, and the additional help given to the students who need it. Obviously, for one adult to lead the behaviors and learning attempts of 30 children is a very complex task. Be sure that students understand specifically what they will be doing during the lesson. Providing clear directions is crucial to the lesson's success. Will students work together or alone? Will they make things? Do seat work? Help your students carry out the assignment. Move around the room, providing assistance as needed. Ask questions, probe, clarify, maintain order, and reassure. Of course, the nature and amount of guidance will vary with such factors as student age, ability, motivation, and the nature of the task itself.

5. *Assessment.* You have a key idea and a learning objective. Your instructional activity has been designed to develop the key idea through experience. Now comes the question of assessment: What did the students learn? How will you know what they learned? What will you do to find out what they learned? All assignments need some pulling together, some summarizing, or some means of looking back. In some cases, a brief discussion will be adequate. In other cases, you will need to analyze the students' work together. In still other instances, you will give a quiz or test. Part of your instructional strategy should be to allow time for students to look reflectively on their work. If you don't, you may inhibit their chances of retaining key ideas and thus limit the lesson's potential to achieve transfer of learning.

6. *Reflection.* At this stage, you and your students have the opportunity to revisit what you have accomplished. You need to spend some time reviewing what has been learned and how it is connected to what has gone before and what is yet to come. Clarify any extended expectations. This is also the time to elicit ideas about the lesson from your students. What do they think they have learned? There will also be times when you assign homework in connection with a lesson. When you do, be certain you are clear about what students are to do at home and what they will be expected to turn in. Remember that they are on their own, so it is not appropriate to expect them to develop new skills. They will continue or build on their classwork.

Together, these steps give you a structure or framework for lesson planning. Don't think of them, however, as comprising a lockstep recipe, in which you must account for every point each time you work with students. The steps are based on known principles of effective learning. Sample Lessons 6.1 and 6.2, at the end of this chapter, illustrate the mechanics of lesson planning more concretely. Read them carefully to see how the steps are fleshed out.

Substance

The other fundamental aspect of a lesson besides mechanics is *substance,* or what is learned. A knowledge of the mechanics of lesson planning is useful because it gives you a framework within which to work. But the framework is of little value unless the substance of the lesson is worthwhile. The substance of social studies lessons is found in four bases: content, concepts, skills, and values.

1. *Content.* The content of a lesson is the knowledge that you have decided is necessary for students to learn. In elementary social studies, the content of the curriculum comes primarily from the social sciences. The most dominant influences of social studies content are history and geography, but economics, government, psychology, anthropology, and sociology are also significant. As you consider lesson content in the planning stages, ask yourself questions to clarify this area of concern: What is important about this content? How is it necessary to students? What information, knowledge, and understanding should students gain from this lesson?

2. *Concepts.* The content of a lesson will be adapted to the ideas or concepts that you want to emphasize. (The teaching of concepts is detailed in the next section.) At the planning stage, consider these issues: What idea or ideas about human behavior are inherent in this lesson? What kinds of questions need to be raised? To what extent will the students be stimulated intellectually? Will they share their ideas? Are the ideas in this lesson transferable to other experiences?

3. *Skills.* As you plan the actual instruction for your lesson, consider what skills you want to reinforce or teach. A later section of this chapter gives specific recommendations addressing this concern. In planning, ask yourself questions such as these: What methods and skills will the students use? Are the skills in this lesson transferable? (see Figure 6.1). Are students becoming increasingly independent in their problem solving?

4. *Values.* To be complete, your planning should take into account the values that will be part of the lesson. Again, some suggestions for doing this are given later in this chapter. As you plan, however, ask yourself: What will the students learn about themselves?

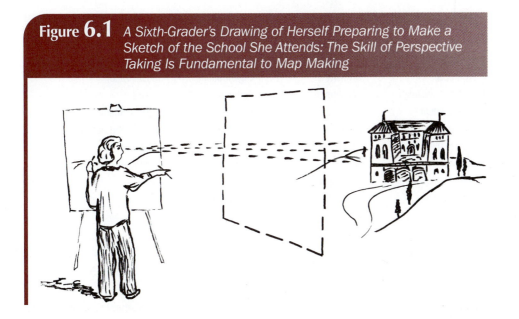

Figure 6.1 *A Sixth-Grader's Drawing of Herself Preparing to Make a Sketch of the School She Attends: The Skill of Perspective Taking Is Fundamental to Map Making*

Will they be exposed to the values of others? Will they have a chance to share their values?

Obviously, not every lesson you teach will provide definitive answers to all the questions suggested here. However, every lesson ought to form part of a total context of instructional experience designed to take all these questions into account. Regardless of whether your philosophy of lesson planning tends to be formal or informal, you need to ensure that your social studies instruction is based on a purposeful rationale, rather than on merely covering topics or spending what is supposedly the appropriate amount of time with social studies. The teaching of concepts, skills, and values is considered in greater detail in the next sections of this chapter.

Teaching Concepts

Concepts in social studies are ideas about human activity. They transcend time and space, and they transfer to new situations. For example, the economic concept of *supply and demand* can be used to understand any economic system, anywhere, at any time. For example, people living in caves faced issues of supply and demand: They had to eat, and they had to gather or hunt in order to supply their demand. But the concept of supply and demand also applies to modern capitalist societies, and it will be an important concept to understand if people establish a base on the moon in the future.

The power of concepts over mere facts and information is that concepts are intellectual tools that can be applied in an endless variety of settings. They provide us with

Figure 6.2 Concepts Commonly Taught in Elementary Social Studies

Adaptation	Diffusion	Norms	Social interaction
Artifacts	Diversity	Organizations	Socialization
Areal association	Enculturation	Patterns	Space
Assimilation	Environment	Power	Spatial interaction
Behavior	Family	Probability	Supply and demand
Cause/Effect	Governance	Problems	Systems
Change	Groups	Resources	Technology
Communication	Interdependence	Roles	Time
Community	Land use	Rules	Tools
Conflict	Life cycle	Scarcity	
Cooperation	Markets	Seasons	
Culture	Needs/Wants	Self	

generalizable ways of dealing with reality. Anthropologists make extensive use of the concept of *culture.* Sociologists attempt to identify and describe *norms of behavior.* Figure 6.2 provides a list of concepts commonly taught in elementary social studies.

Concepts are ideas, not terms whose definitions are to be memorized. Therefore, concepts are learned only through meaningful experiences that are revisited by reflective thinking. Only when people reflect on what they have done or seen do they begin to analyze, to see relationships, to make connections.

Developing Concepts

There are many ways to develop any given concept. However, as just noted, direct experience and reflection on that experience are two proven techniques for concept building with elementary age children. Let's look at two scenarios that illustrate effective ways to get children to think conceptually.

The first lesson, for primary age children, features a problem-centered experience with *supply and demand,* in which the teacher asks students to think reflectively and then to generalize to larger and different problems. This is a very effective way of teaching concepts.

The second lesson uses *webbing,* or *mind maps.* In it, the teacher and class begin their discussion with an organizing concept of theme—in this case, the concept of *culture.* Concepts have attributes or characteristics that define them. In the case of culture, some of those attributes are food, clothing, shelter, customs, work, religion, and technology (see Figure 6.3). Notice the progression from the more abstract webbing, which identifies a kind of rubric of cultural attributes that could be applied to any study (for example, ancient Athens, a medieval village, our community, and so on) to the specific application shown in Figure 6.4, which shows the webbing applied to the Pilgrims of colonial America.

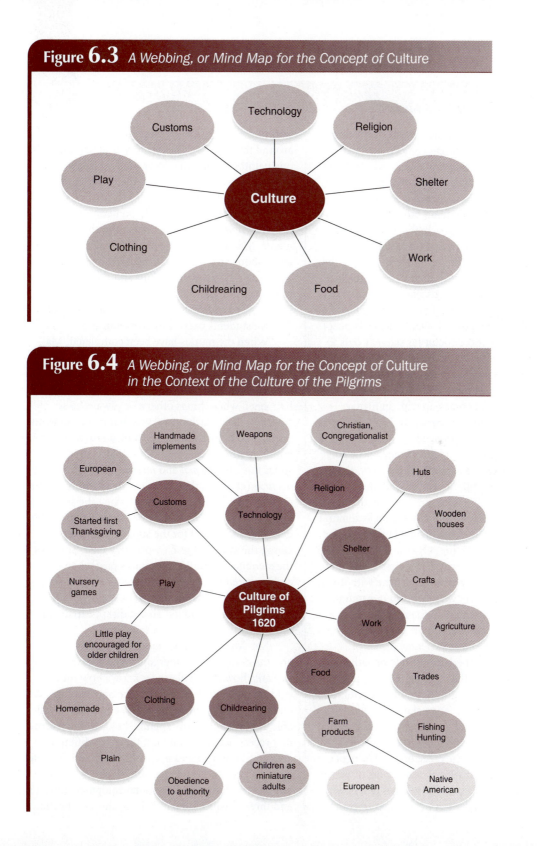

Figure 6.3 *A Webbing, or Mind Map for the Concept of Culture*

Technology

Customs

Religion

Play

Shelter

Culture

Clothing

Work

Childrearing

Food

Figure 6.4 *A Webbing, or Mind Map for the Concept of Culture in the Context of the Culture of the Pilgrims*

Handmade implements

Weapons

Christian, Congregationalist

European

Huts

Customs

Religion

Started first Thanksgiving

Technology

Wooden houses

Shelter

Nursery games

Play

Crafts

Culture of Pilgrims 1620

Work

Agriculture

Little play encouraged for older children

Food

Trades

Homemade

Clothing

Childrearing

Plain

Farm products

Fishing Hunting

Obedience to authority

Children as miniature adults

European

Native American

Ms. Jones, a first-grade teacher, wants to develop the economic concept of *supply and demand* with her students. Since concepts are ideas, not isolated facts, they always transcend time and space. Supply and demand certainly qualifies as a concept because there were supply-and-demand problems in prehistoric times, in ancient Egypt, in the Middle Ages, and in our present society, and there will no doubt be such problems in the future. Thus, we can see that supply and demand is not limited to any one place or any one time; rather, it transcends time and space.

At this point, we know that our first-grade teacher has selected a useful social science concept. But is this concept too difficult for six-year-olds to comprehend? This is where experience is crucial. Ms. Jones must develop an experience for these children that has meaning to them. She thinks about the matter and comes up with an idea to introduce the concept experientially. Let's peek in as she sets up the experience.

Ms. Jones asks the students if they know what holiday is coming up this month. Right away, she has their attention. It is mid-November, and the students immediately answer "Thanksgiving." Ms. Jones asks the children if they would like to make a mural depicting the first Thanksgiving held by the Native Americans and the Pilgrims. Of course they would! She reads the class the story of the first Thanksgiving and discusses the events of that time with them. "Tomorrow," she says, "we will begin our mural."

When the children arrive the next day, they are excited about the mural and want to get started. Ms. Jones shows the class two large pieces of butcher paper, each taped up securely on either side of the room. She tells the children that the class will be divided into two groups and that each group will make its own mural. Then she says, "Jenny, why don't you go over to the paper on this side of the room and get started." Jenny stands up hesitantly and goes over to the piece of butcher paper. In front of her are many brushes and pots of poster paint in a rainbow of colors. Ms. Jones tells Jenny to go ahead and asks the rest of the class to come

over to the other side. Twenty-two children crowd around the second piece of butcher paper. There is one paintbrush and one baby food jar filled with brown paint. The teacher tells the children to go ahead and make their mural.

Confusion reigns. Finally, someone says, "This isn't fair. It won't work." Others echo those sentiments. Ms. Jones asks the children if they have any ideas about how this situation could be improved. They suggest that half the kids should go to each mural site and that the paint jars and brushes should be equally distributed. The teacher agrees, and the students make two great murals.

When the murals have been completed, Ms. Jones reminds the children of the problem they faced and asks if they think their solution was satisfactory. One child asks the teacher why all of this happened when things otherwise always go so smoothly. The teacher explains that it was done on purpose to help the students think about *resources,* both human and material. The children and Ms. Jones talk about *equal* and *unequal distribution of resources* (although they don't use those terms, at least at first). Ms. Jones explains that when the supply is too great for the demand (poor Jenny) or when the demand is too great for the supply (poor rest of the class), the system doesn't work very well. She asks the students to recall Christmases past when every child wanted a particular toy or doll and the supply simply wasn't great enough. Yet usually within a few months, the demand all but disappeared and the supply was more than adequate.

Ms. Jones also talks about the water supply and the demand for water in the summer. She explains how the local grocer knows how much cold cereal to stock on the shelves. She discusses the amount of playground space and equipment available at the school and explains that it is one reason that recess occurs at different times for different classes. She solicits examples of supply and demand from the students—for example, experiences they have had with toys or playground equipment (30 kids and three playground balls). Last, she assigns the students the task of asking their parents if they can think of examples from life at home. The students are to report on these examples the following day.

To reconstruct this example of concept development, Ms. Jones took the students through the experience→mind→meaning continuum. An experience shared by the entire class provided a common point of reference. The teacher then helped the students to reflect on and process the experience, and she developed the meaning of the concept by providing and soliciting from the children other examples of supply and demand.

This supply-and-demand lesson raises an important point in teaching and learning social studies: Why go to all this trouble in order to introduce an economic concept to a group of

six-year-olds? Why not just read the definition from a dictionary or some other source, if you really think the term is important? First, relatively little extra work was involved, assuming that the teacher was going to have the children make Thanksgiving murals anyway. What the teacher did was to capitalize on an every-day situation and teach a concept from it. Second, you can't teach concepts by reading words from the dictionary. At best, you can teach vocabulary that way, but the method isn't very efficient, given what is known about short-term memory learning. The experience itself was the key, and the reflective thinking and mental processing of the process were also instrumental. This teacher taught the students a concept in such a way that they will probably always remember it.

---

in the classroom   Defining *Culture* through Webbing

One of the most fundamental social science concepts is that of *culture.* The sociological or anthropological definition of *culture* is "the sum total of ways of living built up by one group of human beings and transmitted from one generation to another." But what you have just read is a definition of a term. For culture to become a concept, not just a term, you will have to develop appropriate experiences for your students.

The *webbing* approach represents a graphic strategy for developing conceptual schemes. A webbing, or mind map, enables students to bring meaning to information at both the content and conceptual levels. Marzano and Arredondo (1986) suggest that the use of webbing and other graphic approaches can lead students to generate new meaning about the material they study in several important ways:

- Webbing permits and often encourages nonlinear thinking.
- Webbing can be used to synthesize complex information from diverse sources efficiently, helping students to identify patterns and relationships that are otherwise difficult to comprehend.

- Webbing helps the user generate information about the structure of the whole and the relationships among its parts that may not have been clear in the original, nongraphic information.

The webbing shown in Figure 6.3 illustrates how one might begin to imagine the attributes of the concept of *culture.* If culture is about the ways that a group of people live, then it would logically include their food, clothing, shelter, customs, and so on. The webbing in Figure 6.3 contains nine attributes of culture; certainly, others could be added. But this webbing is fairly abstract because it contains no specific content about a certain group of people. In that sense, it could be used as a starting point to describe any culture.

The second webbing, shown in Figure 6.4, illustrates how the attributes of the concept of *culture* can be applied to a specific cultural group—in this case, the Pilgrim settlers of Plimoth Plantation in the 1620s.

Here is a challenge for you: Identify some aspect of human activity—past or present, near or far, small or large scale. See if you can take the concept of *culture* and apply it as a webbing to the group or society you have chosen.

Keep in mind that concepts are *ideas*. Thus, in the first classroom example, if you were asked what the main idea of the lesson is, your response would be that it is the concept of *supply and demand*. In the second example, the main idea is the concept of *culture*. Teachers are sometimes criticized for their failure to teach conceptually. This will not happen if you approach each experience by asking yourself: What is the main idea or concept I want the children to learn?

Teaching Skills

Skills are the *methodological tools* of social science. Being able to use them effectively sets a student free to investigate problems independently. If concepts are ideas about human behavior, then investigative skills are the primary means to further develop and expand those ideas. Social studies instruction often supports a wide variety of skill development:

- *Observing.* Observing phenomena, events, and interactions, both alone and with a partner; eyewitnessing; listening
- *Recording.* Recalling information and observations; photographing; mapping, drawing, and illustrating; tape recording; listing and writing
- *Describing.* Creating written, oral, photographic, and graphic descriptions; identifying attributes
- *Defining.* Defining terms and procedures; developing precise meanings; communicating; stating problems
- *Measuring.* Using standard measures and developing one's own measures; counting and quantifying data; using mathematical computations; developing rating scales; using and developing map scales
- *Estimating.* Guessing distance and size; using experience to make informed guesses
- *Classifying.* Grouping and categorizing; differentiating and labeling
- *Comparing/Contrasting.* Noting differences and similarities; identifying attributes; describing
- *Data gathering.* Identifying and selecting data sources; determining appropriate methods; conducting surveys, historical studies, experiments, and interviews
- *Data processing.* Quantifying data; performing graphic analysis; mapping; making charts; writing summaries
- *Communicating.* Communicating orally, in writing, and through pictures and graphics; engaging in group activities; expressing oneself
- *Constructing.* Building models and dioramas; drawing relief maps and murals; creating displays and exhibits
- *Analyzing.* Discriminating; categorizing; finding patterns; identifying attributes; detecting structures
- *Synthesizing.* Planning; producing; documenting; theorizing; developing systems
- *Hypothesizing.* Guessing in an educated way; developing hunches; testing assumptions
- *Inferring.* Making statements from data; reaching conclusions; making decisions
- *Predicting.* Determining relationships; forecasting outcomes; correlating variables
- *Generalizing.* Conceptualizing; identifying supportive data; testing relationships; finding patterns; summarizing

Collaborative learning works best in an open environment built on trust.

- *Evaluating.* Making judgments and decisions; determining validity; detecting errors and fallacies
- *Question posing.* Developing questions; identifying researchable problems; defining terms
- *Verifying.* Checking sources; validating ideas and sources; referring to authority

Effective teachers plan on incorporating a variety of skills in their lessons. Doing so helps keep students interested and offers them a panoply of ways to process, interpret, apply, and share what they learn. Consider the foregoing list carefully. Every lesson you teach should incorporate one or more of these skills. Let me give you an example of how skills can be put to use.

in the classroom　　**Teaching *Estimation***

Take your class out to the play area of the school. Be sure they bring along some basic tools, such as pencils, pads, and rulers. Have the students work in pairs. Their task is to *estimate* the distance from one end of the play area to the other. Expect wild guesses. This is fine. Remember that children are imaginative.

Next, have the partners work together to measure the length of each person's stride. Depending on the age level, you can teach them about the average length of one of their strides by mathematically averaging 10 strides.

Finally, have the students step off the length of the play area by counting the number of strides from one end to the other end. Now they have *measured* the length. See Figure 6.5, in which a student describes the work she and her partner did in this activity.

Figure 6.5 *Students Write about Measuring Distance*

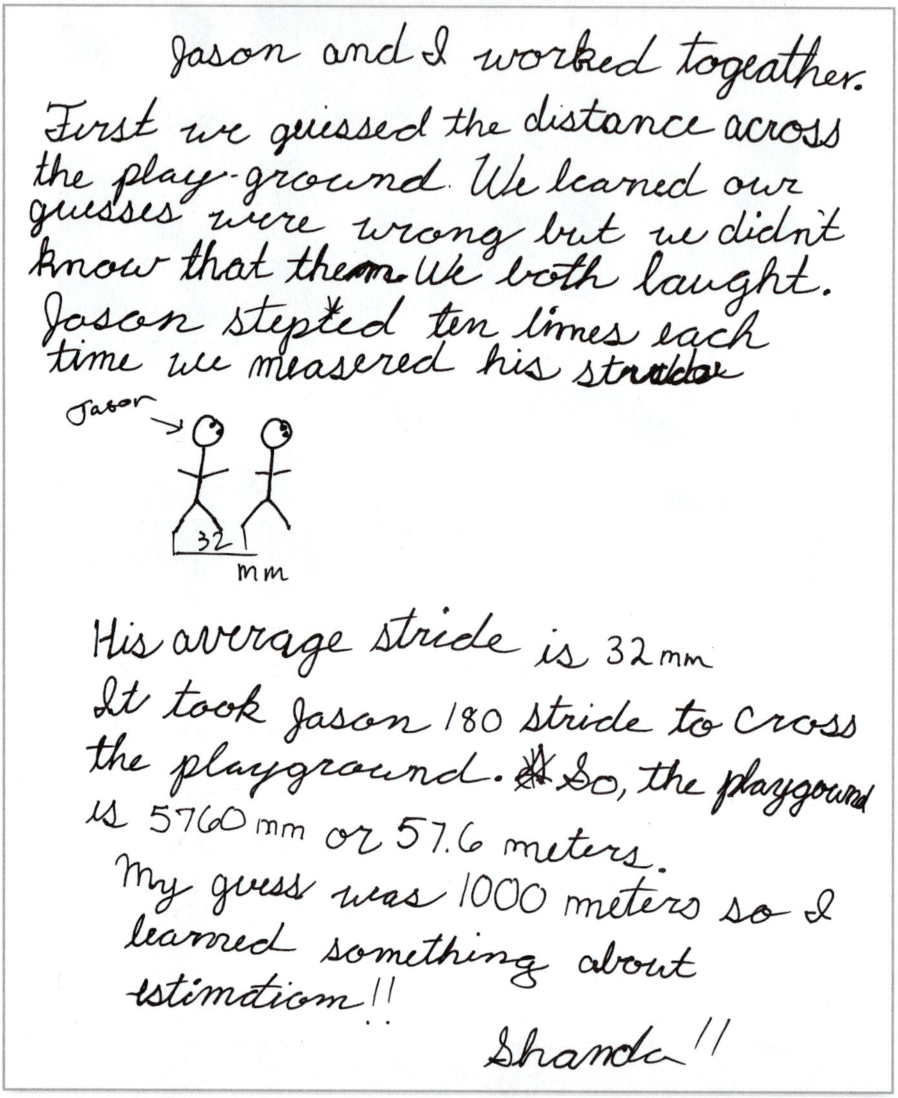

Jason and I worked togeather.
First we guessed the distance across
the play-ground. We learned our
guesses were wrong but we didn't
know that them. We both laught.
Jason stepted ten times each
time we measered his stride

Jason →

32
m m

His average stride is 32 mm
It took Jason 180 stride to cross
the playground. So, the playgound
is 5760 mm or 57.6 meters.
My guess was 1000 meters so I
learned something about
istimation!!

Shanda!!

Teaching Values

The values that we teach in elementary social studies fall into three distinct but related categories, each of which is important to children's growth and development: behavioral, procedural, and substantive. Your task is to ensure that all three are being learned along the way, not just in social studies but throughout the school experience.

English philosopher John Locke noted that teaching and learning can be approached at the simple level of just one variable, as illustrated by the teacher who says, "I teach social studies." What we do can also be approached by addressing several variables, as does the teacher who says, "I teach social studies, but I also teach children to be good citizens and to be critical thinkers." So, when we think of teaching values, skills, and concepts, we can see that good teachers always think in terms of several variables. It is all a part of the art of teaching that separates mediocre teachers from those teachers who aspire to excellence.

Let's consider the three categories of values:

- *Behavioral values* are related to conduct in the classroom and at school. They are what we might consider values of good citizenship. Behavioral values include having respect for others, showing politeness and kindness, taking turns, obeying rules, showing initiative, sharing ideas, and cooperating in group efforts, to name a few. A classroom is a crowded place, and behavioral values are at the heart of the matter of civility.

- *Procedural values* include inquiry, scientific thinking, critical thinking, problem solving, rational thought, perseverance, hard work, organization, and respect for evidence. These are the values we want children to acquire as they study, do their homework, and investigate problems. Procedural values represent the methods of the geographer, historian, and social scientist and are obviously closely connected to the skills mentioned earlier.

- *Substantive values* are those beliefs acquired by individuals as a result of their experiences and feelings about what is true and important. Such values include an individual's ideas of what is enjoyable and not enjoyable, what is right and wrong, and what is worthwhile and wasteful in life. So, if you and I disagree over which season of the year is the best, we can say we have a difference of substantive values. When people express religious differences, it is usually because of their differences in substantive values. One thing you can be sure of is that you will find a wide range of substantive values among students in any class you teach. In a pluralistic society, teachers need to show tolerance and appreciation for differences if they are to expect this from the children they teach.

Values are a part of every lesson and every experience at school, whether we want them to be or not. A teacher's behavior is on constant view by the students. The best way to approach values is at a level of consciousness, in which you determine to teach all three types of values and to organize reflective thinking sessions in which you and your students search for meaning in the social studies experience.

Perhaps you never thought of it this way before, but your values will determine whether you think children should work alone or together in certain situations. Your values will determine how much respect you show to children, especially those whose values seem to be different from your own. Your values will determine whether you can tolerate the messiness of projects and childhood activities. Your values and those of your students will determine to what extent your classroom is a miniature civil society, in which courtesy, politeness, and respect for others are built into the routine. Figure 6.6 is an essay written by a student from that type of classroom, reflecting on what he likes about school.

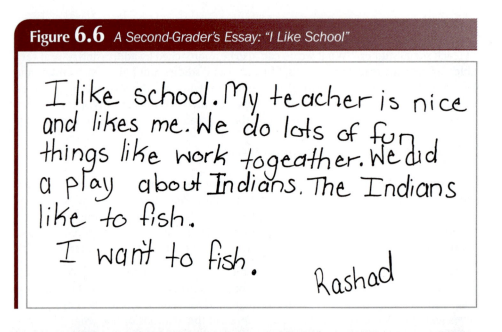

Figure 6.6 *A Second-Grader's Essay: "I Like School"*

> I like school. My teacher is nice and likes me. We do lots of fun things like work togeather. We did a play about Indians. The Indians like to fish.
> I want to fish.
> Rashad

Planning and Developing Units

Unit instruction is a useful approach to most teaching and learning situations because it concentrates your efforts and those of your students on a central theme, organizing idea, or set of concepts. The effect of such a focus is to promote systematic learning toward clearly defined objectives, thus keeping you from falling into the trap of teaching nothing more than activities, worksheets, or pages from a textbook.

What Is a Unit?

A *unit* is a sequential progression of lessons directed toward the development of a theme. Unit themes are developed through articulating content, concepts, skills, and values. The term *unit* implies oneness or wholeness, as opposed to fragmentation. In other words, a unit has integrity; it holds together. Thus, a unit will describe its sense of coherence and oneness.

In social studies, common unit titles might include "Choosing Our Leaders," "Early Explorers," "The Pilgrims," "Minority Rights," "Learning about Latitude and Longitude," and "The Gold Rush." Of course, your textbook and district or state guides provide other sources of information regarding what material (and therefore what unit topics) you are to cover at your given grade level.

How Long Should a Unit Be?

How many days of instruction should be allocated to each unit? There is no predetermined amount of time that must be allocated for any given unit. You, as the instructional expert, need to make that decision on the basis of what needs to be covered in the course of the school year. For instance, if you must cover seven major topical areas in social studies in one school year and a school year is thirty-six weeks long, calculating a simple average will suggest that you should spend about five weeks on each unit. However, that is only an average figure, and various factors are involved.

Much depends on how your units are designed—whether they are based on large themes or smaller, more focused topics. For example, the "Transportation Revolution" could be presented independently as a week-long unit, or it could be taught as part of a broader unit on the United States. A week-long unit on the "Settlers of Massachusetts Bay Colony" could provide a brief overview of the lives of the early colonists in New England; a more comprehensive unit might cover life and times in all 13 original colonies. The same information might also be part of a "Thanksgiving" unit for first grade.

Some teachers prefer to restrict unit length, as narrowing the focus allows more units to be covered in a single year. However, some teachers prefer to keep their unit topics more broadly focused and to develop and teach longer units. A broader focus might support a unit titled "The Movement West," while a narrower focus might support several smaller units, such as "Life on the Prairie," "The Trail of Tears," "Texas, the Lone-Star State," and "Settling the Oregon Country."

Although teaching narrow topics can keep the content focused and manageable, doing so may tend to present learning in small, compartmentalized packages that do not reflect reality. And although broad units can provide a more comprehensive and thus realistic overview, they take seemingly forever to teach and so the focus may well be lost. Developing a *balance* between the two and making connections from one unit to another are among the many challenges facing the instructional expert.

Developing a Unit Plan

In developing a unit, you should always follow these six steps: Set unit goals in context of goals for the year, create an overview, develop objectives, develop a block plan, identify resources, and create an instructional design. Let's explore each of these steps.

SET GOALS IN CONTEXT   The first step in developing a unit is to think of it in terms of your goals for the entire year. You will need to answer such questions as these: Where does this topic logically fit in the flow of my instruction? What skills and knowledge are prerequisite to the skills and knowledge in this unit? And most important, What should children at this level know and be able to do as a result of this year's experience?

CREATE AN OVERVIEW   The second step in the development of a unit is to write the unit overview, which contains a rationale and a brief statement of content. The purpose of a written rationale is to state why you are teaching a particular unit. How is the unit crucial in the process of children's learning in the social studies? This is not terribly difficult to do because people generally agree with the concepts that children must learn to live as social beings in a civilized world and that learning about citizenship, government, history, and geography is necessary to function effectively as a citizen of the world. The statement of content may be written in paragraph form, but more often a table-of-contents format is used. The table of contents tells what topics you intend to teach. (Many teachers map out a plan—a table of contents—for the entire year.)

DEVELOP UNIT OBJECTIVES   Write the objectives for the unit in clear terms; that is, make each objective specify exactly what is expected of the children in performance terms. Thus, while a statement such as "The children need to develop greater capabilities in the area of critical thinking" is fine as part of your rationale, it is probably better stated as a long-term goal than as a unit objective. Here are some examples of clear objectives. Note that each specifies *who* (the child) does *what* (identifies, categorizes, etc.):

- The students are able to identify the symbols used on a map.
- The students can verbally define, recognize, and draw latitude and longitude lines on both a globe and a map.
- The students can locate and identify the four major directions (north, south, east, west) and develop a map key to explain the directional symbols on a map.
- The students can identify examples of cooperative, competitive, and independent learning.
- The students can identify examples of prejudice and bias.
- The students can cite examples of tolerance, justice, and fairness.

When you develop your set of unit objectives, be sure to consider the range of intellectual endeavor, from knowledge and comprehension through such higher levels as application and analysis. Bloom's (1984) *Taxonomy of Educational Objectives* is a useful guide for writing unit objectives. As shown in Figure 6.7, this taxonomy (cognitive domain) is a hierarchical construct that is divided into six increasingly complex levels. Take a few moments to consider each level. Remember that your unit objectives should reflect a representative distribution of each level.

Although you need to develop unit objectives at all six levels, you will write more objectives for knowledge and comprehension than you will for the higher categories. There are two reasons for this: (1) Knowledge and comprehension represent the most basic skills and are therefore fundamental to the learning enterprise and (2) the complexity of tasks at such levels as synthesis and evaluation means that those assignments will usually be of much longer duration.

It is important that you recognize the necessity of developing unit objectives using clear terms and all the levels of Bloom's taxonomy. These objectives will serve to guide your day-to-day instruction, and they will form the basis for writing test items and other means of evaluating students' progress. Thus, there is a natural axis that runs from planning through instruction to assessment:

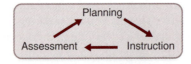

DEVELOP A BLOCK PLAN   The fourth step in developing a unit is to create a block plan. A block plan is a unit calendar, in which the scope and sequence of the unit are laid out

Figure **6.7**   *Bloom's Revised Taxonomy of Educational Objectives*

1. *Remembering.* The issue is recall of information. At this level, it is important that children remember what they have read, were told, or observed. This level is crucial because if children do not possess basic skills in social studies, they are hardly in a position to later carry out meaningful or creative analyses of issues with a social or international scope.

2. *Understanding.* Your objective for children at this level is to ensure that they can explain ideas. It is one thing, for example, to be able to list and identify the requirements necessary to run for president (knowledge) but quite another to be able to explain why these requirements might be important (comprehension).

3. *Applying.* Objectives developed at the application level have as their purpose something practical: actual usage. The issue at this level is whether the child can use such things as skills and concepts in new situations. For example, in spelling, one needs to know how to spell words for a spelling test (knowledge), to define words for a vocabulary test (comprehension), and to use those words appropriately in an explanation or story (application).

4. *Analyzing.* Objectives written at the analysis level are designed to enable children to see relationships, make comparisons and contrasts, and look for patterns. *Analysis,* as the term implies, is an attempt to break down whole entities into their component parts. For example, in a study of communities, you might want the children to identify how various communities (e.g., urban, suburban, rural) function differently to meet the needs of the people living within them or perhaps to identify how daily life might differ among those communities.

5. *Evaluating.* Objectives for the evaluation level include those that encourage children to form their own points of view or to express their ideas on issues. For evaluation to be adequate, this level need not always take the form of the traditionally expected written test. Drawings, stories, and a class panel discussion in which the children explain and support individual opinions can all be considered in evaluation. At the evaluation level, divergent thinking is encouraged and differences of opinion are to be expected.

6. *Creating.* This level requires critical analysis as well as insight, out-of-the-box thinking, and an ability to see things from fresh perspectives. Students are called on to design, construct, plan, produce, and generate new ideas and/or products.

Source: Adapted from B. S. Bloom, *Taxonomy of Educational Objectives* (Boston: Allyn and Bacon, 1984). In the 1990s a team of psychologists led by Lorin Anderson revised Benajmin Bloom's Taxonomy of Educational Objectives in order to make it more adaptable to classroom needs (www.rite.ed.qut.edu.au/oz-teachernet).

on a grid where each square represents one lesson. The filled-in squares show at a glance what will be taught when. Once you have chosen a unit topic that fits logically into your year's sequence of social studies instruction (whatever the level or focus—history, geography, community, or citizenship) and you have developed a set of instructional objectives to guide your teaching, you will be ready to sketch your block plan for the unit. Figure 6.8 illustrates a block plan for a unit on "Consumer Research."

IDENTIFY UNIT RESOURCES   It is quite possible that most of the units you develop and teach will depend heavily on textbooks and your accompanying teacher's guide both for content and direction. When this is the case, the textbook and teacher's guide will

Figure 6.8 *Consumer Research (Economics) Unit: Simple Block Plan*

Monday	Tuesday	Wednesday	Thursday	Friday
Introduction. Discuss quality of products.	Watch film: *Seeing through Commercials.*	Begin testing products.	Do product testing.	Complete graphs, charts.
Present consumer research findings.	Discuss and reflect on product testing.	Write letters to companies.	Prepare advertisements for hypothetical products.	Present advertisements to class.
Analyze videotaped commercials.	Do survey research; skills lesson.	Prepare consumer surveys.	Conduct consumer surveys at primary grades.	Conduct consumer surveys at upper grades.
Analyze survey results. Prepare graphs and displays.	Reflect on pros and cons of consumerism.	Debate topic of advertising on children's television.	Write stories on creative ideas for consumer guidance.	Have test on unit material.

be your primary resources. However, even the teacher who takes a textbook-oriented approach to her or his units should go beyond the given, finding and developing additional source material. A textbook and teacher's guide can give basic direction, but only you, the instructional expert, can design, arrange, and implement the presentation. It is up to *you* to enhance the material and develop a unit that reflects your special style and expertise, as well as the needs of the children in your classroom.

As you consider the development of a unit of instruction (particularly one that goes beyond a series of textbook assignments), you will find it necessary and helpful, as well as challenging, to seek and collect resources that not only help strengthen your own background on the topic but also provide resource material for the children to use throughout the course of study.

CREATE AN INSTRUCTIONAL DESIGN   This section discusses the various elements involved in the development of instruction. It summarizes much of the information just discussed and also provides a guide as you embark on your personal journey of instructional design.

After you have planned your unit, follow these steps:

1. *Time your unit.* Think of your unit in terms of a period of time you must fill from beginning to end. Think of the whole as being made up of segments. Ask yourself: What do I have to cover? Make a list. Then ask yourself: What do the children need to know? Make a list of that, as well.
2. *Design and build a framework of ideas.* Decide how to structure or present those segments. Decide exactly *what* you want to do (the approach you will use in the unit), and then decide *how* you want to do it (the variety of means you will choose to utilize). Remember that the saying "Variety is the spice of life" refers to instructional design, too!

3. *Brainstorm your plan.* Go through an informal planning process, moving energetically from idea, to process, to possibilities, to product. Remember: The creative process is messy! Map out ideas visually, or make lists of them. Dream, think, and imagine. It *will* begin to come together.

4. *Organize your ideas.* The unit needs to be formally organized, so from your outline of ideas or list of themes, activities, and approaches, decide how to do the following:

   - Develop your specific lesson plans
   - Prepare your lecture notes, assignments, and cooperative and individual activities
   - Develop and prepare your handouts
   - Develop and prepare assignments
   - Prepare your classroom to reflect the focus of study in the unit

5. *Calendarize your design.* Organize your unit into a time frame. Decide what you plan to do on a day-to-day basis (including adequate time for children to complete assignments, etc.).

6. *Teach that unit!* First, get the attention of your students by giving them a sneak preview. Next, hit them with the hard stuff: Challenge them, raise their expectations, and explain the need to conquer certain academic material before moving on. Then, proceed through the organized design of instruction. Order and organization are not boring concepts. It's up to *you* to bring your unit to life!

in the classroom   An Archaeology Unit

A unit on archaeology can provide an excellent opportunity to practice a variety of skills and teaching methods. It is also an ideal unit for integrating different areas of the curriculum: history, certainly, but also geography and science; language arts writing and presentation skills; artistic skills (as students create "artifacts" and record "finds" on sketch pads and graph paper); and even skills in mathematics, as children measure their dig areas and take depth measurements on-site. A unit on archaeology also lends itself (as do so many teaching units) to a wide variety of instructional strategies. For example, this unit incorporates cooperative learning, video presentations, creative group storytelling, direct instruction, and a good many hands-on activities outside the regular classroom environment. Critical thinking and decision making are also part of this unit of study, and most of it is conducted by the children while working in dig teams.

Exact instructions on how to teach a unit on archaeology are *not* included here; they are for you, the professional, to assemble and design. However, a good many guidelines are provided to get you started as you explore various ideas, and they might spark you into adding your personal touches to the unit. I encourage you to use the suggestions offered to start your own journey toward filling in the framework. A presentation outline is provided for your reference, but it will be up to you to fill in the blanks and research the content. Reading through the unit materials that follow will present some of the possibilities of what might be done with the children in your unique classroom. For instance, Figure 6.9 shows a sample webbing that you and your students might develop.

Refer to the block plan (Figure 6.10) for ideas and a possible sequence, and remember that the unit can easily be adapted to the age of the children you teach. Obviously, depending on grade level, certain adjustments will have to be made in terms of

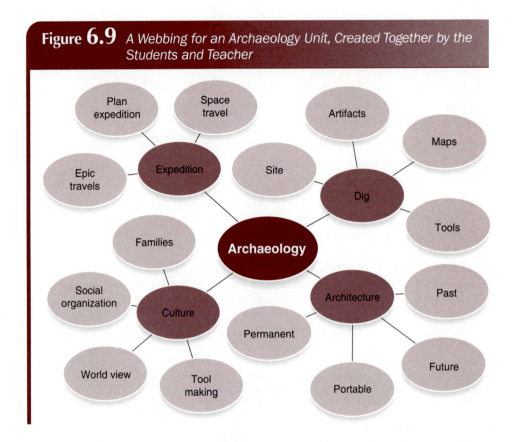

Figure 6.9 *A Webbing for an Archaeology Unit, Created Together by the Students and Teacher*

content, length, and the explanation and execution of the actual "big dig event" (i.e., the excavation). This particular block plan is designed for a 20-day unit, but given your particular circumstances, you may choose to use some of the ideas and teach an abbreviated unit. For example, you might arrange a simulated dig in a sandbox or in a number of sand-filled cartons in your classroom, or you might decide to teach a similar unit but with less comprehensive preparation and fewer after-dig activities.

Be creative in your use of resources. There are many possibilities for obtaining items that can be used in the dig, from your school's art department to the broken items in the storage room of a nearby art or import store. "Artifacts" can come from the most unexpected places. Also keep in mind that vast community resources are available—volunteers

you might ask to assist in preparing the imaginary excavation and to serve as observers at each team's dig area. Research your library and social studies publications for information on archaeological terms and for illustrations of the process of excavating. Again, many resources are available. You simply need to locate them.

With some effort and the application of your instructional design expertise to this model, you and your students can gain much from an archaeological experience—a motivating way to teach units in social studies.*

Presentation Outline Introduction: Mysteries and Antiquities from the Past

I. Historical Records
    A. What *is* history?
    B. What is history based on?

Figure 6.10 Archaeology Unit: Sample Block Plan

Monday	Tuesday	Wednesday	Thursday	Friday
INTRODUCTION: Springboard Tell true stories of discovery Share an artifact Show opening segment *Raiders of the Lost Ark* Start logs	Give hint of upcoming BIG DIG Team Assignment Distribute presentation outline: *HOW do archaeologists actually work?* Reflective thinking Log entries	Garbage can analogy (classroom demonstration and home experiment) Present basic terminology Write letters to museums/universities	VIDEO: *King Tut's Tomb* Discuss Howard Carter Talk about thrill of discovery (use circle discussion)	STORY IN THE ROUND: *The Mystery Dig* (must use archaeology terms learned on Wed; group activity) Introduce idea of field notes
GUEST SPEAKER: Archaeologist from the Children's Museum	TOPIC: Social Scientists (handout, section 2) Class discussion CREATE A POSTER (individual activity): Illustrating and defining one social scientist	SNEAK PREVIEW of big excavation activity Talk about roles and what kinds of things they can expect to be doing CREATE DIG TEAMS Make posters	LIBRARY (cooperative and individual activity): Locate and copy photos, drawings, symbols to assist students in preparing artifacts for dig (art class tomorrow)	ART ROOM (cooperative team activity): Prepare individually designed shards ("artifacts") to be used for the BIG DIG Activity Prepare Hallway Exhibits (use posters made by class)
ARMCHAIR TRAVEL: Teacher slide presentation of her travels to Greece (Mycenae, Delphi, Santorini) Share real stories about archaeologists (Handout, section 3)	PREPARE DIG FOLDERS (cooperative team activity): Select team name; assemble information; illustrate digging methods on graph paper	ORAL REVIEW of terms, social scientists, steps, and dig methods Talk about FIELD and LAB experts Students give briefings	DISTRIBUTE TEAM PACKET for the BIG DIG EVENT: Review all in detail; HOW will it work; time for questions, ideas, clarifications	GROUP DECISION MAKING (cooperative team meetings) Getting Ready for the BIG DIG Event!
THE BIG DIG EVENT (onsite) Videotaping	Groups meet to PREPARE presentations Share ideas from logs	BIG DIG EXCAVATION TEAM PRESENTATIONS	DIG TEAMS CREATE CLASSROOM DISPLAYS for Parent-Friendship Night	REFLECTION: Watch video of dig and discuss experience

143

Young anthropologists experience the process/inquiry approach firsthand as they work on a dig at an actual site.

C. Types of historical records:
   1. Material remains
   2. Written accounts (primary and secondary sources)
II. Social Scientists
   A. Archaeologist
   B. Cartographer
   C. Geographer
   D. Linguist
   E. Political scientist
   F. Sociologist
   G. Economist
   H. Psychologist
   I. Historian
   J. Anthropologist
III. Some Real "Indiana Jones" Experts
   A. The Leakey family (Louis, Mary, and Richard)
   B. Heinrich Schliemann
   C. Your teacher (well, sort of . . .)
IV. Archaeology: Getting to Work
   A. The dig
   B. Plan of work: six steps, from start to finish
   C. Methodology (main ones only; there are others)
      1. Trench
      2. Quadrant
      3. Squares
      4. Numbered squares
V. Experts and Specialists Involved
   A. In the field
      1. Surveyor
      2. Geologist
      3. Photographer
      4. Draftsperson
      5. Preparator

B. In the lab
   1. Geochemist
   2. Paleontologist
   3. Physical anthropologist
   4. Petrologist
   5. Palynologist

The Dig

WHEN: Select a specific day; arrange it with school officials if necessary.

WHERE: Somewhere on the school campus; look for the marked site!

EQUIPMENT: YOUR TEAM PACKET

- Graph paper
- Recording material: paper, pencil, marking pen, clipboard
- Plastic bags that zip close and a shoebox (for the finds)
- Very important: a toothbrush and a spoon. (Each member of the digging team will need both.) These are the only pieces of digging equipment you can use. Archaeologists work slowly and carefully, not wanting to damage potential finds.

OPTIONAL EQUIPMENT: Optional (but potentially helpful in your presentation) is a digital camera to record the stages of discovery and the finished work. (An artist might choose to bring additional equipment to assist in record keeping and documentation.)

CLOTHING: Jeans, sweatshirt, gloves—this is going to be messy!

BASIC TEAM INSTRUCTIONS: You will have to make some decisions together. By the time you locate the excavation site (as soon as possible after fourth period), you should already have decided on the method you will use first and what role each member of the team will play in the actual dig. (We have some time in class before the dig, and you can make your decisions at that time.) Begin digging immediately after you have located your site. All sites will be well marked. Have an alternative method ready, in case the one you select does not work out. An archaeologist would be sure to dig very carefully, as there is always a chance that carelessness will destroy a priceless antiquity. You have no idea what you may find (but believe me—there is something there!), so wield that toothbrush and spoon *very* carefully!

Be sure to keep very careful records of everything you do and everything you find. Remember, you are maintaining a complete record of your dig for next week's presentation.

PROCEDURE: As soon as you come across the edge of something, carefully work your way around it and it will begin to emerge. Your team may have chosen to have members take turns at various tasks, or you may have divided the work evenly so that you each play the same role throughout the dig. However you chose to organize yourselves to accomplish your goal, make sure that all of the following tasks are covered:

- Some members will be engaged in the actual process of digging.
- Someone might use a camera to record stages of discovery.
- Keep track on graph paper of exactly where on the site finds have been located, and illustrate for each the exact method of digging used (trench, quadrant—check your class notes for the different types of methods).
- Be sure to record (draw) each piece as it emerges.
- Maintain a journal of the activity onsite.

When You Have Recovered the Artifact or Antiquity

- Identify and describe. Prepare written copies and graphs—all records of your process.
- Reconstruct and preserve. As archaeologists, your job is to reconstruct and preserve the item(s). Hang on to your sketches and the items themselves. (Put broken bits back together, if possible.)

NOW THAT THE DIG IS OVER, THIS IS YOUR JOB: Let's hope you have kept careful records of everything you accomplished and what you found as it happened. You have been maintaining a complete record of the dig to use in next week's presentation to the museum curator (that's me!)—the sponsor of the dig. As part of the presentation, your team will be sharing the methods and procedures your team chose to use; you will be telling the story of your dig and showing the physical results. (Remember, notes and quick sketches made onsite can be tidied up before the presentation.) During the next few days (and any time you and your team members arrange to meet together), work on your curator (teacher!) presentation, which is due next week. Other noted archaeologists (your classmates) will observe. We're excited to see what you have to share! As part of your presentation, your team will do these two things:

- Share the methods and procedures your team chose to follow.
- Tell the story of your dig and show the results. (Remember, sketchy notes and drawings made on-site can be tidied up before the presentations.)

The Content of Your Presentation

- Decide who will report what.
- As a team, explain the find and the process you followed. Remember, the final job of an archaeologist is to report findings.

- Organize your information so that it will tell the story of your experiences. (Remember the Howard Carter and King Tut video we saw). Unfold the facts gradually. Tell about the methods you used and why you chose them. Take the rest of the class through each step as you share graphs and/or posters with us.
- Show us the reconstructed item (glue is fine). Describe it carefully; tell us what you know.
- Do some research: Can you date the item? Where did it probably come from? What was it used for? Get us excited!

You can mount your sketches and photos on posterboard so we can see everything as you present. Or perhaps you have a better, more creative idea for presenting. (Video? Computers?) Remember to keep *quality* in mind. Don't be sloppy in your presentation, or the curator may not hire you next time!

Finally, hand in an official half-page summary on the Curator Conclusion Form. The whole team should have contributed to this, and the names of all team members should appear on the sheet. What are your conclusions?

(Hey, even Indiana Jones had to start this way!)

*My thanks to Shirley Riley for her contributions to this archaeology unit.

Summary

"Teachable moments"—those serendipitous events that sometimes allow you to support your students' learning in totally unexpected ways—are delightful and rewarding. But the vast majority of what your students learn in your classroom will be the result of what you bring to them. And the more carefully you plan, the deeper and more wide ranging their learning will be. Careful planning of units and lessons will ensure that your instruction meets the goals you set for it—that students understand the content and concepts you envision, that they master the skills you intend, and that they develop the values you incorporate.

Your textbooks and other programs can furnish you with existing lesson and unit plans. It would be exhausting (and counterproductive) for you to attempt to develop all your own lessons and units. In some instances, however—for example, in developing local topics—you will need to make your own lesson plans. But whether you are using plans created by others or developing your own, you should always perceive an underlying rationale designed to expand students' knowledge (content), ideas (concepts), investigative skills (processes), and attitudes and beliefs (values).

Explorations

Reflect On . . .

1. It has been suggested that teachers often teach facts and information, rather than concepts and ideas, in social studies. Why do you think this might be the case? What can you suggest to improve the conceptual aspect of lesson planning?

2. Some teachers might argue that planning takes away from the more creative aspects of teaching—that it inhibits spontaneity in learning. What are the arguments for and against planning social studies lessons? What is your position on planning?

In the Field

3. Examine the teacher's edition of an elementary social studies textbook, and try to find at least five suggested activities that you think would lend an added dimension to social studies lesson plans. Share those ideas in a small-group discussion of effective planning.

For Your Portfolio

4. Develop a one- or two-page lesson plan on the topic of "the importance of reading biographies of key people in American history." Include a few excerpts from actual biographies as part of the material for your lesson plan. Share your plan with several others who have attempted this same activity. What did you learn from them? What did they learn from you?

Continuing the Journey: Suggested Readings

Dell'Olio, J., & T. Donk (2008). *Models of Teaching: Connecting Student Learning with Standards.* Thousand Oaks, CA: Sage.

In a time of standards-based instruction, this book is a valuable guide to how to do it.

Ellis, A. (2010). *Teaching, Learning, & Assessment Together: The Reflective Classroom* (2nd ed.). Larchmont, NY: Eye on Education, Inc.

This book explains 20 practical ways to incorporate reflective thinking into lessons.

McKernan, J. (2008). *Curriculum and Imagination.* New York: Routledge.

Miller, D. (2008). *Teaching with Intention K-5.* (2008). Portland, ME: Stenhouse Publishers. Retrieved from *www.stenhouse.com*

Morris, R. (2007). "Around the Blacksmith's Forge: Interdisciplinary Teaching and Learning." *Social Studies, 98*(3), 99–104.

Delightful article that takes an imaginative look at interdisciplinary teaching of social studies and science.

Planning for Instruction K-12. Retrieved June 26, 2009, from *http://slate.it.uk.edu/~bobannon/index.html*

Online module designed to help teaching develop both units and lesson plans.

10 Steps to Developing a Quality Lesson Plan (2008). Retrieved from *www.lessonsplanspage.com*

A practical template that lays out the major aspects of good lessons.

Websites

Lesson plans and other resources organized by discipline and searchable by key words. *http://teachers.net/lessons/*

This website offers resources spanning all dimensions of the curriculum planning process organized by grade, subject, and themes, *http://www.teachervision.fen.com/*

Lesson plans and more *http://www.education-world.com*

Related NCSS Standards and Principles of Powerful Social Studies

Teaching and Learning Principles

Social studies teaching and learning are powerful when they are meaningful. Meaningfulness is stimulated when:

- Students learn connected networks of knowledge, skills, beliefs, and attitudes that they will find useful both in and outside of school.
- Instruction emphasizes depth of development of important ideas within appropriate breadth of topic coverage and focuses on teaching these important ideas for understanding, appreciation, and life application.

- The significance and meaningfulness of the content is emphasized both in how it is presented to students and how it is developed through activities.
- Classroom interaction focuses on sustained examination of a few important topics rather than superficial coverage of many.
- Meaningful learning activities and assessment strategies focus students' attention on the most important ideas embedded in what they are learning.

Powerful and Authentic Social Studies retrieved from World Wide Web November 23, 2009 *www.socialstudies.org/pass*

SAMPLE LESSON 6.1   What Season Is It?

AGE LEVEL: Primary

NCSS STANDARDS: People, places, and Environments

KEY IDEA: Each season of the year has its own unique characteristics.

INSTRUCTIONAL OBJECTIVE: Students will explore the local environments to observe, record, and gather evidence to show what season it is.

SET: Begin by showing the students a calendar (preferably one with pictures that illustrate the seasons). Ask the following questions to stimulate class discussion:

1. What is a calendar for?
2. Why do we need to keep track of time?
3. How is a calendar like a clock? How is a calendar different from a clock?
4. Calendars keep track of days, weeks, months, and years. Each year is divided into four seasons. Can anyone tell me the names of the four seasons?

INSTRUCTION: Write the names of the four seasons on the board. Ask the students to list various characteristics of each season (e.g., winter might have rain or snow). Write their responses on the board until there is a good list under each season—for example:

Winter	*Spring*	*Fall*	*Summer*
rain	flowers	leaves	blue sky
snow	baseball	football	sunshine
skiing	green grass		vacation

Next, tell the students, "We are going to pretend that we don't know what season it is. We are going to go outside together to see if you can find *evidence* (define) to prove what season it is." Take the class outside, and see how many examples the children can find to show what season it is (e.g., leaves, weeds, kids on the playground playing football). Bring any tangible examples back to the classroom for display.

REFLECTION/ASSESSMENT: Ask the class, "If someone asked us what season it is, how could we prove our answer (with evidence)?"

CLOSURE: Have students complete these statements: "The evidence we found outside shows that it is _____ (name season). When you go home today, I'd like to have you tell someone at home how you proved it was _____ (season). Also, I'd like to have you bring any new evidence that you can to prove that it is _____."

SAMPLE LESSON 6.2 Aleut Maps*

AGE LEVEL: Intermediate

NCSS STANDARD: Teach students to estimate and calculate distance, scale, area, and density, and to distinguish spatial patterns.

KEY IDEA: Distances can be measured in units of space or time. Each culture has invented units of space and time to keep track of those dimensions.

INSTRUCTIONAL OBJECTIVE: Students will construct and use Aleut maps to measure distances on the playground.

SET: Begin by asking students to estimate the following distances or other distances they can think of:

1. The length of a football field
2. The distance from their home to school
3. The height of the classroom door

Next, ask the following questions:

1. How long does it take you to get to school? Can the trip to school be measured using either distance or time?
2. How does using a map help you get from one place to another?
3. How is a map like a plan? A record? A story? A picture?

INSTRUCTION: Tell the students that in times past, when an Aleut hunter or fisherman would leave the village by kayak, he would paddle close to the shore as he voyaged from bay to bay, sometimes going great distances. Because the route was uncharted and bays have a way of looking alike, the Aleuts had to have a method of keeping track of how far they were from their home village. They came up with a simple but ingenious way of doing this: They would take a stick with them, carving a notch in the stick each time they entered a new bay. So, five notches meant five bays away from home.

Tell the children that they are going to make Aleut maps. Give each group of two students a stick (e.g., tongue depresser, Popsicle stick) and a pencil. Take the class out to the playground, and have each pair of students make their way around the edge of the playground, making a mark on their stick for each notable tree, fence post, or whatever they pass.

REFLECTION/ASSESSMENT: Ask the students how such a system of keeping track of distances is similar to or different from the measures they are used to. Give each pair of students time to process this, asking them to make notes. Then discuss insights with the full class.

CLOSURE: Assign students the homework task of making an Aleut map that measures distances at home or in their neighborhoods.

*Aleuts (pronounced "Al-ee-utes") are native people of the Aleutian Islands and the western part of the Alaska peninsula. The traditional Aleut culture is a hunting and fishing culture. They are a resourceful people who are skilled kayak builders and sailors. Their culture is ancient and has been traced back to at least 2000 B.C.

Chapter 7

Successful Strategies for Social Studies Teaching and Learning

Keys to This Chapter

- Five Principles of Effective Teaching and Learning
- What Research Says about Social Studies Teaching and Learning
- Direct Instructional Strategies
- Indirect Instructional Strategies
- Observations on Indirect Instruction

To make social studies interesting, make it social.
—Allysia, sixth-grade student

Social studies instruction demands alternatives, not only in terms of the content learned by students but also—and equally important—in terms of *how* students go about learning. Some evidence exists that social studies is one of the least-liked subjects in the curriculum (Goodlad, 1984, 2008). We simply can't have that! It is especially important that students be motivated by a variety of experiences in social studies and that those experiences be designed to reach students whose interests and needs vary—not only from student to student but from day to day, as well.

The alternatives presented here are not meant to be an exhaustive list of the possibilities inherent in teaching social studies. Rather, they are designed to serve as models. In the pages that follow, each learning alternative is explained and accompanied by examples. Some examples are oriented to primary school-age students; others are oriented to intermediate school-age students.

*T*he *Handbook of Research in Social Studies Education* (2008) informs us that in many ways, social studies teaching has not changed much over the past 50–100 years. It tends to be textbook driven and often not connected to activities. In addition, there is a certain amount of evidence to indicate that social studies has been given less class time since the inception of the No Child Left Behind Act, which seems more focused on reading and mathematics than on subjects like social studies. This thought is seconded by Vogler, et. al. (2007) who state that social studies is often consigned to the "back burner" since so much attention is given to literacy and numeracy. Nevertheless, there is room for optimism because social studies has such great potential for integration with other subjects, especially where project learning is involved, and because social studies in the hands of a good teacher does in fact lend itself quite naturally to active learning.

This chapter is about a variety of ways to teach and learn social studies. Some of the strategies are more teacher directed, or what is known as *direct instruction*, and others are more student initiated, or what is known as *indirect instruction*. Both approaches are needed. They work in concert. The key is to find the proper balance between the two.

However, before we dive into the strategies themselves, I want to share with you several *principles* of good teaching and learning. This will give you a foundation and a set of reasons for doing what you do with kids. The principles of good social studies teaching are (1) active engagement, (2) collaboration, (3) scaffolding, (4) classroom climate, and (5) less is more. Let's examine each in turn.

Five Principles of Effective Teaching and Learning

Active Engagement

Human beings are creatures of motion. We are more alert physically and mentally when we are moving. Young people learn best when they talk, listen, play, work, draw, paint, sing, dance, build, inquire, and discover. These are activities. A curriculum of activity will serve you well. When children are required to stay seated, hunched over a desk for long periods of time, boredom and mental fatigue set in. Sometimes I wonder why children understand child development more clearly than adults.

Collaboration

Collaboration takes many forms: team work, cooperative learning, group projects, and committees, to name a few. Social/moral growth depends on our ability to engage with others, to make shared decisions, to do something we could never do alone, to be part of something bigger than ourselves. Team building in social studies provides opportunities for the give and take of democratic life in the classroom. This is how we create citizens one day at a time.

Scaffolding

The psychologist Jerome Bruner (1996) introduced the word *scaffolding* to educational theory. Scaffolding is a metaphor taken from the construction industry. You have seen scaffolding used when tall buildings are erected. Scaffolding gives support to something new, whether it is a skyscraper or new ideas we wish to teach students. In a nutshell, scaffolding means building on what students already know in order to help them deepen their understanding. When scaffolding is properly employed over time and with patience, students reach levels of understanding and ability that are literally amazing.

Classroom Climate

It has been said that all learning is emotional. In the first century A.D., the Roman teacher Quintillian reached the conclusion that students learn best when they want to learn. He called this phenomenon the *doctrine of interest.* When interest in learning is combined with kindness, fairness, nurturing, and positive discipline, students will respond in a positive way. The psychological principle known as *flow* is a state in which persons or groups become so involved in an activity that they lose track of time, don't want to stop, and have a good feeling about what they are doing. Teaching is such a privilege and a joy when this happens.

Less Is More

This familiar phrase was first used in a poem by the nineteenth century English poet Robert Browning. He meant it in connection with love, but the principle also applies more broadly. It has come to mean learning in depth a few profound ideas, skills, and values as opposed to "covering" many topics. Sometimes teachers stay away from inquiry and discovery because, they reason, they could cover so much in the time it takes kids to "discover" something the world already knows about. Make your classroom a place of depth over superficiality.

With these five principles in mind, let's move on to a number of teaching and learning strategies that will create an aura of excitement and energy as you make social studies everybody's favorite subject!

What Research Says about Social Studies Teaching and Learning

A number of studies have been conducted over the years in which students have been given an opportunity to voice their opinions about social studies. Schug and colleagues (1984) explored the question of how students thought social studies teaching and learning might be improved. The following list shows the preferences that students expressed about social studies learning:

1. Group projects
2. Field trips
3. Less reading
4. Role-play and simulations
5. Class activities
6. Independent work
7. Class discussion
8. Student planning
9. Less lecture
10. Challenging learning experiences
11. Clear examples

Schug's useful study provided insights to the childhood perspective on social studies. However, it was conducted many years ago, and much has happened since then. What do children think *today*?

To answer this question, I conducted a survey, asking children to list ways in which they think social studies could be improved. With a few notable exceptions, the outcomes are remarkably similar to those Schug found. Admittedly, my survey did not involve a random sample, so the results are difficult to generalize. However, I do think they are representative in many ways. Here are the findings:

- Group projects
- Field trips
- Drama and role-play
- Games
- Computer activities
- Construction and hands-on activities
- Animals
- Environment
- Student interest
- Drawing and maps
- Less reading (especially textbooks)

Clearly, the lists are more alike than different. Still, in the more recent list, we see the importance of the computer and its influence on childhood learning and the idea emerging that animals should be studied. Interest in the computer is easy to explain, given the incredible advances in technology in the past twenty-odd years. But the idea of studying animals makes little sense at first glance, since social studies is the study of human beings. Maybe the children know something intuitively that many adults have not considered. When the great psychologist Jerome Bruner put together an experimental social studies program for children many years ago, he was very clear about the idea that in order to understand human behavior, it is necessary to contrast and compare it with the behavior of various animal groups. The second list also shows concern for the environment, a hopeful sign that today's young people take environmental studies seriously.

In yet another study, Fouts (1989) used a questionnaire/survey of students to determine their perceptions of what creates a positive attitude toward social studies. As shown in Figure 7.1, he characterized the findings under positive and negative attitudes.

If you check out the results of these various studies, the obvious and very compelling message from students is that they wish to be actively involved. They also want to work with others, and they would appreciate a certain amount of variety. Now it is up to us to channel these interests in meaningful ways. The evidence is clear that *how* we teach does make a difference. Every now and then, research and common sense come together.

Research in effective teaching supports the use of a variety of teaching strategies. It is useful to vary your strategies in teaching social studies for two reasons. First, students respond differently to various ways of teaching. One student learns effectively

Figure 7.1 *Results of Survey on Attitudes toward Social Studies Instruction*

More Positive Attitudes

- Variety of teaching strategies are used; classroom routines often vary.
- Teacher is involved with students; knows students personally; is perceived as having caring attitude.
- Classroom rules and expectations are fair, clear, and equitable; consistent enforcement of expectations by teacher.
- Students are actively involved in diverse learning activities; structure of class and assignments requires active student participation.
- Positive and frequent student–student interaction; high student support and cooperation.
- Teacher is continually striving to show relevance of subject matter and content; creates interest in subjects by using various strategies.

More Negative Attitudes

- Heavy reliance on a few teaching strategies; classroom routine seldom varies.
- Teacher perceived as aloof and noninvolved with students; perceived as noncaring by students.
- Classroom rules and expectations are arbitrary and unclear; poor communication and possible favoritism by teacher.
- Students play passive learning roles; are simply recipients of information and content.
- Very limited student–student interaction; students usually work in competitive environment.
- Teacher relies on innate importance of subject matter; makes little attempt to show relevance or develop interest.

Source: Based on J. Fouts, "Classroom Environments and Student Views of Social Studies: A Replication Study," *Theory and Research in Social Education* (Spring 1989): 136–147.

through silent reading, but another does not. One student benefits from direct instruction and clear explanations; another benefits from hands-on, self-directed activity. Of course, learners should not be typecast and exposed to only single strategies. You indicate a degree of sensitivity to individual needs when you provide for a wide range of learning styles.

The second reason to use varied approaches is simply for the sake of variety itself. Just as people prefer to vary their diets and other routines, students (and you!) benefit from variety in instruction. A class will be more interesting and appealing when students can look forward to discussions, hands-on projects, games, demonstrations, role-plays, and other strategies. Following a monotonous, predictable routine reduces both motivation and retention of ideas.

Direct Instruction Strategies

Direct instruction, or *expository learning*, is defined as the transmission of knowledge from a source to a receiver. The source of knowledge can vary widely to include teachers, textbooks, films, lectures, records, tapes, trade books, and encyclopedias. The receiver, of course, is the student. Although direct instruction is generally associated in social studies with the transmission of *content* information about events, eras, regions, families, tribal groups, cities, governments, and so forth, it can also be used to impart skills or offer explanations, such as how to read a map or how to write an information-seeking letter.

Those who believe in inquiry and student-involvement approaches to social studies learning are often mistakenly labeled as opponents of expository learning. But in fact, effective teachers always use both direct and indirect instructional approaches in an effort to meet the needs of all the students in their classes. Viewed as one of several viable alternatives, direct instruction can be an effective and stimulating way to learn. Perhaps its greatest strength (as well as its greatest potential weakness, if overdone) is its efficiency. Because direct instruction provides students with information, they are spared the inconvenience of having to discover everything themselves. In reality, none of us would be very far along in our academic development if we were forced to discover on our own everything we needed to learn.

We'll examine three direct instruction strategies: lecture or teacher presentation, class discussion, and demonstration. In each instance, the teacher is directly in charge of the instructional process and the students are challenged to acquire information.

Teacher Presentation

The idea of lecturing or presenting directly to young children may at first seem preposterous, particularly in light of what we have learned from the constructivist movement. Of course, long, didactic presentations are inappropriate. The idea of a well-constructed teacher presentation, however, used in concert with other more involving strategies, can make a lot of sense.

For example, primary students who were investigating the safety of a crosswalk near their school and who had been involved in a number of experiential activities were perfectly willing to listen as the teacher told them how professional traffic personnel do similar investigations. Intermediate students who were producing a product to sell needed to hear their teacher tell them about supply and demand, inventory, advertising, profit and loss, and other economic concepts. These presentations were given in meaningful contexts to students who were able to apply the information. Students who were to prepare a Mexican meal in the context of their study of that country were quite eager to hear their teacher present a talk on Mexican geography, agriculture, and customs. The students' felt need to learn makes all the difference in the world.

Presentations should be reasonably brief, well thought out on your part, and focused on key ideas or concepts. It is important to use numerous examples of the concepts you stress and to make as many real-world applications as you can. Stories also make presentations more appealing to children and adults alike. You should encourage active listening by having students take notes if they can. It also helps students to have listening partners, with whom they can discuss information as you pause from time to time in your presentation. The Keys to Effective Teacher Presentations provide concrete suggestions for making your presentations successful. Study them carefully, and try to use them when you plan presentation lessons.

Class Discussion

Class discussion may not seem like a direct teaching strategy, but keep in mind that the teacher is responsible for structuring the flow of the interaction and for directing the

Keys to Effective Teacher Presentations

- *Remember who your audience is.* These are children of elementary school age. Their attention span is short. Try to make your presentations appealing and contextual.
- *Prepare an outline.* Have just a few key points. Keep in mind the idea that "less is more."
- *Use examples.* Illustrations help people understand and remember. Use multiple examples to make a key point.
- *Speak clearly.* Pronounce your words clearly, speak at a moderate to slow speed, and be sure that you can be heard in the back of the room.
- *Provide an introduction.* Begin with a brief preview of what you plan to say. Build a frame of reference—especially try to relate the topic to previous learning.
- *Emphasize concepts and generalizations.* These are what you really want to teach and what you really want your students to remember. Show how the concepts relate to one another as you proceed.

- *Pause.* Give your students time to think, to write, or to discuss with a partner.
- *Be enthusiastic.* Communicate with your attitude that you think this material is well worth learning.
- *Use props.* Models, transparencies, pictures, diagrams, and so on will bring your presentations to life. These visuals provide variety and support different learning styles.
- *Provide change.* Move around the room. Ask for questions or comments. Pose a question or two. Have students draw illustrations of what they have learned to this point.
- *Summarize.* Remember the adage "tell them what you are going to tell them, tell them, and then tell them what you have told them." It really works.
- *Assess.* Give the students an opportunity to discuss with a partner what they have learned. Have them draw or write about the topic. With older children, you may even want to give a brief quiz.

students' involvement and participation. The secret to effective class discussion is organization. A well-organized discussion has four basic components: a base of information, a central focus, effective questions, and a supportive classroom environment.

1. *Information base.* Information is essential to a purposeful exchange of ideas and points of view. Be sure to get that point across to your students. Even good questions will not rescue a discussion that's floundering because you didn't give students sufficient information on which to build answers.
2. *Central focus.* Provide a central focus of discussion. In a whole-class discussion, you should ensure that the questions keep coming back to the key issues. You can facilitate this by writing out your questions in advance and gently reminding students that extraneous information, while often interesting, is not useful in the process of examining ideas in depth.
3. *Effective questions.* As you develop questions for discussion, use Bloom's (1984) taxonomy to ensure that your questions include knowledge and understanding of the issue and allow for applications to the real world. You also need to include higher-level questions that ask students to analyze, synthesize, and evaluate. The level of the questions you ask sets the tone for the level of thinking by the students. The pacing

Whole-class discussion is an example of direct instruction.

of your questions is also important. Casual observation in elementary classrooms leads to the obvious conclusion that teachers are trying to teach students to be impulsive in providing answers. Seldom does one encounter a classroom discussion in which the wait-time between a teacher's questions and the students' answers exceeds a few seconds.

4. *A supportive environment.* You probably know from your own experience that it is risky to speak up in front of a group. Children need to know that you are there to support them, to challenge them in a nurturing way. The more they realize that trust and support are foundational elements of your classroom, the more they will be willing to express themselves and to respect the ideas of others.

Demonstration

A demonstration lesson represents a direct teaching strategy in which the teacher models the behaviors of presentation, analysis, and synthesis. The student's role is that of observer and recorder of information and/or skills. Demonstrations, often wrongly called "experiments," are in fact carefully rehearsed situations in which the teacher knows the outcome. Demonstrations are most effective when followed by corresponding student activities. Thus, a teacher demonstrating a measuring technique for determining distance on a map would expect the class to use the same technique in a follow-up activity. Or if the class were going to conduct an experiment in product testing, the teacher might demonstrate the appropriate techniques for testing a given product.

Application is the key to a demonstration's worth. If something is worth demonstrating to the students, it is also worth the teacher's time to engage them in a direct application of the skill or activity. Demonstration is an efficient strategy because it allows the teacher to illustrate procedures and to communicate information at the same time.

The danger of the demonstration strategy lies in the passive role of the students, who may or may not understand the concept or skill the teacher is demonstrating. The solution is to accompany the demonstration with an application by the class. Ideally, the students will perform exactly the same activity the teacher has demonstrated in much the same way she or he demonstrated it. In some cases, however, that is not possible. For example, you might demonstrate the working of a volcano, and the student follow-up might consist of completing a diagram or drawing of a volcano. Or you might demonstrate the flow of wealth in the U.S. economic system using a chart, and the follow-up might consist of students keeping records of the money they spend. The Keys to Effective Direct Instruction will help you understand the strengths of this approach.

What are some of the other strategies that you ought to consider in addition to direct instruction? Let's explore them right now.

Keys to Effective Direct Instruction

- Direct instruction usually involves whole-class instruction. Basically, the teacher is the presenter or explainer, and the students are the receivers of information.
- Direct instruction need not be passive learning. It is best to have students involved through questions, note taking, drawing, constructing, and so on, either as an accompaniment or follow-up to a teacher presentation.
- You don't have to do all the talking. Even though a high teacher profile is basic to direct instruction, remember that a textbook, film, filmstrip, video, Website, or guest speaker can also deliver information.
- Timing and pacing are crucial to the success of direct instruction. Children will learn more from you when you lecture or present to them for just a brief time period than when you take a long time to tell them the same thing. If you have too much information, break it up into two presentations.
- Direct instruction works best in social studies when you use other teaching/learning strategies, as well. Too much of anything is not good.

Indirect Instruction Strategies

Indirect instruction is an approach that reorganizes classroom activities in such a way that students take responsibility for much of their own learning. Indirect instruction, which generally draws on the constructivist principles of learning, has been called "democratic learning" because it emphasizes such experiences as student leadership and initiative, group interdependence, shared decision making, and reflective thinking. In the classic *Democracy and Education*, educational philosopher John Dewey (1916) presented his vision of a classroom as a miniature democracy where children participate actively and purposefully. His vision seems even more crucial today.

The teacher's role in indirect instruction is that of facilitator of learning. The teacher often works behind the scenes to prepare the intellectual, social, and moral environment.

One goal is the development of a classroom environment where children feel free to express themselves, to explore actively, and to work together. The teacher ensures that the needed materials and strategies are in place and expects the individual student or the class, depending on the nature of the activity, to assume ownership and responsibility for learning. The teacher questions, suggests, and mediates. A teacher who is accustomed to being the center of attention, direction giver, or autocratic leader often finds this role very difficult.

The student's role is that of active learner. Students are expected to inquire, discover, discuss, plan, act on, and evaluate ideas. The ratio of student-to-student interaction is much higher in classes where indirect instruction takes place. Students seldom sit in straight rows for their work, simply because this configuration is not conducive to working together. Thus, students find themselves playing the role of people who are responsible—morally, intellectually, and socially—for their own learning and that of their fellow students. Figure 7.2 shows certain contrasts between direct and indirect instruction.

Indirect instruction typically means that the student takes on a more active, participatory role while the teacher shifts from the role of director or leader to that of facilitator. Although it may appear that the teacher is doing little except monitoring student involvement during any given activity, the fact is that effective indirect teaching can involve a good deal of behind-the-scenes preparation preceding the lesson itself. In fact, the better the planning, the more the teacher sometimes seems to fade from view. I have visited exploratory classrooms where you have trouble even locating the teacher when you first enter—and then you spot him or her kneeling beside a cluster of desks, helping children with some project.

As noted earlier, indirect teaching and learning generally reflect a constructivist approach. *Constructivism* is based on the theory that we all construct our own knowledge; no one else can do that for us. Constructivist learning is active, engaged, generally hands on, and reflective. See Figure 7.3 for a list of the attributes of constructivist teaching and learning.

The following sections explore 10 different indirect teaching and learning strategies, each of which exemplifies attributes of constructivism. Each strategy places the teacher in the role of facilitator of learning and the student in the role of investigator,

---

Figure 7.2 *Contrasts between Direct and Indirect Instruction*

Direct Instruction	Indirect Instruction
• Students play passive role	• Students play active role
• Teacher serves as director	• Teacher serves as facilitator
• Students receive knowledge	• Students generalize knowledge
• Answers to questions are predetermined	• Answers to questions are discovered by students
• Promotes convergent thinking	• Promotes divergent thinking
• Learning consists chiefly of recall and explanation	• Learning consists chiefly of analysis, synthesis, and judgment

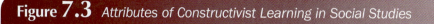

Figure 7.3 *Attributes of Constructivist Learning in Social Studies*

- Emphasis on creativity and hands-on construction
- Emphasis on multiple ways to represent learning
- Real-world connections in meaningful contexts
- Collaboration and team building
- Emphasis on project learning

- Learner inclusion in determining activities
- Emphasis on freedom and opportunity over coercion and restraint
- Emphasis on performance outcomes of work
- Thoughtful reflection on experiences

inquirer, discoverer, constructor, and so on. The process of learning is emphasized as much as the product, and students are invariably actively engaged.

Role-Play

Role-play is an exceptionally versatile strategy used in drama, simulation, play, games, and, of course, counseling. Essentially, role-play is a projective technique in which the role-player either "becomes" someone else or pretends to be performing a task that is different from what she or he usually does. An example of the former could be a student role-playing Martin Luther King Jr. or Harriet Tubman. An example of the latter could be a student pretending to be a nurse, fire fighter, or store clerk.

Role-play comes naturally to children, who do it without ever having heard the term. They use role-play intuitively as a means of learning. It is part of their exploratory nature. A young child becomes a truck driver in a sandbox. Several children play house on a Saturday afternoon. Children pretend to be famous movie stars or popular entertainers. They become traders and bankers in games they play. However, with the exception of the few who go on to try out for the high school play, role-play is often left behind with early childhood. This is unfortunate, because role-play is a viable way to teach and to learn. It helps a child get beneath the surface of learning and begin to explore moods, feelings, and values.

I once had a grant with Harlan Hansen, a nationally known specialist in early childhood education, that enabled us to develop a curriculum for children in kindergarten through second grade. We used an interest-centers approach to learning, and one of the centers that Harlan installed in a first-grade classroom was a shoe shop. It wasn't much on the surface—just a countertop in a corner of the room with a sign saying "Shoe Shop" and a bunch of donated, mostly worn-out shoes. But what was special about that shop was the role-playing the girls and boys did there. The children took turns being the clerk or the customer. Here is a typical exchange at the Shoe Shop:

Clerk: Hello, may I help you?
Customer: Yes, I'd like to buy a pair of shoes.
Clerk: Oh, what kind of shoes would you like?

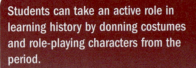

Students can take an active role in learning history by donning costumes and role-playing characters from the period.

Customer:	Well, I would like some brown shoes.
Clerk:	Brown shoes? Yes, we have some. Here, would you like to try these on?
Customer:	Okay. *(Child puts on the shoes with assistance from the clerk.)*
Clerk:	How do they feel?
Customer:	They're fine. I'll take them.
Clerk:	Okay. That will be $10.
Customer:	Here is your money.
Clerk:	Thank you.
Customer:	Good-bye.
Clerk:	Good-bye.

The civility of this exchange seems remarkable for first-graders, yet it is typical of the role-play children are capable of when they are given the chance. Don't underestimate the power of role-play or consign it to the dustbin of "child's play." Language development and gaining a sense of others' perspectives are two of the consistent outcomes of role-play. This strategy can be meaningfully integrated into your social studies program, as the example in the next paragraph illustrates.

The poster reproduced in Figure 7.4 advertises farmland for sale in Illinois in the 1860s and suggests a role-play activity related to the study of the westward movement. In the activity, students are assigned the roles of various family members who live on a

Figure 7.4 *Poster Advertising Illinois Farmland in the 1860s*

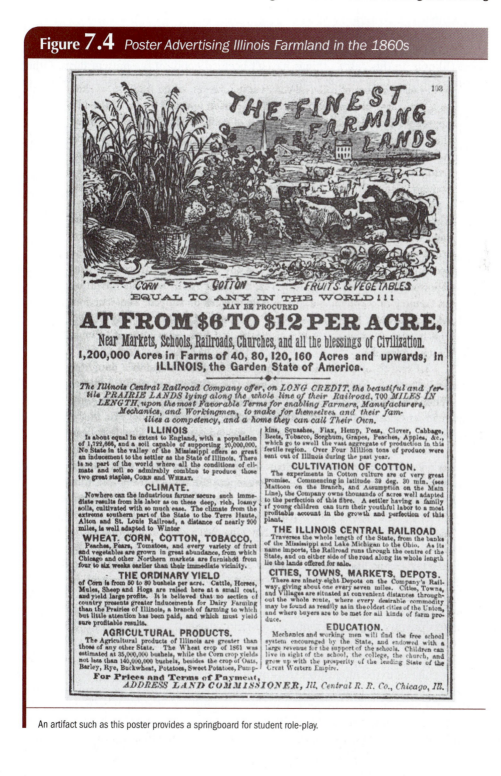

An artifact such as this poster provides a springboard for student role-play.

farm in the eastern United States during the days of the westward expansion of the country. The father in the family is excited about the opportunities for a new chance out West (Illinois, in this case)—things haven't been so good on the present farm. Other members of the family react to the proposed move in several different ways. The mother isn't sure; she would have to give up a great deal. A sickly daughter fears the move. An older son thinks it would be a great opportunity.

I have used this role-play activity a number of times. The dynamics are fascinating. What emerges are the feelings, hopes, and fears that the pioneers must have known. In other words, the activity humanizes history because the role-players (and audience, if there is one) begin to think about actual lives and how people were affected by such changes. Of course, the role-play works best when knowledge of the westward movement is applied. Role-play furnishes the social studies teacher with a perfect intersection of cognition and affect.

One last thought about role-play: You should model it to your class occasionally. Try teaching your students about Sacagawea, George Washington, astronaut Sally Ride, or simply an early American by dressing up like the person and talking to your students as though that is who you are. You will have to do a little background reading about your character, of course, but I think you'll be pleased with the effect your little performance will have on your class. It's fun, and social studies ought to be fun. Don't you agree?

Interest Centers

The interest-centers approach to teaching and learning social studies is primarily a child-centered, exploratory way to get children involved in self-directed, autonomous behavior. Interest centers do not depend on such well-known phrases as "All right, class, take out your books and turn to page 59." Rather, students do different activities of their own choosing.

The key to successful interest centers is to make them meaningful, appealing, and self-sustaining. In order for centers to be meaningful, they should reflect the purposes of your social studies program. Ask yourself: What am I trying to teach my students that they could learn essentially on their own at a center? To make your centers appealing, try to put yourself in a child's position. Games, maps, puzzles, activities, computers, videos, and so on are highly attractive to a child, especially when organized in an attractive way. For example, it doesn't take much to make a reading center appealing—a small rug, some beautiful posters, a table covered with wonderful books, and you're ready to go. The children's imagination will supply the rest of what your center needs. To be self-sustaining, a center must be a place where a child can function successfully and independently. If your presence is constantly needed at a center, it is probably too difficult or ambiguous for the students to understand. Remember: One of the reasons for having centers is to give students a sense of autonomy, not a sense of dependence. The key concept in the interest-centers approach is freedom of choice.

A teacher who uses interest centers is dedicated to the idea that in an attractive, purposeful environment, students make meaningful use of their time based on the pursuit of knowledge and ideas of their own choosing. The teacher has to do much behind-the-scenes work, establishing the centers and providing resources and other types of materials. And during center time, the teacher moves about the room and is available to the children. The roles of the teacher include support person, sympathetic listener, mediator of ideas, and arranger of possibilities.

The teacher assumes a low profile, being careful not to talk too much, not to give too many directions, and not to tell the children how to do things unless it's absolutely necessary. Again, the term *facilitator* is appropriate in this context. A good facilitator is someone who works behind the scenes to make things function as smoothly as possible. The main drawback of being a good facilitator is that it makes the work look so easy. Have you ever watched a really accomplished talk-show host do his or her job? The better the host is, the more people like us are apt to think, "I could do that. It looks so easy." Well, facilitating is not so easy.

The role of students in interest-centers instruction is that of active explorers. The students are decision makers who choose freely from among an array of attractive ways of spending time. They are learning and expressing a great variety of content and concepts in a variety of ways, and they are enjoying their learning.

Group Investigations and Projects

Imagine a group of students who, with their teacher's guidance and support, decide to do something about the environment where they live. Imagine further that these students take up the challenge of asking the school board to ban the use of styrofoam cups and other containers by the schools in their district. This is exactly what happened in Victoria, British Columbia, when some sixth- and seventh-grade students at James Bay School decided to seek such a ban.

The work of these students first came to my attention one fall morning as I drove along the interstate listening to a Canadian radio station. The announcer mentioned the work the James Bay students were trying to accomplish, and I was quite impressed that young people would take up such a challenge. I decided to write them a letter seeking more information about the project, and they replied promptly (see Figure 7.5).

There is something very compelling about positive social action mounted by a group of concerned citizens. It seems to address the very heart of democracy. This is especially true when those citizens are young people who are still in the process of learning how democracy works. The efforts of the students to ban styrofoam use were successful, by the way, but they had to do a considerable amount of work in order to achieve their goal. I'm sure they learned that one has to present evidence and do background work in order to present one's case clearly and persuasively to elected officials.

The James Bay project exemplifies the spirit of group investigation. A group project is an effort by a class—or a whole school—to make a difference in their world. The exciting thing about group investigation is that issues abound in every locality in democratic societies such as Canada and the United States. The teacher just needs to be sensitive to the issues and willing to do the work it takes to keep the students' effort going, ensuring that it is a positive, purposeful effort.

Students of any age can conduct group investigations. I've seen first-graders investigate a potentially dangerous crosswalk near the school and make it safer, possibly saving a life. I've seen third-graders investigate the playground equipment at their

Figure 7.5 *Correspondence Concerning a Group Project*

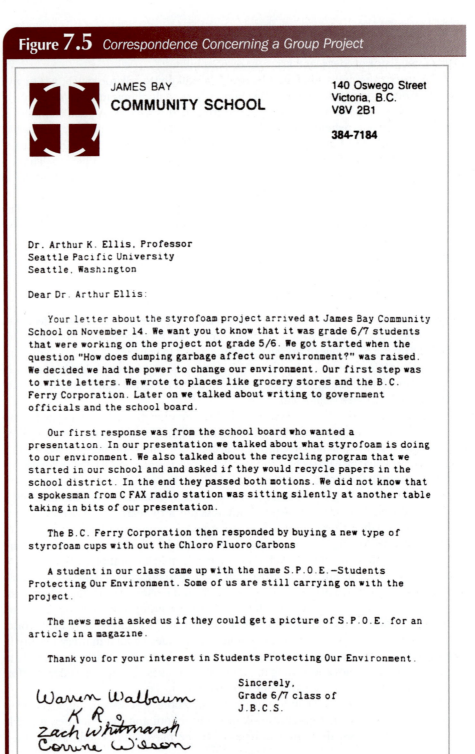

JAMES BAY
COMMUNITY SCHOOL

140 Oswego Street
Victoria, B.C.
V8V 2B1

384-7184

Dr. Arthur K. Ellis, Professor
Seattle Pacific University
Seattle, Washington

Dear Dr. Arthur Ellis:

Your letter about the styrofoam project arrived at James Bay Community School on November 14. We want you to know that it was grade 6/7 students that were working on the project not grade 5/6. We got started when the question "How does dumping garbage affect our environment?" was raised. We decided we had the power to change our environment. Our first step was to write letters. We wrote to places like grocery stores and the B.C. Ferry Corporation. Later on we talked about writing to government officials and the school board.

Our first response was from the school board who wanted a presentation. In our presentation we talked about what styrofoam is doing to our environment. We also talked about the recycling program that we started in our school and and asked if they would recycle papers in the school district. In the end they passed both motions. We did not know that a spokesman from C FAX radio station was sitting silently at another table taking in bits of our presentation.

The B.C. Ferry Corporation then responded by buying a new type of styrofoam cups with out the Chloro Fluoro Carbons

A student in our class came up with the name S.P.O.E.—Students Protecting Our Environment. Some of us are still carrying on with the project.

The news media asked us if they could get a picture of S.P.O.E. for an article in a magazine.

Thank you for your interest in Students Protecting Our Environment.

Sincerely,
Grade 6/7 class of
J.B.C.S.

Warren Walbaum
K R
Zach Whitmarsh
Corrine Wilson

CURRENT EVENTS
Focus on Strategies

Take a strategic view of teaching current events. By doing this, you accomplish more than merely covering stories in the news or, worse yet, falling prey to the unsystematic show-and-tell approach to news reporting by children who are given little leadership. Here is a sampling of proven strategies for emphasizing the productive use of the daily newspaper, television and radio, and Internet news sites:

1. *Read from news sources to your students.* Take a few minutes each morning or at some convenient time of the school day to read to your students from the newspaper, Websites, magazines, and the like. This gives you the opportunity to focus on stories of importance and those items in the news related to your current course of study. This time is crucial because it provides students with a model of an adult thoughtfully going through the news and reflecting with them on the significance of different stories.

2. *Headlines and their significance.* Newspapers, Websites, magazines, and other sources of the news carry headlines of different sizes and locations. A front-page, above-the-fold headline in bold type is considered to indicate a lead story, especially if it is a "banner" headline, stretching across the width of the front page. But headlines are written under the pressure of deadlines. One strategy that allows your students to show their comprehension is to challenge them to rewrite headlines, improving on them from their reading of a story. A second strategy is to present the class with the headlines from a current newspaper. Ask students to work in groups of two to determine what they think will be the long-term significance of each of the various stories. Ask them to rank order the stories and defend their choices.

3. *Special topics.* A special-topics approach to the news takes into account students' interest and motivation. Teams of students can take responsibility for reporting on special topics that appear in the news, including the following: animals, politics, weather, disasters, major countries, science, medicine, military, transportation, and trade.

4. *Categories in the news.* Newspapers, magazines, the Internet, and even the evening newscast all carry stories by departments or categories; for example, the news is often broken up into international, national, regional, and local. Then there are special sections for sports, weather, business, lifestyle, travel, comics, classified ads, and so on. Give your students choices of categories, and allow them to become "experts" in those categories by reading and analyzing particular sections. This strategy takes advantage of student interest. One child may be interested in sports, another in the comics, and so forth.

5. *Advertising and want ads.* It is a useful exercise in economics to go through a newspaper or magazine looking at the advertising and want ads. The daily newspaper carries grocery ads, department store ads, and advertising of other kinds. A historical perspective can be reached by comparing prices now with those found in an old newspaper. A similar comparison can be made of jobs, salaries, and the like listed in the want ads, using a current newspaper and one from the past.

Cross-age tutoring experiences are rewarding for both younger and older students.

school and make it safer and more creative. I've also seen intermediate-grade students make their school cafeteria a more appealing and sane place to eat lunch. You ought to try the approach—it works!

The role of the teacher in group investigation is complex. She or he must facilitate group processes, keep the focus on the problem to be solved, ensure that *all* students are involved actively, help the students locate appropriate resources and information, and evaluate the group's progress as it conducts its investigation. Some teachers find this overwhelming and fall back on traditional seat work assignments. Admittedly, it does take a lot of energy to guide a group of children through an investigation, but the rewards of seeing students grow and learn to work effectively with each other are considerable.

Independent Study and Presentations

It goes without saying that children need to learn to work together, but they also need to find out what they can do largely on their own. Children learn interdependence when they collaborate as well as when they work alone. In life we need both. Independent study can be conducted as a solo investigation or as a piece of a larger group investigation. It is ideal for invoking the *doctrine of interest*, which states that students should study what they are personally interested in.

When a student studies something he or she is curious about or wants to learn more about or simply chooses for whatever reason to study something, a powerful energy is already in place: *motivation*. When teenagers get to take driving lessons, we typically do not have to worry about their motivation to learn. They bring that commodity along with them. When a young child asks a parent if she or he can bake some cookies, we know that motivation is already in place. And when a child learns to ride a bicycle, painful as it is, the child typically won't stop until he or she can do it, no matter how long it takes. The motivation is there.

So, what I am saying to you is, let students decide for themselves some of the things they want to study. The following scenarios demonstrate the role you can play in providing independent study opportunities for your students.

in the classroom   Finding Students' Interests

In a primary-grade class, the teacher asked the students what seasons, games, and activities interested them the most. The students volunteered their ideas while the teacher wrote them on the board. When the board was filled with ideas, the teacher talked with the students about how they could learn more about the topics of their choice. The teacher gave each student three tasks to carry out:

1. To talk with her or his parent(s) about the topic and have them help write down some of the things they discussed
2. To draw a picture showing something he or she learned or enjoyed about the topic
3. To tell the class about her or his findings

This assignment involved the home. It also asked the child to inquire on his or her own and to express herself or himself artistically. Finally, it gave each child an experience with presentation skills. As simple as this independent study is, consider that it involved choosing freely, carrying out a task, talking to an adult, and presenting before an audience.

In an intermediate-level class that was studying Native Americans, the teacher showed the class a large map that illustrated the locations of various nations on the North American continent. The

teacher spent a little time telling the class about various tribal groups, including information about their customs, habits, food, and shelter. The teacher stressed the idea that each nation had its own unique identity and way of life.

The independent study flowing from this overview/introduction was to challenge each student to make a booklet and accompanying display on one of the Native American nations. Each student chose a different nation and did research, including writing letters to people of the nation to learn of modern-day life, reading accounts of tribal life in the past, and learning as much as possible in order to become an "expert." As the study progressed, the room began to fill up with maps, pictures, drawings, artifacts, stories, letters, and so on. Each student reported his or her findings to the class during a culminating activity, and a number of students taught a "lesson" on their chosen nation to a class of younger students in the school.

In both of these cases, the teacher played the role of facilitator, helping students with sources of information and providing guidance when they needed it. But in both cases, the ultimate responsibility for learning was with the individual students.

Reflective Thinking

Reflective-thinking activities are designed to give learners the opportunity to be philosophical—to consider, discuss, and argue issues. Reflective-thinking sessions are often used to help students analyze certain tasks they have performed. This strategy is also involved in situations where the teacher wants students to speculate on how a certain chain of events might take place under certain conditions.

Reflective thinking and inquiry share the idea of active student involvement in problems and questions. They differ as learning strategies in that inquiry learning is predicated on the notion that sufficient data will enable a student to answer a question or solve a problem, whereas reflective thinking often deals with questions that cannot be answered solely by data. The following questions provide a simple contrast:

Inquiry question: How do messages flow in our school?
Reflective-thinking question: What are the advantages of written versus oral messages?

The first question can be answered on the basis of data gathered, whereas the second may be a matter of opinion. The following examples demonstrate how reflective thinking can be implemented in your classroom, as does Sample Lesson 7.1 at the end of the chapter.

in the classroom   An Incident In Human Behavior

A teacher told her third-grade class the following story:

> Mary, a third-grader, checked a book out of the library. When school was over, she took the book home to read. On the way home, Mary's friends asked her to play outside. So Mary ran into her house, changed into play clothes, left the book on a chair in the living room, and went outside to play. Her brother Tim, who was three years old, found the book and colored on the pages with crayons. The book was ruined.

The teacher then asked the class this question: "How many people could we name who *might* be responsible?" The class listed Mary, her mother, her father, Tim, Mary's teacher, and the librarian. The teacher did not ask the students to reach conclusions about responsibility at this point. She just told the students to think about it and that they would discuss it the next day.

During a discussion period the next day, the teacher asked the students to tell who they thought was responsible. Here are some responses:

- "Mary is responsible. She shouldn't have left the book where her little brother could get it."
- "Her brother is three. He shouldn't be coloring in books. A two-year-old might."
- "Her mother didn't watch her little brother very carefully."
- "The teacher shouldn't let kids take books home."

Some students took issue with certain responses. Others supported their classmates' reasoning. Others had asked their parents and gave their parents' opinions. The teacher then asked, "How do we know the right answer?" One student said, "Some families are different, so it might not be the same for everyone."

The teacher asked another question: "What should be done, now that the book is ruined?" Some students had ready answers, while others made such suggestions as "We could ask the librarian what she thinks about it."

in the classroom   Looking Forward and Looking Back

The Roman god Janus (for whom the month of January is named) could look forward into the future and back into the past. So can we, at least to some extent. Many learners (not just children) tend to be impulsive when it comes to carrying

out an assignment. Reflective thinking can improve one's work substantially.

Let's say that you want your students to make maps of the school and play area. Prior to the activity itself, allow your students to meet in groups of two or three to think and plan about the qualities of a good map. Depending on the age of the pupils, you may want to list some key terms on the board, including *scale, key, cardinal directions, color, perspective, accuracy,* and so on. Following the activity of making maps, give your students an opportunity to talk about the assignment, including such issues as these: What was difficult about it? What did you learn? What would you tell someone who was going to make such a map?

Having before-and-after sessions like this raises students' levels of consciousness about their work. In doing so, they practice *metacognition*, or thinking about thinking. It's time consuming but eminently worthwhile.

Brainstorming

One proven method for tapping into the creativity of a group is brainstorming. It is particularly useful at those times when the teacher wants to give students an opportunity to think expansively about a problem, activity, project, or the like. Brainstorming in problem solving, for example, typically is done early in the process. If your class is studying economics and the children have decided to manufacture a product that they will then market, you might begin with a brainstorming session in which you allow students to think of as many possibilities as they can. Eventually, you and the children will decide on a single product to manufacture, but for now, you want to let the creative potential of the students flower.

There are three essential elements of brainstorming, and you must honor all three for the process to work effectively. First, there is the rule of *quantity over quality*. This means that you want the children to come up with as many possibilities as they can—the more, the merrier. The second rule is *no judgments*. There will be plenty of time later to decide whether an idea is practical, achievable, whatever. For now, refrain from judging; to do otherwise kills creative instincts. The third rule is *inclusion*. Everyone in the class needs to feel welcome to take part, not just the more vocal or more opinionated students.

Two alternative grouping possibilities are available, and I suggest you use them both from time to time. First, there is the whole-class group with the teacher at the chalkboard. Students simply speak up while you record their ideas. Generally speaking, you will have no trouble filling an entire board with suggestions. A follow-up session can be devoted to discussing the feasibility of the various suggestions. The second procedure is to put students in small groups of three or four and allow them to brainstorm. Each group will need a recorder or some way of keeping track of their ideas. The class then comes back together for a time of sharing.

The last thing to keep in mind is how much you want to structure the process. Free-form brainstorming allows people to speak up spontaneously. Its advantage is obvious—the spontaneous nature of the process. Its disadvantage is that the more vocal, outgoing types will dominate, while others will be reluctant to compete. Structured brainstorming is a process whereby a group (class or small group) actually gives each person a turn either to make a suggestion or to pass. The great advantage is that everyone has an equal opportunity to participate; the disadvantage is some slight loss of spontaneity. Try both approaches.

Creative Expression

Social studies offers great potential for students to express themselves creatively in a variety of ways. Although consuming knowledge, inquiring into problems, and discussing ideas are important uses of students' time in social studies, it is also important that they be given opportunities to build, act, draw, paint, and photograph as means of involving themselves in learning and sharing. See the Keys to Creativity for guidelines on encouraging creative thinking among your students.

Keys to Creativity

The teacher's behavior is crucial in establishing conditions that are conducive to creativity. The following suggestions are designed to help you establish a creative climate in your classroom:

- Give freedom and space.
- Promote discovery learning.
- Create a playful atmosphere.
- Encourage projects.
- Allow students to make choices.
- Bring interesting things to class.
- Be a good listener and sounding board.

- Give open-ended assignments.
- Encourage students to help each other.
- Encourage fresh perspectives on ordinary things.
- Model and encourage trust and respect.
- Encourage student initiative and risk taking.
- Have a sense of humor.
- Give unusual assignments.
- Encourage involvement with good literature and the arts.

Here are some examples of creative expression by students:

- A second-grade class presented a slide show to the PTA, illustrating their work on improving the safety of a crosswalk near the school.
- A sixth-grade class constructed a diorama in the school showcase, illustrating life in a medieval manor during their study of a unit on life in the Middle Ages.
- A student constructed a model of the school playground and presented his recommendations for improving its use during recess periods.
- A group of fifth-grade students made puppets and presented shows to kindergarten and first-grade classes on the topic of school safety.
- A third-grade class put together a directory of mini–field trips in the local area that students could take with their parents.
- Some sixth-graders developed and constructed a simple game designed to teach cardinal directions. They mass-produced the game and made copies available to children in the lower grades.

What kinds of products do creative students produce? There are some you might expect—poems, stories, drawings, paintings. But there are also others that might not immediately come to mind—murals, booklets and instruction pamphlets, models, puppet shows, games, plays, dioramas, radio and television programs, photographs, and a wide range of computer-assisted slide shows and Websites. The following example tells about students becoming "journalists" and writing newspaper stories about nursery rhymes.

in the classroom   **Nursery Rhyme Newspaper Stories**

One way to support children's creative instincts is to let them write newspaper stories about nursery rhymes. Give each child a nursery rhyme (find nursery rhyme books in your school or local library), and ask him or her to write a newspaper article about the story the rhyme tells. Here is an example of how one child wrote up the story of "Jack and Jill":

> Jack and Jill went up the hill,
> to fetch a pail of water.
> Jack fell down and broke his crown,
> and Jill came tumbling after.
>
> Now up Jack got and home did trot,
> as fast as he could caper.
> He went to bed and covered his head
> with vinegar and brown paper.

"Youngsters Hurt in Tragic Fall"
by Shandra, Room 17 (5th Grade)

Jack and Jill, both aged 10, were injured today when they fell while running down the hill from the town well. Witnesses said they tripped over each other in their hurry to bring the pail of water back to the Old Washerwoman. Jack apparently broke his crown. He ran home and covered his head with vinegar and brown paper and is expected to make a full recovery. Jill needed no treatment. Safety Officer Billy Bones said that children should *never* run down the hill because it is too steep. Concerned citizens will meet at Town Hall on Friday night to discuss this important safety issue. Officer Bones will lead the opening flag salute. Both Jack and Jill said this sure has been a lesson to them, and from now on, they will *walk* down the hill. The Old Washerwoman said in an interview that maybe she had been working the children too hard and that is why they fell. No charges are expected to be filed in the case.

Content Analysis

Because so much of what people learn and know comes from secondary sources, it is important to develop the skill of content analysis. Content analysis is a means of examining content more closely than if one merely wanted to know what it stated. Content analysis raises such questions as interpretation of meaning, significance of material, and even accuracy or bias. It is also a way for students to take information presented globally and break it into categories that are more manageable.

The content that students can analyze can come from any source: a film, story, textbook, newspaper, Website, and so forth. Practice at content analysis should make students more critical thinkers and critical readers. The interpretive activities involved in content analysis enable students to construct meaning as they read, view, or listen to information. Take some time to consider the following examples, as well as Sample Lesson 7.2.

Content Analysis

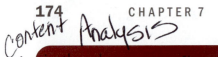

Nursery rhymes have the potential for content analysis at several levels. In that respect, they are appropriate content at both the primary and intermediate levels. At the primary level, you might focus on the sequence of events within a nursery rhyme. After memorizing "Humpty Dumpty," for example, you might ask the children to draw a series of pictures showing what actually happened. Figure 7.6 illustrates a young child's sequence content analysis of the nursery rhyme.

At the intermediate level, you can use the same content to get at different things. Here are two possibilities:

1. Have students write about what they think the message really is in the story of "Humpty Dumpty." The literal meaning is obvious: He fell off the wall. But is there a moral to the story?
2. "Humpty Dumpty" was written in a historical context. Have students investigate the origins of this nursery rhyme. Does it portray an actual king? What were the conditions that led to his fall? What were the consequences?

All textbooks, by definition, contain content. A very useful exercise in content analysis for a team of intermediate-level researchers is to take two social studies textbooks designed for their particular grade level and to compare and contrast them. A good place to start is the books' tables of contents; then look at the indexes.

Ask the students to focus on these questions: To what extent are the two books alike and different in coverage? How difficult and how interesting is the writing in each book? How do the illustrations compare? How complete and how fair is the coverage each book gives to certain cultural groups? To women? To minorities? Which of the two texts do you prefer?

Differentiated Assignments

Often, assignments are given to the whole class as though all the students have the same needs and the same learning styles. In fact, they do not. If you provide choices for children, they have an opportunity to practice decision making and to fulfill your requirements while serving their own interests. Of course, not every assignment needs to be differentiated, but many should be, if only to provide variety.

The idea behind differentiated assignments is to give students choices. In a true differentiated assignment, there are a number of ways each student might achieve this goal. Learning style, interest, and motivation are factors that will guide the student's choice of activities. In most cases, a differentiated assignment will take several days for each student to complete because of the research, construction, drama, and other activities involved. Time should also be allowed for class presentations, because much additional learning will take place as the children share what they have learned. The following examples show how you can offer differentiated assignments in your classroom.

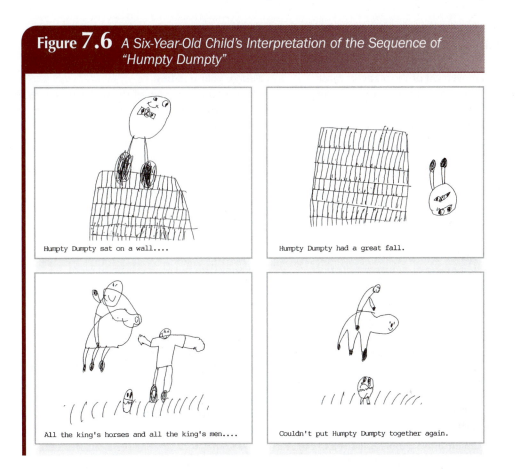

Figure 7.6 *A Six-Year-Old Child's Interpretation of the Sequence of "Humpty Dumpty"*

Humpty Dumpty sat on a wall....

Humpty Dumpty had a great fall.

All the king's horses and all the king's men....

Couldn't put Humpty Dumpty together again.

in the classroom   The Pioneer Treks*

The teacher's goal in this example is for students to learn about the westward expansion of the United States across the Great Plains and on to the territories of California and Oregon. As you examine the following assignment options, keep in mind Howard Gardner's (1983) *multiple-intelligences theory,* as well as what you know about student learning styles:

- Find a book that has a picture of a covered wagon in it. Sketch a copy of the covered wagon.
- As the covered wagon trains moved along the trail, they would stop for the night. Find a picture of a covered wagon encampment, and draw a sketch of it.
- Using craft sticks, cloth, glue, and other materials, make a model of a covered wagon.
- Most families that traveled west had to leave many of their possessions behind. Prepare a list of the things you think a family might have had to leave behind and a list of things a family would have needed to take with them on the trail.
- Write a fictional story about a family and their decision to leave the eastern United States and move west.

- Draw a map that illustrates the Oregon Trail, the California Trail, and the Mormon Trek.
- The westward movement of the pioneers must have seemed strange from the perspective of the various native peoples through whose territory they traveled. Write a story explaining the westward movement from a Native American point of view.
- Read the book *The Children of the Covered Wagon* by Elizabeth Carr. Present a brief oral report to the class on the life of children in a wagon train as described in this book.
- Pretend you are a child journeying west on a wagon train. Write a letter to a friend who stayed behind, telling her or him about life on a wagon train.
- Some people who went west went to the gold fields of California and Colorado. Draw a sketch of a gold-mining camp.
- Write a song about life along the trail.
- What job would you have liked to have on a wagon train? Wagon master? Scout? Write a paragraph telling what job you would have liked and why.
- Look through the index of a book on the westward movement. Find a topic that looks interesting to you and research it, using this book and other sources.

- Find a play about pioneer days or the westward movement. Round up enough students to put it on, and present it to a primary-grade class in your building.
- Make a salt/flour map of the westward movement. Show the major trails, forts, and other important features.
- Find out what songs were sung along the trail by the pioneers. Learn a song and teach it to the class.
- How fair do you think the westward movement was to the Native Americans? Do some research into this question, and report your findings to the class.
- What was the typical diet along the trail? Find out and (with the teacher's help) prepare a meal for the class to eat.
- Where will pioneers go in the future? Under the oceans? To the Antarctic? To outer space? Do some research and write a report on future pioneer efforts.
- Look through the school district's film catalog for a good film on the westward movement. Ask your teacher to order the film you select. Preview it so that you can introduce it to the class for showing.

*Thanks to Anne DeGallier for many of the differentiated assignment options for this activity.

in the classroom   Archaeology

Using differentiated assignments helps ensure that you will reach children who have a variety of learning styles and preferences. The type of differentiated assignment illustrated here, which includes three modes of learning (verbal, activity, production), is really a template that you can use for any unit or area of instruction. Just change the focus of the assignment to whatever content you are teaching.

Direct each student to choose *any two* assignments from *each list*, for a total of *six* assignments.

List A: Verbal

- Read one of the books on our Unit Resource List.
- Write a letter to a museum that asks how curators do their work.

- Read an article on archaeology from *National Geographic* or *Smithsonian* magazine, and write a report on it.
- Write an essay on archaeology. Be sure to include at least three references.
- View a video on archaeology (select one from the video list), and write a report on it.
- Write a short play or skit about an actual archaeological expedition.
- Write a story about a fictional archaeological expedition.

List B: Activity

- Make a model of an ancient dwelling.
- Construct a diorama of life in an ancient setting.
- Draw a series of pictures that illustrate an archaeological dig.
- Use clay and sticks to make a model of an ancient city.
- Make a reproduction of an artifact from ancient times.
- Draw sketches of several ancient tools.
- Use magazine pictures to make a collage of an archaeological expedition.

- Make a time capsule filled with artifacts from our culture.
- Tour a local museum, and draw pictures of the exhibits.

List C: Production

- Help stage a play about an archaeological expedition.
- Do a role-play in which you become an actual archaeologist who tells about his or her work.
- Prepare and present a group presentation on an actual archaeological expedition.
- Prepare and teach a lesson on archaeology to another class.
- Have a discussion on archaeology at home with your family members.
- Be an archaeologist. Carry out your own expedition using artifacts from your home or neighborhood.
- Visit a garage sale or yard sale. Pretend that you are an archaeologist and the items for sale are artifacts.

Jigsaw/Peer Teaching and Cooperative Learning

The jigsaw strategy, developed by Elliot Aronson (2009), is an interesting combination of cooperative learning and individualistic goal structure. The idea of this teaching/learning strategy is that each student in a cooperative learning group of, say, three students is responsible for peer teaching his or her companions a portion of the material that they all need to learn. Thus, each student teaches one-third of the information, skills, or whatever and is taught two-thirds of that content. It is important that students do their best to teach their compatriots, because all the members of the group are depending on each other. This truly creates a "We're in this together" mentality.

The jigsaw strategy is illustrative of the broader idea of *cooperative learning*, which is dedicated to the idea of having civil conversations and working together in an atmosphere of mutual interest and collaboration. Cooperative learning is based on the idea of shared goals. If you and I want the same thing, why don't we work together to achieve it? The work of such theorists as Lev Vygotsky, Jean Piaget, and Jerome Bruner points to the need for children to express themselves civilly in social situations for language and thought to codevelop.

Johnson and Johnson (2004), pioneers in this area, cite cumulative research findings that support cooperative learning. Positive outcomes include the following:

- Higher achievement and better retention
- Growth in moral and cognitive reasoning
- Enhanced motivation to learn
- Improved attitude toward school and school subjects
- Improved attitude toward teachers
- Enhanced self-esteem
- Better liking of one another

The teacher's role is to act as a consultant, mediator, and facilitator in keeping the process going forward. The teacher also serves as a strategist who carefully considers who should work with whom. She or he teaches students the skills needed to work together, helping them know when to listen, when to talk, how to be supportive, how to ensure participation by all, and so on. The teacher creates an atmosphere in which students are able to construct knowledge, reflect on what they are learning, practice good citizenship, and build one another up in an academically and socially supportive atmosphere.

Keys to Cooperative Learning

Cooperative learning is based on these six principles:

- Positive interdependence
- Small groups (two or three students)
- Face-to-face interaction
- Individual accountability

- Development of small-group skills
- Time for reflection and analysis

Source: Based on D. Johnson, R. Johnson, & E. Holubec, *Circles of Learning* (Edina, MN: Interaction Book Company, 2002).

The student's role is to work with others to achieve common goals. Many students today come from small families, where there is little of the give and take that occurs with a clan of brothers and sisters. These students need to learn to share, give, listen, care, and experience the transcendent moments of life that come only when people are part of something larger than themselves. When students come to learn the skills of cooperation, the projects, productions, committee work, and other experiences found at the heart of social studies are greatly facilitated.

I'm convinced that peer teaching is one of the best ways for children to learn. Piaget noted that children are more effective than most adults realize in teaching each other, especially if teachers provide some structure and support. This is so, he claimed, because of a language issue—namely, greater syntactic compatibility is found within the peer group than exists when, for example, adults talk to children. What this means in simple terms is that adult language is far more complex than children's language; therefore, a child talking to another child does not take linguistic shortcuts, use sophisticated terminology, or assume years of experience. John Dewey noted that one of the biggest problems in teaching is the false assumption by teachers of experience on the part of students.

All of this in no way diminishes the importance of your role as a teacher. It does, however, shift the center of gravity from you to the students, making your job one of organizer and facilitator of learning, rather than lecturer or presenter. See the following example of how to use cooperative learning.

---

in the classroom   The American Revolution

You can use the jigsaw or cooperative learning method to help students understand three events that took place leading up to the American Revolution: the Boston Tea Party, the Battle of Lexington, and Paul Revere's ride. Break the class into groups of three, and assign each group the responsibility of learning about all three events. Using the jigsaw strategy, have one student within each group study one of the events thoroughly. Provide enough time for students to study their respective events. Then convene the small groups and ask each student to teach the other two members of his or her group about the event assigned.

You will need to coach your students in techniques for making the information they present interesting, significant, and involving. With practice, the students will improve their teaching, especially if they have learned a variety of teaching strategies from what you have modeled.

Simulations

Simulations are attempts to represent and model social systems, often through the medium of a game. Those social systems may be economic, political, spatial, or cultural, or they may be some sort of combination of systems. *Reality* is the key word in simulation activities. If students are to learn how a market system or a governing system works, then it is important that they not only play the roles and use the processes but also that those roles and processes accurately reflect the reality of the system they are intended to represent.

Of course, in every simulation, some compromise must be reached between the attempt to represent the reality of the system and the limitations imposed by such factors as the age and maturity of the students, the resources available, the size of the classroom, and the constraints of time. Oversimplifying processes and interactions in order to make a simulation easier or more exciting can be dangerous. Developing an effective simulation requires making wise choices about which elements of reality need to be included in order to make the activity valid and which elements can be factored out as extraneous to the fundamental processes involved.

Thus, in any social system you choose to model or in any simulation you select for use in social studies, it is crucial for you to determine whether the elements included accurately represent the ideas you think children should learn. One way to ensure this is to determine exactly what your learning and valuing objectives are and to choose or develop a simulation on that basis. Sample Lesson 7.3 provides a simulation that's not tied to any particular unit of study that you can use in the classroom. In adition, two commercially developed examples of simulations are described in the following examples.

in the classroom **Starpower**

Starpower has been used extensively in age groups ranging from third grade to college graduates and business personnel. It is designed to set up a three-level, low-mobility socioeconomic society, in which the low group remains low in power and the high group remains high in power and ultimately is allowed to make the rules for continuing the game. The middle group isn't sure what to think. The wealthy power group generally makes rules that maintain its own wealth and power rather than benefit the poorer groups. The dramatic parallels with real-life society are missed by few participants. Participation and interest are reliably high, with most participants becoming highly emotionally involved.

Although recommended for 18 to 35 participants, Starpower has been successfully used with groups as small as 13 and as large as 70 or 80. The use and abuse of power demonstrated by the game is particularly appropriate to a number of factions in today's society. Discussion during the debriefing of the highly stimulating activity is frequently intense and heated, even for fifth- and sixth-graders. Although the facilitator's guide recommends a 50-minute period for playing Starpower, experience dictates that a 3-hour time block should be allowed, excluding preparation time of about 30 minutes. At least 1 hour should be allowed for debriefing and discussion, since emotionally charged topics often come up and should be dealt with thoroughly during the course of the debriefing.

During the game, interaction among the participants is spirited, basically cooperative within each of the three groups, and allowed to occur naturally, with little or no outside control on what is said or what roles are portrayed. The roles of the three groups are allowed to develop naturally along the lines dictated by the power structure involved. Overall, this is an excellent simulation that is highly recommended for fourth grade or higher.

in the classroom **Bafà Bafà**

In this simulation, participants are divided into two groups. Each group is taught certain rules and develops its own culture. Then visitors are exchanged between the groups to experience the foreign culture instituted by the other group. The game helps students understand the meaning of the term *culture* in graphic and physical ways, how cultural misunderstandings and miscommunications occur, and how stereotypes and prejudice evolve.

Although the simulation may at first seem complex to participants, after a few minutes of practice at their given culture, participants generally find the experience enjoyable, exciting, and interesting. The cultural exchange and subsequent debriefing provide many opportunities for eliciting cultural stereotypes and misunderstandings and provide for an emotional understanding of what it is like to be a visitor to another culture. Bafà Bafà also helps illustrate that values are culture laden and that no culture is necessarily better but merely different. This understanding is essential to increasing world harmony in a modern, technological society.

This is an excellent cross-cultural simulation that has been used successfully with Peace Corps volunteers, teachers, and legislators, as well as students. It is highly effective in creating an understanding of cultural attitudes and cultural norms.

Computer Simulations

Simulations have taken a great leap forward with the advent of videodiscs, video and computer games, and the whole theory of computers as learning environments in themselves. The early days of so-called drill-and-kill computer programs have come and gone. Those programs have been replaced by exciting ways to access and interact with stored knowledge.

The videodisc encyclopedia is a good example. A child reading about the origins of World War II can virtually watch and listen to President Franklin D. Roosevelt's speech to the nation following the attack on Pearl Harbor in 1941. Or a child using videodisc technology can suddenly find herself or himself on the banks of the Zambesi River in Africa, surveying the landscape.

At a heightened interactive level, computer simulations allow learners to take part in making decisions, solving problems, and otherwise applying their knowledge and skills to situations where they have consequences. Computer simulations range from those suitable for one or two students at a time to whole-class simulations. At their best, they represent situations much like those that students will encounter in real life. One of the first computer simulations to achieve widespread popularity was Oregon Trail. It is perhaps primitive by the standards of the new generation of simulations, but it remains no doubt one of the most played school-related simulations. Students take on roles of pioneers traveling west and must make decisions regarding food supplies, safety, health, and various other issues all along the trail. The idea is to survive and reach the Oregon Territory. Three of the most widely used and successful computer simulations of recent times are Where in the World Is Carmen Sandiego?, Sim City, and Science 2000.

- *Where in the World Is Carmen Sandiego?* This game begins with the whole class playing; the game is projected from the computer onto a large monitor or screen (see Figure 7.7). The students practice observation, note taking, and other skills needed to capture the wily criminal, Carmen Sandiego. The teacher guides the class at first, teaching students to use reference materials that they will need for tracking and apprehending the criminal. Because Carmen Sandiego travels all over the world, geographic knowledge builds as the game proceeds. In time, students work in pairs to solve the problem and to prepare a report about the state or region they have researched. A newer game is Where in Time Is Carmen Sandiego? In this version of the popular simulation, the focus is on history. Various "time doors" are available from which to choose, with different possibilities for exploring eras.

- *Sim City.* This and a related simulation, Sim Earth, place students in the roles of planners and builders of cities. They must take into account the systems that cities depend on, including transportation, water, industry, communications, recreation, and housing. Problems occur along the way that must be solved, whether they be traffic congestion, water supply, or inadequate residential zoning. The complexities introduced in Sim City give students a far more sophisticated sense of urban planning, development, and maintenance than they could obtain in a less interactive way. The Sim City series continues with simulations such as Sim City 4. These complex games offer a variety of

Figure 7.7 *Where in the World Is Carmen Sandiego?*

Discover *Where in the World Is Carmen Sandiego?*, where the chase first began in popular computer software games by Broderbund Software.

Learn about countries and cultures as you search for the elusive Carmen in beautiful locations rich with history, culture, and music. Software, animated adventures on DVD, and other Carmen products are available worldwide.

Where in the World Is Carmen Sandiego? was also a PBS television game show for kids that built knowledge of geography. It was on the air for five seasons and nominated for seven Emmys, which it won in 1995 and 1996.

As they chase Carmen Sandiego and her gang through countries around the globe, or through all fifty United States and Washington, DC, kids learn about geography and cultures. Carmen has also been known to challenge kids to learn more about history, music, and the solar system.

Carmen Sandiego began her career in 1985 as an original character in an innovative detective software game that broadened kids' knowledge of languages. Over seven million copies have been sold for use in schools and homes worldwide.

thinking skills and intellectual challenges for children. The problems are realistic and offer role-playing opportunities in which players test their wits as urban planners and problem solvers.

- *Science 2000+.* This thematic curriculum uses hypertext databases connected to videodiscs. Students encounter problems found in real life, including pollution, fragile ecosystems, water supplies, soil conditions, climate factors, and so on. The approach is based on cooperative group learning in which students take on roles ranging from farmers, developers, elected officials, and law enforcement personnel to naturalists and representatives of the Environmental Protection Agency. The rich databases enable the students to access information that's useful in representing their positions and reaching decisions made in the best interests of society.

Observations on Indirect Instruction

The strengths of the indirect instructional strategies are exemplified by the contrasts between direct and indirect instruction. Although the contrasts seem on the surface to be heavily weighted in favor of indirect instruction, keep in mind that it is not practical for students to learn from any one strategy exclusively. Knowledge of events, eras, and places and explanations of spatial, cultural, and economic systems, which are certainly major objectives of a social studies program, are often better suited to direct teaching.

Perhaps the major contribution of indirect learning is that it gives students opportunities to become involved in the processes used in forming knowledge. Such intimate contact with knowledge formation gives learners an important perspective as they read, see, and hear what others have to show and tell them about human beings through books, films, lectures, Websites, and other sources of information. But when the subject lends itself to indirect learning, the rewards of this democratic learning strategy are great both for the facilitator/teacher and for the active, independent learners.

Summary

This chapter defined and illustrated the wide range of approaches you might use to teach and students might use to learn social studies. Two categories, direct and indirect instruction—each with numerous permutations—were discussed. The search for curricular balance in teaching and learning is particularly important. Keep in mind as you combine lessons into units that students need a certain amount of meaningful reception learning balanced with a certain amount of construction of knowledge and meaning on their own part. Also keep in mind the social aspect of social studies. Whenever possible, students should learn and work together. A final thought is that yet another kind of balance should be sought: one that ensures students will learn through verbal modes, through construction and related activities, and through productions and presentations they carry out themselves.

Explorations

Reflect on . . .

1. Choose a key idea or concept from one of the social sciences—for example, the concept of *culture* from anthropology. Consider what three instructional strategies you might use to teach this concept. Try to achieve balance in your choice of strategies.

2. Discuss with a partner, a small group, or your whole class the issue of how a teacher might decide

how much time to devote to particular strategies in teaching social studies.

In the Field

3. Try teaching one or more of the In the Classroom lessons or activities illustrated in this chapter, either in a student-teaching environment or to your peers.
4. Get a copy of the teacher's guide for a social studies textbook being used in an elementary school.

How many teaching/learning alternatives does it suggest? How might you enhance the unit or otherwise improve on it using the suggestions found in this chapter?

For Your Portfolio

5. For the activity or lesson that you taught in item 3, write about what worked and didn't work. Would you choose a different strategy if you were to teach this content again?

Continuing the Journey: Suggested Readings

Aronson, E. (2009). Jigsaw Classroom Official Website. *www.jigsaw.org*

Techniques for using jigsaw in a variety of classroom settings.

Kirman, J. M. (2008). *Elementary Social Studies: Creative Classroom Ideas.* Upper Saddle River, NJ: Pearson.

Lestvik, L., and C. Tyson (2008). *The Handbook of Research in Social Studies Education.* New York: Routledge.

Schmidt, L. (2007). *Social Studies that Sticks.* Portsmouth, NH: Heinemann.

Stone, R. (2008). *Best Practices for Teaching Social Studies.* Thousand Oaks, CA: Corwin Press.

Sunal, C., & Haas, M. E. (2008). *Social Studies for the Elementary and Middle Grades.* Upper Saddle River, NJ: Pearson.

Thombs, M., Gillis, M., & Canestrari, A. (2008). *Using Webquests in the Social Studies Classroom: A Culturally Responsive Approach.* Thousand Oaks, CA: Corwin Press.

Vogler, K., et. al. (2007). "Getting off the Back Burner: Impact of Testing Elementary Social Studies as Part of a State-Mandated Accountability Program." *Journal of Social Studies Research* (October).

Websites

Find research-based ways to organize your teaching at the Doing What Works Clearinghouse Website, *http://dww.ed.gov*, an information-dispensing branch of the U.S. Department of Education. Recommended practices include (1) space learning over time with review and quizzing, (2) alternate worked examples with problem-solving practice, (3) connect abstract and concrete representations of concepts, and (4) use higher-order questions to help students guild explanations.

Strategies on reading, writing, classroom management, integrating technology and more. *http://teacher.scholastic.com/teachingstrategies/*

Geared toward higher education educators but the topics are imminently practical for any teacher. Also, the sources are reviewed, simple to navigate, and well organized. Topics include assessment, teaching strategies, teaching challenges, course design, and more *http://pedagogy.merlot.org*

Related NCSS Standards and Principles of Powerful Social Studies

Teaching and Learning Principles

Social studies teaching and learning are powerful when they are meaningful. Meaningful learning activities and assessment strategies focus students' attention on the most important ideas embedded in what they are learning (p. 12).

Social studies teaching and learning are powerful when they are challenging. Teachers model seriousness of purpose and a thoughtful approach to inquiry, and use instructional strategies designed to elicit and support similar qualities from students" (p. 13).

Pedagogy Standards

1. Learning and Development

Social studies teachers should possess the knowledge, capabilities, and dispositions to provide learning opportunities at the appropriate school levels that support learners' intellectual, social, and personal development.

2. Differences in Learning Styles

Social studies teachers should possess the knowledge, capabilities, and dispositions to create at the appropriate school levels learning experiences that fit the different approaches to learning of diverse learners.

3. Critical Thinking, Problem Solving, and Performance Skills

Social studies teachers should possess the knowledge, capabilities, and dispositions to use at the appropriate school levels a variety of instructional strategies to encourage student development of critical thinking, problem solving, and performance skills.

4. Active Learning and Motivation

Social studies teachers should possess the knowledge, capabilities, and dispositions to create at the appropriate school levels learning environments (p. 51).

Source: Excerpted from National Council for the Social Studies. *National Standards for Social Studies Teachers.* (Silver Spring, MD: Author, 2002).

SAMPLE LESSON 7.1 Economics: Making Choices

AGE LEVEL: Primary

NCSS STANDARD: Theme VII. Production, Distribution, and Consumption

Knowledge—learners will understand what they gain and give up when they make a decision. *Source:* Excerpted from National Task Force for Social Studies. (Draft 2008). *Expectations of Excellence: Curriculum Standards for Social Studies:* Waldarf, MD: National Council for the Social Studies, p. 86.

KEY IDEA: The choices we make depend on the resources we have.

INSTRUCTIONAL OBJECTIVE: Students will work in groups to decide how to spend "tokens" to purchase a school lunch. Students will also evaluate how choosing one item limits other possible choices.

SET: Begin the lesson by showing students two different lunch items. Tell students that you have one "token" to buy one of these items and that each item costs one token exactly. Have students help you decide which item you should buy for lunch. Once you have chosen one of the items, discuss with students how you won't be able to get the other item because you have used your token.

INSTRUCTION: Organize a simple school menu with five or six lunch items on it. Show the menu to the class and tell them that you have three "tokens" to spend on lunch. Have the class help you decide how you should spend your tokens by placing a token on that item to indicate that you plan to buy it. Discuss with students what it means to choose one item but then have one less token to spend elsewhere.

REFLECTION/ASSESSMENT: Organize students into pairs or triads and give them three tokens each.

Have each student decide how he or she will spend the tokens, but use a menu with different items so that students are not tempted to copy the choices you made during instruction. Work with each group and discuss which item students chose and why. Also discuss which items students did not buy and why.

CLOSURE/ENRICHMENT: To increase students' understanding of making choices with limited resources, you can increase or decrease the number of tokens that students have to work with. Another option is to add items to the menu or use alternative menus that you rotate between groups. For higher grades, have students create their own "menus" or lists of things to buy with tokens. Then have groups roll dice to assign the number of tokens that they get to spend. With higher-grade students, you may also want to formally define economic terms such as *resources, alternative,* and *scarcity.*

SAMPLE LESSON 7.2   Geography: Interpretive School or Classroom Map

AGE LEVEL: Primary

NCSS STANDARD: Theme III: People, Places, and Environments

Learners demonstrate their knowledge by constructing a map depicting the school, community, state or region that demonstrates understanding of relative location, direction, boundaries, and significant physical features. *Source:* Excerpted from National Task Force for Social Studies. (Draft 2008). *Expectations of Excellence: Curriculum Standards for Social Studies,* p. 45.

KEY IDEA: Maps tell us about people, places, and environments.

INSTRUCTIONAL OBJECTIVE: Students will create an interpretive map of their school or classroom, showing relative locations, boundaries, and significant physical features or objects. Students will also answer geographic questions related to their map.

SET: Show students a map of your home or a floor plan that you invent. While you show the map, identify objects that go in different rooms. For instance, a bowl goes with the kitchen. Discuss with students how each room has its own special set of objects and activities.

INSTRUCTION: On sketch paper, have students draw an interpretive map of their school or classroom, identifying significant locations such as the cafeteria, gym, playground, and so on. Direct students to illustrate important objects such as the basketball hoop on the playground, the reading center in your classroom, or the cafeteria table where they sit during lunch. In addition to identifying rooms and objects, have students illustrate the boundaries of the school or room such as fences, parking lots, sidewalks, walls, and the like.

REFLECTION/ASSESSMENT: When students finish illustrating their maps, have them share their work with one another. One technique for sharing is to have students compare maps looking for similarities and differences. For instance, one student might have included the principal's office while another student included the music room. Students can write about the similarities and

differences or simply discuss them. With this, have students talk about the following questions: What do people do in each of the locations on the maps? What objects can be found in each of the locations? What path does a person walk to get from one location to the next? In what ways are maps helpful?

CLOSURE/ENRICHMENT: To extend the activity, younger students can make a map of their room at home, maybe with the help of a parent or guardian. The map could include illustrations of objects that are important to them. For higher grades, have students list the names of locations on their map into the first column of a two-column table. In the second column, have students summarize objects and activities related to that location.

SAMPLE LESSON 7.3   Anthropology: Studying and Describing Artifacts

AGE LEVEL: Primary or Intermediate

NCSS STANDARD: Theme II: Time, Continuity, and Change

   Students demonstrate their knowledge of Time, Continuity, and Change by using artifacts to offer guesses to reconstruct events and life of the past participating in role-playing and reconstructing events. *Source:* Excerpted from National Task Force for Social Studies. (Draft 2008). *Expectations of Excellence: Curriculum Standards for Social Studies.* Waldarf, MD: National Council for the Social Studies, p. 34.

KEY IDEA: Studying and describing an artifact to learn about the people who made it.

INSTRUCTIONAL OBJECTIVE: Students will study an artifact for 2 minutes and describe its features.

Students will sketch, measure, note the color, material, and any numbers, words, letters, symbols, or defects on the artifact. Students will make an educated guess about the purpose of the artifact and what the artifact tells us about the people who made it.

MATERIALS: Collect artifacts from various cultures that are mostly new to students such as foreign currency, books, clothing, or souvenirs. If these kinds of artifacts are difficult to find, use objects from around your classroom or home that would be novel to students; it doesn't have to be foreign for students to analyze it.

SET: Show students an object that fits the definition of an artifact; in other words, an object made or shaped by humans. Discuss with students what they think the purpose of the artifact is. Spend 1 or 2 minutes extending the discussion so that students are making educated guesses about what the artifact tells us about the people who made it.

INSTRUCTION: Show students another artifact. Lead the class in describing the artifact and recording the results on the board. Some ideas for the description include a sketch, measurements, color, material, texture, words, numbers, symbols, and defects. While you are doing this, have students record the results of the discussion/board work on their own paper. After making a thorough study and description of the object, discuss with students what they think the purpose of the artifact is and what the artifact tells us about the people who made it. Record student responses on the board as students write their own thoughts to these questions on their paper.

REFLECTION/ASSESSMENT: Organize students into groups of three or four. Present each group with one artifact. Have groups work through the steps for studying and describing an artifact: (1) study the artifact for 2 minutes, (2) describe the artifact, (3) make an educated guess regarding its purpose, and (4) make an educated guess about what it tells us about the people who made it. Have students record their findings on a poster-size piece of paper as a group. Once students have finished their work, have them share their posters with the class. While students share, use formative assessment techniques to determine students' progress toward meeting the instructional objective.

CLOSURE/ENRICHMENT: As an extension of the day's artifact lesson, have students locate "artifacts" at home to study and describe on their own or with their parents/guardians.

SAMPLE LESSON 7.4   Political Science: Defining Values of American Government

AGE LEVEL: Primary or Intermediate

NCSS STANDARD: Theme VI: Power, Authority, and Governance

Knowledge—the learner will understand fundamental American values of the common good, liberty, justice, equality, and individual dignity. *Source:* Excerpted from National Task Force for Social Studies. (Draft 2008). *Expectations of Excellence: Curriculum Standards for Social Studies.* Waldarf, MD: National Council for the Social Studies, p. 77.

KEY IDEA: American systems of authority and governance include certain democratic values.

INSTRUCTIONAL OBJECTIVE: Students will define five characteristics of American government

systems and create images to illustrate their meaning.

SET: Locate a picture or short video about the Statue of Liberty. Show the picture or video to students and discuss the ideas that the statue represents. The same procedures could be done with other symbols such as the American flag or Liberty Bell.

INSTRUCTION: Conduct a class discussion and ask students how they think each of the following values should to be defined: common good, liberty, justice, equality, and individual dignity. Create a poster with the class that defines each value in simple, student-friendly terms but that still captures the meaning of each value. Have students write down each value and its agreed upon definition. Next brainstorm with students possible images that communicate the meaning of each value. For example, a piece of chain broken in half would communicate the idea of liberty. Then have students make a small drawing next to each value that they think communicates its meaning.

REFLECTION/ASSESSMENT: Organize students into groups of three or four. Have groups select one value to define and illustrate on a poster for the class. Then have each group share its poster and explain to the class how each image or picture explains the meaning of the value.

CLOSURE/ENRICHMENT: Invite students to gather news reports that are related to any of the values thus discussed. For instance, a report on the selection of a new Supreme Court judge would correspond to the value of justice. Have younger students, look for images or ideas that communicate the values discussed above. For example, playground rules represent the idea of common good.

SAMPLE LESSON 7.5 · History: Analyzing Historical Photographs

AGE LEVEL: Intermediate

NCSS STANDARD: Theme II: Time, Continuity, and Change

Processes—The learner will be able to identify and use a variety of primary and secondary sources for reconstructing the past such as photos. *Source:* Excerpted from National Task Force for Social Studies. (Draft 2008). *Expectations of Excellence: Curriculum Studies for Social Studies.* Waldarf, MD: National Council for the Social Studies, p. 33.

KEY IDEA: By studying and analyzing historical photographs, we can understand our community better.

INSTRUCTIONAL OBJECTIVE: Students will study and analyze historical photographs and learn about their nearby community.

SET: Gather several historical photos about the nearby community in which students live. These photos can be from one or more time periods. Inform students that the photos they will be looking at are from their community. Show students one of these photos and ask them the following questions: What activities, objects, people, or animals does this photo show? About how old is this photo? What would be a good title for this photo? What is one thing we can learn from this photo?

INSTRUCTION: Show a second photo to the class to study and analyze together. Begin by having students make a 2-minute sketch of the photo on paper. Next, make lists according to the activities, objects, people, or animals that are shown in the photo. These lists are primarily descriptive and can be made next to the 2-minute sketch that students have drawn. Then have students answer the following questions on their paper: What can we learn from this photo about our community? What question does this photo make me think of? Where could I find an answer to the question that I have about this photo?

REFLECTION/ASSESSMENT: Organize students into groups of three or four. Give each group one historical photo to study and analyze. Have students follow the procedures above including sketch, description, and questions. Each student can record the results on her or his own lesson. As groups finish their photo analysis, have them report their findings to the class as they show the photo.

CLOSURE/ENRICHMENT: Once groups have shared their findings, have students write one thing that

they learned about their community from the activity. Students can write what they learned on their assignment and share it with their neighbor. Then as a class, take all of the photos and place them in the front of the room from oldest to newest. Ordering the photos may involve a bit of guesswork, but it serves as an introduction to the skill of constructing a visual timeline.

SAMPLE LESSON 7.6   Sociology: Comparing Groups

AGE LEVEL: Intermediate

NCSS STANDARD: Theme V. Individual, Groups, and Institutions
    Knowledge—the learner will understand that individuals, groups, and institutions share some common elements but also have unique characteristics. *Source:* Excerpted from National Task Force for Social Studies. (Draft 2008). *Expectations of Excellence: Curriculum Standards for Social Studies.* Waldorf, MD: National Council for the Social Studies, p. 68.

KEY IDEA: The groups that students participate in share similarities and differences.

INSTRUCTIONAL OBJECTIVE: Students will choose two groups that they are part of and compare the characteristics of these groups in a Venn diagram.

SET: Show students pictures of yourself, or someone else, taking part in activities with two different groups. For instance, show a picture of you with your family and another at school with students. Conduct a class discussion about the characteristics of each picture. Also talk about the similarities and differences that the pictures show.

INSTRUCTION: Take and post each picture on the board a few feet apart. Draw a Venn diagram so

that each picture occupies the center of one of the circles. Using information from the introductory class discussion, list features of each picture in the Venn. Renew the class discussion, and have students remind you of the similarities that the pictures show as well as the differences.

REFLECTION/ASSESSMENT: Have students draw their own Venn diagram on paper. This would be a good time to integrate some mathematics and show students how to use a hinged compass for drawing circles. Next, have students brainstorm different groups that they participate in such as family, school, church, soccer, and the like. Have students choose two groups to compare using their Venn diagrams. As students complete the assignment, invite them to share their diagrams with one another and with the class. This sharing time is an opportunity for students to practice the learning objective and to become more familiar with classmates.

CLOSURE/ENRICHMENT: For closure, discuss with students general similarities that groups seem to share. For instance, all groups involve people and special events. As you discuss general rules that apply to groups, write your findings on the board under the title "Things We Know about Groups." Have students record these general rules on their Venn assignments.

SAMPLE LESSON 7.7   Settlement of the United States

AGE LEVEL: Intermediate

NCSS STANDARD: Understands how early European exploration and colonization resulted in cultural and ecological interactions among previously unconnected people.

KEY IDEA: History is affected by a variety of factors, some random.

INSTRUCTIONAL OBJECTIVE: Students will develop alternatives that might have occurred given a changed historical circumstance.

SET: Begin by asking the following question on a Monday morning and telling students that the class will spend about 15 minutes on Friday discussing their responses. Post this question on the board:

> In what ways would the United States be different if it had been settled west to east instead of east to west?

Tell students they may discuss the question with parents or friends during the week.

INSTRUCTION: On Friday, ask students to give their responses to the question, and write their responses on the board. Here are some answers provided by a fifth-grade class to this question:

- "We'd have a different language. Maybe Chinese."
- "People would have come mainly from Asia."
- "The capital city would probably be in the West."
- "We'd have easterns instead of westerns on TV."
- "We probably wouldn't be here."
- "The western areas would probably have a larger population."
- "The high mountains of the West would have been a barrier to early expansion."
- "There might be several countries where Canada and the United States are today."

REFLECTION/ASSESSMENT: Ask students to comment on one another's responses. Which ones seem the most realistic? Why?

CLOSURE: Point out that sometimes the historical events we take for granted are the result of random circumstances, such as the fact that Europeans landed on this continent before (or perhaps with different motives than) Asians.

SAMPLE LESSON 7.8   The Zuni Culture

AGE LEVEL: Intermediate

NCSS STANDARD: Human beings create, learn, and adapt culture.

KEY IDEA: Most cultures are founded on central cultural concepts, which are observed through various behaviors and rituals.

INSTRUCTION OBJECTIVES: Students will identify concepts followed by the Zuni Indians and describe how they observe those concepts.

SET: Have students read the following narrative about the Zuni and study the accompanying picture.

Zuni

In the fine craftsmanship of their turquoise and silver jewelry, in the fabulous designs of their dance masks and in their wealth of ceremonial observances, the Zuni Indians have displayed a creative spirit which has brought great beauty to their desert home.

The Zuni now occupy an area along the Zuni River, south of Gallup, New Mexico. Their old home was a terraced, stone and adobe pueblo on a hill overlooking the river. Originally they lived primarily by agriculture, raising corn, beans, squash and chiles. During the last hundred years, or so, Zuni Indians developed skills

A visual description of Zuni life.

as jewelry-makers—and are now famous for this work.

Zuni use a variety of jewelry designs—deer, butterflies, eagles, dance figures in flat relief and more—in which turquoise stones are individually set or arranged in mosaics. Different colors of stone, shell and coral pieces, delicately elaborate designs and silverware trim often distinguish Zuni creations. Jewelry-making has joined agriculture as their important economic activities.

The artistry expressed by the jewelry-makers was traditionally found in the fertile imagery of the abundant religious dances and ceremonials of the Zuni. Kiva groups, priesthoods, fraternities and medicine societies played important roles in preserving sacred traditions and observances. For it was through proper attention to ritual and prayer that rain, fertility and a joyful life were granted by the gods.

Religious dances were not diversions from a rigorous life, but a highly important unifying element in the Zuni harmony with life. Dances were held often throughout the year, except during the crucial planting and harvest seasons.

Masks became a vital element in these dances. The Zuni were renowned for the skill in construction, imagination in design and the sheer variety of their masks. They were bizarre, often grotesque creations, symbolically painted and, at times, impressively large. The masks used for the Shalako festival after the harvest were as much as three meters (nine feet) high and enclosed the men who danced within them.

The Zuni sun priest set the dates for the dances. In the summer, rain dances were held. In winter, members of the Wood Fraternity—men and women—performed the dances of the sword swallowers. With great dexterity they combined dancing with swallowing red-colored swords made of juniper and decorated with feathers. Their rites lasted for several days. The medicinal powers of the Wood Fraternity were said to have been most useful for treating sore throats.

The climax of the year was the Shalako ceremonial, held in November or December. This was a symbolic representation of the Zuni's creation and migration to their homeland. Dancers completely enveloped in huge, awe-inspiring masks personified the Shalako, divine messengers from the rain gods who devoted prayers to the happiness and fruitful life of the Zuni.

Preparations for this festival went on throughout the year. Participants honored special rites to prepare themselves for their roles. As the great time approached, special houses built for the Shalako were decorated, great amounts of bread baked and meals readied. Finally a masked, nude youth painted black with red, yellow, blue and white spots, representing the fire-god, appeared carrying a burning cedar brand. He was followed by a Council of Gods and finally, by the six Shalako. These figures were striking, enormous masks with eagle-feather headdresses, turquoise faces with rolling, bulging eyes, clacking beaks, and accents of long black hair and ravens' feathers. These marvels were received in their houses where they danced through the night. Truly, the gods seemed to be among their people.

The Zuni have preserved much of their heritage to this day. Many of their dances survive.[*]

INSTRUCTION: Ask students to consider the concepts list that follows. First, have students decide how the Zuni observe the concepts. Second, have students decide how they themselves observe the concepts.

Culture Concepts	How the Zuni Observe Them	How I Observe Them
Food	_____	_____
	_____	_____
Shelter	_____	_____
	_____	_____
Seasons	_____	_____
	_____	_____
Religion	_____	_____
	_____	_____

Festivals   _____   _____

              _____   _____

Ceremonies   _____   _____

              _____   _____

Heritage   _____   _____

              _____   _____

Artistry   _____   _____

CLOSURE: Ask students to read entries from their lists aloud, and write these on the board.

REFLECTION/ASSESSMENT: Have students discuss whether they could identify their own cultural concepts from the lists that the class has developed. What do students in the class have in common with one another? What differences are there among students? Is it possible to draw comparisons between the classroom culture and Zuni culture?

EXTENSION: Have students take their lists home and talk with their parents about the cultural traditions of their own ethnic groups.

*Text and image from Price Stern Sloan, Incorporated. Reprinted by permission.

SAMPLE LESSON 7.9   The Bicycle Path

AGE LEVEL: Intermediate

KEY IDEA: The role of special interests in making public decisions.

INSTRUCTIONAL OBJECTIVE: Students will demonstrate understanding of the role of a particular participant in a public decision-making process.

SET: While showing students the map, explain that the town plans to build a bicycle path from Lower Town to the Little Red Schoolhouse that will enable the children who live in Lower Town to ride their bikes to school. Explain that several obstacles lie along the way from Lower Town to the school, including hills, swamps, roads, and houses, and that various groups are concerned about these obstacles:

- The City Engineers do not want to build the path over hills because doing so raises construction costs.
- The Wildlife League does not want the path built through swamps because it might harm animal habitats.
- The Safety Commission does not want the path to cross streets because that would be dangerous to young bikers.

- The Housing Commission does not want the path built through people's homes and yards.

INSTRUCTION: Divide the class into four groups, and assign each group one of the four roles listed above (City Engineers, Wildlife League, Safety Commission, or Housing Commission). Explain that the object of the game is for each group to draw a path from *any* of the southernmost squares to any of the northernmost squares and to acquire the least number of points. For each square that a path passes through, the group must add 5 points. In addition, the group must add 5 points to its total for each square they enter that causes problems for their particular role: for example, the City Engineers must add 5 points for every square with hills; the Wildlife League must add 5 points for every square with swamps; the Safety Commission must add 5 points for every square with streets; and the Housing Commission must add 5 points for every square with houses. Thus, for the Engineers, a square with hills in it adds 10 points—5 for the square and 5 for the hill. Give students enough time to complete the task.

CLOSURE: Have a spokesperson for each group talk about why the route they have established is more appropriate than the other routes. Allow the groups time to negotiate. Can the groups together establish a route for the path that is least objectionable to the town as a whole? Which group created the path that accumulated the least points?

EXTENSION: Assign the students to investigate a local issue that is controversial. Ask them to try to identify the particular interests of each group involved and how those interests are reflected in the group's position on the issue.

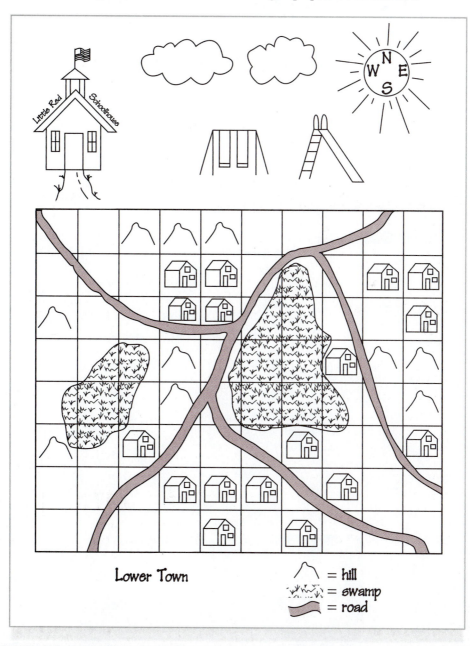

Lower Town

⌒ = hill

꙳ = swamp

▬ = road

Assessing Social Studies Learning

- An Overview of Assessment
- Integrated Assessment Strategies
- Assessing Assessment: Why Is It Important?
- Testing and Assessment
- Portfolio Assessment
- Assessing Your Own Effectiveness
- Standards and Achievement

I guess I lost track of time.
　　—A child's self-assessment of why
　　　she came back late from recess.

Assessment. Tests. Grades. Report cards. Do these terms bring joy to your heart? Is this why you decided to go into teaching? Maybe not.

Well, now that I've cheered you up with these opening remarks, let me just mention that assessment is more complex in social studies than in, say, spelling. I think you already know that. Social studies assessment calls on the imagination to seek out grand strategies that can be integrated with teaching and learning as a seamless whole. When you elevate assessment to this level, it becomes something to anticipate with, yes, a sense of joy, rather than a sense of dread. It becomes part of the "big picture" of teaching and learning.

Most teachers are not particularly enthusiastic about assessment. This is so for a variety of reasons, including the perception and reality that it can dampen spontaneity, affect trust, and take away from the joys of learning. Beyond that, young children often do not understand why they must take tests, and teachers of the young often question why they have to test their students.

Recently, a parent of a fourth-grade student told me that his child, a high achiever, was extremely worried about the standardized tests she would be taking in connection with statewide assessments of student learning. Apparently, the school principal had summoned the fourth-grade classes to the school gym to tell them how to prepare for the tests: Get a good night's sleep, eat a good breakfast, don't worry too much, and do your best. For this child, and probably many others, the principal's well-intentioned advice was a recipe for disaster. The child couldn't get to sleep and had trouble eating breakfast because of her worried state of mind. It's easy for adults to forget that a nine-year-old child does not necessarily see certain purposes of school in the same way adults do. For this child, school was fun, playful, and generally a happy experience. Then, seemingly from nowhere and connected to nothing, came this test announcement.

Such stories should make us ask ourselves, *why* do we assess children's academic progress? Or, to turn the equation around, why *don't* we assess their happiness quotient, their ability to get along with others, or their love of learning? I will not go to great lengths to defend high-stakes standardized testing of children. But I will attempt to explain some reasons why assessment can be a good thing and why my own bias is toward small-scale, classroom-based *formative* assessment. Basically, there are three forms of assessment: assessment of learning, assessment for learning, and assessment as learning. Sounds a little like Lincoln's "of the people, by the people, for the people," doesn't it?

Assessment of learning is perhaps the most widely known of the three. It is typically retrospective, that is, we want to know what a student has learned. Therefore, it assumes learning has already taken place, and now we will test knowledge, skills, and so on. One of the main objectives of assessment of learning is to categorize students. Some students are A students, and some are less than that. The most difficult matter in assessment of learning is to make assessments valid. How valid is a test based on a textbook and given to individual students when so much of the experience is hands on, experiential, and collaborative? We do the best we can.

Assessment for learning is often diagnostic. It involves planning lessons, units, and activities. It also involves providing teacher guidance in helping students learn how to learn. It should provide opportunities for students to improve. A century or so ago, this form of assessment was paramount in the Child Study Movement. In classrooms where children are immersed in activities and interest centers, where a great deal of self-direction is encouraged, teachers are able to carry out systematic observations of students, charting and recording their strengths and weaknesses, getting to know students better through observation and conversation. For example, if an educational goal is that of socialization and civil behavior, a teacher is able to diagnose a student's (or a whole class's) behaviors and to make recommendations for improvement. Assessment for learning is a wonderful tool at the elementary level, and it should become standard practice by teachers.

Assessment as learning implies seamless connections among teaching, learning, and assessment. They all become one when assessment as learning is at its best. Perhaps it is useful to give you an example from a research study conducted by my doctoral student, Laurynn Evans. Students in the experimental groups were asked to write down an "I learned" statement at the end of each class session during a month-long unit. In time, their statements became so insightful that the teacher would use them to begin class the next day. This is student empowerment. The kids were helping the teachers create connections from one day to the next with their insights. The teachers began to report that this was changing the social structure of the class. Students were more engaged and were far more willing to volunteer to have their work shared with others than were students in comparison classes. Interestingly, the students who practiced assessment as learning also scored significantly higher on the unit post test than did their comparison group counterparts (Evans, 2009).

We have a basic human need to know how we are doing. Most of us want to make progress in life, and most of us know that assessment, at its most meaningful, is really just a way of showing how we're doing so that we can improve. I think there is a discussion in this—one between you and your students. It could bear real fruit if it is an open, honest discussion of feelings and dreams and even fears.

It is easy to forget that social studies is about more than history and geography and civics. It is about the very life of the classroom. In that sense, if you were to assess yourself as a social studies teacher, you might make one of the self-test questions: "Have I talked with the kids about why assessment is necessary?"

Meaningful assessment is an integral part of effective planning and teaching. At its best, assessment is ongoing and reflective, meant to help make improvements along the way. Still, a problem exists at the level of childhood education because it is never easy to determine what young children know using either traditional or innovative measures. We know that their thinking abilities typically transcend their abilities to read and write. I firmly believe that the students in your class are learning a lot. The issue is how to capture it.

This chapter addresses that very issue. The major focus is authentic, integrated assessment strategies. In that sense, many of the techniques I will propose are themselves activities for teachers and students in the spirit of teaching, learning, and assessment as seamless whole.

An Overview of Assessment

Assessment is best perceived as a natural and logical part of the teaching/learning process. Try not to think of it as something set apart or as a kind of outside event. Perceptions of assessment as integrated into the routine of school life are not easily held, given the experiences we've all had with tests through the years. Let's consider three key questions about assessment: Why should we assess? What should we assess? How should we assess?

Why Should We Assess?

My guess is that assessment is not one of the leading reasons you got into teaching. Most of the teachers I know and have known over the years, myself included, don't particularly enjoy assigning grades, even though they have come to accept that part of the job as a necessary part of school life. Assessment certainly has its critics—probably more than any other aspect of teaching. Common complaints include such comments as "It takes the joy our of teaching" and "It hurt me to give out the report card to that child." Many people feel that nothing takes the joy out of learning more than a test.

There is some merit to that sentiment, especially where young children are concerned. Children are often not testwise and may not understand school assessment purposes in general. They tend to see the world as a whole, and only gradually do they begin to perceive that there are activities and there are tests. As this unfortunate dualism becomes a reality, some children, often high achievers, fall prey to learning not for its own sake but for getting good grades. Others find assessment traumatic, worrisome, or lacking in meaning.

Of course, there is another side to this argument. I could tell you stories about the look of joy on the face of a child who has done something very hard, very well. There are compelling reasons for assessing student progress. First of all, students need to know how they are doing. Their parents need and want to know, as well. And you need to know to what extent your students are learning important ideas, skills, and content. Your own concerns will range from the professional to the personal as you consider your students' progress. Finally, there is the role of assessment as a means of getting students to take learning seriously, to realize that accountability is a fact of life.

What Should We Assess?

The question of what to assess is not as simple as it may seem at first glance. You can't assess everything. This argues for a strategic use of assessment. In social studies, we can start with the standards as our long-term goal structure. From there, we should consider the age level and the specific course of study at a particular grade. Within that structure lie the various units you will teach during the year. And finally, we come to the day-to-day experiences. So, when we arrive at the place where you and your students are involved concretely in reading, discussing, writing, constructing, and otherwise performing in some meaningful manner, we can reflect on the idea that goals, plans, activities, and assessment make up our social studies curriculum. Furthermore, we can reflect on the idea that each of these separate pieces must be joined together in ways that make sense. Figure 8.1 shows the flow among these pieces.

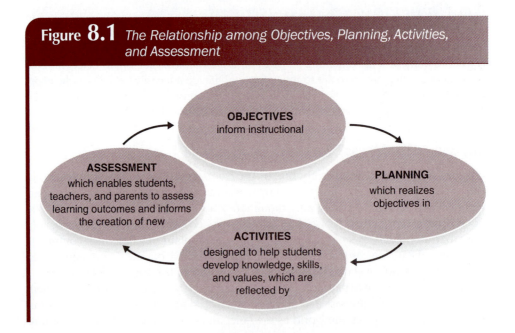

Figure 8.1 *The Relationship among Objectives, Planning, Activities, and Assessment*

OBJECTIVES inform instructional

PLANNING which realizes objectives in

ACTIVITIES designed to help students develop knowledge, skills, and values, which are reflected by

ASSESSMENT which enables students, teachers, and parents to assess learning outcomes and informs the creation of new

How Should We Assess?

Let's say, for example, that one of your unit teaching objectives is "students will develop a sense of chronology or time order." This objective fits NCSS Standard II, "Time, Continuity, and Change" (see Chapter 3). Obviously, your plans will call for activities that give your students opportunities to develop their sense of time. Such activities might include having students make timelines of their lives to date with speculation about their lives into the future or family trees showing parents, grandparents, and other relatives. Another activity might include a whole-class project on the history of the community and how local history fits into state, national, and world history. Assessments might include writing or otherwise explaining how time lines or family trees work. The point is that goals, objectives, plans, activities, and assessments should be aligned.

So, when you think of how you should assess, think of how you should teach, how your students should learn, and keep the assessment procedures in line with experiences. A balanced curriculum will contain a balance of experience, including reading, writing, listening, speaking, constructing, inquiring, and performing. In addition, keep in mind that some experiences are individualistic and some are collaborative. A balanced curriculum leads naturally to balanced assessment.

See what you think of the teacher's use of assessment in the following scenario.

in the classroom   Assessing a Lesson

Mr. Hayward, a fourth-grade teacher, brought a large number of Brazilian artifacts to class one day. He placed them on a display table in a corner of the room. The students eagerly examined the artifacts and asked their teacher many questions. He said he would rather let them guess about the artifacts for a while. On the next day, Mr. Hayward gave two artifacts each to small groups of four and asked the groups to consider the following questions: (1) How are the two artifacts alike and different? (2) Who might use them? (3) What uses might they have? (4) How many uses can you suggest for them? On the third day, he told the name and use of each artifact and explained that the items were from Brazil. He told the class that they would be involved in a unit on Brazil and he just wanted them to be inquirers. He said he was pleased with their guesses and their active involvement.

To evaluate the outcome of this experience, Mr. Hayward gave the class a test in which he selected 20 of the artifacts, numbered them, and asked the students to write the name and use of each artifact beside its number on a sheet of paper.

How fair do you think this test was to the learners? What might have been a fairer evaluation?

In my opinion, Mr. Hayward was not totally fair because he tested only for the third day's experience. Before that, he had the students hypothesizing, probing relationships, communicating in groups, and making inferences. After they engaged in these high-level activities, he tested the students only on their ability to recall. If you feel the evaluation was fair, as Mr. Hayward obviously did, I think you made a very common error: You defended an assessment strategy that is attractive because the test is easily developed, easily scored, and provides an objective progress check. Unfortunately, the students deserved more in this case.

This scenario illustrates the use of an essentially invalid test. For an assessment to be *valid,* it must be a representative measure of the material that was taught. Mr. Hayward had three days of instruction, but his test measured only the learning that took place during a portion of that time. He used an inquiry-teaching strategy but not an inquiry-testing strategy.

What could Mr. Hayward have done to make his assessment strategy valid? He overlooked a simple procedure, which, if followed, helps ensure that assessments provide accurate reflections of potential learning outcomes. Objectives, activities, and assessment must parallel one another. Take a moment to study Figure 8.1.

For a portion of the inquiry activity, Mr. Hayward might have stated the following objective: "Students will be able to state ways in which two artifacts are alike and different." The statement of such an objective, clearly present in the activity in which the students were involved, would have helped focus the assessment. Obviously, another objective was the following: "Students will be able to list the name and use of each artifact." As we saw, the teacher taught toward that objective and tested for it.

Following are a sample objective, some activities, and a test item that Mr. Hayward might have used to assess learning outcomes other than recall of information:

- *Objective.* Students will be able to state ways in which two artifacts are alike and different.
- *Activities.* Students discuss and record similarities and differences between two artifacts in small groups. Student groups share their analyses with the class. The teacher helps students consider the physical properties, form, and potential uses of artifacts.
- *Sample assessment.* The teacher gives groups two new artifacts and asks them to record differences and similarities.

You may be wondering about the propriety of such a group assessment procedure. Remember that the students learned in groups. They should therefore be given some opportunity to illustrate how effective that strategy was. This is not to say that all group activities need to be tested in groups. However, some provision should be made for such a procedure if for no other reason than students should sense that you have confidence in group activities as a way to learn effectively. Do the exercise in Figure 8.2 to see how you feel about assessment of social studies learning.

Integrated Assessment Strategies

For the teacher of elementary social studies, authentic, integrated assessment strategies are completely necessary. They accomplish several important teaching/learning goals at once: They enable you to get a clearer picture of how well you are teaching. They provide both you and your students with a far clearer idea of how well you and they are learning. They promote a reflective atmosphere in which you and the students begin to become more consciously aware of what is being learned and how meaningful it is. (This is known as *metacognition,* or thinking about thinking.) And they help provide a classroom experience that is itself more integrated and seamless.

Figure **8.2** *An Assessment Survey*

Let's consider two questions: (1) Should children's learning in social studies be evaluated? and (2) Why or why not? To answer the first question, place a check at the point on the continuum that describes your feelings.

Elementary students should *never* be assessed in social studies. They should just enjoy it and learn what they will. Tests are evil.

Low-key assessment is okay but not formal tests.

Some form of assessment is necessary—not always in the form of tests. A wide variety of measures should be used.

Formal tests are necessary, but other measures can be used to supplement assessment by tests.

Elementary students *must* be assessed by formal tests, better grades are necessary in order to assess student progress, and only formal assessment procedures can give reliable grades.

I can tell you this: If you use these strategies faithfully, two things of great and lasting significance will happen. First of all, student achievement will increase. You will definitely see improvement on standardized tests. Second, the social/moral fabric of life in your classroom will improve. Your classroom will be a better place for you and your students, and citizenship will be something real, not just an academic study.

Writing about Learning

"I LEARNED" STATEMENTS   This is a simple and durable strategy that you should use often. At the end of an activity or lesson, ask your students to write down (or tell you if they are too young) something they learned. When you have your students write down what they learned and turn in their papers, you have given each of them the opportunity to think about the experience and to reflect on it. You will also notice that the aggregate of what is turned in is an excellent measure of what your students thought was significant. Don't be disappointed if the first time you try this, many students don't write or say anything. Why should they? No one has ever asked them such a question. They will get the idea in time. Use "I learned" statements a couple of times a week—in other words, often enough to keep the students thinking that you just might ask them following any given experience.

KEY IDEA IDENTIFICATION   At the close of a lesson or activity, ask your students to explain—preferably in writing, if they can—what they think was the key idea. Researcher John Goodlad (1984) has faulted teachers for failing to teach ideas. That can't happen if you teach your lessons with a key idea in mind and you ask your students to identify it. Don't worry if they identify something other than what you were looking for or if different students identify different key ideas. That becomes the essence of a good discussion. By using this strategy from time to time, you will raise your own level of consciousness about the importance of ideas in learning while you raise your students' consciousness.

THE WEEK IN REVIEW   This is a small-group assessment strategy best done on every Friday afternoon. Place students in groups of two or three, and challenge them to look back over the week with the idea of identifying some of the most important things the class did and learned. Each group should submit a written statement or verbally explain their findings. When the students know that they will always reflect back on the week, they begin to think about what they are doing and learning, especially if you remind them that on Friday, they will do the Week in Review. It makes a great way for you to begin on Monday. You start the week by saying, "Well, here were the big stories from last week. Let's see what happens this week."

SEARCH FOR MEANING   One of the most important assessment strategies you can utilize is to search for meaning in learning. From time to time, you need to ask your students to write (or tell) you what they are learning that is meaningful to them. This takes trust on your part and theirs, but I guarantee you that it is rewarding.

Ideally, all learning should be meaningful, but we know that is not always the case. However, as a search for meaning becomes a part of the goal structure for you and your students, meaning will begin to develop if for no other reason than that you and they are looking for it.

CLEAR AND UNCLEAR WINDOWS   Have you ever tried to look through a window that was dusty, dirty, or foggy? You can't see much, can you? Or have you ever noticed a child whose glasses are so smudged that you wonder how he or she can see anything?

Sometimes, social studies can be that way for some students. Why not ask your students now and then how clear things are? Give them an opportunity to show you by putting things that they understand in a clear window and things that are hard for them in an unclear window. Here is an example of Sarah's windows:

Sarah

Clear Window	Unclear Window
I loved doing the rol play, It was fun to be a astonott.	I hav trubbel reading the book. It was to hard for me.

RECORD KEEPING   Record keeping uses Skinnerian reinforcement techniques and, at the same time, turns a measure of responsibility over to the student. In order to carry out accurate individualized record keeping, your students will need to record the assignments they have completed, the scores or grades they received on each assignment, the pages they have read, the films they have seen, the books they have read, the projects they have participated in, the maps they have made, and so forth.

It sounds complicated, doesn't it? It's not, though, if you have your students record each item as soon as they complete it or as soon as you return it to them. I would also encourage you to have your students make a brief notation beside each entry. The notation should include the main idea or most important point of the activity. Here is an example:

Noah M.
Social Studies Record

Date	Assignment	Grade	Note
Mon. 6th	Film on traffic safety		Don't just depend on cars to stop for you.
Tue. 7th	Worksheet on traffic safety	100%	Rights and responsibilities of pedestrians
Wed. 8th	Make map of crosswalks by Oak Point School	A	My map shows what the crosswalks look like, only flat.

I guess every teacher wants to teach his or her students ways of becoming more responsible. Record keeping is a tangible way to do that. It is also a kind of metacognitive strategy, because it enables students to increase their awareness of the work being done in social studies.

SELF-REPORTING   An obvious but often overlooked assessment strategy is to have students assess their own progress. It's their work, after all. Why not let them help to assess it? Self-reporting gives students an opportunity to be analytical about their own progress. A good self-report should deal with both the strengths and weaknesses of progress as viewed by the student.

Because self-analysis is rarely encouraged in school settings, you will have to be patient at first. In fact, some students may even consider self-reporting inappropriate. But what, after all, is the purpose of learning if it is not to encourage independence on the part of the learner? I think that in time, you will be gratified with the ability students develop in this area. Following is an example of a self-report turned in by a fourth-grade student:

February 10
Mark Goldberg

I liked learning about the feudal economy. I'm glad we don't have it anymore though. The best thing I did was when Jason, Maria, and me made the feudal manor out of cardboard. I really did a lot of work and so did everyone. We showed where the lord of the manor lived and where the serfs were. The poor serfs loved holidays. So do I! Do you know where we got most of our information? We got it out of a book called *Life in Medieval Times*. Part of it was hard to understand.

QUESTION AUTHORING   This seldom-used strategy can provide brilliant insights to your students' sense of what is important and just how curious they have become about learning. Simply ask the children to write down (do this orally with young children) any questions they would like to ask about the content and experience in general.

This activity provides you with a context for telling the class about higher-level questions. In time, if you are patient, you will see a tremendous improvement in the nature of the children's questions. Also, many of the questions they raise will help you with your teaching because the children are, in effect, acting as diagnosticians for you.

JOURNAL ENTRIES   One of the greatest improvements in teaching and learning in recent years has been the idea of student journals. Although journals serve a variety of purposes, they are quite useful as an assessment tool. Encourage students to make entries about the subject matter they are studying, including their feelings about it as well as their thoughts and ideas. Their entries will provide them with an ongoing record of their perceptions of social studies. You should collect student journals periodically and make brief comments of encouragement and support.

SPOT-CHECK INVENTORIES   The spot-check inventory is a simple strategy that allows you to obtain from your students a brief synthesis about what they think they have learned during a particular amount of time. To do a spot-check inventory, merely stop whatever is going on at a given time (class discussion, group work) and ask each student to list several things that he or she has learned during the activity. Be patient and allow students to become better at this metacognitive strategy over time.

Younger children will simply have to tell you what they have learned as you list their thoughts on the board. Older children can write down their own lists to share with the class. A useful alternative to the listing approach is to have students write a paragraph or essay telling what they have learned. The example in Figure 8.3 was written by a Scottish girl, Diane, age 9, after a discussion about life in America.

THANK-YOU   There is a powerful idea known as *serial reciprocity*. Simply put, it means that if someone does something kind, helpful, or thoughtful for you, you need to pass it along. This is different from merely giving back directly to the person who helped you. It goes around and comes around.

This is an assessment technique that will in time make your classroom a truly civil place to be. It is based on the notion that in a classroom, everyone is a teacher in one way or another. We can all help each other. Make it part of the routine to encourage students to write or draw thank-you notes and notes of appreciation to each other. You might be surprised how many come your way!

Talking about Learning

PYRAMID DISCUSSIONS   Have you ever thought of class discussion as assessments? Probably not, if for no other reason than that most class discussions involve only the teacher and a handful of more talkative students. But what if you wanted everyone to discuss and reflect? Here's how you can do it.

Figure 8.3 *A Scottish Child's Essay on Her Knowledge of America*

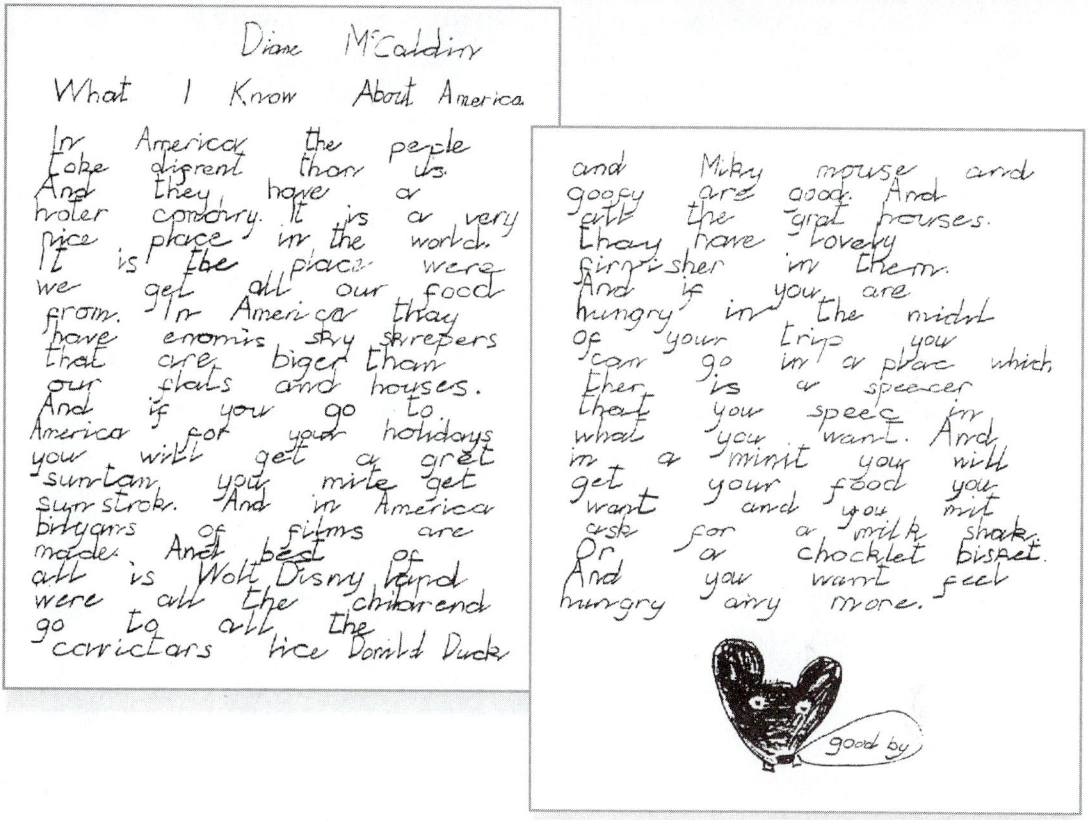

Diane McCaldin

What I Know About America

In America the peple are diffrent than us. And they have a holer condtry. It is a very nice place in the world. It is the place were we get all our food from. In America thay have enomis sky skrepers that are biger than our flats and houses. And if you go to America for your holidays your will get a grat suntan, you mite get sun strok. And in America biliyons of films are made. And best of all is Walt Disny land were all the chilidrend go to all the carictars like Donld Duck

and Miky mouse and goofy are good. And all the grat houses. Thay have lovely firnisher in them. And if you are hungry in the midst of your trip you can go in a place which ther is a speecer that you spee in what you want. And in a minit you will get your food you want and you mit ask for a milk shak. Or a chocklet bispet. And you want feel hungry any more.

good by

Begin by asking or writing on the board one or two important questions related to what your students should be learning. Place students in groups of two and have them discuss the questions. When the groups of two have had a chance to discuss, place students in groups of four and have them discuss the same questions. Groups of eight come next, discussing the same question. Then go to the whole class.

This accomplishes two things. First of all, everyone has a chance to talk. Second, if the questions are important, then the students should have the chance to consider and reconsider them. By the time you reach whole-class discussion, everyone will have had an opportunity to think through something important.

I CAN TEACH   We've all heard the expression "The best way to learn something is to teach it." There is some profound wisdom in the saying, for teaching involves expression and performance, two commodities often sadly lacking in school learning. So, the assignment is for the students to teach an idea, skill, or some content they have learned in social studies to someone else. Typically, you would ask your students to teach one

CURRENT EVENTS
Focus on Assessing Critical-Thinking Skills

One easy way to evaluate both literacy and critical-thinking skills is to ask students to give occasional oral reports on current events. Emphasizing themes in the news encourages students to do in-depth investigating and reporting and discourages them from reporting on the many sensational and bizarre events that are reported. A focus on a given theme also creates a conceptual framework for students, and many themes create an exciting potential for learning.

You may want to post a "Theme of the Week" on the bulletin board and ask students to focus on it as they report the news. Some themes are so powerful that you will find yourself returning to them several times during the school year. Here are some suggested themes:

- *Energy:* conservation, production, supply and demand, new developments, controversial issues
- *Air and/or Water Issues:* supplies, sources, pollution, clean-up efforts, exhaust, run-off, conservation
- *Helping People:* volunteer efforts, clubs, organizations, heroes, service people, advice columns, leaders.
- *Transportation:* inventions, energy-saving ideas, mass transit, modes of travel, space flight, travel by water, air, and land
- *Climate and Weather:* droughts, disasters, tourism, ideal places, clothing, shelter

Here are some websites that students may want to explore:

> www.ecologyactioncenter.org
> www.eia.doe.gov/kids
> www.mhwest.com/NTCSC
> www.kidsnet.au/kidscategories/kids
> www.whyfiles.org/021climate

Doesn't anybody worry about the day when the stream might run dry?

Editorial cartoons furnish students with excellent nonverbal material for the analysis and display of current events topics.

Source: Arthur Poinier, courtesy of *The Detroit News.* Reprinted by permission.

of their parents or a brother or sister. This accomplishes the goal of having your students revisit what you taught them from a different perspective, that of a teacher.

CHOICES AND FEELINGS   At the end of a lesson or at the end of a week, give your students a few minutes to reflect on the choices they were able to make in social studies.

Did they get to decide anything? What was it? How do they feel about how things are going? Let them express their feelings in a conversation with you or a brief note.

CIRCLE MEETINGS   The circle meeting is a very helpful way to gauge the class's feelings and thoughts about how things seem to be going. Everyone's seat, including yours, is arranged in a circle. You begin the meeting by telling about what you have been trying to accomplish and how you think it is going. After your introduction, simply go around the circle and give each child an opportunity either to say something or to pass, if she or he does not wish to talk. Don't be discouraged if, at your first try, the children do not offer up gems of wisdom and insight. They will, in time, if you are patient and supportive.

This technique, which draws on Lev Vygotsky's ideas of social intelligence, is one of the surest ways of getting at the truth of things based on the group's collective perceptions and impressions. Primary school–age children take to this format naturally. By the intermediate grades, some children have become reluctant to speak up in a group setting. Your job is to overcome that unfortunate phenomenon.

Circle meetings take anywhere from 10 minutes to an hour, depending on how deeply the class gets into the matters at hand. Once a week is probably a good target for circle meetings.

THINKING ALOUD   The simple technique of thinking aloud is one of the best ways to prevent the "in one ear and out the other" syndrome that seems to haunt children's learning of social studies (not to mention other subjects!). This should be a 5- to 10-minute activity in which you ask students to talk and listen with partners about what they are learning. Sometimes you may want to place a question or two on the board for the pairs to discuss. However, if you leave the discussion open, you will find that you get a wider range of student input. It is useful to have a whole-class discussion following the thinking-aloud session, in which students can volunteer aspects of their talks together.

Illustrating Learning

LEARNING ILLUSTRATED   At least once a week, you should ask your students to draw pictures or make maps of interesting or important things that they have learned recently in social studies. Their drawings and maps make excellent displays, and they should find their way into the students' portfolios in time. It is important to remember that some children who may not be adept verbally are actually learning a lot, and this provides one way for them to show it.

DISPLAYS   It has been noted that doing schoolwork is like preparing for an athletic event or a drama production that never happens. You just *prepare.* Imagine spending time rehearsing a play and never putting it on. Doesn't that strike you as strange? But this is what happens with schoolwork all the time. Perhaps this is one reason it seems unreal to some children.

You might be surprised at the number of nursing homes, hospitals, clinics, restaurants, shopping malls, stores, and so on that would welcome the chance to display your students' work. Parents and children alike are proud when they see student work put on public display. By the way, it is very good public relations for the school.

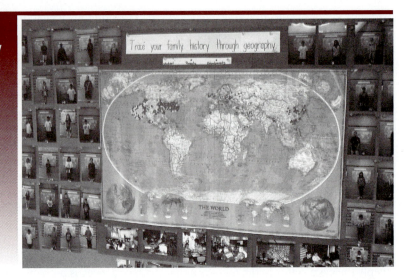

Students combine historical and geographical inquiry as they participate in a project tracing the origins of their ancestors.

Keys to Getting Parents Involved

Parents send their children to you, hoping that you will do a good job of teaching them. In most cases, they are extremely interested in how their children are doing. Report cards give parents a sense of a child's progress, but only a general sense. Here are several strategies you can use to inform parents of the progress their children are making in social studies:

- *Send a note home.* If someone in your class did a nice job on an assignment, worked effectively in a group, or whatever, send a brief note home that explains to the parents what happened.
- *Make a phone call.* You and your students' parents are busy people. But a one-minute phone call in the evening for the purpose of telling a child's parent that he or she is doing very well (it helps to be specific) in social studies doesn't take very much of anyone's time, and it will be appreciated.

- *Have a conference.* In most schools, conferences are held once or twice a year for the purpose of reporting pupil progress. It is important to be prepared for such an important meeting. First, don't sit behind your desk at a conference; it is too threatening and official. Rather, sit at a table with the parent. Try to be positive; remember, you are discussing the parent's own child. If you do have some negative comments, be sure that they are specific and that they are not a personal attack against the child. Balance any negative comment with something positive. Perhaps the most important thing at a conference is to have numerous examples of the child's work. Parents are impressed with maps, artwork, and so forth. Above all, express genuine interest in the child. That won't be hard, because you really do care.

Assessing Assessment: Why Is It Important?

Perhaps at this point you are thinking something like, "OK, Arthur, those may be good metacognitive strategies for assessing student learning, but where on earth am I supposed to find the time for them?" I have an answer for you. The saying "Less is more" is really quite profound. As applied to education, it has been attributed to Theodore Sizer, a leader in the school restructuring movement. But the idea is actually rather an old one, dating back at least to Jean-Jacques Rousseau, who wrote in the preface to his book *Emile,* "Teachers, teach less and teach well." A so-called coverage mentality is self-defeating. The more you try to cover, the less your students will learn and retain. The strategies I have presented here are time consuming, but they have several advantages.

1. *They will facilitate language development.* This is one of the most important goals of teaching. As Piaget, Vygotsky, and others have pointed out, children need to reflect and talk about what they are learning. Speech and thought co-develop; they are not separate functions. So, by giving children time to talk about, draw about, and reflect in general on what they are learning, you actually create a more efficient system.
2. *They build opportunities for citizenship.* This is one of the major goals of social studies. The participating citizen is basic to our democratic way of life. The kinds of activities and conversations you focus on during assessment of learning represent fundamental practice in speaking one's mind and in publicly expressing oneself.
3. *If you are patient, you will begin to see a group intelligence start to emerge.* This is something that simply cannot happen when people are denied the opportunity to reflect on and talk about ideas publicly. So, yes, it does take time. Anything worthwhile takes time.

My advice is to take these strategies seriously and integrate them into your teaching. It will mean less talking time for you and more for the children, but since their growth and development is at stake, it is well worth it.

Testing and Assessment

The assessment procedures described to this point are essentially unobtrusive; that is, they are designed to be integrated into the flow of instructional activities. The idea is to create a seamless whole. Tests, on the other hand, are typically perceived by students as disconnected events that they must prepare for and that often cause nervous discomfort.

Formal tests are a fact of classroom life, but you should use them sparingly and strategically. Make a sincere effort to help your students understand that the purpose of such testing is to identify where they still need instruction—not to embarrass them! This is not easy to do. Some educators feel that testing causes problems of trust between students and teachers. That may be somewhat extreme, but the point is valid. Children are natural learners. They like to explore, create, talk, and do projects. They do not always understand the adult agenda that mandates accountability measures that they would not choose to participate in: namely, formal tests.

Part of your task as a social studies teacher is to help children understand the role that accountability plays in their learning. Tests help us, as teachers, know how our students are doing and what progress they are making, as well as what they are not learning and what needs to be revisited. More and more, tests are mandated by state and federal law. But when you move from authentic, integrated assessment into the realm of formal tests, proceed with caution.

Let me tell you a story. Recently, a fourth-grade teacher told me that her son had come home from school after a long day of taking statewide standardized tests. She asked how things had gone. She could tell her son was upset. He told her that he hadn't had time to finish the test. Sympathetic, she reassured him that we often can't complete tests because the questions are difficult. He said no, it wasn't that the questions were hard. He knew the answers. What had taken time was filling in all the circles. He explained, "The teacher told us we had to fill in each circle for a right answer with our pencil, and we couldn't go outside the lines." This boy had spent a lot of time filling in each circle completely and then carefully erasing all the places where his pencil had strayed outside the line. That was why he didn't finish the test.

It's easy for adults to forget that children are not testwise. It's also easy to forget how literally they take what we say. And it's easy to forget how much children worry over getting things right.

I'm not arguing that children should not be tested, although I do think the current fad for standardized testing is not particularly helpful to learning in many cases. (Do you ever wonder how children managed to grow up into contributing, thoughtful, responsible adults in the days before standardized testing existed? It's a pretty good bet that George Washington and Abraham Lincoln never took a multiple-choice test in their lives. Neither did Jane Austen or Thomas Edison.)

We live in an era of testing, and that is a reality you must face. But you can do everything in your power to make testing more humane and children less anxious. Review the most important foundations of assessment in the Keys to Humane Assessment.

Keys to Humane Assessment

- *A teacher's first job is to care.* You are there because you care about children. You want the best for them. Never lose sight of the fact that great teachers make it their central concern to care for their students, to make them whole.
- *Social studies is about human beings.* Always make it a point to treat the human beings in your classroom with respect, care, and support.
- *Students need to understand the purpose of tests.* When you do formal testing of your students, explain that the purpose is not to punish them but to help them and their parents get a better idea of what is going on in the classroom. You want to identify what

children have learned and plan for future learning.

- *Students need to be prepared.* Be as certain as you can that the children in your classroom are prepared to take a test—not only by reviewing the content that will be covered but also by explaining test procedures and strategies. Maintain a firm, friendly classroom atmosphere, one where learning is prized. Help children understand exactly what is expected of them when they do take tests.

- *The classroom needs to be a safe place.* Help your students understand that your classroom is a place where they can relax, be comfortable, and feel free to share concerns. If they are worried about tests, make sure they know they can express that worry.

- *Model the importance of learning.* Be certain that each lesson and each activity contains important knowledge, skills, and values. And take the time to reflect on important concepts with your students. You might be surprised how well prepared they are for formal tests as a result. The prepared mind always has the advantage!

Essay Tests: Extended-Response Questions

In social studies assessment, an *extended-response question* requires the student to write an answer that explains his or her position, reasoning, and conclusions. A good extended response contains something more than the correct answer. In fact, students are sometimes given credit for their reasoning, even if they have certain facts wrong. Often, extended-response answers include interpretations of data, identifications of relationships, analyses of problems, and so on. The one thing that all extended responses have in common is that they require the student to supply information, rather than merely pick an alternative, as with a true-false or multiple-choice question.

You should have at least two purposes in asking extended-response questions: (1) You want to gain some idea of how much each student knows, and (2) you want to help students learn to present their ideas in a logical, coherent manner. To accomplish these two goals, extended-response questions should have these qualities:

1. *Be focused on main ideas.* Because they require providing developed answers to a few global questions, rather than a wide range of specific knowledge, extended-response questions should always review the main ideas you have covered in instruction. When you prepare for a unit, identify the main ideas you wish students to learn; then write extended-response test questions that parallel those ideas. Consider these examples of good and bad test questions:

   Poor: What caused the fight between Peter and James? (This question seeks recall of a specific event.)

   Better: Peter and James fought over who would take Bob's paper route. List some reasons such conflicts happen. Explain how you think this conflict might have been avoided. (This question seeks students' understanding of the concept of *conflict.*)

2. *Be designed to elicit higher-level thinking.* Lower thought levels, such as recall, are more easily tested by objective tests. Again, consider some examples:

Poor: Why were Iroquois longhouses made of wood? (This question seeks lower-level information that could readily be incorporated into a higher-level question.)

Better: Do you think an Iroquois longhouse is more like an apartment building or a one-family house in our culture? Why? (This question gives students an opportunity to choose between alternative answers and seeks criteria in defense of the answer they select.)

3. *Be written in clear, unambiguous language.* Children need to know what is expected of them. One way to ensure that your questions will be reasonably clear is to list the criteria you will use in judging student responses. Compare the following:

Poor: Discuss the causes of the American Revolution. (This question invites rambling answers and does not specifically seek alternative perspectives on the issue.)

Better: (a) List two reasons the American colonists felt they should break away from England. Do you think these were good reasons? Why or why not? (b) List two reasons the English wanted to keep the American colonies. Do you think these were good reasons? Why or why not? (The questions are broken down so specific criteria can be applied. The questions guide students toward developing reasons that reflect alternative perspectives.)

Objective Tests: Selected-Response Questions

Two types of items for objective tests are (1) true false, and (2) multiple choice. These types of items have certain common characteristics. For instance, tests containing such items are easily scored. Also, a relatively high number of questions can be included on a test, thus ensuring adequate representation of topics and ideas. Elementary students who lack the capability to develop an essay that conveys their true understandings of a topic are often able to demonstrate their understanding by discriminating among alternative answers. Also, objective tests are potentially fairer than essay tests, in that they prevent teachers from favoring student responses on the basis of penmanship, personality, and other essentially irrelevant variables.

Perhaps the greatest potential shortcoming of objective tests involves the tendency teachers have to develop questions that seek answers based only on recall or explanation. This is certainly a difficult obstacle to overcome, and having a certain number of lower-level questions is acceptable on an objective test. However, if you taught higher-level thinking during a social studies unit, you should logically attempt to assess whether your students profited from that instruction.

Let's examine the two types of objective test items and strategies for their effective development.

TRUE FALSE   Following are some suggestions for developing true-false test items for social studies:

1. Statements should be entirely true or entirely false.

Poor: The population of California grew rapidly as settlers moved east during the gold rush of 1849.

Better: The population of California grew as settlers moved west during the gold rush of 1849.

2. Include only one idea or thought in a true-false item.

Poor: Producers offer both goods and services in our economy, and consumers help regulate supply and demand.

Better: Producers offer both goods and services in our economy.

3. Use terms that are clear and unambiguous.

Poor: Trading things is better than buying and selling them.

Better: Trading goods and services is more common than using money in our country.

MULTIPLE CHOICE   Multiple-choice items permit inclusion of a wider range of possible answers to items than do true-false items. Obviously, a person responding to multiple-choice items has less chance of surviving questions on the basis of guesswork. It is important that the test writer attempt to keep all potential responses plausible and ensure that the stems to each item are parallel.

Poor: Persons everywhere have unlimited wants and limited resources. James and Heidi are persons who live in different countries.
   a. James and Heidi have unlimited wants and limited resources.
   b. James lives on the moon and Heidi lives in Switzerland.
   c. Heidi is a young girl.

Better: Persons everywhere have unlimited wants and limited resources. James and Heidi are persons who live in different countries.
   a. James and Heidi have unlimited wants and limited resources.
   b. James and Heidi can have all their material wants fulfilled.
   c. James and Heidi must produce all the goods that they consume.

Portfolio Assessment

One of the most promising ideas to come along in recent years is authentic assessment of learning. The term *authentic assessment* implies that the assessment of student learning should be more reality based. This is not to say that standard paper-and-pencil tests are of no value; rather, it is to say that the more natural forms of assessment are not only less threatening to children but also make more sense to them. Perhaps the best-known approach to authentic assessment is *portfolio assessment.*

The idea of children putting together and keeping track of their own portfolios comes from such professional areas as architecture and art. An architect keeps a folder or portfolio of her or his sketches, designs, plans, drawings, photographs, ideas, and so on. The architect will show the work to interested people who will then decide if they want her or him to do architectural work for them. It is a way of showing what one has accomplished and is capable of doing.

For children in social studies classes, the building of a portfolio makes good sense. A good portfolio will contain a variety of entries that provide a record of authentic student accomplishments. Here are some suggestions for what a portfolio should contain:

- Daily work samples; ordinary papers that are part of the daily routine
- Various data entries—for example, research notes, graphs, and surveys

- Student writing samples, such as essays and stories
- Rough drafts of work in progress
- Finished products, final drafts, and papers turned in for final grading
- Group or cooperative efforts that illustrate the work of several students
- Sample journal entries
- Reflections, such as "I learned" statements
- Tests, exams, and so on
- Major projects or pictures of displays
- Teacher comments and feedback
- Creative thoughts, ideas, insights, and personal-growth reflections

Each child is responsible for building and maintaining her or his own portfolio. Of course, some teacher guidance and support is necessary, especially with younger children, but it is important that children assume as much responsibility as they can for their portfolio. Sometimes we are tempted to include only a child's very best work in a portfolio. But good portfolios demonstrate progress and real learning. These suggestions can help students assemble materials for genuinely useful portfolios:

- A sample that reflects a problem that was difficult for you
- Work that shows where you started to figure it out
- A sample that shows you reached a solution
- A sample that shows you learned something new
- A sample of incomplete work and where it will lead
- Two items of which you are proud
- An example of something that did not work out well

Several interesting moral issues arise in connection with the keeping of portfolios. For example, whose property is the portfolio? Should the school keep it and pass it along to next year's teacher? Is it a private possession to be viewed only by the child and the teacher? Who decides what goes into the portfolio? Remember, a portfolio can, at most, hold a mere sample of the child's work. Should only his or her best work be included? These are important moral issues for you and your students to discuss.

My own position on ownership is that the portfolio belongs to the child and is hers or his to take home at year's end. Does the teacher have the right to examine the portfolio? I think, yes, he or she does, but I hope that the trust level is such in your classroom that the child wants you to see the portfolio. Actually, portfolios are wonderful to share with parents at conference time. As for the last question: What should go into the portfolio? I think it's the child's decision.

Assessing Your Own Effectiveness

When people think of assessment, such things as tests, conferences, and report cards typically come to mind. I've attempted to persuade you in this chapter that there is much more to assessment, even though those things are important. I do want to impress on you how meaningful informal assessment strategies can be. I hope that you will use them often.

Let's now take the process of assessment a step further. How do you, the teacher, know whether you are doing an effective job of teaching your subject? Read the Keys to Being an Effective Assessor, which provide some strategies that will help you probe deeper than most teachers ever go in assessing the effectiveness of their instruction.

These strategies are metacognitive strategies, in that they enable you to think reflectively about your work. I'll pose them as questions for you to answer from time to time. In fact, I guarantee you that if you tape these questions to the top of your desk and read them occasionally, your teaching will improve. Use these questions to shape your thoughts about social studies teaching. Ask them of yourself often. Take them seriously, but have fun with them as well. Relax and enjoy social studies. After all, as I told you earlier, social studies is about people, so it's a pretty exciting subject to teach.

Keys to Being an Effective Assessor

- Am I trying to learn more about the content I'm teaching? What books have I read lately?
- Am I talking with the children about how they feel about the material we are studying? Am I genuinely interested in their thoughts about social studies? Do I seek to know their interests?
- Are my lessons organized appropriately? Are we studying ideas in depth, or are we just covering the material?
- Do I attempt to make connections? Do I relate social studies to other areas of the curriculum? Do I attempt to build continuity from one day to the next?
- Am I teaching key ideas and concepts and not just information? What are some of those ideas?
- What values are the students and I exploring? Do we have conversations that take us into depth? When was the last time the children and I really explored feelings?
- Am I developing lessons and activities that allow for many ways to learn? Are my students involved in making things, talking to each other, and doing cooperative projects, artwork, music, role-play, drama, and so on?
- Am I getting the students involved in making decisions and participating in democratic processes? Does my class ever get involved in the community?
- Am I making real readers out of my students? Do they read biographies, historical fiction, stories about other lands, and so forth?
- Would I want to be in this classroom if I were a child? Is this room an interesting place to come to every day?

Standards and Achievement

Beginning in the 1990s and continuing into the first decade of the twenty-first century, teachers have found themselves in an age of standards and assessment. The No Child Left Behind legislation, passed in 2002, has been called by some No Child Left

Untested. Considerable anxiety has been expressed by child-centered teachers who feel not only that childhood should be a time of exploration, wonder, and joy, not rigorous testing, but also that overtesting encourages "teaching to the test," not true learning.

Can assessment work effectively? The key is to integrate assessment into the everyday classroom routine as organically as possible. I am convinced that using the 20-odd integrated assessment strategies presented in the first part of this chapter will go a long way toward ensuring that children both learn and enjoy learning.

The most powerful means of integrating informal assessment procedures into the routine of classroom life is reflective thinking. Reflective thinking causes both teachers and students to slow down, to go back over what has been taught, and to search for meaning. By returning to an activity or lesson, students revisit it with a fresh perspective. Take, for example, the "I can teach!" strategy, which asks the student to teach to someone else what she or he learned in social studies that day. The student will need to go back over the material learned, organize it, and think about what to emphasize. The child's role, in other words, will change from student to teacher. This approach supports learning through the power of repetition, insight, and altered perspective.

Figure 8.4 shows an assessment activity from the Michigan State Social Studies Assessment for the fifth grade called "Colonial Comparison." Students are presented with pictures of the interior and exterior of a typical colonial house of the 1700s, where various items are labeled with letters of the alphabet, and then are asked to answer multiple-choice questions. Let's assume that you want to use the "I can teach!" strategy with this material. You might ask your students to teach this lesson at home and report back on their experiences the next day. Your students will not only need to know what the items in the picture are and how they are used, but they will also need to be able to explain which answers are correct and why. By adding this task to their learning, you will be well on the way both to ensuring that their learning meets appropriate standards and to preparing your students for the more complex kinds of reasoning that will be required of them by the new generation of assessments.

Most of the new generation of standards and accompanying assessments are based on learning at three levels: knowledge, understanding, and application. See, for example, Figure 8.5, which shows an assessment framework from the National Assessment of Educational Progress (NAEP). The terminology used in these materials may vary from state to state, but you will typically find these three concepts embedded in every set of standards.

Knowledge

Students are always expected to be able to recall information. Assessments for knowledge typically include *what, when,* and *where* questions. The idea behind them is that students must possess a certain amount of basic information—a basic *schema,* as we talked about in earlier chapters—to be able to build on what they already know and comprehend, analyze, synthesize, and apply new social studies concepts.

Figure **8.4** *An Assessment Activity Using Graphics and Multiple Choice Questions*

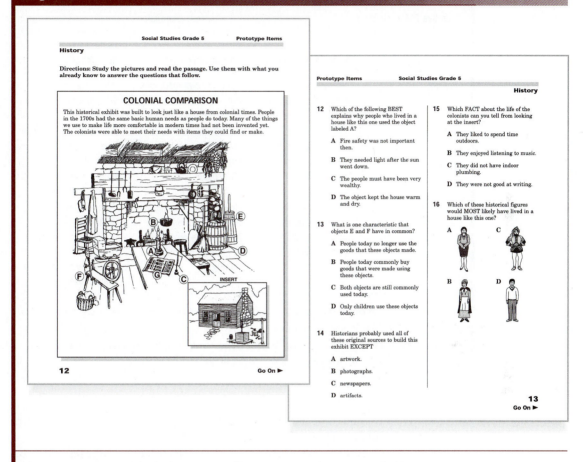

Source: Michigan Department of Education, Michigan Educational Assessment Program (MEAP). Reprinted by permission.

Understanding

Assessment of understanding often calls on students to tell *why,* or to explain the information they possess. It is one thing to know the location of a city (*where*), but it is another to explain the reasons the city might have been built where it is (*why*).

Application

Assessments that measure whether students can apply their knowledge and understanding of a certain topic typically ask them to support their conclusions, reason through an

Figure **8.5** *Elements of the NAEP Geography Assessment Framework*

Cognitive Dimension	Content Dimension		
	Space and Place	**Environment and Society**	**Spatial Dynamics and Connections**
Knowing	Where is the world's largest tropical rain forest?	What mineral resources are often extracted by strip mining?	What factors stimulate human migrations?
Understanding	Why are tropical rain forests located near the equator?	Explain the effects of strip mining and shaft mining on the landscape.	Explain the motivations of modern-day Mexicans and Cubans for immigrating to the United States.
Applying*	Support the conclusion that tropical rain forests promote wide species variation.	How can both economic and environmental interests be reconciled in an area of strip mining?	Compare current settlement and employment patterns of Cuban and Mexican immigrants in the United States.

Note: Example questions are illustrative only and not meant to represent the full array of assessment content.

*Applying = A range of higher-order thinking skills.

Source: National Assessment Governing Board. *Geography Framework for 1994 and 2001 National Assessment of Educational Progress,* (Washington, DC: U.S. Department of Education, 1994, 2001).

issue, make contrasts and comparisons, transfer knowledge from one situation to another, and provide a reasoned analysis of an issue.

Although educators are concerned about too much "teaching to the test," the curriculum can often follow readily from the frameworks created by various standards and assessments. For example, the NAEP's U.S. History Framework (NCES, 1994, 2001) stresses the use of themes as a way of thinking about history. Theme 2 is "The Gathering and Interactions of Peoples, Cultures, and Ideas." An associated question asks:

1. What were the family patterns, religious practices, and artistic traditions of Native Americans, Western Europeans, and West Africans on the eve of Columbus' voyage?

Questions for Theme 3, "Economic and Technological Changes and Their Relations to Society, Ideas, and the Environment," include the following:

1. How did Europeans, Native Americans, and West Africans live and make a living on the eve of Columbus' voyage?
2. How did European inventions and technological developments (particularly in navigation and armament) lead to exploration and early conquest? What individuals and groups contributed to these developments?

Can you begin to imagine the unit objectives that might flow from these questions? How about stimulating classroom activities? Engaging in drama, construction, music, foods, dance, artwork, and so on is the key to blending child-centered experiences with the demands placed on teachers and students by the standards and testing movement.

Summary

Assessment of student learning in some form is necessary. If you are planning social studies experiences that focus on content, concepts, processes, and values, you and your students will certainly want to obtain some measure of their progress. The most effective way to assess student progress is to use a variety of measures.

Perhaps you have strong feelings about formal tests for children. If you feel they are harmful or ineffective, then you will need to depend more heavily on such unobtrusive measures as checklists, observations, and interviews. If you favor the use of formal tests, you will have to justify their use as an effective means of finding out how much learners really know. The balance you achieve among the various assessment measures available to you will be a function of your teaching style and the ages and capabilities of the students you teach.

Explorations

Reflect On . . .

1. Write an "I learned" statement about something you have learned in this chapter. Share it with a classmate.
2. Interview some elementary school students to find out their attitudes toward testing and being tested. What, if anything, do their responses tell you about the relationship between student success and attitude toward tests?

In the Field

3. Collect student social studies work from several classrooms. See what inferences you can make about what is happening in those classrooms.

4. Make a list of 10 different social studies activities. Have the children in a classroom rank order them from most to least favorite.

For Your Portfolio

5. Make a list of some of the things that children might do in social studies that cannot readily be evaluated. Then figure out ways to evaluate the outcomes of those activities. Keep the results in your portfolio.

Continuing the Journey: Suggested Readings

Belgrad, S., Burke, K., & Fogarty, R. (2008). *The Portfolio Connection*. Thousand Oaks, CA: Corwin.

Black, P., & William, D. (1998, 2008). "Inside the Black Box: Raising Standards through Classroom Assessment." *Phi Delta Kappan. www.pdkintl.org/kappan*

This insightful article explores the positive effects of ongoing formative classroom assessment.

Briggs, L. (2009). "Keeping Students Engaged with Classroom Assessments." *Campus Technology.*

Written with college students in mind but useful ideas for elementary and middle school assessment.

Darling-Hammond, L., & McCloskey, L. (2008). "Assessment for Learning around the World" *Phi Delta Kappan,* v. *90* (4), 233–272.

A look at worldwide comparisons and assessment methods used in different countries.

Ellis, A. (2010). *Teaching, Learning, & Assessment Together: the Reflective Classroom, 2nd ed.* Larchmont, NY: Eye on Education, Inc.

Provides 20 research-tested strategies for raising achievement through reflective thinking.

Fisher, D., & Frey, N. (2007). *Checking for Understanding.* Alexandria, VA: Association for Supervision and Curriculum Development.

"How Should We Measure Student Learning? The Many Forms of Assessment." (2009). The

George Lucas Foundation. *www.edutopia.org/comprehensive-assessment-introduction*

Underscores the importance of higher-order thinking skills such as comparison and inference but also traits not typically measured such as teamwork, collaboration, and moral character.

Kingore, B. (2007). *Developing Portfolios for Authentic Assessment.* Thousand Oaks, CA: Corwin.

McMillian, J. H. (2007). *Formative Classroom Assessment.* New York: Teachers College Press.

Moss, D. M., Osborn, T. A., & Kaufman, D. (2008). *Interdisciplinary Education in the Age of Assessment.* New York: Routledge.

Popham, J. (2008). *Transformative Assessment.* Alexandria, VA: Association for Supervision and Curriculum Development.

Wright, R. J., (2007). *Educational Assessment.* Thousand Oaks, CA: Sage.

Websites

Custom design rubrics online. *http://rubistar.4teachers.org/*

This Website thoroughly outlines the basics of classroom assessment practices. *http://fcit.usf.edu/assessment*

Teacher resources and professional development programming across the curriculum. *http://www.learner.org/*

Related NCSS Standards and Principles of Powerful Social Studies

Curriculum Standards

Not much to report other than discussion/examples teachers assessing student work, and students assessing their own work via self-assessment, and so on.

Source: National Task Force for Social Studies. *Expectations of Excellence: Curriculum Standards for Social Studies.* (Silver Spring, MD: National Council for the Social Studies, 2008). The Council's website is www.socialstudies.org

Teacher Standards

Social studies teaching and learning are powerful when they are meaningful. Meaningfulness is stimulated when:

Meaningful learning activities and assessment strategies focus students' attention on the most important ideas embedded in what they are learning (p. 12).

Teaching and Learning Principles

7. Assessment

Social studies teachers should possess the knowledge, capabilities, and dispositions to use formal and informal assessment strategies at the appropriate school levels to evaluate and ensure the continuous intellectual, social, and physical development of learners. They should be able to assess student learning using various assessment formats, including performance assessment, fixed response, open-ended questioning, and portfolio strategies (pp. 51–52).

Source: Excerpted from National Council for the Social Studies. *National Standards for Social Studies Teachers.* (Silver Spring, MD: Author, 2002). The Council's website is www.socialstudies.org

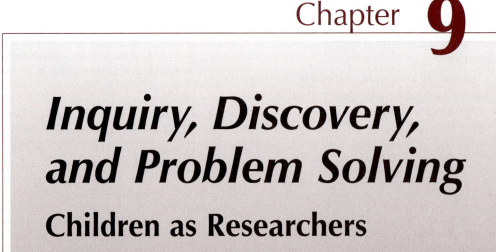

Chapter 9

Inquiry, Discovery, and Problem Solving

Children as Researchers

These children can do wondrous things, if only we would let them.
　　　—Akmed Akbar

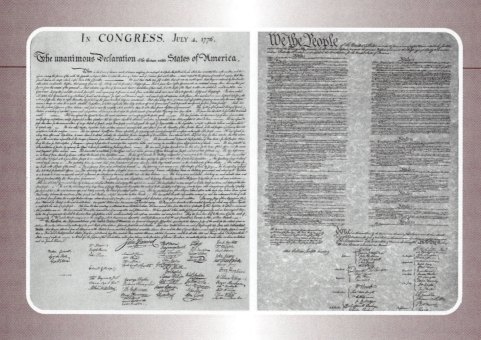

Here are four research questions to ask your students:

1. What was school like for our grandparents? (historical research)
2. What are the most used areas of the playground? (descriptive research)
3. What day of the week do people like best? (survey research)
4. Does the teacher reading to the class after lunch have a good effect? (experimental research)

These investigations can be carried out at any level. The spiral curriculum informs us that the studies can be carried out at deeper levels of sophistication as children grow and develop, and, importantly, as they begin doing research early in their school careers.

Exploration, research, inquiry, and discovery come naturally to children. I challenge you to watch a young child sometime as the little one goes about exploring the environment. Young children especially like to touch things, to pick things up, and to look at them. You may know from experience that they

like to put things in their mouths even when they shouldn't. Children use what psychologist Jerome Bruner calls *intuitive learning;* that is, they use their five senses. Actually, these are investigations. Aristotle called such inquiry *sense realism.* Whatever you call it, such learning invokes the five senses of sight, touch, taste, smell, and hearing.

Sensory learning is the beginning of the inquiry/discovery process. It is hands-on learning. It involves a lot of trial and error. But it is the foundation, the beginning, of social science. Children also ask many questions. Why is the sky blue? Why can't our dog talk? Why do I have to go to bed? These questions represent early attempts to understand and explain as the young child tries to make sense of the world around us. Children are natural historians (Remember when my tooth fell out?), geographers (Are we there yet?), economists (Please buy me some candy.), anthropologists (Why do I have to dress up?), and sociologists (Can everyone come to the party?). Of course, they don't think in terms of any particular scholarly discipline; rather, their inquiry is spontaneous, filled with wonder, and open to the possibilities. Their curiosity is a gift. We should view it that way. We should reward it. We should encourage it. We should make it part of social studies, and the whole day for that matter.

Introduction

A fascinating chapter titled "The Science of Deduction" appears early in Arthur Conan Doyle's book, *A Study in Scarlet.* It describes the methods of crime detection used by the world's greatest detective, Sherlock Holmes. Holmes observes, smells, tastes, listens carefully, takes notes, and gathers bits and pieces of evidence. He sifts through his clues and findings, reflecting on their possible meanings. He spends time thinking aloud with his associate, Dr. Watson, who marvels at Holmes' ingenuity. Using all these strategies of observation, hypothesis, analysis, and reflection, Holmes is able to put the evidence together—almost like someone assembling a jigsaw puzzle without having the picture on the box cover as a guide to the outcome. In time, when a sufficient number of "puzzle pieces" have been assembled, the great detective reaches his conclusion and solves the crime.

The only problem with this description is that the author, Conan Doyle, has confused *deduction* with *induction.* Holmes' inquiry methods are, in fact, inductive. I mentioned puzzle pieces. If you have children assemble a puzzle with the picture on the box cover as a guide to the finished product, then you have a deductive experience on your hands. Contrariwise, if you have them assemble the puzzle *without* the cover, then you have created an inductive experience.

Inquiry and discovery methods and social science research procedures, in general, are based on inductive reasoning. *Induction* is the process whereby information and evidence are pieced together to the point that reasonable conclusions, based on evidence or data, can be reached. These conclusions then lead to inferences about some time, place, event, or phenomenon. We often call this process *inquiry.* Inquiry and induction go together in social science problem solving. For example, if a survey of students indicates that Saturday is the favorite day of the week while our survey of their parents indicates that Friday is the favorite for them, then we would want to know why.

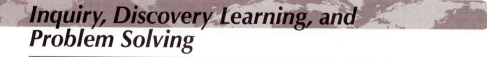

Inquiry, Discovery Learning, and Problem Solving

Are there differences among the terms *inquiry, discovery,* and *problem solving?* Yes, but the differences are subtle.

- *Inquiry* is an investigative process based on the examination of evidence, often using questioning, hypothesis testing, and other means of information or data gathering. Typically, the inquirer reaches a conclusion based on the evidence and then makes inferences. Inquiry is generally the method of choice for the historian, geographer, anthropologist, economist, and sociologist. The conclusions based on inquiry are always accepted tentatively and open to revision when new evidence is offered.

- *Discovery learning* is the search for something. (Of course, some discoveries are completely accidental, but that is another matter.) In history, geography, and the social sciences, discovery implies a search that results in bringing something to light—new information of some kind. Distinctions are sometimes made between "big D" *Discovery* and "small d" *discovery.* For example, the discoveries made by Christopher Columbus in the New World changed the world (for better or worse, depending on one's point of view) and are therefore "big D" Discoveries, while the discovery made by a child that the native people of the Pacific Northwest were quite peaceful is a "small d" discovery, since this knowledge is already available to historians. Regardless of these differences in scope, the process of the discovery is the same: An investigation takes place, and an idea emerges.

- *Problem solving* is the process of attempting to answer a question in some systematic way. Typically, the problem solver tries to resolve some doubt, come to some solution, or satisfy those involved to the best extent possible. Problem solving is closely related to inquiry and discovery in that it attempts to bring to light an answer that enables us to know more, do more, or have greater insight. For school purposes, problems can be thought of as real or contrived. As we will discuss later in this chapter, *real problems* involve the issues that arise naturally in school life and that a thoughtful teacher turns into social studies content. *Contrived problems* are those that are not directly part of students' lives but that are beneficial to their growth and development.

Inquiry, discovery learning, and problem solving are far more alike than they are different. They all involve active learning. They typically (but not always) require some teamwork, they work best when students utilize good information, and they all teach a disciplined way of reasoned thinking and acting. They generally share the steps that I have placed in a circular diagram (see Figure 9.1) to emphasize that they are not necessarily linear, resulting in a final outcome. Rather, as John Dewey once noted, the purpose of problem solving is *more* problem solving. Sample Lesson Plan 9.1, found at the end of this chapter, illustrates the inquiry, discovery, and problem-solving processes.

The Tradition of Inquiry

The inquiry tradition is an ancient one, dating back at least to Aristotle, who emphasized the use of the five senses in learning. In fact, although John Dewey is generally

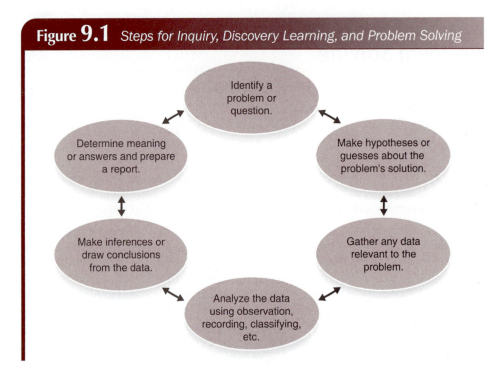

Figure 9.1   *Steps for Inquiry, Discovery Learning, and Problem Solving*

credited with the idea of "learning by doing," Aristotle himself wrote, "It is in doing that we learn best."

Sensory experience is fundamental to discovery learning, and all people employ it, at least in casual fashion, on a daily basis. If, for example, you decide to go for a walk, step outside, and realize you had better go back in the house for a coat, you are using sensory learning. You *felt* the chill or damp, or you *looked* at the sky, *saw* threatening clouds, and predicted rain. Perhaps you *heard* the wind whistling around the buildings or through the trees. Some people say they can *smell* rain in the air. These sensory experiences, of course, are direct encounters with the environment—a hallmark of discovery learning.

The teacher who wants to emphasize discovery learning capitalizes on the built-in tendency for people to use their senses to help them learn. The keys to discovery learning in a school setting are twofold: (1) provide your students with sensory experiences and (2) help them develop the skills of systematic inquiry.

Fortunately, children are natural inquirers. They excel at the art. Unfortunately for them, most teachers spend no time on problem finding whatsoever. It is simply overlooked as a skill in school life. On the other hand, from the first day they enter school, children are given problems to solve. These "problems," which are actually exercises, appear in seemingly unlimited quantities in their workbooks and textbooks.

Let's see what we can do to remedy that. I think a good place to start the process of inquiry is with children's stories and nursery rhymes. For example, Aesop (620–560 B.C.), a slave who lived in ancient Greece, collected and wrote a large number of animal fables that contained moral problems within them. Consider the story of the moles and porcupine:

> Once a porcupine asked a group of moles if he could live with them in their safe, snug, warm underground tunnels. Feeling sorry for the porcupine, the moles agreed to let him live with them. But the porcupine's quills stuck the moles, making them uncomfortable when they tried to sleep.

What is the problem in this fable? Can you offer a solution?

In the Gospel of Luke, Jesus tells the parable of the good Samaritan:

> A man was going down from Jerusalem to Jericho when he fell into the hands of robbers. They robbed and beat him, leaving him half dead. A priest going down the road saw the hurt man but crossed over to the other side to avoid him. Another man came along, and he too passed by the hurt man. But a Samaritan traveling the road stopped to help the hurt man. He bandaged his wounds, put the man on his donkey, and took him to an inn to take care of him. The next day, he gave the innkeeper two silver coins and asked him to care for the hurt man. He said if there were more expenses, he would pay for them when he returned from his business.

Can you state the problem or key issue in the story?

Stories, parables, nursery rhymes, and other tales have been used for centuries to help children frame problems, think about right actions, and consider moral issues. I encourage you to draw on the wealth of stories that already exist in folklore, fable, myth, and legend to find and solve problems with the children you teach.

Real and Contrived Problems

Now let's look at a few of the characteristics that distinguish *contrived* and *real* problem solving in the inquiry process. A contrived problem may deal effectively with the inquiry process; however, it is imposed on learners by the teacher or the program. A contrived problem does not arise directly from the life experiences of the students. Obviously, textbooks and other social studies programs cannot anticipate and make provision for the real problem that may confront a given group of students located in a particular geographic/economic/social setting at a particular time.

Proponents of real problem solving point out that because the learners are attempting to deal with an issue that they helped to develop and that is part of their lives, the learning process has more meaning. Proponents of contrived problem solving point out, on the other hand, that many worthwhile issues in historical, economic, and anthropological inquiry might never come to the learners' attention if they had not been guided into them by a creative teacher working with a good program. Rather than take sides in an either/or dichotomy, let's assume that both approaches have their merits. Note the steps of inquiry process in the following two examples.

Before the formal introduction of a unit on Japan, a fourth-grade teacher brought a number of Japanese artifacts to the classroom. He divided the class into research teams of five students each. He gave each team three artifacts, which he asked them to spend a few minutes examining and discussing. He then placed the following questions on the board for each team to answer:

1. How would you describe each artifact?
2. How are the artifacts alike and different?
3. Are these artifacts like any tools that we use?
4. What uses would you guess these artifacts might have?
5. Who might use these artifacts?

The small groups of students discussed the questions and recorded their answers. As the discussion progressed, the teacher moved around the room and helped students focus on their analysis of the artifacts. When the discussion groups had completed their tasks, each group was given an opportunity to present its conclusions. When each group made its presentation, students from other groups were allowed to ask questions about the artifacts and their possible uses.

Later each group developed a chart based on its speculations about the artifacts, and the chart and accompanying artifacts from each group were displayed in various areas of the room. The teacher asked the students to treat the statements on the charts as hypotheses that they would either accept or reject as the unit progressed and more information was acquired.

Thus, in this lesson, students were given a *problem*. The teacher *gathered appropriate data sources*, which the students examined. The students then *processed the data* through oral discussion and the development of their charts. The charts contained the students' *inferences*, which were to be treated as *hypotheses* that could later be verified.

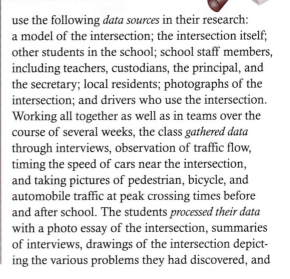

One morning, members of a second-grade class were excitedly telling their teacher and each other about a near accident that had occurred at a pedestrian crossing next to their school. A primary-age child had nearly been struck by a car as she was crossing the street. The students exclaimed that the intersection was dangerous, especially during the winter months when ice and snow were present. The teacher asked the students if they would like to conduct an investigation of the intersection to see how dangerous it really was and to see if they could suggest ways to make it safer. The class agreed that this would be a worthwhile project.

The class wrote a *statement of the problem* as follows: "How can our school crossing be made safer?" With the teacher's help, the class decided to use the following *data sources* in their research: a model of the intersection; the intersection itself; other students in the school; school staff members, including teachers, custodians, the principal, and the secretary; local residents; photographs of the intersection; and drivers who use the intersection. Working all together as well as in teams over the course of several weeks, the class *gathered data* through interviews, observation of traffic flow, timing the speed of cars near the intersection, and taking pictures of pedestrian, bicycle, and automobile traffic at peak crossing times before and after school. The students *processed their data* with a photo essay of the intersection, summaries of interviews, drawings of the intersection depicting the various problems they had discovered, and charts showing the volume of foot, bicycle, and auto traffic at peak hours. They *made the following inferences:*

1. The crossing is dangerous, especially for younger children, and a safety awareness campaign is needed.
2. Four safety patrol students should be placed on duty rather than two, the present number.
3. Larger, more visible warning signs should be posted along the streets leading to the intersection.
4. The crosswalk lines should be repainted.

The students' report was given to the school principal and to the police department. They were pleased to see that all four of their recommendations were enacted.

Differences and Similarities

Although these examples of contrived and real problems are intended as models, rather than exhaustive explanations of the possibilities inherent in each approach, let's take a moment to review their differences and similarities as teaching strategies.

The most obvious point of contrast is that the intersection investigation came directly from the life experiences of the students, whereas the artifact lesson was imposed on students at least partly to broaden their life experiences. A second contrast is found in the ways in which the students dealt with the steps in the inquiry process. In the artifact lesson, the statement of the problem, the selection of data sources, the means of gathering and processing data, and the making of inferences were predetermined by the teacher. In the intersection problem, the structure of the inquiry problem was much less obvious. A third contrast involves the outcomes of the students' findings. The intersection investigators were able to effect changes in the community. The artifact investigators were given an opportunity to become actively involved in previewing a forthcoming social studies unit.

The two examples also have similarities. Both used the steps in the inquiry process presented at the beginning of this section. In each case, students moved through a progression from problem statement to inference making. Second, both problems provided for a high degree of student interaction. Third, both problems provided for the development of the following skills: observation, description, problem definition, classifying, decision making, hypothesizing, verifying, and inference making. Fourth, in each lesson the teacher played the role of facilitator, guiding but not dictating to the students. A further similarity is the active involvement of the students. Finally, both lessons had transfer value; that is, they had the potential to be used by learners as models for investigating and solving problems in many situations other than the actual lesson situation. The next section expands on the idea of transfer of learning.

Reflective Thinking as a Follow-Up to Inquiry

Perhaps either of the foregoing inquiry examples could be justified on the grounds of student motivation and active involvement. But it should be emphasized that problems such as these have an inherent potential for helping students make applications of their learning that are generalizable beyond the specific problem. A useful strategy to facilitate learning transfer is a short *reflective thinking session,* held either at the conclusion of a given lesson or on the following day before the introduction of new material.

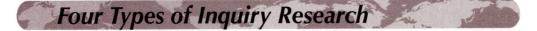

Four Types of Inquiry Research

Historians and archaeologists attempt to reconstruct past events and eras. Anthropologists observe and try to describe cultural aspects of human behavior. Sociologists deal with the behavior of groups. Psychologists conduct experiments with human subjects in an effort to expand our knowledge of human responses and behavior.

What do these investigators have in common? They share a common subject matter—human beings—as well as a respect for evidence and a desire to increase the world's knowledge of human behavior. In each case, their investigations represent attempts to answer questions by seeking appropriate sources of data, gathering and processing data, making inferences, and reaching conclusions about human behavior. Differences exist as well. The historian cannot replicate a situation, as a psychologist often can, nor can the historian mail questionnaires to subjects in many cases.

In the next few sections, we'll look at historical research, descriptive research, survey research, and experimental research. There are many illustrations of ways these inquiry methods can be implemented in the classroom, turning your children into researchers and active learners. As you read about the investigations, try to view them from the dual perspective of teacher and researcher.

Historical Research

Historical research represents an attempt to put together the pieces of a puzzle known as the past. Because historical research deals with events that have already happened, it is often difficult to acquire accurate knowledge, especially when it comes to the distant past. We do our best to reconstruct life in Ancient Egypt or China, but it is not easy given the passage of centuries.

Historians cannot control the events they wish to recapture; more often than not, they cannot even find enough documentation to ascertain full knowledge of an occurrence. Even though such tragedies as the assassination of Martin Luther King, Jr., and the attack on the World Trade Center in New York on September 11, 2001, happened within recent memory, there is much controversy about exactly what happened in either case. Eyewitness accounts of the Battle of Lexington at the beginning of the American Revolution vary considerably. How is the historian to know the truth?

Because history is such a major part of the social studies curriculum, an entire chapter to this important topic is included in this book. Therefore, I ask you to refer to Chapter 12, "Making History Come Alive," for activities, methods of investigation, and the involvement of children as active historians themselves.

Descriptive Research

Descriptive research, as the term implies, has as its purpose the description of human behavior, primarily through observation. Groups and/or individuals are the descriptive

A young inquirer makes a careful descriptive study of the Sacagawea dollar coin.

researchers' data sources. For example, it has been common practice for anthropologists to live among tribal groups in order to make direct observations of their behavior. Such a method of investigation is known as *participant observation* because the investigator plays the dual role of participant in the daily life of a group and observer of that group.

Another form of descriptive research is *direct observation*. One can observe without actually becoming involved in a situation. Although participation puts the observed at greater ease and thus produces a more natural situation, it may make the observer less objective because of personal involvement in the activities of a group.

Another type of descriptive research is *indirect observation*. This often involves the use of such data as pictures, artifacts, written accounts, books, and maps. Of course, someone engaged in direct or participant observation might also use such tools as the camera, tape recorder, and field notes as aids to ensure the accuracy and permanence of her or his record keeping.

Another means of gathering information for use in descriptive research is the technique of *interviewing informants*. Members of a group often provide a valuable source of data. In addition to observing their behavior, an investigator can obtain information by interviewing them—asking individuals questions about leadership, customs, rapport, and so on within the group.

As an illustration, let's see how the four descriptive research techniques of participant observation, direct observation, indirect observation, and interviewing informants might be used in investigating the activities and behavior of a Cub Scout pack. As a participant observer, you would join the Cub Scout pack, attend meetings, and take part

Young social scientists observe nature and sketch what they see.

in the rituals and activities. You would, in effect, become one of the group. As a direct observer, you would watch the pack at its meetings but refrain from taking part. In addition to keeping notes, you might photograph and tape-record events. As an indirect observer, you might examine crafts made by members of the pack. You might also examine minutes of meetings, the *Cub Scout Handbook*, and other relevant artifacts. As an investigator interviewing informants, you would seek out one or more members of the pack and ask such questions as: How do you usually spend your time in meetings? and Who do you think are some leading members of the group?

Obviously, to do a thorough study of the scout pack, it would be advisable to use all the foregoing techniques, because (1) to use all four would provide a greater and more varied base of information and (2) the different approaches might provide cross-checks on the validity of the information obtained.

As is the case with all social science research, descriptive research attempts to answer questions or solve problems by gathering and processing data and making inferences from those data. The following sections illustrate various techniques students might use in doing descriptive research.

OBSERVATION   Observation can take many forms and should be used as often as it takes to see real improvement in the children's ability to observe systematically, a very valuable skill. Here is one example: Take the class out to the playground or to some interesting scene near the school. Each student should have a pencil and a sketch pad.

The idea is to let the students look at the scene for a couple of minutes or so. Then ask them to turn around and sketch or map what they saw. A variation on this theme is to ask students to write down a description of what they saw. Older students, of course, can and should do both. After students have finished their descriptions, ask them to turn around and check their work against what they see. How accurate was it?

Another example of this form of descriptive research is to have students make a drawing of an object such as a vase, a toy, or whatever. The brain begins to function elaborately in such a situation. The concentration, the careful observation, and the attempt to render what you see brings out subtleties that are too easily overlooked in casual observation. I suggest that you put on a recording of Mozart or Haydn when you do this activity. I think you'll find the students will like it. Finally, another variation is to describe the music. See the activity called The Five Senses Game for other possibilities.

INTERVIEWING   The interview, as a descriptive research tool, provides investigators with an informant's perspective on a group or event. Obviously, investigators could add validity to their research by interviewing more than one group member. Also, it is important that investigators consider a member's status within a group. For example, the perspective of the president of a club is likely to be different from that of a member with lower status who attends meetings only occasionally. When an interview is expanded to include larger numbers of respondents, it becomes a *questionnaire*. Figure 9.2 illustrates an interview situation in which a third-grade investigator questioned a four-year-old about her membership in a YMCA group.

To summarize, the task of the descriptive researcher is to pose a question or problem about human behavior and to attempt to answer that question by gathering data through observation and/or interviewing. Thus, descriptive researchers add to the existing base of knowledge of human behavior through their investigations.

Figure 9.2 *The Interview Guide*

I talked to .... Robyn .... Age ... 4 .. She belonged to .... YMCA ....

She goes there ...... 2 .... times a week. This is how she feels about it. ... ☺ ......

Her favorite things to do at .... YMCA .... are ...... swimming and gym ....

I asked her if she thought other .... 4 .... year olds would like to be in.

She said ...... Yes ....

Comments. ...... She likes to go there. ....

COMMUNITY STUDY   The community study descriptive investigation can become a whole-class project. The object of the study is to describe the community around the school. Students can work in teams to develop their descriptions. Among the descriptive research tools they might use are drawings, maps, photographs, and interviews. The following elements of the community would be worth describing:

Types of trees	Streets
Parks	Churches/temples/mosques
Businesses	Vacant lots
Houses/apartments/condominiums	Playgrounds

MAP MAKING   Map making begins with observation and description. In fact, a map is a spatial (as opposed to verbal) description of a place. Make sure everyone has a notebook or sketch pad and a pencil and ruler, and take your class outdoors. If you can find one, choose an elevated spot, such as a hillside, and put the children to work sketching what they see. Don't be too concerned with some of the details at first. Things like which way is north and how does one draw to scale can come along gradually. The key is to observe and describe, not in words but using a spatial approach (drawing) to description. I guarantee that you will gain some new insights regarding students' abilities. Some of the children who don't shine verbally will surprise you with their spatial abilities.

in the classroom   The Five Senses Game

The Five Senses Game, which takes on many variations, can be played as often as you like. It takes its cues from the work of Francis Bacon and before that from Aristotle, who were both convinced that sensory learning was the foundation of scientific inquiry. I would recommend that you try the game with your class as a whole, at least for starters. If you have a primary class, you may have to do most of the note taking. Older children can do their own.

The key idea of this game is the ability to *describe*. It is useful to isolate one of the senses each time you play the game. If you decide to emphasize the sense of touch, you can take your students outside and ask them to identify various objects in the environment they would like to touch—for example, a leaf, a mud puddle, a worm, grass, bark, the air, the side of the building, and so on. The idea is to draw out of your students descriptive terms related to texture, feel, and touch. You can do the same for the other senses: sight, hearing, smell, and taste. (You may want to elicit taste descriptions in the classroom using some things to eat that you have brought.)

Survey Research

Taking a survey is a means of gaining information about groups of persons. Often an investigator will be interested in discovering the attitudes, preferences, or opinions held

A young sociologist conducts survey research.

by large numbers of people concerning particular ideas or issues. This precludes the possibility of mere observation because of the difficulties posed by such factors as time and distance.

Assume, for example, that a student investigator at Washington Elementary School wishes to assess the attitudes of the students at the school toward some newly installed playground equipment. Although it might prove instructive to observe who uses it, it could be difficult to provide observation coverage during the many recess periods throughout the school day. Additionally, an observer would probably see only students who chose to use the equipment, thus failing to tap the attitudes of nonusers who might have a preference for different kinds of equipment. Thus, the survey offers an alternative to the observation/descriptive approach.

The student researcher should bear in mind three important considerations when conducting surveys: (1) what to measure, (2) how to measure, and (3) whom to measure.

The question of *what* to measure needs to be defined with precision. For example, a surveyor who wishes to determine how students feel about school assemblies must decide exactly what it is about student attitude toward the assemblies it is important to know. Consider the following two questions:

1. What do you think of school assemblies?
2. Are you in favor of school assemblies?   yes   no

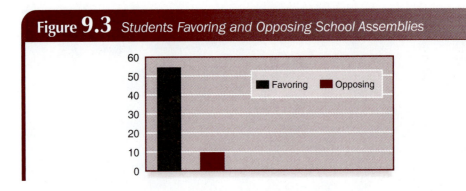

Figure 9.3 *Students Favoring and Opposing School Assemblies*

Although Question 1 may provoke interesting responses, it is a vague question and thus it may be difficult to quantify the responses. Question 2 is more precisely defined, and it allows one to quantify the responses given to it. Figure 9.3 illustrates the processed data for Question 2.

The question of *how* to measure involves the idea of *sampling*. A survey researcher need not ask all the students at the school whether they favor school assemblies in order to make valid inferences about the opinions of students at the school. Rather, an effective method is to sample student responses from the school's population. These are three different sampling techniques:

1. *Simple random selection.* If our school has a student population of 500 and we wish to sample 10 percent, or 50 students, we need only ensure that the 50 we choose are selected on the basis of pure chance.
2. *Stratified random selection.* Because we might wish to ensure equal numbers of primary and intermediate students, we could take room lists and randomly select three students from each room in the school.
3. *Stratified selection.* To do a stratified sampling, a researcher would take, for example, every tenth name from room lists. This might be useful if we wished to ensure equal boy/girl representation, in which case we would use separate boy/girl lists.

All three procedures provide fairness in the selection of samples and allow investigators to make inferences about a population without interviewing every person in that population.

The question of *whom* to measure is important because survey researchers need to ensure that their samples adequately represent the various types of groups and/or individuals found in the population. Thus, in a student preference poll, it may be crucial to ensure that primary-age as well as intermediate-age students are given an opportunity to respond and that teachers, clerks, custodians, and cooks are not included.

Let's consider two examples of surveys done by elementary classes. The first, a playground equipment survey, was conducted by a second-grade class. The second, a Halloween survey, was conducted by a fifth-grade class.

in the classroom   A Playground Investigation

Students in a second-grade class had experienced a number of problems with the use of the playground equipment at their school. They wondered if students in other classrooms were having similar difficulties. Among the problems the class listed were the following:

1. Some things are too crowded, so we don't get to use them.
2. People get hurt on some of the equipment.
3. We would like to have some new equipment.

The students randomly chose five students from each room in the school and asked them the following questions:

1. Have you ever been hurt while using playground equipment at school?

       yes   no

   If so, on which piece of equipment?

   _____

2. Do you ever have to wait to use playground equipment?

       never   sometimes   often

3. Would you like to have some new playground equipment?

       yes   no

   If so, give the name of the new equipment.

   _____

4. Are you a boy or a girl? _____

5. What grade are you in? _____

The results of the survey indicated that few children had ever been hurt using the playground equipment. However, 83 out of 110 students indicated that they often had to wait to use equipment. The most asked-for piece of new equipment was a tetherball pole. Two such poles were installed at the principal's request after he had reviewed the students' findings.

in the classroom   A Halloween Study

Students in a fifth-grade class were interested in the question of who trick-or-treats. To investigate the question for their school's population, they devised a questionnaire:

Trick or Treat Survey Form

_____ Boy   _____ Girl   _____ Age

Do you plan to trick-or-treat on Halloween this year?

_____ Yes   _____ No

The class decided to try each of the three sampling procedures described in this chapter to see if different results would be obtained. Here are their results:

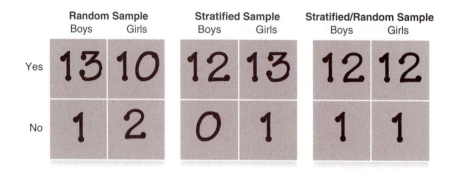

In addition, the father of one of the students agreed to gather age and gender data from the trick or treaters who came to his house that Halloween. (All the students were busy trick-or-treating themselves!) That information is collated in this bar graph:

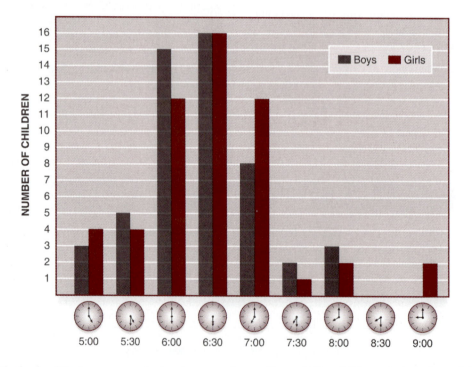

On the basis of their survey work, the class made the following inferences:

- Trick-or-treating is popular among all age groups at our school.

- From 6:00 to 7:00 P.M. is the prime trick-or-treating time.
- There don't seem to be many differences between the trick or treat habits of boys and girls.

Students need to understand that for the results of a survey to have real meaning, their work in gathering, recording, and graphing data must be accurate. The next example shows an effective way to develop students' survey skills by conducting a weather station survey.

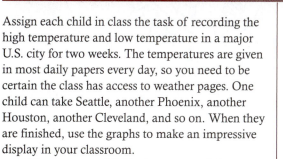

in the classroom   A Weather Station Survey

Assign each child in class the task of recording the high temperature and low temperature in a major U.S. city for two weeks. The temperatures are given in most daily papers every day, so you need to be certain the class has access to weather pages. One child can take Seattle, another Phoenix, another Houston, another Cleveland, and so on. When they are finished, use the graphs to make an impressive display in your classroom.

Of course, an additional outcome of the weather stations survey is the introduction of geographic concepts and how geography affects weather and climate. Here are some questions you will want to consider with the class:

- How does latitude affect temperature?
- Does closeness to large bodies of water have an effect on temperature (Seattle versus Minneapolis, for example)?
- How do mountains affect temperature?

With younger students, you may wish to do the project together as a class, selecting only four or five cities. With older students, you may wish to include international temperatures.

CURRENT EVENTS
Focus on Gender Roles

Cartoons, political or otherwise, can provide insights into current issues and provide inspiration for student surveys. Look at the following cartoon about gender roles. A cartoon like this one could be used to stimulate students' thinking about current attitudes toward women through a classroom or wider-ranging survey.

First, ask each student to answer the following questions about the cartoon. Then ask each student to show a copy of the cartoon to his or her parents or another adult and ask the same questions.

1. What does this cartoon tell you about women?
2. Can a girl own a ranch?
3. Should a girl consider ranch owning as an occupation?
4. Do you think most ranch owners are men or women? Why?

Finally, tabulate all the results. What do the answers say about how people feel about women's roles? Are there differences between how your students responded and how their parents and other adults responded?

Little Bo Peep had lost her sheep
and couldn't tell where to find them—
So when she grew up and had her
own ranch, she hired someone
to take care of lost sheep for her.

Reprinted by permission of Allen Glenn.

A survey can serve more of a purpose than mere information gathering. Sometimes, the results of a survey can help people take positive action. If you send your surveyors (your students) out around the school environment to look for potential problems, they can no doubt come up with a list of them: litter, vandalism, faulty playground equipment, pollution, noise, dangerous intersections, and the like. Thus, your students' survey can serve as the basis of a list of concerns that they can survey the whole school about. Then they can determine the rank order of the student body's concerns and try to involve the whole school in taking positive action to remedy the situation.

Getting a whole elementary school mobilized to study and correct a pressing problem is a wonderful experience. Having an impact beyond that is even more wonderful. That's what happened in the following example.

in the classroom   Consumerism

This example of a child researcher using survey techniques is from Evelyn Kaye's (1974) book *The Family Guide to Children's Television*. An 11-year-old girl named Dawn Ann Kurth from Melbourne, Florida, became interested in advertising to children because of her younger sister:

> My sister Martha, who is seven, had asked my mother to buy a box of Post Raisin Bran so that she could get a free record that was on the back of the box. It had been advertised several times on Saturday morning cartoon shows. My mother bought the cereal, and we all (there are four children in our family) helped Martha eat it so she could get the record.
>
> It was after the cereal was eaten and she had the record that the crisis occurred. There was no way the record would work.
>
> Martha was very upset and began crying and I was angry too. It just didn't seem right to me that something could be shown on TV that worked fine and people were listening and dancing to the record and when you bought the cereal, instead of laughing and dancing, we were crying and angry.

Dawn had been chosen with 35 other students at Meadowlane Elementary School to do a project in any field they wanted. She decided to find out how other children felt about deceptive advertising. She began by watching television one Saturday morning. She clocked 25 commercial messages during one hour, 8:00 to 9:00, not counting ads for shows coming up or public service announcements. She also discovered that during shows her parents liked to watch there were only 10 to 12 commercials each hour, which surprised her.

Dawn devised the following questionnaire and asked 1,538 children the following questions (answer these questions yourself):

1. Do you ask your mother to buy products you see advertised on TV?

    yes   no

2. Did you ever buy a product to get the free bonus gift inside?

    yes   no

3. Were you satisfied?

    yes   no

4. Write down an example.

    _____

    _____

5. Do you believe that certain products you see advertised on TV make you happier or have more friends?

    yes   no

6. Please write an example.

    _____

    _____

7. Did you ever feel out of it because your mother wouldn't buy a certain product?

    yes   no

8. Did you ever feel your mother was mean because she wouldn't buy the product you wanted?

    yes   no

Dawn got the following responses to her questionnaire: (1) yes 1,203; no 330. (2) yes 1,120; no 413. (3) yes 668; no 873. (5) yes 1,113; no 420. (7) yes 802; no 735. (8) yes 918; no 620.

Dawn's teacher sent the results of Dawn's work to a local paper, the kind known as an advertising shopper that carries a few stories of local interest. To their surprise, Dawn was invited to testify before a U.S. Senate committee that was investigating the effects of advertising on children. In her testimony, she explained her concerns and how she conducted her research. Her work is now part of the *Congressional Record.*

Source: From *The Family Guide to Children's Television* by Evelyn Kaye, text copyright © 1974 by Action for Children's Television, Inc. Used by permission of Pantheon Books, a division of Random House, Inc.

Experimental Research

In social science, experimentation involves the manipulation of variables to determine whether a particular treatment has an effect. In its simplest form, this generally means that subjects are placed in control and experimental groups and an assessment is made at the end of the experiment to see which group receives a higher average score on a test or performs better according to some other criterion. Commonly, the experimental group is given a special or "experimental" treatment, whereas the control group is given "other" (perhaps traditional) treatment. Experimental treatments often involve a special group of lessons or a special way of teaching those lessons. For example, an experimenter might wish to know whether learning pioneer history through stories (the experimental treatment) is as effective as learning history from the textbook (the control treatment).

The next two examples engage students in experiments about products: first, paper towels and then, a health drink.

in the classroom   The Great Paper Towel Experiment

Here is an example you can try with a class of students. It's an experiment I've done many times with children, and I can tell you they do a remarkably good job.

Begin the session by asking the class if anyone has ever bought a product that she or he thought was very good. Perhaps students will tell about bicycles, toys, or video games. Give them plenty of time to tell about what makes a product good. Then ask them if they have ever had a product that was not so good. Let the children reflect on what makes a product not so good.

Tell the class that they are going to become experimenters who do research on products. Of course, their scientific work may take several days, and they will want to be very careful that they do a good job. The first product they will examine is paper towels. You will need to get three rolls of paper towels, each a different brand. You will also need a little bit of equipment: rulers, water, oil, containers, and calculators.

Place the students in groups of three, and have them begin their plans for how they will conduct their research. Be sure to tell them that their challenge is to determine which of the towels is the best buy, second best, and third best. When the groups are ready to proceed, let them go ahead and begin their testing. (Your job is that of coach, to make sure the students are considering how good their tests are.)

When the tests are completed and each group has its ranking of the towels, you can put all the data on the board to see how the groups' results compare. This will be a time of discussion as each group reports to the class.

Of course, there are many other products to test: brands of popcorn, orange juice, crayons, peanut butter, or other products the children may suggest. Your research may lead to letter writing, analyses of advertising, or even suggestions for improvements in various products.

This problem-solving experiment challenges students to invent and advertise a new health drink. Working in small groups of about five, students will need to test various formulas, figure ways to keep costs down, and plan a promotional campaign for their product. You will need to supply such raw materials as fruit, juices, and kitchen measuring instruments.

Assessment and Inquiry

Part of the process of inquiry is being able to understand and apply the information that is gathered. Students not only need to understand how to conduct research; they also need to understand how to analyze it, comprehend the results, and use their analysis to form opinions or make decisions.

Moreover, as the emphasis on assessment continues at every level of American education, we are starting to see the analysis and application of survey results in various assessment tools. Even standardized tests can require that students understand the process of inquiry, including how to comprehend and apply results. Figure 9.4 is part of the Michigan State Social Studies Assessment for the fifth grade. In this test item, students are asked to interpret the results of a survey and then to form an opinion based on those results.

Metacognition and Inquiry

As students become inquirers, discoverers, and problem solvers, they can also explore the process of their own learning. Thinking about one's own learning and knowledge is called *metacognition*. With virtually any of the projects we have talked about in this chapter, the simple act of reflecting on the results can provide an added dimension to the learning experience. Let me give you some examples.

Earlier in this chapter, we looked at the strategy of observation. A simple way for you to extend any observation activity is to have students try it both alone and in groups

Figure 9.4 An Assessment Activity Using Survey Research

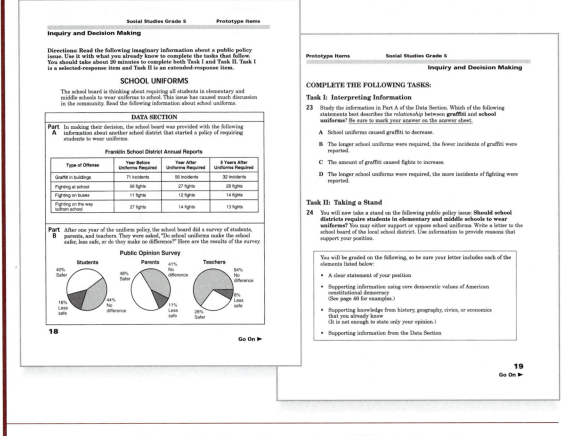

Social Studies Grade 5   Prototype Items

Inquiry and Decision Making

Directions: Read the following imaginary information about a public policy issue. Use it with what you already know to complete the tasks that follow. You should take about 20 minutes to complete both Task I and Task II. Task I is a selected-response item and Task II is an extended-response item.

SCHOOL UNIFORMS

The school board is thinking about requiring all students in elementary and middle schools to wear uniforms to school. This issue has caused much discussion in the community. Read the following information about school uniforms.

DATA SECTION

Part A In making their decision, the school board was provided with the following information about another school district that started a policy of requiring students to wear uniforms.

Franklin School District Annual Reports

Type of Offense	Year Before Uniforms Required	Year After Uniforms Required	5 Years After Uniforms Required
Graffiti in buildings	71 incidents	56 incidents	32 incidents
Fighting at school	56 fights	27 fights	28 fights
Fighting on buses	11 fights	12 fights	14 fights
Fighting on the way to/from school	27 fights	14 fights	13 fights

Part B After one year of the uniform policy, the school board did a survey of students, parents, and teachers. They were asked, "Do school uniforms make the school safer, less safe, or do they make no difference?" Here are the results of the survey.

Public Opinion Survey

Students: 40% Safer, 16% Less safe, 44% No difference

Parents: 48% Safer, 41% No difference, 11% Less safe

Teachers: 84% No difference, 8% Less safe, 28% Safer

18   Go On ▶

Prototype Items   Social Studies Grade 5

Inquiry and Decision Making

COMPLETE THE FOLLOWING TASKS:

Task I: Interpreting Information

23   Study the information in Part A of the Data Section. Which of the following statements best describes the *relationship* between **graffiti** and **school uniforms**? Be sure to mark your answer on the answer sheet.

A   School uniforms caused graffiti to decrease.

B   The longer school uniforms were required, the fewer incidents of graffiti were reported.

C   The amount of graffiti caused fights to increase.

D   The longer school uniforms were required, the more incidents of fighting were reported.

Task II: Taking a Stand

24   You will now take a stand on the following public policy issue: **Should school districts require students in elementary and middle schools to wear uniforms?** You may either support or oppose school uniforms. Write a letter to the school board of the local school district. Use information to provide reasons that support your position.

You will be graded on the following, so be sure your letter includes each of the elements listed below:

• A clear statement of your position

• Supporting information using core democratic values of American constitutional democracy (See page 46 for examples.)

• Supporting knowledge from history, geography, civics, or economics that you already know (It is not enough to state only your opinion.)

• Supporting information from the Data Section

19
Go On ▶

Source: Michigan Department of Education, Michigan Educational Assessment Program (MEAP). Reprinted by permission.

---

or pairs: How effectively do they observe on their own, as opposed to observing with a partner? Try this: One day, ask students to observe a painting for 5 minutes. Then remove the painting and ask each student first to draw a picture of it and then to write down everything he or she can recall about the painting—colors, size, subject matter, composition. The following day, using a different painting, put the students into pairs and ask them to observe for 5 minutes, during which time they may discuss what they are seeing. Then ask them, as you did the day before, to draw and write about what they observed. Did talking about the painting with a partner improve their ability to remember it? Or did having a partner simply distract them from the task at hand? You can't generalize too much from this brief exercise, but repeating it several times might allow your class to reach firmer conclusions.

Here's another possible experiment with a metacognitive element: Does listening to classical music help a person think better as she or he studies? Some experts think it does (and, of course, most teenagers will argue that listening to rock, rap, or heavy metal will do the same), but most feel there is not enough evidence to support this conclusion. Try something like playing a Mozart or Haydn piece in the background during a spelling lesson each day for a week. Then give a quiz on the words studied. The following week, have the daily lessons without the music and then give the quiz. Are the quiz results any different? (This not only gives you an opportunity for studying the learning process, by the way, but also provides you with a good time to teach students how to compute an average score for the class.) Finally, compare attitudes. Whether or not there was a difference in quiz scores, did students find studying with music or without music more enjoyable? Do all the students agree? Which do they prefer? What might be some weaknesses in this study?

Summary

This chapter illustrated a number of ways in which children can themselves become social science researchers. All too often, children are exposed only to the results and conclusions of the research of others. They therefore gain little insight into the processes of producing knowledge. By allowing them to conduct descriptive, survey, and experimental research, you give your students the opportunity to move toward the forefront of knowledge. A student who has helped to develop new knowledge is in a far better position to consume knowledge because he or she understands what is involved in gathering the original ideas from which conclusions are made.

No school-age child is too young or immature to conduct research of the kind described in this chapter. Allowances must be made for students' abilities to work independently of the teacher as they mature. Younger students often profit from whole-class investigations supervised by the teacher. So, whether your students are primary or intermediate or perhaps older than that, get them involved as inquiring, curious researchers.

Explorations

Reflect on . . .

To review what you have just read about the use of social science research methods in elementary social studies, take the following quiz:

1. Indicate whether you think each of the following research problems would best lend itself to descriptive, survey, or experimental methods.

a. _____ A study to determine which of two ways of studying our spelling words produces higher average test scores.

b. _____ A study in which investigators observe the flow of the school lunch lines in order to determine whether improvements could be made.

c. _____ A study to determine local residents' preferences concerning topics the PTA might present at its monthly meetings during the school year.

Problem (a) is experimental. Investigators could randomly assign students in the classroom (or classrooms) to two groups, each of which would study the same spelling list in a different fashion for a certain time period—perhaps 15 minutes per day for 4 days. Both groups would then be tested on the fifth day to determine which received the higher average score.

  Problem (b) is descriptive. Observing, photographing, mapping, and drawing the flow of traffic through the lunch lines in order to recommend improved procedures would make this a descriptive study. However, you might have thought of experimenting with alternate flow routes, staggered serving times, and so on. Also, investigators could certainly survey students, teachers, and lunchroom personnel to see if they had ideas for improving the lunch line service.

  Problem (c) is survey. Students could make a valuable contribution to the PTA or other parent group by consulting with the group's leadership about potential offerings for that year and then surveying community interest in proposed topics.

2. Explain the differences among the following types of sample selection: simple random selection, stratified random selection, stratified selection.

In the Field

3. Choose any one of the three methods of research presented in this chapter, and develop a possible investigation at a grade or age level of interest to you. Use the following form to outline your proposed study.

Topic:

_____

_____

Problem or question to be investigated:

_____

_____

Data sources:

_____

_____

For Your Portfolio

4. Carry out an investigation, from problem posing to conclusion. Use the methods of inquiry and discovery in much the same way you would want students to use them. Make maps, charts, and illustrations and also write up your results. By doing this, you will have an artifact showing your own knowledge of how inquiry works.

Continuing the Journey: Suggested Readings

American Academy of Pediatrics. (2005). *The Smart Parent's Guide to Kids' TV.* Elk Grove, IL: Author.

 Wise advice for limiting, assessing, and selecting programs for kids.

Barell, J. (2007). *Why Are School Buses Always Yellow.* Thousand Oaks, CA: Corwin.

Block, C. C., Morrow, L. M., & Parris, S. (2008). *Comprehension Instruction.* New York: Guilford Press.

Chambers, D. (2007). *How to Succeed with Problem-Based Learning.* Carlton South Vic, Australia: Curriculum Corporation.

Janzen, R. (1995). "The Social Studies Conceptual Dilemma: Six Contemporary Approaches." *Social Studies, 86*(3): 134–140.

 This article challenges the reader to think through a variety of social studies emphases.

Kellett, M. (2005). *Children as Researchers.* Thousand Oaks, CA: Sage.

This book identifies both topics and procedures for carrying out research by children.

Kuhlthau, C. C., Caspari, A., & Maniotes, L. (2007). *Guided Inquiry.* Santa Barbara, CA: Libraries Unlimited.

Lintner, T. (2005). "A World of Difference: Teaching Tolerance through Photographs in Elementary Schools. *Social Studies, 96*(1): 34–37.

A good example of the exciting use of original source material.

Maxim, G. (2003). "The Local Cemetery: Exploring a Primary Source." *Social Studies and the Young Learner, 15*(4): 21–23.

Children become historians doing first-person field work.

Merryfield, M. (2004). "Elementary Students in Substantive Culture Learning." *Social Education, 68*(4): 270–274.

The concept of culture so central to social studies comes alive in this article.

Moore, K. (2008). *Effective Instructional Strategies.* Thousand Oaks, CA: Sage.

West, M. (2007). "Problem Solving: A Sensible Approach to Children's Science and Social Studies Learning—and Beyond." *Young Children, 62*(5): 34–41.

Websites

A Web-based index of learning theories and models. *www.learning-theories.com/*

Free professional development workshops related to inquire learning and other teaching concepts. *www.thirteen.ore/edonline/concept2class/about.html*

Strategies and perspectives on problem-based learning. *www.studygs.net/pbl.htm*

The role of metacognition through the lens of teaching reading comprehension. *http://metacognition.org/*

Related NCSS Standards and Principles of Powerful Social Studies

Curriculum Standards

What social studies is and its importance:

Civic competence requires the ability to use knowledge about one's community, nation, and world, apply inquiry processes, and employ skills of data collection and analysis, collaboration, decision-making, and problem-solving"(p. 6).

Essential social studies skills and strategies, specifically, examining and evaluating consequences students utilize. . .

Inquiry Learning

Be curious, ask powerful and complex questions

Observe, investigate and explore to develop understanding

Organize, create and communicate ideas and results

Discuss, connect and/or compare with other works

Reflect to monitor progress and self-evaluate" (p. 134).

Source: Excerpted from National Task Force for Social Studies, *Expectations of Excellence: Curriculum Standards for Social Studies.* (Silver Spring, MD: National Council for the Social Studies, Draft 2008). The Council's website is www.socialstudies.org

Pedagogy Standards

Pedagogical standards for social studies teachers:

3. Critical Thinking, Problem Solving, and Performance Skills

Social studies teachers should possess the knowledge, capabilities, and dispositions to use at the appropriate school levels a variety of instructional strategies to encourage student development of critical thinking, problem solving, and performance skills (p. 51).

5. Inquiry, Collaboration, and Supportive Classroom Interaction

Social studies teachers should possess the knowledge, capabilities, and dispositions to use at the appropriate school levels verbal, nonverbal, and media communication techniques that foster active inquiry, collaboration, and supportive interaction in the classroom (p. 51).

Social studies teaching and learning are powerful when they are challenging.

Social studies becomes challenging when:

- Students are expected to strive to accomplish the instructional goals, both as individuals and group members.
- Teachers model seriousness of purpose and a thoughtful approach to inquiry, and use instructional strategies designed to elicit and support similar qualities from students.
- Teachers show interest in and respect for students' thinking and demand well-reasoned arguments rather than opinions voiced without adequate thought or commitment (p. 13).

Teacher expectations

have learners explain and apply ideas, theories, and modes of inquiry drawn from anthropology and sociology in the examination of persistent issues and social problems (p. 20).

Source: Excerpted from National Council for the Social Studies. *National Standards for Social Studies Teachers* (Silver Spring, MD: *National Council for the Social Studies*, 2002). The Council's website is www.socialstudies.org

SAMPLE LESSON 9.1   The $1.50 Inquiry

NCSS STANDARD: Identify and use various sources of information

This lesson plan will involve your students in an inquiry activity that has potential to extend itself in a number of ways into history, geography, economics, and anthropology. To carry out this lesson, you will need enough nickels so that each child in your classroom can have one. Always provide drawing paper, notebook paper, and pencils.

KEY IDEA: Social Scientists make inferences by piecing together evidence.

INSTRUCTIONAL OBJECTIVE: Students will learn the skills of observing, recording, classifying, and inference making as they examine an artifact (a nickel).

Students will practice the communication skills of speaking, listening, drawing, and writing.

1. Give each of your students a nickel, and ask all students to spend some time observing it and taking notes about what they see. Tell them to write down anything they think is important about the artifact. Each student should work alone at this stage of the lesson.
2. Ask each student to draw two pictures of the nickel: one of the coin's head and the other of the tail.
3. Place students in groups of two, and ask them to research and discuss the following questions:

- What different inscriptions do you find? (Liberty, date, five cents, etc.)

- Whose face is on the nickel? (Thomas Jefferson)
- What is the drawing on the back side? (Lewis & Clark's flatboat)
- Who were Jefferson, Lewis, and Clark? (third president; nineteenth-century explorers of the American West)
- What does *e pluribus unum* mean? (Latin for "one out of many") What is the significance of this Latin phrase for the United States? (one nation out of many states)
- What kinds of things do you learn about an artifact by drawing it?

4. Have each pair of students put their findings into categories and label the categories (for example, "Words or Phrases," "Pictures").

CLOSURE: Ask each student individually to write as many "I learned" statements as he or she can about the activity.

REFLECTION: Ask students to share their "I learned" statements, and record them on the board. Have the class discuss what they learned.

EXTENSIONS:

- Make an illustrated poster portraying today's activity.
- Research the origin of the U.S. motto: *e pluribus unum.*
- What is a nickel made of? What other materials have coins been made of over the centuries?
- Make a brief report on Lewis and Clark and their expedition of 1804–1806.
- Make a report on the life of Thomas Jefferson.
- Compare a nickel from the 1990s with a new nickel. How are they alike and different? Illustrate the differences.
- Interview an older, retired person. Ask her or him what a nickel would buy years ago.

Chapter 10

Social Studies and the Integrated Curriculum

| Keys to This Chapter | • What Is Integration?
• Projects: The Building Blocks of Integrated Studies
• Significant Themes for Integration |

All things are connected.
    —Chief Seattle

Young children don't think in terms of separate subjects, academic disciplines, or a world fragmented by specialists. They inhabit a seamless world of daily adventure and discovery. That is their nature. They ask questions, take risks, make mistakes, and attempt to fit what is new (to them) into what they already know. In a sense, they are conducting an ongoing experiment about how things are, how they turn into other things, and why things are the way they are. By adult standards, their methods may seem clumsy, repetitive, and inefficient. But actually, children are incredibly effective learners. Some experts suggest that half of what a person will know in the course of a lifetime has been learned by the age of five. It takes all the other succeeding years to learn the other half.

One aspect of children's efficiency is their ability and tendency to see everything as being connected. The separate subjects that we are taught in the name of learning come along the way, as we work our way through our school years. Ironically, these divisions are introduced in the name of efficiency. It is efficient to separate reading from writing, mathematics from geography, and so on. In time (predictably), children stop seeing things as connected, and they enter a world in which school subjects are routinely separated from one another. But what if they are intuitively right about learning, and we are mainly wrong? How might the curriculum be different? Well, in a single word, it would be *integrated*.

In his insightful book *The Schools Our Children Deserve,* Alfie Kohn (1999) writes that often he will ask teachers which of two fractions is larger: 4/11 or 5/13? He writes that nearly everyone he asks gives the wrong answer, especially

mathematics teachers. The right answer, according to Kohn, is "Who cares?" His point is that isolated facts and skills are not particularly important in the greater scheme of things.

This brings us quickly to a deeply imbedded problem in the school experience. The problem is that bits and pieces of information are all too often taught to children outside any meaningful frame of reference or context. The stuff literally goes in one ear and out the other. All of us were taught at some point in our school days (probably around fifth or sixth grade) how to compare the sizes of fractions by dividing the numerator by the denominator. It isn't difficult, so why don't we remember that particular skill or others? I'll let you answer that.

Integrated studies represent a kind of seamless whole in learning. Children see the world as a whole. They don't think in terms of separate disciplines. Incidentally, so do great philosophers and other profound thinkers. Leo Tolstoy, author of *War and Peace* and other great novels, was himself deeply interested in childhood education. He even started his own school for poor children. Tolstoy observed that children, unlike most adults, are drawn to and enjoy complex themes. He also noted that unfortunately, most teachers are not drawn to complex themes; they prefer the oversimplified world of textbooks, separate subjects, facts, skills, and so on.

Of course, the secret is to see the world as children see it. The purpose of this chapter is to stimulate your thoughts about the possibilities inherent in integrated teaching and learning.

What Is Integration?

When you think of the word *integration,* perhaps the first thing that comes to mind is the Civil Rights Movement. This is really a good place to begin. When such leaders as Martin Luther King Jr., Ralph Abernathy, Rosa Parks, and others pioneered the movement, the idea was that in order for one person to be free and equal, all people must be free and equal. The word *segregation* implies that not all people in a society can work, play, and be together, that they must be kept apart. *Integration* means the opposite, that is, that people ought to be together. Think for a moment about a classroom—your classroom. You want it to be integrated. You want your students to work together, play together, and care about each other. That cannot happen if they are segregated by being told, "Keep to yourself. Don't talk to your neighbor. Do your own work." The famous educational researcher John Goodlad once wrote that "students come to school to learn alone in groups." How ironic. Goodlad's insight reminds us that just because there are 25 to 30 kids in a classroom, we can't know that they are learning together.

John Dewey wrote that the primary purpose of school is social. Of course, he knew that academic achievement is important. But he also knew that this is a democracy. He knew that students can and should practice democracy on a daily basis while they are learning academics. There is a moral thread here, just as there was in the Civil Rights Movement. Segregating people in a free society is immoral. It is wrong. Segregating students in a classroom is wrong. They desperately need to talk to one another for both intellectual growth and for social reasons. They need to experience the give and take of working together, sharing, deciding, organizing, compromising, and supporting each other. In his book, *The School and Society* (1899), Dewey mentions four characteristics of students that he calls their natural tendencies or instincts. Those four instincts are:

1. They like to talk.
2. They like to construct.
3. They like to express themselves artistically.
4. They like to inquire and discover.

In order for students to realize the potential value of these natural tendencies, they must work and play together. As your classroom becomes a miniature society, a democratic community in which students are integrated, you set the stage for them to grow and develop academically, socially, and morally. This must happen before we worry about integrating school subjects. But just as we integrate people, we will do well to create an integrated curriculum. Young people do not think and act in terms of separate academic subjects. This is all well and good for advanced students at university levels, but in childhood and adolescence, learning is improved when connections are made. We could ask the question, What does mathematics have to do with social studies? Or we could ask whether reading and writing are important in learning social studies. To what extent should the arts become linked to social studies? If you are able to see some natural connections here, then you are on the right track.

Projects: The Building Blocks of Integrated Study

Integrated studies in the form of great projects have an energizing quality about them. At their best, they are what psychologists call *flow experiences.* When people are "in the flow," they tend to lose track of time, want to keep going, and feel engaged in something personally meaningful and rewarding. You'll know your kids are in a flow activity when they say, "Can't we just work on this a little longer?" or something to that effect.

Psychologists today say that human beings are "wired" to do projects. Some have gone so far as to say that projects are the single most purely human activity. I think there is much to this; for example, how often do people think, "One of these days I've got to spend a day getting all my stuff in order," or "Let's plan a trip to the mountains," or "Maybe we can organize a neighborhood cleanup campaign." Actually, something as simple as a trip to the grocery store is, in fact, a project. We may not call it that, but that's what it is. Some projects, of course, are larger than others.

Characteristics of Good Projects

Projects, whether they are ours alone or something we try with a class or even a whole school, have several interesting characteristics. First of all, a good project is a *defining activity*. If a project is about reconstructing Native American life in your area from 200 years ago, then it is clear what you are doing. You are not studying history or anthropology; rather, you are using both to help you complete your project.

The second characteristic of a good project is that it is *interdisciplinary*. A project on "Activities of the Night" will use music, art, mathematics, language, science, and, most of all, social studies. Projects have what can be called *syntactic complexity*. A project really is more complex than reading a text and answering questions. One truly needs all the help one can get from the various areas of the curriculum. The difference is that textbooks and questions are contributors to, not controllers of, the curriculum.

A third characteristic of a good project is that it allows a person the luxury of setting *boundaries*. A project has a beginning, a middle, and an end. If students in your class decide to create an art museum, then they must go through the stages of purpose, planning, development, exhibition, and evaluation. That's pretty straightforward compared to the seemingly endless voyage through a textbook. Most projects have a definite time frame; otherwise, students couldn't accomplish their goals.

The fourth and perhaps most significant characteristic of a project is that it has an *outcome*. A good project is undertaken with a clear purpose of achieving something. If your class decides to build a greenbelt along the edge of the school grounds, then you all know what needs to be done. You may not initially know *how* to do it or even what it will look like, but you know you are heading toward a culminating event—that of a finished greenbelt. An outcome is important, because it addresses the much-needed aspect of reality in learning and gives one a sense of closure.

Group versus Individual Projects

Projects can be done alone or with others; indeed, this is true of all learning. My position on working together or alone is that students must learn to do both. But in social studies, let's not forget that most of what a class does should be *social*, and that argues for group projects whenever possible. People need to cooperate with each other in life for a variety of reasons. One of those reasons is that many of the worthwhile things in life (a play or pageant, for example) are simply too complex and demanding to orchestrate alone. Another reason for working together on projects is that it gives children a chance to actually practice citizenship. So, a few projects can and should be done alone, but most projects should be group enterprises (see Figure 10.1).

The advantages to group projects are that they allow children to experience the give-and-take of community life and that they create a much more process-centered learning environment. The first advantage is pretty straightforward; working together comes closer to mirroring real life in a democracy than does working alone. The second advantage takes some explaining. To miss the underlying point is to miss something extremely important in learning theory.

When learners work together, a more complex learning environment is established. This is so because there is less opportunity for teacher control of intellectual and social forces. Although this may seem like a drawback at first glance, it is actually a step in the

Figure 10.1 *Ideas for Individual and Group Projects*

Individual Projects

- Role-playing a famous person in history
- Constructing a model of a ship, clothing, or village from another time or culture—specifically, its architecture, food, and festivals
- Reporting on another culture—specifically, its architecture, food, and festivals
- Conducting an investigation or neighborhood survey
- Building a kite after the fashion of Japanese kites
- Making a musical instrument from another culture

Group Projects

- Putting on a pageant of pioneer or Native American life
- Creating a museum in the classroom
- Investigating different brands of the same product
- Producing a weekly "radio" news program to be broadcast over the school intercom
- Conducting a schoolwide effort to improve safety conditions
- Creating displays or exhibits of schoolwork
  - Issuing a class challenge to read a certain number of books
  - Putting on a schoolwide social studies fair
  - Mapping the local environment

right direction. Learning becomes more process centered simply because students get to share their thoughts and feelings with each other. More conversation means more complexity; more complexity means more opportunity for language development, for perspective taking, and for moral development.

The best way for language development to proceed for children is to put them into social situations with their peers and allow them to solve problems together. They learn to express themselves, to find their own voices, to listen to others, and to decide things together. Thus, the social and intellectual aspects of learning become intertwined, rather than separated.

The ability to see something from more than one perspective is useful whether one is viewing the Grand Canyon (it looks rather different from the top of the canyon than it does from the bottom) or finding ways to solve a problem. Weighing different perspectives on an issue is something one can learn from practice. Group projects afford children the opportunity to see things from other points of view. For example, if children want to build a greenbelt on the school grounds, they need to learn that their own viewpoint may be somewhat different from that of the school board or even from the viewpoints of students in other classrooms.

The richly textured environment that arises when children work together on projects is filled with opportunities for the thoughtful examination of moral issues. For example, children working together will have more disagreements than children working alone, but this is good in an atmosphere where people are free to express their thoughts and feelings. Such conditions help students confront real moral issues, such as sharing, reaching consensus, doing one's fair share, and learning through experience that different people have different innate gifts in life. In short, group work makes it clear that people need each other and that there is no room for condescension toward another if anything is to be accomplished.

Kinds of Projects

Four distinctly different kinds of projects will be discussed here: service-learning projects, production projects, problem-solving projects, and schoolwide projects.

Keys to Creating Effective Projects

- *Clear tasks.* Be as clear as possible about what students will be doing and about the purpose of the experience.
- *Common experiences.* As you begin the challenge, ensure that the whole class has a set of common experiences. This will enable the groups that emerge to share a knowledge base so that communication will be meaningful.
- *Content versus process.* One of the problems in curriculum development is that developers give undue emphasis to process and little emphasis to content. You want to be able to say at the conclusion of the project that your students have a body of knowledge, as well as an array of skills and values.
- *Focus groups.* Once you have established a common body of knowledge, you will be ready to move ahead with smaller groups that will work on subchallenges of the larger challenge. Assume that you will have three or four groups, and identify specifically what each group will be doing.
- *Seminars, class meetings.* The groups will need to keep each other informed. Create some kind of checkpoint to ensure that this happens.

- *Presentation.* Once the groups have completed their work and the efforts have been synthesized, they make a presentation to parents, the principal, the school board, or other interested parties. A second presentation will come when the students have actually finished the project.
- *Reflection.* Some ways of providing both formative and summative reflective thinking must be built into the process. Journals and informal assessment strategies seem to work best.
- *Connections.* A legitimate criticism of schoolwork is that it is often unconnected. Identify connections with literature (specific titles), science, geography, history, language, the arts, mechanical drawing, or landscape architecture.
- *Skills.* What specific skills will be employed and where?
- *Concepts.* What key ideas or generalizations should students learn?
- *Flowchart or webbing.* Provide some sort of diagram to show how the unit works. The webbing shown in Figure 10.2 is an example of how you might proceed.

SERVICE-LEARNING PROJECTS   Service-learning projects, as the name implies, are about contributing to community, school, and family life. The purpose of such a project is to provide services or goods to others who can benefit from your work. An example of this would be a project in which children become involved with the residents of a retirement home, attempting to include them in their lives. Many teachers have commented on the beneficial effects of such a service-learning project, both to the children

Figure 10.2   *The Tasks Needed to Complete a Project*

and to the residents of the retirement home. The singing, artwork, plays, and reports bring joy to the residents and fulfillment to the children.

One service-learning project done by elementary school children that especially impressed me was at a school that had a considerable turnover of enrollment. New children were continually enrolling in the school. The students entered into a service project that involved making "Welcome to Our School" kits, which were given to new children when they enrolled during the school year. The kits were shoeboxes that contained names of friendly children to meet, a map of the school, a letter from the principal, a free lunch ticket, and activities and puzzles. The students who did that project learned about moral development and caring for others who might be scared, anxious, or just plain feeling alone, and that was worth a lot more than some abstract discussion of fairness, caring, and other virtues. But more than that, when teachers get the children involved in such projects, they have concrete experiences to enhance the discussions.

Many children today do not even know elderly people. They are denied the wisdom and comfort that older people can share with the young. Others may never have considered what it would be like to be a new student in an unknown environment. The beautiful thing about service-learning projects is that they are truly win/win situations in which it is difficult to know who gains the most.

PRODUCTION PROJECTS   Anyone who has ever been in a play, helped to set up a school carnival, or participated in any equally ambitious project knows how much fun and how much work it can be. The key to production projects is that the focus is on *producing* something. The event itself represents only the outcome. It's what happens along the way that is so great: the rehearsals, the late-night hammering and sawing, the camaraderie, the worry over whether things will ever come together, and so on.

One of the best tests of school experience comes when one looks back from a perspective of time. In fact, Aristotle noted that such things as happiness are best defined in retrospect. Some of the great memories of school experience are created by production projects. To this day, one of my clearest, best memories of school comes from third grade (in my case, about a million years ago), when our class did a production of the play *The Shoemaker and the Elves*, which was broadcast over a local radio station. What a great teacher Mrs. Knott was to do that with us. Another great production that I recall was in fourth grade, when our class made a huge wrap-around-the-room mural of life in ancient Egypt, Greece, and Rome. Thanks to Mrs. Emery for making social studies come alive. Oh, what vision teachers have who get their students involved in group productions!

Teachers and students bring history alive through sociodrama and role-play.

PROBLEM-SOLVING PROJECTS Solving problems using the project approach is great because it gets you and the students into the business of *applying* ideas and skills, rather than merely learning them for their own sake. A problem-solving project is best organized around an empirical question, one that can be answered by gathering information and reaching a solution on the basis of an analysis and synthesis of the information. Problem-solving projects use methods and ideas from every discipline, combining mathematics, language, science, music, art, social studies, and anything else that might be helpful.

Problem-solving projects are experiences with real problems that have real solutions. For example, if your class wants to improve communication in the school, you might begin with the question: How can we improve communication in our school? Once the question is framed to everyone's satisfaction, you are ready to go. The class will have to do surveys, experiments, and whatever it takes to solve the problem.

Here are some other examples of questions that can result in problem-solving projects:

- How can we make the pedestrian crossing near our school safer?
- How can we determine which of several brands of a product is the best buy?
- How can we establish ways for kids of different grades/ages in this school to work together?
- How can we find out about different ways to learn?
- How can we create a schoolwide celebration of Arbor Day?
- How can we redesign our classroom to make it a better place to learn?
- How can we get a schoolwide literacy campaign going?

SCHOOLWIDE PROJECTS It is great to involve all the students in a classroom, or even all the students at a grade level, in projects of one kind or another. But schoolwide projects are particularly wonderful because they have the potential to bring the whole student body, faculty, and staff together to focus on a common topic. It takes energy and leadership to mobilize a whole school, but when it is done well, a different ethos will prevail.

Schoolwide projects create an esprit de corps that you can't achieve any other way. It is indeed heartwarming to see children of different ages working together, sharing, teaching, and learning from each other. School assemblies take on new meaning as the entire K–6 student body gathers to hear the outcome of a school project on helping the homeless, the elderly, or the needy; to present the culminating activities of a school-wide fitness and nutrition project; or to present awards and certificates to the children who have taken part in a literacy campaign.

in the classroom   Constructing a Greenbelt

Many school environments are dominated by pavement and noise. In recent years, *greenbelt theory*, first developed in England and Australia by urban geographers, has led to ecologically sound, aesthetically pleasing, and economically feasible ways to bring about positive change in even the most paved-over, congested areas. People around the globe have responded to the need to maintain places of beauty, animal habitats, and areas to play and relax.

People have developed the capacity to dominate most plant and animal species. For better

or worse, human beings have become the main stewards of the planet. We need to teach our children positive stewardship in order to ensure a productive ecological balance of nature.

In the Greenbelt Design Project (Sharp & Ellis, 1994), students are challenged to explore the possibilities of designing and developing a green-belt. The students take part in all facets of the project, from gathering information, doing feasibility studies, creating models, planning, and convincing others of the need to the final stage, the actual construction of a greenbelt.

The purpose is clear: to design and construct a functional and beautiful greenbelt at the school. The greenbelt, no matter how small or large, must be something the children can themselves produce. The design considerations are beauty, cost, animal habitat, plant choice, safety, and low maintenance. The students will need to take into account ecological factors, such as growing conditions, soil, climate, and so on. This will demand a good deal of research. They will also need to study elements of design, architecture, and safety.

Here is how one primary teacher approached the project with her class (see Figure 10.3):

In creating our greenbelt, it was important for us to know all the basic needs of the plants we wanted in our little park, and how we could supply those needs. It was a small, bare lifeless corner of the school yard. What a challenge we faced if we wanted it to be beautiful! We learned all about the plants and animals (everything from dogs and rabbits to earthworms and bugs) that might inhabit the area. We learned how to test soil and how to enrich it. We studied the weather and climate patterns. Each day, we took temperature readings, checked sun angles, shade, and so on. We measured the rainfall faithfully. We took pictures, we drew maps, we interviewed kids, citizens, and experts. We watched films about parks and greenbelts, looking for ideas. We

Figure 10.3 *Constructing a Greenbelt*

even figured out fund-raising ideas to pay for the plants and other work related to planting. We made designs, drew pictures, built models, had landscapers come to class—whatever it took!

Every day, committees met. They discussed, they argued, they listened to experts—they were becoming experts themselves. I was really proud of the kids. At *long* last, we presented our model to the school board, complete with drawings, sketches, and even cost estimates. They were surprised when we told them we had developed a budget and had raised the money to pay for the project. I wish you could have been there on the beautiful spring morning when we dedicated the greenbelt. What a crowd! And such beautiful music and dancing. Everyone was excited. I just watched from the side while the kids gave speeches and graciously accepted the praises of the Parks Commissioner, the principal, and the chairman of the school board. Those kids and I know what it means to be a citizen!

Significant Themes for Integration

The search for significant common themes is at the heart of integrated studies. Once established, themes become the rallying point of the curriculum, the place to go when you want to be sure that the pursuit is meaningful and excellent. Themes provide a means for the various contributing disciplines to be different, showcasing their unique properties yet at the same time carrying out a similar conceptual purpose. The liberating aspect of a carefully chosen, content-enriching theme is that it is supportive of connected, integrated experiences across the disciplines. Moreover, it prohibits a superficial tyranny of integration for its own sake from taking over the curriculum.

Of course, there are many significant themes that teachers and children might pursue. I will suggest here eight broad themes that have the potential to be encountered and reencountered in spiral fashion at gradually increasing levels of sophistication and complexity. Each theme, in order to qualify, must meet several important tests:

1. Is the theme truly conceptual—that is, is it representative of ideas that transcend place and time? If so, it has the potential for transfer and utility beyond the bounds of specific subject matter.
2. Does the theme lend itself to all three knowledge modes—that is, knowledge received, knowledge discovered, and knowledge constructed? If so, then the theme is suited to knowledge acquisition, cultural literacy, problem solving, experiential learning, and constructivist thinking and doing.
3. Is the theme fundamentally worth pursuing in each of the separate content areas—that is, social studies, science, arts, humanities, mathematics? If so, then the integrity of the curriculum can be ensured. After all, if a theme cannot be pursued within any given discipline, then it is not actually interdisciplinary but in fact peculiar to certain subject matter.
4. Does the theme have the potential to enrich the curriculum and therefore the lives of students and teachers? If so, then the theme is useful, beautiful, and truthful and it addresses an underlying sense of moral goodness.

There are many interesting and possibly worthwhile themes that teachers can use to integrate the curriculum. By applying this fourfold test, we can reduce the list to manageable, meaningful proportions. I do not mean to suggest that I have developed the one magic list; other themes no doubt could be readily added. The following themes, however, will do for purposes of illustration.

Cause and Effect

Children and adults, amateurs and professionals, and young and old notice effects all around them. Any given effect assumes one or more causes. Leaves fall from the trees in October. Someone is in a happy mood. War breaks out in a region of the world. People speak the same language but with different accents. These are all outcomes—that is, they are the effects of certain causes. How do things come to be the way they are? Why do things sometimes turn out differently from the way one had hoped they would? What are the causative agents? How can one know? It seems to be in people's nature to want to identify the cause or causes of the effects they perceive. What were the causes of the Civil War? Why did the cake taste differently this time when you thought you followed the same recipe? What were the lasting effects of Lewis and Clark's epic trek to the West?

Commonality and Diversity

One of the hallmarks of investigation is the attempt to document similarities and differences. People ask themselves how they are like their parents and how they are different from them. They explore the similarities and differences between the travels of Marco Polo and those of Francis Drake. They wonder, if reading and writing are both branches of language arts and therefore similar, how then are they different? They contemplate how students studying such similar material at school can be so different in their learning preferences and learning styles. They ask how history and historical fiction are as different as a factual and make-believe account of something, yet at the same time, both can move one nearer to the truth about the past.

Three of the most basic processes of the arts and sciences are at the heart of exploring commonality and diversity. Observation, description, and classification are excellent points of departure. Young children notice differences and similarities in the patterns and shapes of leaves. Flowers are alike and different, beginning with simple and composite blossoms. Foods fit into different groups. Paintings can be classified by schools, time periods, and means of expression. Separate subjects or disciplines arose over time because enough perceived difference developed between and among them. Interdisciplinary teaching and learning turns the equation around and asks: What are the similarities?

Systems and Patterns

Children learn early in their lives to think and feel in terms of the patterns of holidays, birthdays, and special events. They intuitively perceive a system of special days and times of the year that take on a rhythm. The start of school in the fall, along with Halloween, Thanksgiving, Christmas, New Year's Day, Valentine's Day, spring break, and summer vacation, are all touch points in the elaborate culture of childhood. As students grow older, many of them relate to the patterns of the sports calendar of the school: football, followed by basketball, followed by baseball, and so on. For teachers, the system is often divided into reporting periods of three or four per school year. Units of study begin and culminate following a pattern. The school itself is a complex social/academic system, complete with roles, expectations, rules, checkpoints, diplomas, and so on.

As part of the solar system (see Figure 10.4), Earth is itself a system of water, land, creatures, plants, and atmosphere. Earth's system has an established pattern of seasons, with a time to sow and a time to harvest, a time to work and a time to rest. Within families, patterns of behavior and traditions are established, complete with histories and mythologies. People search for patterns in their ancestry. Geneticists look for patterns in the work of such scientific undertakings as the human genome project, an intricate mapping of the the DNA structure of human beings. Each atom of each element is itself a system with certain valences that place it in a family of similar elements.

Cycles and Change

The life cycle of the monarch butterfly illustrates four major changes in the growth and development of that beautiful creature: from egg, to larva, to pupa, to adult. The idea of a *cycle* is that of an interval of time during which a sequence of a recurring succession of events or phenomena is completed. Thus, the life cycle of the monarch butterfly has a sense of predictability in terms of time and form.

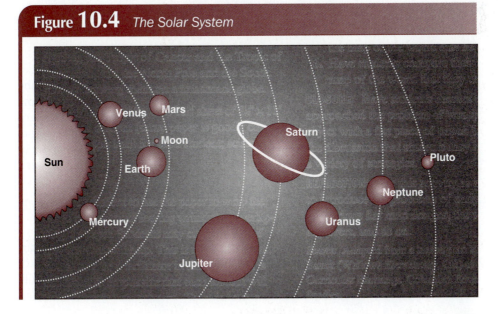

Figure 10.4 *The Solar System*

A cycle not only has a theme of recurrence but also a theme of circularity that makes it different from a pattern of linear development. The classic Greek sense of time and history was cyclical—that is, no beginning and no end—as opposed to the Hebrew sense of time and history, which was set more to a vector with a beginning point (creation), direction, and end time (judgment).

Cycles vary greatly in scale so that some are more immediately distinguishable as cycles—for instance, the cycle of day and night or of the seasons. Others—for example, the recurrence of ice ages that appear at least to have some cyclical pattern—are known only on the basis of serious scientific investigation. Comet Halley, which will reappear in the skies in the year 2061, has a cycle of 76 years, so some people are able to see the recurrence of the cycle in their lifetimes.

Historical change often occurs in cycles, just as change occurs cyclically in the lives of living things.

In music, any compositional form characterized by repetition from an earlier movement in order to unify the structure is called a *cycle*. The familiar children's tune "Row, Row, Row Your Boat" is a simple example. The need for cyclic devices became crucial during the times of Mozart and Haydn, when the romantic novel took the place of classical drama and narrative poems as the basic model for instrumental music. Thus, the idea of the cycle in music took on somewhat new meaning as changes in forms of expression happened in literature and other arts. The relationship between cycles and change, then, can also be seen between and among different art forms.

Scale and Symmetry

Human beings are bilaterally symmetrical; that is, one side of the body is nearly a mirror image of the other, which could be demonstrated by drawing an axis from the top of the head to the place between the two feet. A hen's egg would be shown to be bilaterally symmetrical if an axis were drawn on it longitudinally but not if it were drawn around the middle of the egg, as if the line were an equator. A circle, no matter where one draws a line from one side to the other through the center, is biradially symmetrical.

Forms of symmetry, more or less, are found everywhere in nature and in the constructed environment. One finds forms of symmetry in a daffodil; in the Parthenon of ancient Athens; in the shell of a chambered nautilus; in Jane Austen's book *Pride and Prejudice*; in the yin and yang of Eastern philosophy; and in Beethoven's symphonies. One also finds a certain symmetry in the seasons, in day and night, and in the configuration of the solar system. Symmetry is found in the leaves of a tree, in the three branches of U.S. government, in the design of the space shuttle, in the balance a teacher brings to the curriculum, in the need for both work and play, and in the graceful contours of a Grecian urn.

In cartography, scale is represented by the ratio between distances on a map and distances on the earth's surface. A scale drawing showing the floorplan of a classroom is an attempt to illustrate the relative size and distances of objects from each other as they exist in the actual classroom. The more closely the size of features on a map or sketch approaches actual size, the larger is the scale. Thus, a map showing the whole earth is considered small scale, whereas a map showing a backyard would probably be considered large scale (see Figures 10.5 and 10.6).

Athletic fields and gymnasiums are built to certain scales and symmetries. A football field must be built to an exact size, as must a tennis court, but a baseball field or a basketball court can vary in size. A basketball court must be a true rectangle, even though it may be somewhat different in size from one court to another. A baseball field, on the other hand, must be regular only in its infield proportions (i.e., from one base to another). The outfield may be allowed to vary so that the distances from home plate to the right-, center-, and left-field walls are quite different within a given park as well as from park to park. Thus, a baseball field has qualities of symmetry as well as of asymmetry.

Children, by nature, are marvelous sketch artists and map makers. As they begin to learn about scale and symmetry, they need to be encouraged to observe, draw, sketch, map, chart, talk, and sing and dance about what they see. Observing and recording are the two most basic skills of science, both social and natural. When a child begins to observe carefully and to record in some way what she or he sees, subtleties begin to emerge. Elements of color, line, texture, size, distance, symmetry, and scale become clearer, and the child's sense of consciousness is heightened. The doors leading to a world of real learning begin to open.

Interaction and Relationships

In a classroom of 25 people, the number of paired person-to-person combinations is 300! Assuming that you and a fellow teacher's classes have 25 students apiece for a total of 50, the three-to-a-group combinations of students the two of you could put together numbers 19,600! Just imagine the possibilities you have to allow your students to really get to know each other.

Of course, people interact not only with people but also with nature, the built environment, texts, films, and so on. A child's relationship with others is very different in a

Figure 10.5 *Large-Scale Maps Represent Small Areas of the Earth's Surface*

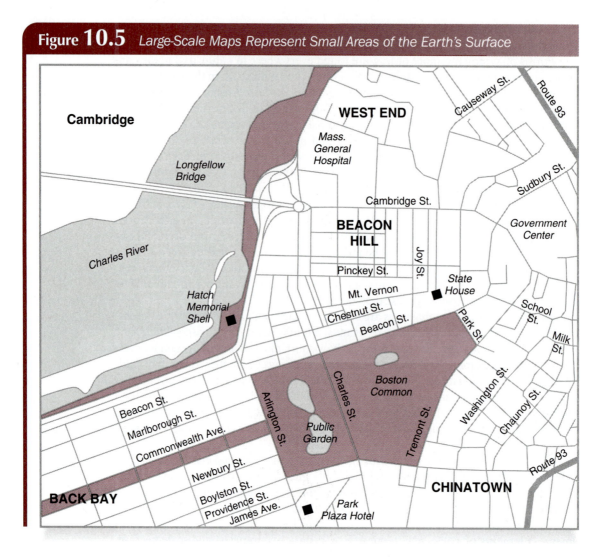

classroom where each student works alone at his or her desk versus a room where group projects and collaborative learning are emphasized. A child's relationship with the teacher is very different in a warm, supportive, caring, challenging environment versus an autocratic, aloof, and unfair environment.

School subjects can themselves be related and allowed to interact, or they can be isolated, unrelated, and unconnected. Whether there is interaction among people or school subjects in the teaching/learning equation is a fundamental pedagogical question. Where school life is dominated by what German philosopher Jürgen Habermas (1968) calls *technical interests*, then predictability and control become paramount pedagogical concerns. The technical interest focuses primarily on means–ends questions.

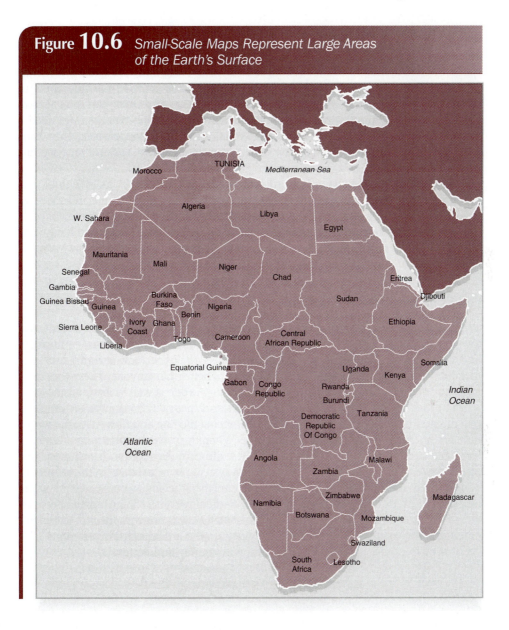

Figure 10.6 *Small-Scale Maps Represent Large Areas of the Earth's Surface*

Examples of this are the use of behavioral objectives and a tightly scripted lesson plan. In other words, any attempt to predict and therefore control the behavior of students toward a predetermined outcome is indicative of the technical interest at work. The result of such a preoccupation is a socially, morally, and intellectually simplified syntax of classroom life.

Time and Space

History and literature provide insights to time. Geography, art, and geometry illustrate space. Studied in integrated fashion, these disciplines bring time and space together as powerful themes for orienting oneself to one's place in the world. To a child, an hour can seem a long time. Adults often think in terms of projects of several years. Nineteenth-century pioneer Marcus Whitman who together with his wife, Narcissa, founded a mission settlement near present-day Walla Walla, Washington, once wrote, "My plans require time and distance." Today, someone flies from New York to San Francisco in a matter of hours.

Although modern conveniences such as jet planes, telephones, fax machines, and the Internet are wonderful devices, they tend to distort our sense of time and space. In this limited sense, the people of the past had a deeper understanding of these concepts than we do today. For instance, if you've walked or hiked somewhere, you have a different sense of time and space than you do if you've gone to the same place in an air-conditioned car.

Equilibrium and Disequilibrium

When disequilibrium occurs—for example, in war or in family problems—disorder follows close behind. When feelings, thoughts, and actions are harmonious, equilibrium and order result. Young people desperately need balance (equilibrium) and predictability (order) in their lives. Teachers know this better than anyone. They work daily with students who bring with them equilibrium and order as well as its opposite.

The idea of equilibrium applies well to systems theory. For instance, a traffic system maintains much of its equilibrium by balancing the rate and flow of traffic with a network of lights, signs, patrols, and the like. When the system is in a state of equilibrium and good order, traffic flows smoothly. Untoward events (e.g., a rush-hour pile up), however, can quickly throw the smoothest system out of balance. In the balance of nature, disequilibrium can occur in an ecosystem when previously outside elements are introduced. An example of this is the introduction of rabbits to the Australian ecosystem. The system, in its more natural state of balance, was not equipped to accommodate the influx of the fast-breeding and wide-ranging animals. Many attempts have been made to restore balance to the system, with mainly limited results.

Summary

The project approach to social studies is an effective way to create an integrated studies learning model. Projects have a real-world flavor to them, and that makes them appealing to children. They also have a beginning and an end, which allows students and teachers a better sense of what they are accomplishing. Projects offer splendid opportunities for children to work together, experiencing the give-and-take, shared decision making, and camaraderie that happens only in group activity.

There are four different but related kinds of social studies projects: (1) service-learning projects, (2) production projects, (3) problem-solving projects, and (4) schoolwide projects. Each is necessary along the road to childhood growth and development.

Group projects put the *social* back in social studies, and they provide the syntactic complexities needed to enhance moral development, language development, perspective taking, problem-solving ability, and citizenship.

Explorations

Reflect On . . .

1. Some people feel that social studies becomes watered down when it is incorporated into integrated teaching and learning. Do you agree? Why or why not?

2. How are service-learning projects beneficial to students? Production projects? Problem-solving projects? Schoolwide projects? What are the essential differences among these?

In the Field

3. Observe a classroom where students are doing a project and one where students are doing more traditional schoolwork. Do you see any differences between the two? If so, what kinds of differences?

4. Recall a project from your own days in elementary school. Describe it to another student. Have that colleague describe a favorite project to you. Discuss what made these projects enjoyable.

For Your Portfolio

5. Make two lists of projects students could do: one for primary grade students and one for intermediate grade students. Note objectives for each project.

Continuing the Journey: Suggested Readings

Benson, T. (2004). *Integrated Teaching Units.* PBS Teachers. *www.pbs.org/teachers/earlychildhood*

Drake, S. (2007). *Creating Standards-Based Integrated Curriculum.* Thousand Oaks, CA: Corwin.

Ellis, A. (2010). *Teaching, Learning, & Assessment Together: The Reflective Classroom.* Larchmont, NY: Eye on Education.

Fogerty, R., & Stoehr, J. (2007). *Integrating Curricula with Multiple Intelligences.* Thousand Oaks, CA: Corwin.

Fredericks, A. (2000). *More Social Studies through Children's Literature.* Englewood, CO: Teacher Ideas Press.

Gardner, H. (2006). *Multiple Intelligences.* New York: Basic Books.

Gregory, G., & Chapman, C. (2006). *Differentiated Instructional Strategies.* Thousand Oaks, CA: Corwin.

Lare, G. (2006). *Social Studies Teaching Activity Books.* Lanham, MA: Scarecrow Press.

Mindes, G. (2006). *Teaching Young Children Social Studies.* Westport, CT: Greenwood.

Stone, R. (2007). *Best Practices for Teaching Writing.* Thousand Oaks, CA: Corwin.

Whitebread, D., & Coltman, P. (2008). *Teaching and Learning in the Early Years.* New York: Routledge.

Websites

Thematic teaching and integrated lessons. *www.pbs. org/teachers/*

"A project based learning method is a comprehensive approach to instruction. Your students participate in projects and practice an interdisciplinary array of skills from math, language arts, fine arts, geography, science, and technology." *http://pblchecklist. 4teachers.org/*

"Project learning is a dynamic approach to teaching in which students explore real-world problems and challenges. With this type of active and engaged learning, students are inspired to obtain a deeper knowledge of the subjects they're studying." *www.edutopia.org/proiect-learning*

WebQuest, sample units of instruction; a wonderful resource for interdisciplinary teaching. Retrieved from *www.multiage-education.com* June 17, 2009.

Related NCSS Standards and Principles of Powerful Social Studies

Curriculum Standards

Ten themes are seen as vital to a comprehensive social studies program. These themes can be adapted to content in discipline-based courses, such as those primarily focused on U.S. history or economics, but likely to draw on other disciplines as well. The themes also support an organization for more highly integrated courses that cut across disciplinary boundaries such as Problems of Democracy or World Cultures (p. 3).

The Ten Themes are organizing strands for the social studies program. The ten themes are:

I Culture
II Time, Continuity, and Change
III People, Places, and Environments
IV Individual Development and Identity
V Individuals, Groups, and Institutions
VI Power, Authority, and Governance
VII Production, Distribution, and Consumption
VIII Science, Technology, and Society
IX Global Connections
X Civic Ideals and Practices (p. 8).

The standards recommend that students demonstrate their knowledge of each theme using project learning. For instance:

Possible Student Products—Learners might demonstrate their knowledge of Time, Continuity, and Change by: developing a project or exhibit representing an historic era or event (38).

Source: Excerpted from National Task Force for Social Studies, *Expectations of Excellence: Curriculum Standards for Social Studies* (Silver Spring, MD: National Council for the Social Studies, draft 2008). The Council's website is www.socialstudies.org

Teacher Standards

Social studies teaching and learning are powerful when they are integrative.

Integration is encouraged when:

• Social studies subject matter is taught topically across disciplines.

- The subject matter cuts across time and space.
- The instruction interconnects knowledge, skills, beliefs, values, and attitudes with effective social/political action.
- The teaching makes effective use of technology.
- Social studies teaching and learning are connected to other subjects.

Source: Excerpted from National Council for the Social Studies, *National Standards for Social Studies Teachers.* (Silver Spring, MD: National Council for the Social Studies, 2002), p. 12. The Council's website is www.socialstudies.org

Exploring Our Geographic World

When it comes to the fusion of beauty and useful information, is there anything as glorious as a map?

> —Roberta Smith

The more I work in the social studies field the more convinced I become that Geography is the foundation of all.

> —James Michener

"At one time, the earth was supposed to be flat. Well, so it is, even today, from Paris to Asnieres. But that fact doesn't prevent science from proving that the earth as a whole is spherical. No one nowadays denies it. Well . . . we are still at the stage of believing that life itself is flat, the distance from birth to death. Yet the probability is that life, too, is spherical and much more extensive and capacious than the hemisphere we know."

—Vincent Van Gogh

When visitors to the Washington state capitol in Olympia enter its massive front doors, one of the first sights they see is a statue of nineteenth-century pioneer Marcus Whitman, with this quote from him inscribed at the bottom: "My plans require time and distance." How remarkably apt these words are for those of us who teach elementary social studies. In fact, *time* and *distance* are two of the most crucial concepts in the social studies curriculum: Time is the key to history, and space, or distance, to geography. An integrated social studies curriculum brings the two together.

Children's sense of time—past, present, and future—develops gradually and experientially through the elementary years. So, too, does their sense of distance—far away, nearby, exact, and approximate. In everyday speech, we often fuse these two concepts: "How far is it from your home to your office?" "Oh, about half an hour, unless there's heavy traffic." Or "What's the distance from Denver to Minneapolis?" "About two hours by plane—about a day and a half if you drive it." Indeed, in traditional desert cultures, time and space are intertwined, as people think of a certain distance as being so many days' ride by camel or horse.

Maps and globes are spatial essays. They tell stories about location, direction, area, distance, scale, and proportion. They convey information primarily in graphic and symbolic terms. Maps are graphic representations of space. In this sense, they are qualitatively different from the reading and writing that dominate the school day. Reading a map is different from reading a story. Making a map is different from writing a paragaraph. Don't be surprised if some of your best mapmakers and map readers are children who do less well with typical reading and writing activities. Different children have different gifts.

Experience, as always, is important. It has been noted, for example, that children who play a great deal with Lego blocks and other building materials often develop remarkable spatial-reasoning abilities. This should serve as a reminder to all teachers that concrete activities are especially important for elementary-age children. Playing with blocks is a developmentally appropriate precursor to map making, as is playing board games like checkers and chess. Playing with blocks and board games enhances spatial reasoning.

Understanding the Tools of Geography

The earth is a sphere, but most maps are flat. Thus, it's important to keep in mind that any map, of any portion of the earth, represents an attempt to show part of a sphere on a flat surface. This cannot be done without compromising something—size, distance, proportion—which means every map contains distortions.

The distortions are not particularly important if we are attempting to show a relatively small area, as we do in a treasure map, a map of a park, or even a map of one of our states. Problems arise, however, when we attempt to show a whole continent, and things become even more troublesome when we attempt to show the entire earth (a sphere) on a flat map. You may have grown up thinking that Greenland is larger than South America, for example. After all, it appears to be larger on many world maps, especially those based on the familiar *Mercator projection.* But, in fact, it would take more than seven Greenlands to equal the size of South America.

All this is merely a way of saying that for children, maps take some getting used to. Children (and adults) live in a three-dimensional world, and maps portray that world graphically in two dimensions. That's why good map making and map reading by children begins with observation, discussion, drawing, photograhy, and other more concrete means of representing the space around us.

Maps and globes are universal means of expression in geography, history, and the social sciences (and for teachers—see, for example, Figure 11.1). They provide to the geographer, historian, political scientist, and anthropologist graphic portrayals of great economy. In the social sciences, maps are intended as selective and abstracted representations of reality. In contrast to a photograph, which is nonselective (that is, it shows everything seen by the camera's eye), a good map portrays only what is central to the message of the researcher (such as the locations of cities and states, reconstructed battle lines from military engagements, results of voting by states in a presidential election, the hunting and gathering territory of a tribal group) and factors out the details not essential to the researcher's message.

Figure 11.1 An Aerial View of an Ideal Classroom Learning Environment, as Conceived by an Elementary Teacher

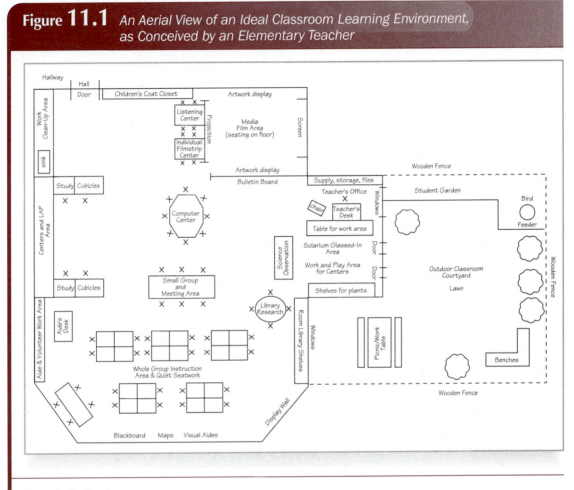

Source: Dy Ann Dennie.

At its most basic, a map shows one variable. The map in Figure 11.2, for example, offers the map reader nothing more than the spatial distribution of tropical rain forests throughout the world. Most maps illustrate a number of variables, but for young learners, a one-variable map is often a good starting place.

A map, then, is a basic communication tool that represents reality in an arbitrary and selective way. In creating Figure 11.2, we arbitrarily decided to select tropical rain forests for illustration. We could just as well have shown river systems, mountain ranges, or major cities. Keep this idea in mind when you are working with students of elementary school age. The selectivity that makes a map a powerful means of communicating spatial relationships renders that same map potentially confusing to the child who has not had experience in making the developmental transition from real and pictorial representations to abstract representations.

Figure 11.2 *Tropical Rain Forest Map*

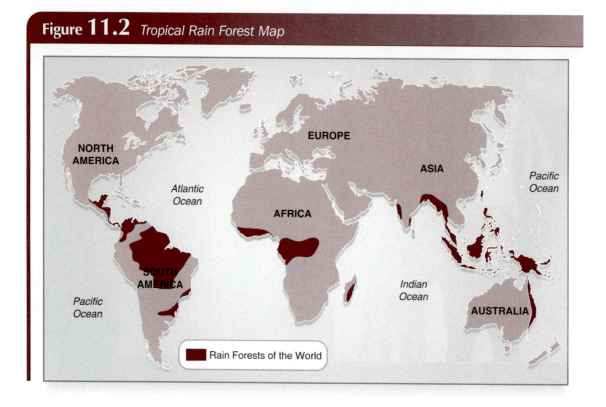

NORTH
AMERICA

EUROPE

ASIA

*Pacific
Ocean*

*Atlantic
Ocean*

AFRICA

SOUTH
AMERICA

*Indian
Ocean*

*Pacific
Ocean*

AUSTRALIA

Rain Forests of the World

A child's ability to conceptualize space develops with age and experience. For example, compare the bedroom map drawn by a 6-year-old (Figure 11.3) with that drawn by an 11-year-old (Figure 11.4). What differences can you see between the younger and the older child's conception of space?

With regard to mapmaking and map interpretation, in particular, experiential approaches to teaching the underlying concepts and skills are much more effective than are traditional textbook approaches. The younger the children, the more hands-on (and feet-on!) experiences are needed to allow them to make the connection between the landscape and its graphic representation. Sample Lesson 11.1 provides a wonderful introductory experience with maps for children who are new to a school. Famous educator Maria Montessori once noted that children actually learn to write before they learn to read. This may seem backward, but she was right. Children's scribbling often represents their early attempts to put their thoughts on paper.

Montessori's insight is especially appropriate to map reading. Children begin making maps—in the form of the drawings and pictures they create—before they begin reading maps. They are, in fact, natural map makers. Consider the child's drawing in Figure 11.5. It demonstrates perfect readiness for mapmaking and map interpretation. The child has developed a sense of perspective, distance, and scale, all of which are basic elements of cartography.

Finally!

Figure 11.3 *A Map of a Bedroom Drawn by A Six-Year-Old*

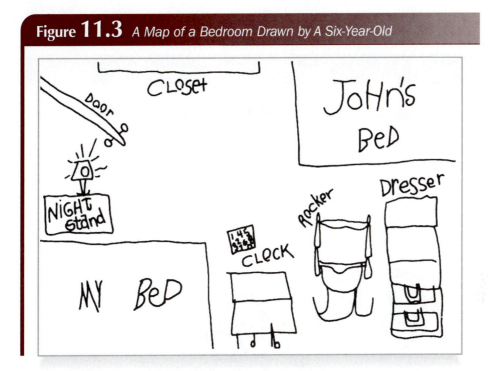

Figure 11.4 *A Map of a Bedroom Drawn by an 11-Year-Old*

Figure 11.5 *A Child's Drawing of a Sheep Pasture*

Applying the Five Themes of Geography

Before we begin thinking about specific techniques for making and interpreting maps and globes, let's step back and look at the larger picture. In 1984, the National Council for Geographic Education (NCGE) and the Association of American Geographers (AAG) cooperated in the development of five themes on which to base the curriculum of geographic education. Those five themes—location, place, human/environment interaction, movement, regions—provide a conceptual foundation on which to build appropriate learning experiences for children. The themes can provide points of reference for all the activities you undertake related to geographic learning (see Figure 11.6).

You can begin with the world around you and your students. Your school, for example, has an *absolute* location. It is located at a particular intersect of longitude and latitude on the Earth's surface. It has an address that locates it within the city or town. Your school also is located *relative* to other places, such as stores, houses, parks, churches, and the like. So, your school, like all places, has both a particular absolute location (longitude and latitude) and a particular relative location (proximity to other places). Your school can also be described in terms of *place*—that is, the characteristics

Figure 11.6 *The Five Themes of Geography*

The five themes of geography were presented in 1984 by the Joint Committee on Geographic Education of the National Council for Geographic Education (NCGE) and the Association of American Geographers (AAG).

Theme 1: Location. Geographers use latitude and longitude to identify a place's absolute or precise location. Relative location means the location of one place on the Earth's surface relative to other places.

Theme 2: Place. A particular place on the Earth's surface can be described in terms of its human and physical features and characteristics.

Theme 3: Interaction. Human beings interact with their environments by changing them, using them for various purposes, and so on.

Theme 4: Movement. People change their locations, move across the landscape, and migrate from one place to another. Goods and services are transported from certain locations to other sites.

Theme 5: Region. A region is an area that displays physical, political, or cultural unity. There are three types of regions: (1) formal regions defined by political boundaries; (2) functional regions defined by a specific purpose such as trade, distribution, or service; and (3) vernacular regions defined generally by people's perceptions, such as New England or Southeast Asia.

Source: Adapted from the National Geographic Society. *www.nationalgeographic.com*

of its setting, whether hilly or flat, and so on. And your school represents a human modification of the environment from its natural state. Perhaps a century ago, the very place on which the school stands was used for some other purpose.

Then there is *movement*. People move in and out of your school every day. Students and teachers come in the morning and leave in the afternoon. Visitors also arrive and leave. In addition to people, communication goes in and out: Mail and e-mail are sent by and received at your school. And finally, your school is located in a particular *region* of the state and country. That region might be described as suburban, industrial, middle class, rainy, western, or whatever.

The five themes of geography should be used by childen as tools for investigation and as ways of thinking about the earth and how we occupy it. The themes are inherently interdisciplinary. They can form the conceptual point of reference for studying the environment, literature, art, music, history, health, and practically any topic you and your students decide to investigate. Geography may, in fact, be the most integrative subject in the curriculum. The study of geography involves not only the other areas of social studies education—history, economics, sociology, and so on—but also the skills and strategies of other disciplines: math, language arts, and even science. Geography is not merely the centerpiece of social studies; it goes beyond that, offering the possibility to connect well with every subject you teach.

Helping Students Learn to Make and Read Maps

To help students participate in the transition from reality to abstraction in representing space—that is, making maps and understanding how to read them—encourage them to develop the basic skills of the geographer: observing and recording. You can do a number of activities to move students forward in this process. An ideal way to lead students from a realistic understanding of an area to an abstract one is to use your school as a starting point. Follow these eight steps:

1. Have your students take a walking tour of the area surrounding the school. Note the various landmarks, such as streets, businesses, houses, parks, and so on.
2. Using a digital camera to record the sights, work with your students to put together a "slide show" of the area surrounding the school, in which various landmarks are portrayed.
3. View the school area from some elevated perspective, such as a hill or a tall building. Take some pictures and review them in class.
4. Have the class or several small groups do murals depicting the school and the surrounding area. Teams can illustrate the playground, the cafeteria, gym, and the like.
5. Make a model of the area from cardboard, wooden blocks, and paper. This can be done by the entire class or even better by small groups.
6. Borrow an aerial photograph of the area around the school from the local office of the U.S. Department of Agriculture or the local public library. Pick up a map of your city or area. Locate the school. Let the students compare the aerial photograph with the map.
7. Make an enlargement of the portion of a map that shows the area around the school, and give each student a copy. Compare this map to the aerial photograph, the model, the map mural, and the photos you and your students took of the area.
8. Take another walk around the area. Have each student bring along his or her copy of the map from step 7. As students see landmarks, have them point to them on their maps. Be sure to bring along sketch pads so students can draw items of interest.

This activity uses a series of developmental steps to take students from the concrete experience of walking through and observing an area to understanding its eventual abstract representation. The steps could be used in a daily sequence of eight lessons or scattered over a longer time period.

Mental Maps

Making and interpeting so-called mental maps ranks high on the list of national geography standards. All of us carry images, or *mental maps,* of spaces and places in our heads. Take a moment to refer to your own "atlas" of mental maps. Can you visualize your bedroom? (I hope you remembered to make the bed!) Can you visualize the route from your home to the grocery store? Can you imagine a tropical island paradise that you would love to visit? Can you see your fourth-grade classroom in your mind's eye? The fact is that you have literally thousands of mental maps stored in the atlas of your mind and memory.

Mental maps are more or less accurate, depending on a number of factors, including the reliability of one's memory, how often one visits a place or traverses a certain distance, and how important it is for one to know how to get someplace. For example, even very young children have pretty good mental maps of the rooms in their houses or apartments. They typically have little trouble navigating from one area to another. But if a very young child lives in a house with a basement that she or he never or seldom ventures into, then the mental map of that basement may be quite inaccurate. In fact, the basement may seem like a mysterious and frightening place.

On a different scale, the mental map of western North America contained about as much fiction as fact for many years. In fact, in 1804, President Thomas Jefferson sent Meriwether Lewis and William Clark from the Missouri River to the Pacific Ocean across North America for the purpose of finding the so-called Northwest Passage, an imagined water route from the Great Plains to the Pacific. Many maps of the day already showed the Northwest Passage in one location or another (see Figure 11.7). The only trouble was that it never existed except in people's imaginations. The mental

Figure 11.7 *Map of Northwest Passage*

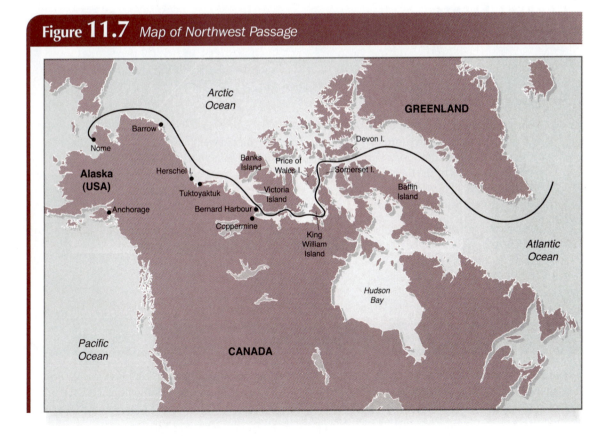

map of the West changed dramatically as the vast region was explored over time. Mapmaking has become much more scientific in modern times, but looking at certain maps from ancient times will tell you that imagination played as great a part in creating them as did surveying and cartography.

An individual has literally dozens of mental maps stored in her or his mind. Many of them are so accurate that the person navigates flawlessly, perhaps from his or her residence to the shopping mall or grocery store or Aunt Margaret's house. Certain other maps may be a bit on the hazy side, especially if the person is the type to get lost occasionally. Some mental maps cover small distances; others cover great distances. We are all mapmakers and navigators—some, better than others.

Generally, a mental map is retrieved only when the person needs it to go somewhere or to explain to someone how to get somewhere. In this sense, mental maps are quite functional. However, they have other uses, as well. Sometimes people just like to think about places that they've been to and even places they've never visited. Other times, we may use mental maps to respond to requests for directions ("How do you get from here to the aquarium?") or rely on the mental maps of others when we need directions ourselves. It is always a good idea to bear in mind that mental maps are not necessarily *accurate* maps; they just represent the maps we have in our heads.

CURRENT EVENTS
Focus on the Weather Page

Every major newspaper carries a complete weather page each day, providing an incredible almanac of information. Here are two mapmaking activities in which to engage your students:

- Assign each student a city in the United States, and have her or him record the high and low temperatures for that city as reported daily on the weather page of the newspaper. Do this for a period of at least two weeks. Have each student create a line graph of the daily high (in red) and low (in blue) temperatures for this time period.
- Repeat this process using international city temperatures.

In each case, the work that results makes a wonderful display in your classroom. A bulletin board map should be posted during each activity that shows the cities for which records are being kept.

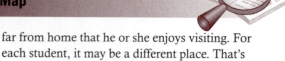

in the classroom   Drawing from a Mental Map

Provide your students with opportunities to get their mental maps out of their heads and onto paper. Ask each student to think about a place not far from home that he or she enjoys visiting. For each student, it may be a different place. That's good, because you will have more variety when the children put their maps up for display. (On the other hand, if you want to start with a place students have in common, have them make mental maps of the playground or how to get from their room to the principal's office.) Then have the students do the following:

1. Make a list of landmarks along the way—things that stand out in their minds. Younger children can tell you what landmarks they intend to include when they draw their maps, and older children can make a written list.
2. Draw their maps as they see them in their minds.
3. Take their maps home and verify them against reality—that is, check to see if their maps are

more or less accurate. The process of verification is a very important skill that children need to learn.

4. Make new maps based on the knowledge gained in the verification process. This is a good time to reflect with students on the idea of making errors, because their first maps may have contained some. Point out that errors are not bad, as some children and adults think, but merely items to be corrected. Error analysis is used a great deal in problem solving, especially in the form of a technique called *reverse engineering,* where one takes a look at some product she or he has constructed and works backward to see what needs to be improved.

Traverse Maps

One of the simplest map forms for children to understand is the traverse map. A *traverse map* represents a line or linear path through an area—usually an obvious one, such as a street, a lakeshore, a river, or a boundary of some sort. Traverse maps are very easy to make, and I encourage you to have even the youngest children construct them.

To do a traverse, begin with observation and recording, the two most basic skills of the investigator. For example, if you wish to map a single block of a city street, simply walk along the block, recording everything on either side—storefronts, signposts, and so on. Similarly, to map a brook or creek for, say, 200 feet, merely walk along the side of it and record the significant things you see along the way (trees, docks, bridges, houses, and so on).

These activities are called *fieldwork.* When your fieldwork has been completed, you are ready to make your traverse map. Figure 11.8 shows the development of a child's traverse map.

in the classroom   Conceptualizing a Common Traverse

Constructing a map of the route from home to school affords children an excellent opportunity to conceptualize a common spatial traverse. It's more complicated, of course, if students ride a bus to school over some distance than if they live a block or two away. The assignment progresses like this:

1. For several days, have the children observe carefully as they walk or ride to and from school. They should notice the street names

and other important landmarks. This period of incubation and reflection about the landscape is crucial. Don't hurry the children into making a finished product. Instead, at this point, stress the skills of observation and mental recording.

2. Encourage older children to learn the particular cardinal directions they travel. For example, a child might walk two blocks south before turning east and so on.

3. Have the children begin taking field notes. They should write down street names, draw rough sketches, and so forth.

4. Have the students use their field notes to draw maps during class time. Be sure that several city maps are available, so students can refer to them as they construct their own maps.

5. Have the students give brief oral reports, in which they show the class their maps and verbalize the way they come to school.

6. Display the maps on the wall of the classroom. Encourage students to study them and make comparisons of the various routes used to get to school.

Figure 11.8 *A Child's Traverse Map of the Fremont Neighborhood*

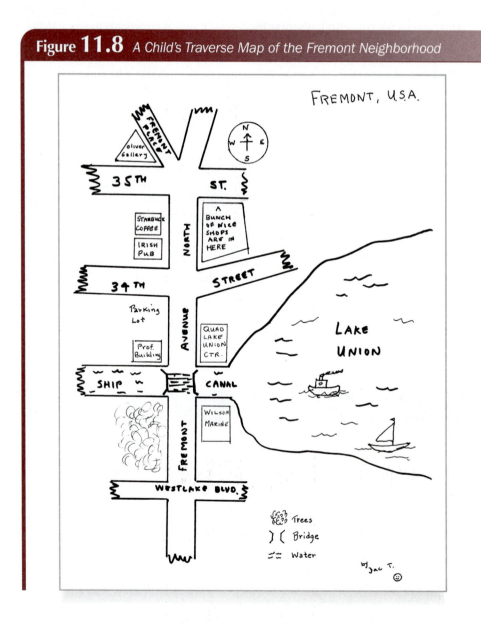

Visualizing Space

Visualizing space is a useful intellectual exercise for children. At the primary level, you can challenge students by asking them to verbalize the directions for getting from their homes to school. At the intermediate level, you might want to assign students the task of giving directions for getting from the school to certain landmarks, such as the city center, airport, zoo, park, or athletic stadium. Children can use their mental maps to help with this task.

Children also enjoy visualizing imaginary space. Instead of doing a standard book report, ask students to map the location in which a story takes place, or read a story aloud and have them note the landmarks mentioned and then draw maps. Figure 11.9 shows a map of Narnia, the setting for C. S. Lewis's popular tale *The Lion, the Witch, and the Wardrobe.* Other children's books that provide a lot of mapping possibilities are J. R. R. Tolkein's *Hobbit* books (*The Hobbit* and the *Lord of the Rings* trilogy) and J. K. Rowling's *Harry Potter* books. For many children, such a project is a welcome relief from the usual book report.

Aerial Photographs and Maps

To give younger students some insight into the overhead vertical perspective generally portrayed by maps, let them use a camera to take pictures of a terrain model or a set of blocks laid out to simulate a village. By standing directly over the model while photographing it, the student achieves the physical perspective of the mapmaker. Such a perspective is known as a *bird's-eye view* of a landscape.

Aerial photographs are widely available from a variety of sources and can be used to help students construct their own maps. Students can produce original and very accurate large-scale maps by placing tracing paper over an aerial photograph and tracing the roads, cities, water forms, wooded areas, farmland, and so on. Such a map is an interpreted form of the photograph, in which the child has made decisions about what to portray and what to leave out. Figures 11.10A and B illustrate the translation of an aerial photograph into a base map.

Changing the Scale of a Map

There are three basic techniques for changing the scale of a map: mechanical, optical, and mathematical.

- *Mechanical method.* The mechanical method uses a *pantograph,* which is an inexpensive instrument in the shape of a parallelogram. By using a pantograph, which may be set to various scale changes, the student can make a very accurate enlargement or reduction of an existing map. Also, junior cartographers can decide exactly what change of scale they want to make. You can order a pantograph from any school supply store.
- *Optical method.* The elementary school counterpart of the precision optical instruments available in certain cartography laboratories is the opaque projector. To use

Figure 11.9 *A Child's Map of the Fictional Land of Narnia*

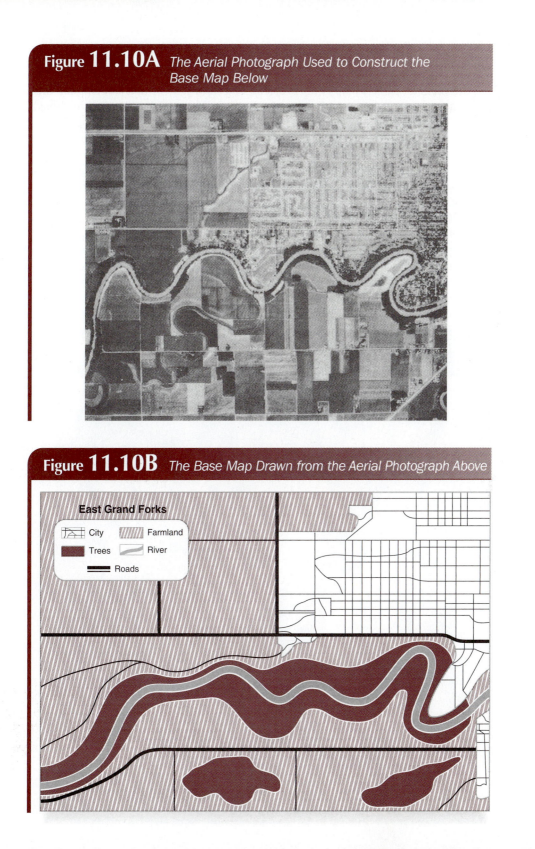

Figure 11.10A *The Aerial Photograph Used to Construct the Base Map Below*

Figure 11.10B *The Base Map Drawn from the Aerial Photograph Above*

East Grand Forks

City
Trees
Roads
Farmland
River

this method, place a map in the projector and show it on a wall; students can then trace the enlarged map outline onto a sheet of paper taped to the wall. Although the opaque projector is probably the most commonly used scale-change instrument, it is the least satisfactory, for several reasons. First, it is not possible to reduce a map with an opaque projector. Second, students using this method do not really know what the change of scale is; they only know that the new map is larger. Third, distortions often occur because the book page does not lie flat in the projector or because the instrument is projecting at a slight angle to the wall.

- *Mathematical method.* The mathematical method, which is also called the *method of similar squares,* is useful for making both enlargements and reductions. After plotting points on a grid of larger or smaller dimension than a grid superimposed on an existing map, the student can then connect the points in a line to construct a new outline. Points for cities, mountains, and other features can also be plotted. Figures 11.11A and B illustrate this method.

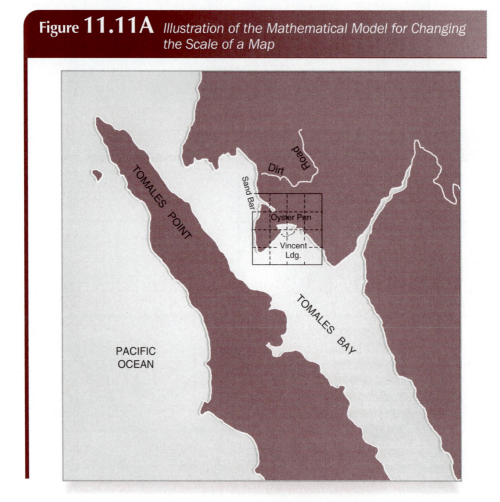

Figure 11.11A *Illustration of the Mathematical Model for Changing the Scale of a Map*

Figure **11.11B** *Illustration of the Mathematical Model for Changing the Scale of a Map*

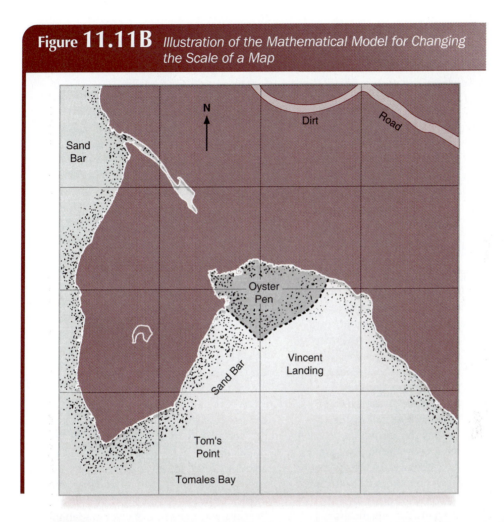

Keys to Understanding the Language of Maps

The following terms will help you and your students understand the vocabulary of maps.

- *Absolute and relative location. Absolute location* refers to a particular point on the earth's surface. Absolute location is fixed by longitude and latitude. For example, Cairo, Egypt, is located at 30 degrees east longitude and 30 degrees north latitude. *Relative location*

refers to a particular place and its relation and access to other places. For example, Greybull and Cody, Wyoming, are located not far from each other in the same county. However, the summit of the Rocky Mountains lies between the two towns, making travel difficult in winter.

- *Symbols. Symbols* are used on maps to represent both natural features (such as mountains, rivers, forests, lakes, deserts) and constructed features (such as roads, bridges, schools, airports, towns). Most maps have a *key* or *legend* that explains the meanings of the symbols used. Symbols allow mapmakers to display a variety of information. (See Figure 11.12 for a list of common map symbols.)

- *Projection*. The globe is a sphere that accurately represents the shape, size, and distance of the earth's features. An attempt to show the earth's curved surface on a flat map is called a *projection*. Small areas of the earth's surface can be portrayed more accurately on flat maps than large areas. When the entire surface of the globe is projected onto a flat map, distortions always occur. (As noted elsewhere, the familiar Mercator projection, used to create many maps of the world, makes land areas near the poles seem larger than they are. That's why many people think Greenland is larger than South America.)

- *Scale*. *Scale* is used to determine size and distance on a map or globe. A large-scale map shows a close-up representation of space (for example, a neighborhood), while a small-scale map may show the entire earth. A map's key usually contains a scale of feet or miles, centimeters or kilometers. Scale on a map describes the proportion of the size of the map to the reality it represents (for instance, 1 inch = 1 mile). Map scale makes it possible to determine real distances (for instance, if 1 inch = 1 mile, then cities shown 3 inches apart are actually 3 miles apart). Maps are nearly always smaller than the realities they represent: The larger the scale, the smaller the area depicted on a map (for example, a map of your bedroom is large scale; a map of the world is small scale). Conversely, the smaller the scale, the larger the area depicted on a map (a map of the United States is small scale; a map of your classroom is large scale). To help

students understand scale and how to use mileage keys, try Sample Lesson 11.2.

- *Direction*. Map directions are generally set to the points of the compass. It is a common misconception that north is always at the top of a map (or up) and that south is always at the bottom (or down). The *cardinal directions* of the compass are north, south, east, and west, but a *compass rose* (the map symbol that indicates direction) can show as many as 32 directions on a map.

- *Lines and space*. On a map, lines define the boundaries of space. For example, a river is a line that separates land on one side from land on the other. Often, rivers form political as well as physical boundaries; Indiana and Kentucky are separated by the Ohio River, for example.

- *Elevation*. Elevation is the extent to which a particular place is at, above, or below sea level. In the Netherlands (Holland), much of the land is below sea level and is kept from flooding by dikes. Nepal is often referred to as the "roof of the world" because the Himalayan Mountains, and in particular Mount Everest, the world's highest peak, are located there. California contains rugged mountains, land below sea level, the great flat Central Valley, and just about every kind of landform imaginable. Elevation is typically shown on maps by using either shading or color gradations.

- *Areal association*. Areal association indicates the relationship of one area to another and can refer to both natural and humanmade associations. For example, cities are often located on major rivers and harbors. Shopping malls are located regionally to accommodate large numbers of residents in a local area. Schools and shops are located in neighborhoods to facilitate walking or short rides. Hotels are located near beautiful beaches and other sites of interest. Athletic facilities are located on the grounds of high schools and universities.

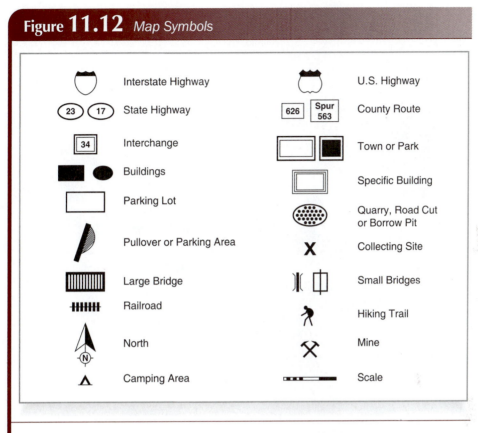

Figure 11.12 *Map Symbols*

Symbol	Label	Symbol	Label
	Interstate Highway		U.S. Highway
23 17	State Highway	626 Spur 563	County Route
34	Interchange		Town or Park
	Buildings		Specific Building
	Parking Lot		Quarry, Road Cut or Borrow Pit
	Pullover or Parking Area	X	Collecting Site
	Large Bridge	)(	Small Bridges
	Railroad		Hiking Trail
	North		Mine
	Camping Area		Scale

Note that these symbols represent features of both natural and constructed environments.

Understanding Map Projections and Globes

I am convinced that it is difficult for most children to understand that maps are, in fact, projections of the earth's curved surface onto a flat piece of paper (see Figure 11.13). That is why the *constructivity principle,* which states that activity must precede analysis, is so crucial. In other words, *drawing* maps should come before *studying* maps, especially maps drawn by someone other than the child.

Any attempt to portray a sphere (the earth) onto a flat surface meets with difficulty. Nevertheless, it is necessary to do so, simply because we can't use a globe as efficiently as a flat map that's posted on a wall or bound up in a book. A map can also portray details and show particular regions using different scales.

When the round earth is portrayed on flat paper, the result is called a *map projection* because the sphere is projected onto a flat surface. There are many map projections of the earth, but they all have one thing in common: They distort something. As noted earlier in this chapter, the most well-recognized case of distortion is that of Greenland. Many children (and some adults) assume that Greenland is larger than it is. In fact, Greenland

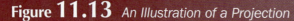

Figure 11.13 *An Illustration of a Projection*

Attempts to portray a sphere (the earth) on a flat surface are called *map projections*.

is about one-seventh the size of South America. The most common source of distortion arises from the attempt to portray lines of longitude and the spaces between them. As you know, lines of *longitude* converge at the earth's poles; they have to, since the earth is shaped like a ball, not a table top. But when they are shown on a flat map, the lines of longitude are often shown as straight vertical lines running from the North Pole to the South Pole, thereby distorting the sizes of land masses in the far north and south. To help your students understand the difficulties of making flat maps, see Sample Lesson 11.3.

The three most common projections of the round earth onto a flat surface are the following:

- The cylindrical projection
- The conic projection
- The plane surface projection

These three projections are illustrated in Figure 11.14. I suggest that you demonstrate them to your students and let them practice the activity, as well. It's a hands-on way of experiencing the difficulties of representing a sphere on a flat surface. In Figure 11.15,

Figure **11.14** *Examples of Portraying the Round Earth on Flat Paper*

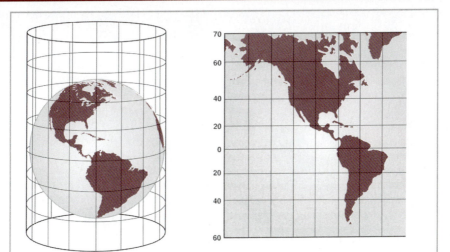

A cylindrical projection is based upon the projection of the globe onto a cylinder.

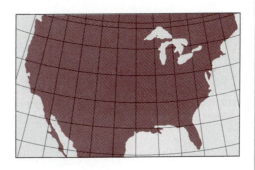

Projection of the globe onto a cone becomes a conic projection.

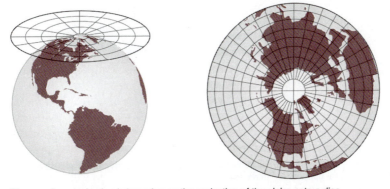

Plane-surface projection is based upon the projection of the globe onto a disc.

295

Figure **11.15** *Various Portrayals of a Globe*

When the globe is portrayed as a rectangle, the correct shapes are shown, but notice how large Greenland and Antarctica appear to be.

When the globe is portrayed as an oval, the sizes are shown correctly but the shapes are distorted.

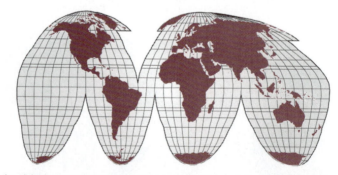

When the globe is portrayed as an orange peel, both size and shape are accurate, but notice what happens to Antarctica.

we see the different results of attempts to project the globe onto flat surfaces. In each case, something is sacrificed. Notice that the three main distortions are size, shape, and the sense of what the map should really look like.

in the classroom   A World Globe Activity

To help students understand the relationship between maps and globes and the relative sizes and locations of continents on the globe, have them do the following activity.

Simply photocopy Figure 11.16, which includes outlines of the six settled continents. Divide the class into pairs, and give each pair a photocopy. Have them cut out the individual continents. Then

provide each pair of students with a blue balloon, and have them glue the continents onto the balloon. Make sure they consult a map of the world before trying to do this, so they have a clear idea of each continent's location.

The students—and perhaps you!—will be surprised at the amount of blue still showing and the way the continents fit together.

Helping Students Learn to Use Maps

Obviously, one of the main purposes of a map is to help a person find his or her way from one place to another. Children benefit greatly from practice games in which they are challenged to tell how they would go from point A to point B. For example, on the map of Lancaster, England (Figure 11.17), how would you explain to someone how to get from St. Peter's Cathedral to the Maritime Museum? From Town Hall to the Grand Theatre? From the City Library to the Roman Bath House? From the Police Station to the Sports Centre? Encourage your students to use maps to understand locations in relation to one another and ways to get from here to there.

in the classroom   Mapping Directions

This activity is designed to help students visualize oral or written information spatially. Any story or written information that includes directions for traveling around a given space will do. Here is one example. You and your students can develop others.

Read your students the following story, and have them draw maps of the places involved. (One such map is shown in Figure 11.18.)

One morning, Little Red Riding Hood decided to visit her sick grandmother. After she left her

house, she went to the Muffin Man's to get some muffins for Grandmother. Then she went to the Flower Lady's for some nice fresh flowers to take to Grandmother. Next, Little Red Riding Hood entered the south entrance to the woods and walked along the path toward the Woodcutter's house, which was west of her house. When she reached the Wood-cutter's house, she stopped for a drink of water. She then walked north to feed some squirrels, and from there, she went by the most direct path to Grandmother's house.

Figure 11.16 *The Six Continents*

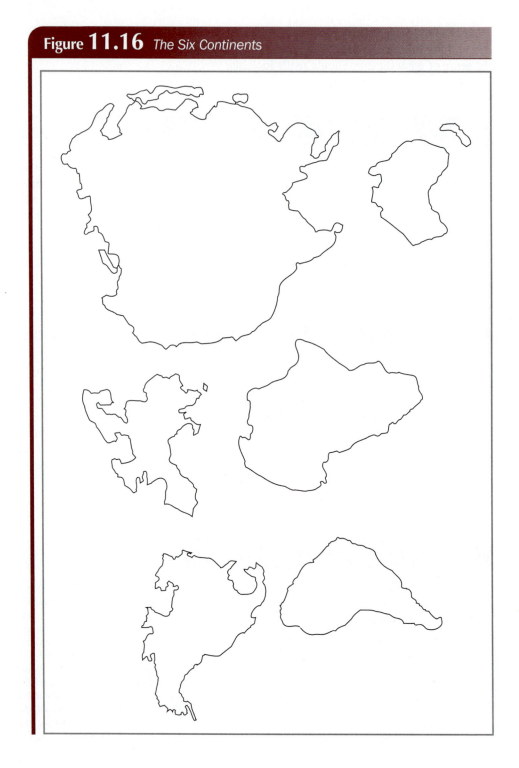

Figure 11.17 *A Map of Historic Sites in Lancaster, England*

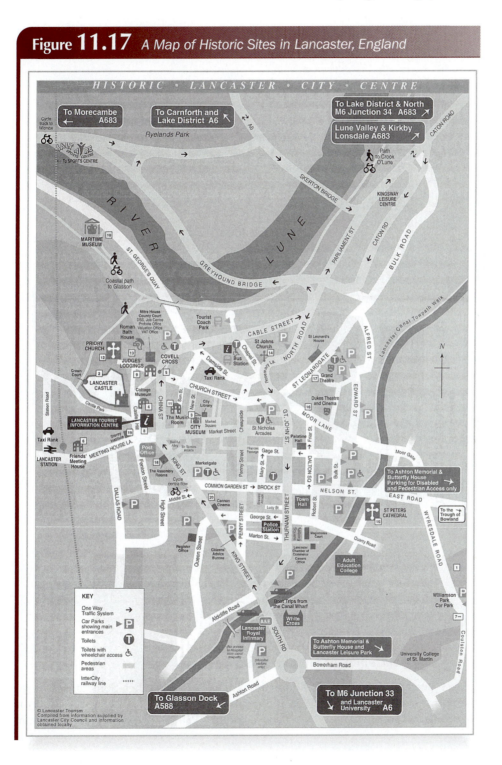

Figure 11.18 *The Road to Grandmother's House*

Considering Variables in Finding Your Way

People spend much of their time going from one place to another. Sometimes they go on foot, and sometimes by bicycle, and sometimes by bus or subway or car. Rarely is there only one way to go from one place to another. When a person decides to go from point A to point B, she or he usually considers the purpose of the trip, how much time there is to accomplish it, what means of transportation are available, and so on. All these things are called *variables*. Thus, a child walking to school must consider several variables: time, safety, friends, and perhaps scenery.

in the classroom   Mapping Variables

Here is a problem-solving challenge for you to present to your students. Have them work in pairs for this exercise in cartography. Choose any two points in the local environment. The challenge is for students to illustrate three routes on a single map: (1) the fastest route; (2) the safest route; and (3) the most scenic route.

Such an activity does several things. First of all, it encourages careful observation and exploration. Second, it creates a situation in which the junior mapmakers must plot three variables on a single map. And third, it requires decision making on the part of the participants. See Figure 11.19 for an example of a child's map showing three routes.

Figure **11.19**   *A Child's Map Showing Alternate Routes from Home to School*

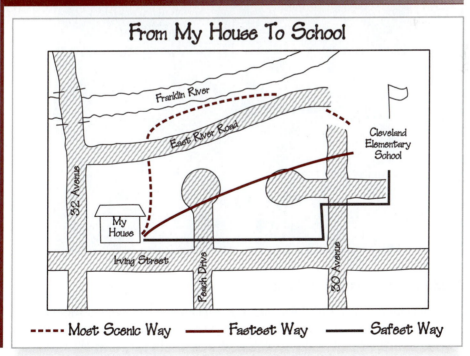

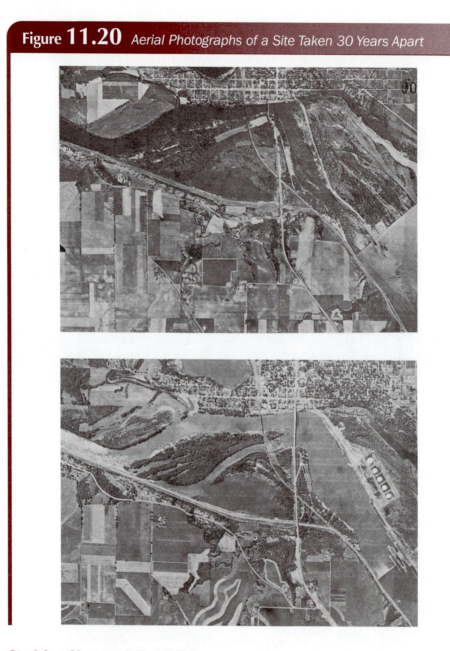

Figure 11.20 *Aerial Photographs of a Site Taken 30 Years Apart*

Studying Changes in Land Use

Maps and other spatial depictions, such as aerial photographs, can illustrate clearly the changes that people and nature have made to particular areas over time. Figure 11.20, for example, shows two aerial photographs of basically the same site taken about 30 years apart. Using photographs like these or historical maps, have students study two depictions of the same site and then document as many changes in the landscape as they can. You can use the two photos here for this task, but you may want to obtain two such photos of your school site or of the landscape in your local community. Aerial photographs are available from the Department of Agriculture and may also be available from local real estate agencies.

in the classroom   Learning Geography from Chocolate Bars

A typical chocolate bar contains the following ingredients:

Sugar	Milk
Chocolate	Soybeans
Cocoa butter	Almonds
Cacao	Vanilla

Where do these ingredients come from? The answer is that it takes many places from around the world to put together a chocolate candy bar.

Give the children a world map, and challenge them to discover where each ingredient comes from. (Don't forget the wrapper—it's probably made of paper and metal foil.) Let them use the Internet for research or look things up in the library. Then ask the students to plot the products on the map, encouraging them to make a pictorial representation of each product. Next, committees can report on each of the various products, as well as on how the products get from field to factory and how the candy bars are made at the factory. And finally, how do the candy bars get to the store so that we can buy them?

This activity will provide learning in a wide range of areas—beginning with mapmaking but including history, nutrition, and economics.

Understanding Perspective

There is nothing like a map to teach children the concept of *perspective*. The best way to use maps, of course, is developmentally. By that, I mean that lessons should come from direct experiences, which are then thoughtfully considered and discussed.

For example, to help students understand how perspectives may differ, find a picture of a bird in flight—a magazine photograph, for example. Ask the students to talk about what the bird would see from its vantage point in the sky. Perhaps students who have flown in an airplane can describe the perspective as they recall it. Next, have the students draw maps using a bird's-eye view. To do this, have each student create a model of a small village from construction paper, complete with streams, forests, roads, houses, and so on. When the villages are done, ask each student to place his or her village on the floor, so that he or she can look straight down on it. Then have each student draw a sketch, or map, of what he or she sees.

Following this activity (perhaps the next day), take the class outside to an elevated place (if there is one) on the playground. Have them draw maps of what they see. Now you are ready to have a good discussion of the differences in perspective between an aerial view and a view from the ground.

The map in Figure 11.21 is a good example of perspective taking. Notice that the centerpiece of the map is the North Pole; therefore, this map is called a *polar projection*. The space shown on the map is projected out from the North Pole. In this case, the horizon of

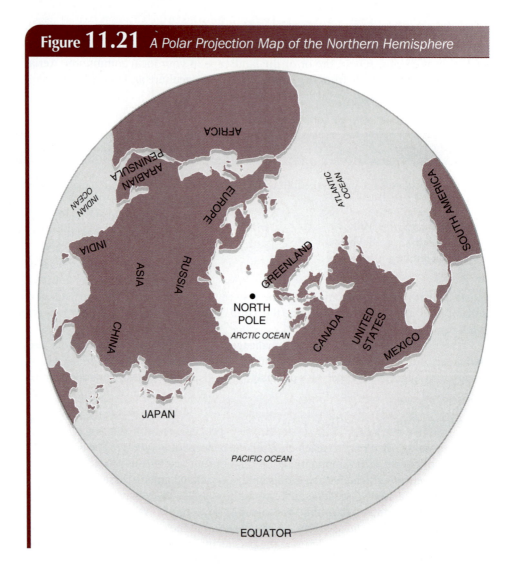

Figure 11.21 *A Polar Projection Map of the Northern Hemisphere*

the map is the equator, so we are looking at half the world's surface. This map makes it apparent that the vast majority of the earth's land surface is in the Northern Hemisphere.

Make copies of this map (one for each student), and have the students cut it out along the equator. Then ask them to rotate the map and examine it from Africa, Asia, North America, and so on. Ask students to express their thoughts about how the earth appears from these various vantage points. Ask them if they have ever considered looking at North America from such a perspective. Next, have each student draw the map. This enables them to let the perspective sink in. North America may appear upside down in their drawings, but that's only because they are used to a different perspective (see Figure 11.22).

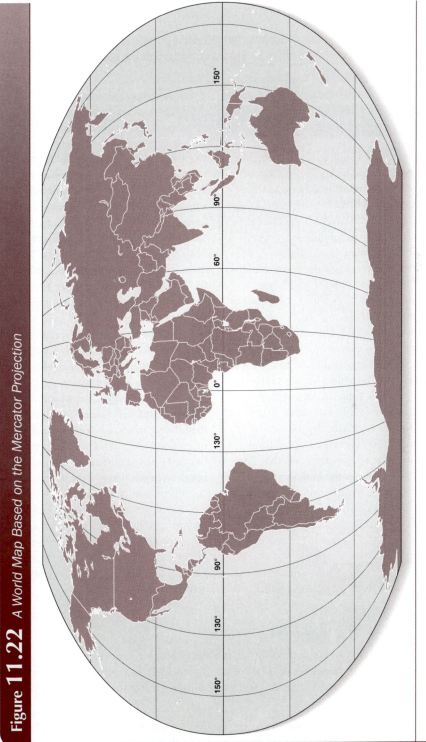

Figure 11.22 *A World Map Based on the Mercator Projection*

Compare this perspective of the world with the polar projection perspective shown in Figure 11.21.

Of course, the concept of *perspective* is pervasive. Even the perspective on a class-room lesson will be different for a child sitting in the back versus the front of the room or near a window.

---

in the classroom   Four-Color Mapping Theory

Your students can have fun exploring the theory of *four-color mapping,* which allows them to differentiate all bordering areas from one another by means of color. This technique is used by professional cartographers, or mapmakers, to make borders clear. Intermediate-age children can quickly learn the idea and use it in their own map making.

Four-color map theory is based on a mathmatical theorem that allows any series of bordering areas to be differentiated by color, using only four colors and without ever duplicating colors along any given border. A key for the United States is provided in Figure 11.23, but let your students try to figure this out themselves. It will take many tries!

Students may find four-color mapping relatively easy in the western United States, where most states have regular geometric shapes. There are two reasons for this regularity, by the way: (1) There are fewer major rivers to create natural boundaries, although there are exceptions (like the Columbia River, which forms the Washington–Oregon boundary); and (2) the boundaries for these states were mostly created long after the territories had been settled by mapmakers sitting in offices in Washington, D.C., who seemed to love drawing long, straight lines!

But just notice the squiggly lines created by the Mississippi and Ohio Rivers! These two mighty rivers create the boundary lines between more than a dozen states. The Mississippi creates a natural boundary all the way from Minnesota to Louisiana, where the river runs into the Gulf of Mexico. Trace it with your finger from north to south. Notice how the Ohio River forms the entire northern boundary of Kentucky. Trace the Ohio from its origin in Pennsylvania, where it begins at the junction of the Allegheny and Monongahela Rivers, all the way to where it joins the Mississippi in southern Illinois.

The four-color theory is really put to the test by such states as Tennessee and Kentucky. Just count their neighbors! But still, it works. Maine has only one neighbor, so it's easy.

I suggest that you create an inductive lesson for your students. Give them each an outline map of the United States. Challenge them to color the map using only four colors, without ever duplicating colors along any state boundary line. Have a few extra maps on hand, just in case the trial-and-error process doesn't work at first.

Activities such as this are powerful ways of anchoring the concepts of space and place in the minds of children. A map begins to take meaningful form, it begins to make sense, and it takes its place in the memory when a person engages in activities such as these.

Estimating Distances

The ability to estimate distance is a very valuable skill (e.g., in driving). The National Council of Teachers of Mathematics (NCTM) lists estimation as one of its 10 goals for learning mathematics. You can do many things to develop this skill; here are two suggestions:

- Take the class out on the playground (or into a long hallway), and set two markers a certain distance apart. Have everyone write down or tell her or his best guess about

Figure 11.23   *The Key to Four-Color Mapping Theory for a U.S. Map*

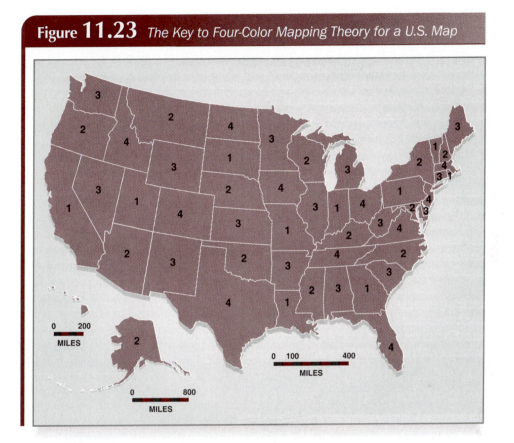

the distance between the markers. Then measure the distance between the two markers with a tape measure, like the kind used for measuring distances in track meets. (Your school probably has one.) Measuring is an important skill, and in this instance, it allows students to employ yet another skill: that of verifying their guesses. With repeated practice, students will become quite skilled at estimating distances.

- Have your students work in cooperative groups of two and use a yardstick or meterstick to measure each other's typical stride. The best thing to do is to work in a little math here. If you measure your stride, say, five times, you can add the total of all five strides and divide it by 5 to derive the average or mean stride. Once a child knows the approximate distance of his or her stride, he or she can use it to pace off distances. This becomes a built-in tool for estimating, measuring, and verifying distances anywhere.

The Internet and Maps

The explosion of electronic information has made maps and other geographic information readily accessible for both students and teachers. Figure 11.24 provides a list of Websites that you may find worth exploring.

> ## Figure **11.24** *Useful Geographic Education Websites*
>
> U.S. Geological Survey (USGS) *www.education.usgs.gov* Provides map collections, resources for meeting social studies standards, digital libraries, information about Earth Week, and a host of links.
>
> For Geography Teachers *www.members.aol.com/bowermanb/teach.html* Provides links to more than 30,000 social studies lessons, information about geographic professional associations (such as NCSS) and global education, as well as puzzles, maps, and games.
>
> Education World *www.education-world.com* Provides links to the five themes of geography and lessons to achieve them, holidays and special days around the world, a lesson plan of the day, geography A to Z, and more.
>
> Global Issues Gateway *www.gig.org/departments/gig_k12* Provides links to the National Geographic Education Guide, Newsweek Education Program, Discovery Channel School, PBS, and other valuable sources for bringing geography to life.
>
> City of San Antonio Library *www.sanantonio.gov/library/geography* Provides links to country profiles, currencies, flags, weather, maps, teaching materials, lesson plans, activities, curriculum resources, and other geography Web resources.

Summary

Maps are abstract representations of the surface of the earth or some other sphere that help people see certain spatial relationships. Maps are particularly useful to social scientists as a means of illustrating spatial data, such as political boundaries, population distributions, the relative locations of goods and services, and the distribution of land and water forms. The interpretation and development of maps by elementary-age students gives them a clearer picture of spatial phenomena. Using aerial and satellite photographs can help students view the earth's surface features more concretely.

The ability to interpret and develop maps is most effectively taught through experiential approaches. This chapter described a wide range of strategies and activities to help students learn map concepts and skills.

Maps and globes are iconic representations of the earth's surface. In a sense, they are word pictures that enable us to see spatial relationships such as distance, scale, size, and location. They are communication tools that are illustrative, rather than alphabetical. A map is different from a photograph, however, in that a map is a selective representation of space, whereas a photograph includes everything the camera sees. Using aerial and satellite photographs provides a useful foundation for understanding maps because children can make maps from them (by tracing or copying).

In this chapter, we focused mainly on the developmental processes of making maps. Children begin by sketching and drawing, tracing and copying, and gradually make the transition from seeing a concrete representation of the earth's surface to understanding the abstract representation shown on a map or globe.

The five themes of geography provide a conceptual point of reference for understanding the spatial world. Using a spiral approach, in which the same themes are revisited each year at an increasing level of sophistication, we set in motion a process of geographic literacy. Children at the primary level are introduced to these themes through reading stories, making drawings, and investigating the world around them. This sets the stage for acquiring the increasingly complex knowledge of location, place, interaction, movement, and region in the intermediate grades.

Explorations

Reflect On . . .

1. Take a few moments to reflect on your own thoughts about how children learn. Address the following issues: interest, motivation, activity, exploration, and collaboration. Write a brief paragraph about each topic.

In the Field

2. Become a social scientist for a brief period of time. Find an appropriate time and place to observe a group of children who are engaged in an activity. The size of the group can vary from two to many. Take notes as you observe. What conclusions do you reach about childhood learning on the basis of your systematic observation?
3. Ask the weather bureau or your local television station for satellite images of your area. Trace one of these images to make a map. What skills do you think your students might learn from doing this activity? What did you learn?
4. Go to a local playground and take photographs or make sketches of the equipment and the setting. What do you think this area looked like before the playground was built? What changes were made (in addition to simply installing equipment) to make the area "friendly" to children? What can you and your students learn about the relationships of natural and humanmade phenomena from this activity?

For Your Portfolio

5. Using the imaginary map below, create a lesson plan for students that will help them understand one of the five themes of geography: location, place, human/nature interaction, movement, and region.

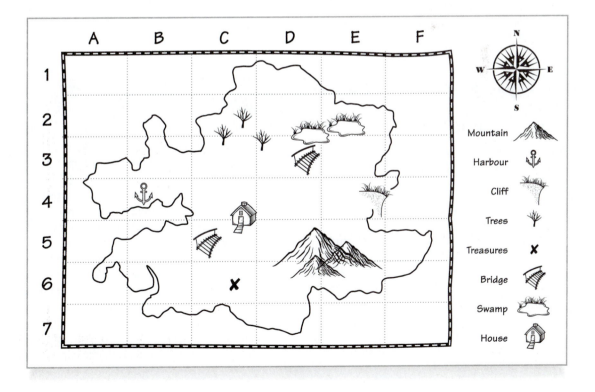

Continuing the Journey: Suggested Readings

Britt, J., & LaFontaine, G. (2009). "Google Earth: A Virtual Globe for Elementary Geography." *Social Studies and the Young Learner, 21*(4): 20–23.

Cheyney, A. (2005). *Geography Challenge.* Tuscon, AZ: Good Year Books.

Gersmehl, P. (2008). *Teaching Geography* (2nd ed.). New York: Guilford.

Golden, N. (2005). *Exploring the United States with the Five Themes of Geography.* New York: Roesn.

Leeder, A. (2006). *100 Ideas for Teaching Geography.* New York: Continuum.

Morgan, J., & Lambert, D. (2005). *Geography.* New York: Routledge.

Wiegnand, P. (2006). *Learning and Teaching with Maps.* New York: Routledge.

Websites

"NCGE is a non-profit organization, chartered in 1915 to enhance the status and quality of geography teaching and learning." *www.ncge.org*

"The Association of American Geographers (AAG) is a scientific and educational society founded in 1904. Its 10,000 members share interests in the theory, methods, and practice of geography and geographic education." *www.aag.org/*

Amazing satellite images of planet Earth. *http://geography.usgs.gov/*

An interactive Website for kids sponsored by National Geographic. *www.mywonderfulworld.org/*

This site presents a table of other Websites related to teaching and learning about geography. *www.sabine.kl2.la.us/zes/geography/default.htm*

Related NCSS Standards and Principles of Powerful Social Studies

Curriculum Standards

Social Studies Themes

III. People, Places, and Environments

Social studies curriculum should include experiences that provide for the study of people, places, and environments.

Technological advances connect students at all levels to the world beyond their personal locations. Geography helps students understand the world they live in and gives them insight into where things are located, why they are there, and why students should care. The study of people, places, and human-environment interactions assists learners as they develop their spatial views and geographic perspectives of the world. This area of study helps learners make informed and critical decisions about the relationships between human beings and their environment (p. 14).

In schools, this theme typically appears in units and courses dealing with regional studies and geography. In the early grades, young learners draw upon immediate personal experiences in their neighborhoods, towns and cities, and states as well as peoples and places distant and unfamiliar to explore geographic concepts and skills. They also express interest in and have concern for the use and abuse of the physical environment. During the middle school years, students relate their personal and academic experiences to happenings in other environmental contexts as they explore peoples, places and environments in this country and in different regions of the world (p. 14).

Source: Excerpted from National Task Force for Social Studies, *Expectations of Excellence: Curriculum Standards for Social Studies,* (Silver Spring, MD: National Council for the Social Studies, draft 2008). The Council's website is www.socialstudies.org

Teaching and Learning Principles

Geography

Teachers who are licensed to teach geography at all school levels should possess the knowledge, capabilities, and dispositions to organize and provide instruction at the appropriate school level for the study of geography (p. 39).

Teacher Expectations

Teachers of geography at all school levels should provide developmentally appropriate experiences as they guide learners in their study. They should

- guide learners in the use of maps and other geographic representations, tools, and technologies to acquire, process, and report information from a spatial perspective;

- enable learners to use mental maps to organize information about people, places, and environments in a spatial context;
- assist learners to analyze the spatial information about people, places, and environments on Earth's surface;
- help learners to understand the physical and human characteristics of places;
- assist learners in developing the concept of regions as a means to interpret Earth's complexity

Among Others (p. 39).

Teachers of the early grades can provide learners with experiences that give them an understanding of the characteristics and purposes of geographic representations, such as maps, globes, and satellite-produced images. Learners can be helped to understand their local community and nearby communities. They can be taught the location of major physical and human features in the United States and on Earth and how these physical and human processes together shape places and ways of living (p. 40).

Source: Excerpted from National Council for the Social Studies, *National Standards for Social Studies Teachers* (Silver Spring, MD: author, 2002). The Council's website is www.socialstudies.org

SAMPLE LESSON 11.1 Learning a New Environment

GRADE LEVEL: Appropriate for grades K–2.

NCSS STANDARD: Understand how human actions modify the physical environment

PURPOSE: To orient students to their surroundings.

OBJECTIVES: As a result of this activity, the students will:

1. Locate specific places in the school on a map.
2. Visit specific places in the school setting, such as the principal's office, restrooms, lunchroom, and playground.

3. Learn the rules and responsibilities associated with specific settings, including places within the school that are off limits.

RESOURCES/MATERIALS: Butcher paper, markers, maps of the building (one per student), crayons, construction paper, scissors, storybook.

PROCEDURE:

1. Make a large wall map of the school and its grounds on butcher paper, identifying specific places with different colors (classrooms, hallways, bathrooms, the gym, the lunchroom, etc.).

Doors, water fountains, and the like can be cut from construction paper that's the same color as the specific place shown on the classroom map.

2. Give students small outline maps of the school (one map per student). Have them locate the specific areas and color them to match the large wall map.

3. Take the students on a building tour. Let each student bring her or his map and a marker. As you visit each area, tell students the roles of the area. Have them mark on their maps any special features that they want to remember, such as water fountains, outside doors or exits, and so on.

4. If possible, arrange to have the students make a special trip to the principal's office, and as a special treat, ask the principal to read a story to them. Similarly, visit the school nurse, the librarian, and other special people in the school.

5. On returning to the classroom, have the students cut their maps into pieces, creating jigsaw puzzles, and reassemble them to learn the relationship of one area to another.

CLOSURE: Use this unit at the beginning of the year for students who are new to the school building. They will not only learn the layout of the building, but they will also begin to learn mapping skills. Doing this activity will help students feel comfortable and welcome, and that will enhance the learning process. When they know and respect the rules of the school setting, the environment becomes a better place for everyone involved.

Source: Adapted from a lesson plan submitted by Dianne Elaine Hill (West Junior High School, Muskogee, OK) to OFCN's Academy Curricular Exchange, Columbia Education Center, Social Studies.

SAMPLE LESSON 11.2   Map Mileage

GRADE LEVEL/SUBJECT: Grades 3–6.

PURPOSE: To give students experience in using the mileage key on a map.

OBJECTIVE(S): The students will be able to use the mileage key of a map to plan a trip and keep within a set amount of miles given by the teacher.

RESOURCES/MATERIALS: A map with a mileage key for each team of students; rulers, pencils, paper; small inexpensive plastic cars; and certificates.

PROCEDURE:

1. Announce that everyone in the class has the chance to win a brand-new car by doing one simple thing: planning a vacation.

2. Divide students into teams of three, and give each team a small toy car and a map of one state. It can be your state or a vacation state (like Florida, New York, or California), or it can be a region (like New England or the Southwest). Tell each team that their

car is brand new and has 0 miles on its odometer.

3. Tell each team to plan a trip of not less than 1,000 miles and not more than 1,200 miles that includes at least three places of interest. If when they "return" from the trip, their odometer reads between 1,000 and 1,200, the car is theirs to keep.

4. Each team should plot their trip on their map and make a chart of the legs of the trip with the mileage noted. They must begin and end in the same place but cannot visit any place along the route more than once.

5. To add an element of history and culture to the activity, students can use the Internet, an atlas, or tourist brochures provided by the teacher to get information about things to see and do and to decide which places to visit. Teams should also try to find interesting routes with interesting scenery, which doesn't necessarily mean following interstate highways.

6. Have teams check one another's mileage totals. All teams who plot trips of the correct mileage win their cars.

CLOSURE: Have each team present their trip to the class orally, as though they are travel agents. They should talk about the places they visited and the routes they took. The class can vote on which is the most interesting route.

EXTENSION: For homework, have students use maps and mileage keys to plot their own dream vacations anywhere in the world.

Source: Adapted from a lesson plan submitted by Faun White to OFCN's Academy Curricular Exchange, Columbia Education Center, Social Studies.

SAMPLE LESSON 11.3 Mapmaking

GRADE LEVEL/SUBJECT: Grades 4–6; Map Skills.

NCSS STANDARD: Understand how to use maps and other geographic representations

PURPOSE: To help students understand that a map is a representation of all or part of the surface of the earth on a plane. To acquaint students with some of the problems associated with mapmaking. This is a very effective first-day activity, not only to introduce a map unit but also to set the class tone for emphasizing problem solving as a way of addressing learning.

OBJECTIVES:

1. Students will identify the placement of the continents and the oceans by drawing them on a handmade globe.
2. Students will identify the placement of the equator, the Tropic of Cancer and the Tropic of Capricorn, and the North Pole and the South Pole by drawing them on a handmade globe.

RESOURCES/MATERIALS: One-half sheet of $8\frac{1}{2}'' \times 11''$ paper for each student (scrap paper is good); one tennis ball (or soft ball) for each student; scissors, tape, pencils.

PROCEDURE:

1. Ask each student to use the paper to wrap the tennis ball, without leaving wrinkles or overlapping the paper. Students may cut the paper, if they feel that will help. This is not an easy task. You should be a facilitator in this activity; it is important to emphasize that each student will find his or her own solution. There is no one right answer. Stress that each student can develop his or her own strategy but also that students are free to get ideas by looking around the room.

2. Have each student tape the wrapping in place.
3. Ask each student to sketch the continent on his or her globe, using a classroom map as a guide. For older children, add the North and South Poles, the equator, and the Tropics of Cancer and Capricorn.
4. As students finish, have them bring their globes to the front of the room and compare them to a commercial globe. They can make adjustments to their own globes as necessary.
5. When each student has completed the drawing, have her or him remove the covering from the tennis ball, lay it flat on the desk, and study the map of the world that he or she created.
6. Have students compare their maps to the flat map of the world that they used initially.

CLOSURE: Have students discuss the ways they approached the problem of wrapping a round object with a flat piece of paper. Underscore in the discussion that students may have developed a variety of strategies.

REFLECTION: Use this activity as a springboard to introduce the problems of early cartography, the various flat map designs, the voyages of early explorers, and so on.

Source: Adapted from a lesson plan submitted by Linda Bauck (Wallowa Elementary, OR) to OFCN's Academy Curricular Exchange, Columbia Education Center, Social Studies.

Making History Come Alive

*It is commonly acknowledged that an understanding of the past is fundamental to an understanding of the present. There is another reason to study history: **it's fun.***

—Frank Luttmer, historian

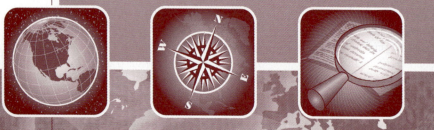

To say that it is fun to study history may come as a surprise to some people. Here are some examples of children who agree that studying history is fun:

Jason, age 11: "I love studying about the Aztecs. They had a very advanced civilization. I found out that they did, invent the wheel. Their toys had wheels on them. But they didn't have big carts with wheels because there weren't any roads and they didn't have any big animals like horses to pull them."

Carlita, age 8: "I made this picture of people in Holland a long time ago. My favorite thing is windmills and my other favorite thing is drawing."

These two kids love history. Because they are young, the students we teach don't have much of a past themselves, of course. As the insightful scholar, S. I. Hayakawa, once wittily observed, "Children are the most recent immigrants to our land." But in spite of the fact that they haven't been here very long, they do refer to the past surprisingly often. Talking with children about the past is instructive. Their thoughts serve as reminders that they are, in fact, historians. Young children are especially good at oral history. They love to tell about things they have done, places they have been, things they have heard, and sights they have seen. They also never tire of hearing the stories of adults—parents, grandparents, older siblings, aunts and uncles, teachers, and friends. "Tell me about when you were little," they ask.

What is history? Is it a collection of dates, names, and facts from the past? Some people seem to think so. Is it exciting as Jason and Carlita seem to think?

The *Random House College Dictionary* defines *history* as the record of past events, especially in connection with the human race. Others define *history* simply as a record of everything that has happened.

These two definitions are more alike than different: Both define *history* as a record of the past (although the second encompasses more), and both acknowledge the potential for change, because the record of the past is itself constantly changing. New discoveries happen daily. Here are two examples:

- On the western coast of Mexico, historians and archaeologists have unearthed large stone heads with features that appear to be Chinese. Who created these heads? Do they suggest that there was contact between Old World and New World civilizations long before Christopher Columbus?
- In 2005, a collection of ancient manuscripts was rediscovered in storage at Oxford University in England. Some of the manuscripts are as much as 2,000 years old and would previously have been indecipherable. But new technologies now make the print legible to scholars.

What Is History?

Let's accept the definition of *history* as a record of the past. But what exactly do we mean by the word *record*? Surely, text qualifies—the written record. So does film, a more recent innovation. But what about artifacts? Cave drawings? And what about the writings whose origins have been disputed or even proven false? What about religious writings, which were produced sometimes centuries after the events they recorded, but are now taken as perfect fact?

Our libraries and museums are outstanding repositories of history, making it readily available to us. Old books, ancient maps, and exhibits can bring the past to life in wondrous ways, thus stimulating the childhood imagination. But should we include as history the stories handed down from one generation to the next?

The family is the social unit that young students relate to most intimately. Alex Haley, author of the Pulitzer Prize–winning book *Roots: The Saga of an American Family,* wrote, "In every conceivable manner, the family is link to our past, bridge to our future." Haley's book traces the history of a family (a fictionalized reality) from its African roots, through its arrival in the United States via the slave trade, to its eventual growth into a diverse African American family. Like Haley's creation, every family has a history, a set of stories, a saga. In recent years, oral history—which is often about everyday life, as it was lived by ordinary people—has become a respected and legitimate form of historical inquiry.

Is yesterday's newspaper history? Are old television reruns history? What role do the Internet and the World Wide Web play in keeping the historical record? History is all around us, from the statue in the park to the evening program on the History Channel.

But that may be a very real problem for us and especially for our children: the overload of information that we face in today's world.

How does a teacher know what history is of most worth? Fortunately, most social studies curricula are grounded in a scope and sequence designed to help you with this. To some extent, the district and state in which you teach will help you make decisions about what comprises history. But beyond that, your own professional judgment must come into play. No two teachers teach in the same contextual setting. In fact, local studies often provide the richest opportunity for searching and researching the past with your students.

Why Should Young People Study History?

For some of us, World War II was the stuff of our childhood. We remember hearing radio newscasts in our parents' cars; perhaps we even remember our fathers going off to war. For others, the cold war looms large in our memories. Bomb drills were conducted in school, where we were asked to hide under our desks to escape nuclear annihilation. And for others, the memories are of Vietnam—all those people in the streets, all that long hair. For those of us with these memories, it can be hard to understand that the first Gulf War is a distant memory for today's high school students and that for the next generation of elementary school children, the 9/11 attacks on New York and Washington will be as unreal and far away as Hiroshima.

Why do children need to understand history? One answer to this question is that history is a fluid continuum. The present in which we live is also the future of the past and the past of the future. Children living in the present can benefit greatly from understanding the past—the sense of continuity, the inheritance, the traditions, the changes, and the reminders that are all around them.

Historian Peter Stearns (1993, 2006) writes, "History should be studied because it is essential to individuals and to society." Stearns goes on to list these six reasons that we should study history:

1. *History helps us understand people and societies.* History is our "laboratory" of the past. It shows us how people solved problems in the past. We can learn from their behaviors, whether good or bad.
2. *History helps us understand change and how society came to be.* The children we teach are changing every day. Their own history bears evidence of physical, mental, emotional, and social growth. And just as individuals change, so do families and even societies change. Sample Lesson 12.1, for example, helps students understand the Civil War from different viewpoints.
3. *History is important in our own lives.* Reading biographies, works of historical fiction, and other histories informs us not only about other people but also about ourselves. In learning about the lives of others, we can also reflect on our own lives.
4. *History contributes to moral understanding.* History provides examples of human behavior. We learn about courage, honesty, perseverance, and integrity from the stories of those who have gone before us.

5. *History provides identity.* One of the important questions of childhood is: Who am I? When children construct family trees, research their genealogy, and hear stories from parents and grandparents, they gain a greater, deeper sense of self.

6. *Studying history is essential for good citizenship.* The rights and responsibilities we enjoy today did not just happen. They came about because of the contributions of caring and courageous leaders from the past. The habits of heart and mind that characterized persons from years past become part of us when we learn of their dedication and sacrifice.

Henry Ford once suggested that "History is bunk." But in fact, history is a noble subject, filled with human behavior at its best as well as its worst. History reminds us that we have obligations to citizenship, morality, identity, and heritage. As philosopher George Santayana famously wrote, "Those who do not learn from the past are condemned to repeat it."

The Power of Storytelling as History

Encouraging students to learn history should not be difficult. In fact, learning about the past can be one of the most exciting and engaging activities you will undertake with your students. In part, that's because history is so much about stories, which almost all children enjoy both telling and hearing.

Surely, your family has stories about its history that you heard over and over again as a child. Those stories became part of who you are. They are your history. In the largest sense, history is simply storytelling. Some of the best historians—or at least, the ones who have had the most impact on our understanding of history—have been

A teacher in traditional African costume teaches his students.

story-tellers. The stories they tell are of adventure and hardship, love and cruelty, and an entire range of human emotions. They touch us deeply.

As children study history, it becomes important that they learn about sources. Some of the most exciting sources available are children's trade books, especially biographies and works of historical fiction, although these also pose some challenges. Children must learn, of course, how to tell fact from fiction. Historical fiction, in particular, can be challenging in this respect. But a classroom stocked with a wealth of good children's books, both nonfiction and fiction, can go a long way toward learning history.

Perhaps the very best way to learn history is through *primary sources:* texts, images, and artifacts produced at the same time the events being recorded took place. Although original primary sources are often available only through libraries and museums, facsimiles can almost always be found, especially with the electronic help of the Internet and World Wide Web.

Of course, the most common resource for learning history in most elementary school classrooms is the social studies textbook. Many textbooks are engagingly written; even so, support from trade books and primary sources can only make learning more exciting. Let's take a look at some of the resources available to you.

Biographies

A biography tells the story of someone's life and times. Children in the intermediate grade levels are especially ready for biographies. The life stories of people like Martin Luther King Jr., Abraham Lincoln, Jane Addams, Marie Curie, and George Washington can be particularly inspirational for young readers. But be sure to find well-written trade books for your classroom. (See the end of this chapter for Websites that provide lists of appropriate, high-quality children's books.) You have only to contrast a well-written biography with a typical social studies textbook to know why I make this suggestion!

Primary-age children depend more on oral forms of learning than older children do, so your own role as a storyteller is significant as a means of teaching and learning about the past. When teachers role-play certain persons from the past by dressing in period costume and becoming that person, children watch and listen with rapt attention. And just in case you think storytelling is only for the young, I can tell you about a friend of mine, a high school history teacher, who electrified his classes by showing up dressed as Andrew Jackson and being him for the entire day.

Historical Fiction

Learning to differentiate fact from fiction is an important skill, especially when students read books in which the authors have included both real and fictitious characters. Help your students understand how historical fiction works. Good historical fiction provides examples of real settings—for example, everyday life in colonial America, the suffering of the soldiers in the American Revolution, the hardships endured on the American frontier. Historical fiction can create context, setting, characterization, and plot in ways designed to attract young readers, who might well find textbook accounts less appealing than fictionalized ones.

Using Historical Sources

Most of what children learn at school about history comes from what are known as *secondary sources:* textbooks, workbooks, encyclopedias, Websites, and even biographies and works of historical fiction. Secondary sources are fine, up to a point. Their primary limitation is that they provide the reader with already formed conclusions. The best contribution of secondary sources is to provide the context and background for children's inquiry into primary sources. *Primary sources,* which are original texts and artifacts, are filled with potential, not with conclusions. The reader, not the writer, must analyze, synthesize, and draw conclusions.

Children need to know and have access to primary sources as well as secondary sources and to understand the differences between them. The two types of sources are not opposed one to another; rather, they have a symbiotic relationship when teachers use them wisely.

Again, primary sources include materials such as interviews, newspapers, letters, diaries, journals, drawings, maps, paintings, photographs, artifacts, and even stories told to children by adults inside or outside their families. Only when children and teachers use primary sources do they *become* historians. This is the excitement of discovery, the excitement of doing one's own thinking and reaching one's own conclusions.

To understand the differences between primary and secondary sources, consider the two excerpts that follow. The first, dated November 20, 1805, is from the journal of Captain Meriwether Lewis of the Lewis and Clark expedition of 1804–1806. It was written some two centuries ago, when the expedition was camped at a site where the Columbia River meets the Pacific Ocean, and it includes Lewis's reflections about a day on which his party had encountered several parties of Chinook Indians.

> It rained during the course of the night. A hunter dispatched to kill some food, returned with eight ducks on which we breakfasted. We then followed the course of the bay [where the Columbia meets the Pacific Ocean]. As we went along the beach we were overtaken by several Indians who gave us dried sturgeon and wapato roots.
>
> We met several parties of Chinooks returning from the camp and two of them were chiefs. We went through a ceremony of giving to each a medal and a flag to the most distinguished. . . . One of the Indians had a robe made of two sea otter skins which was the most beautiful fur we had ever seen. The owner at first resisted every attempt to part with it but length could not resist the offer of a belt of blue beads which Sacagawea wore around her waist. (Scheuerman & Ellis, 2004, pp. 162–163)

Reading this excerpt might lead to any number of possible activities. You might begin your inquiry by having students draw pictures of what they think this scene must have been like. From there, you might challenge your young historians to reflect on how this scene would have been considered differently by the Chinook or perhaps by Sacagawea herself, either in drawings or in words. The journal excerpt is rich in possibilities for research by students into native clothing, foods such as the wapato root and sturgeon, and the relationships between various Native American tribes.

Now consider how a textbook treats the same moment from the Lewis and Clark expedition:

> Lewis and Clark explored much of what is today the Columbia River region. They established a camp near the mouth of the Columbia River. While they were there, they hunted for food and traded with the local Indians. Their camp was near the beach of the Pacific Ocean so this made it possible for them to live off fish, birds, and other animals. The Indians were especially fond of bright beads, and Lewis and Clark were able to trade beads for robes and skins. They also gave medals and a flag to the Indian leaders. (Scheuerman & Ellis, 2003, p. 24)

Here, we have much the same scene, but we have traded a narrative account, written by the explorer himself, for information that, while accurate, has little character or sense of adventure. Of course, a good teacher could give many of the same follow-up assignments suggested for the original source material, but students might find less to inspire their creations.

In 1863, President Abraham Lincoln delivered the Gettysburg Address, the most famous speech in American history, on the battlefield at Gettysburg, Pennsylvania, where only months before, the decisive battle of that great armed conflict between the Union and the Confederacy had taken place. No television cameras were present, no tape recordings were made, and conflicting reports of the speech itself and how it was received were filed by different newsmen. Figure 12.1 presents what is thought to be the most accurate version of the address.

Figure **12.1** *The Gettysburg Address*

Four score and seven years ago our fathers brought forth on this continent a new nation, conceived in Liberty, and dedicated to the proposition that all men are created equal.

Now we are engaged in a great civil war, testing whether that nation or any nation so conceived and so dedicated, can long endure. We are met on a great battlefield of that war. We have come to dedicate a portion of that field, as a final resting place for those who here gave their lives that that nation might live. It is altogether fitting and proper that we should do this.

But, in a larger sense, we can not dedicate—we can not consecrate—we can not hallow—this ground. The brave men, living and dead, who struggled here, have consecrated it, far above our poor power to add or detract. The world will little note, nor long remember what we say here, but it can never forget what they did here. It is for us the living, rather, to be dedicated here to the unfinished work which they who fought here have thus far so nobly advanced. It is rather for us to be here dedicated to the great task remaining before us—that from these honored dead we take increased devotion to that cause for which they gave the last full measure of devotion—that we here highly resolve that these dead shall not have died in vain—that this nation, under God, shall have a new birth of freedom—and that government of the people, by the people, for the people, shall not perish from the earth.

Abraham Lincoln

Figure 12.2 *Previous Versions of "Of the People . . ."*

- "a government of all the people, by all the people, for all the people."—Theodore Parker, at an antislavery convention in Boston, May 20, 1850
- "the people's government, made for the people, made by the people, and answerable to the people."—Daniel Webster, January 26, 1830
- "a government made by ourselves, for themselves, and conducted by themselves."—John Adams, 1798
- "I am in favor of democracy . . . that shall be of the people, by the people, for the people."—Attributed to Cleon, 420 B.C.

Note that the speech is only 10 sentences long. It contains only 271 words. It is hardly the length of an essay that a child of 10 or 12 might write. Most of the words are simple and common. What makes this speech so powerful? What ideas are found in it? What values does it contain?

The Gettysburg Address could be used to prompt a whole-class inquiry, in which you lead the class through the investigation. To begin, ask your students to illustrate each of the 10 sentences. Have some students memorize the speech, or even a sentence from it, and deliver it as a role-play. Have others look up any unknown words and report their meanings. Still others can investigate the context of the time Lincoln spent before and after delivering the speech. Using the library or the Internet, some might be able to find contemporary news articles about the address or other instances in which Lincoln's powerful language echoed. See, for example, prior uses or variations of the famous phrase "government of the people, by the people, for the people," as discovered by Lincoln scholar William Barton in 1930 (see Figure 12.2). And of course, you will want to have a class discussion or two devoted to the meaning of the speech.

For how many speeches would this activity be possible? Not many, I think, which may explain some of the power of Lincoln's words. Regardless, make sure that your students have access to the actual words of historical figures, along with contemporary accounts of historical events and other primary sources. History will be so much richer for them! That point is well proven in the following example.

in the classroom   **Thomas Jefferson and Meriwether Lewis**

Students must be exposed to original source materials as they conduct inquiry. Far too often, even university-level students read only textbooks and other secondary interpretations—the academic equivalents of frozen dinners! Original resource materials, such as the following exchange of letters between Thomas Jefferson and Meriwether Lewis, represent rich text—*real* food for learners!

First, have your students read the letters that follow. You may want to read the letters to your class or have members of the class role-play (in costume, perhaps!) and read them aloud. You may need to explain certain words (*relinquish,* for example) and phrases, and walk students through difficult passages, but that's what real teaching and learning are all about. Don't worry: The students can understand the ideas. Trust them. If you don't believe me, go back and read the quote at the beginning of this chapter!

Jefferson to Lewis

Washington, February, 23, 1801

Dear Sir

The appointment to the Presidency of the U.S. has rendered it necessary for me to have a private secretary, and in selecting one I have thought it important to respect not only his capacity to aid in the private concerns of the household, but also to contribute to the mass of information which it is interesting for the administration to acquire. Your knowledge of the Western country, of the army and of all its interest & relations has rendered it desirable for public as well as private purposes that you should be engaged in that office. In point of profit it has little to offer; the salary being only 500. D. which would scarcely be more than an equivalent for your pay & rations, which you would be obliged to relinquish while withdrawn from active service, but retaining your rank & right to rise. But it would be an easier office, would make you know & be known to characters of influence in the affairs of our country, and give you the advantage of their wisdom. You would of course save also the expense of subsistence & lodging as you would be one of my family. If these or any other views which your own reflections may suggest should present the office of my private secretary as worthy of acceptance you will make me happy in accepting it. It has been solicited by several, who will have no answer till I hear from you. Should you accept, it would be necessary that you should wind up whatever affairs you are engaged in as expeditiously as your own & the public interest will admit, & adjourn to this place and that immediately on receipt of this you inform me by letter of your determination.

It would also be necessary that you wait on General Wilkinson & obtain his approbation, & his aid in making such arrangements as may render your absence as little injurious to the service as may be. I write to him on this subject. Accept assurances of the esteem of Dear Sir your friend & servant.

Th. Jefferson

Lewis to Jefferson

Pittsburg, March 10, 1801

Dear Sir,

Not until too late on Friday last to answer by that day's mail did I receive your much esteemed favor of the 23rd Ult. In it you have thought proper so far to honor me with your confidence, as to express a wish that I should accept the office, nor were further motives necessary to induce my compliance, than that you Sir should conceive that in the discharge of the duties of that office, I could be serviceable to my country, or useful to yourself Permit me here, sir, to do further justice to my feelings by expressing the lively sensibility with which I received this mark of your confidence and esteem.

I did not reach this place on my return from Detroit until late on the night of the 5th instant, five days after the departure of General Wilkinson. My report therefore on the subject of your letter was immediately made to Colonel Hamtramck, the commanding officer at this place. Not a moment has been lost in making the necessary arrangements in order to get forward to the City of Washington with all possible despatch. Rest assured I shall not relax in my exertions. Receive I pray you, sir, the most undisassembled assurance of the attachment and friendship of your most obedient, & very humble servant,

Meriwether Lewis

Next, use a discussion guide, like the following one, to help students understand and evaluate the historical information in these letters.

Discussion Guide

DIRECTIONS: Please check each statement that you can support and be prepared to cite your evidence from your reading and experience.

DEFINITIONS AND KNOWLEDGE:

———— 1. President Jefferson invited Meriwether Lewis to be his private, presidential secretary.

———— 2. President Jefferson liked Lewis's knowledge of the western country and the army.

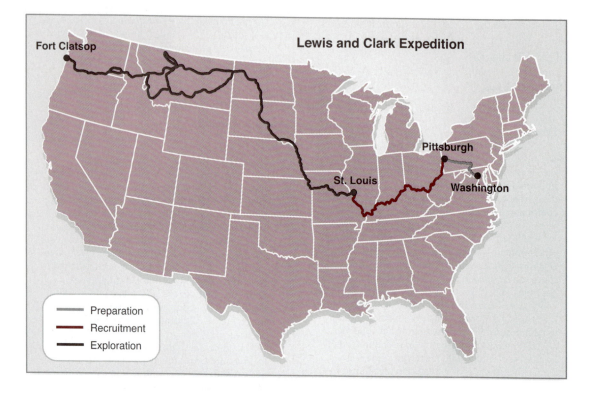

Lewis and Clark Expedition

Fort Clatsop

Pittsburgh

St. Louis

Washington

Legend:
- Preparation
- Recruitment
- Exploration

-------- 3. Jefferson pointed out that Lewis could serve his country and also get to know important people.

-------- 4. Jefferson offered to make Lewis a member of his family, which meant Lewis would receive both food and lodging.

-------- 5. Lewis retained his rank in the army.

-------- 6. Lewis accepted Jefferson's invitation to become his private secretary.

-------- 7. Lewis had to travel from Pittsburgh, Pennsylvania, to Washington, DC, to accept the position.

COMPREHENSION (RELATE AND APPLY KNOWLEDGE TO EXPERIENCES AND CONCEPTS):

-------- 1. Jefferson was a good judge of character and loyalty.

-------- 2. Lewis was honored to serve his country.

-------- 3. Salary was not an important factor in Lewis's decision to take the job.

-------- 4. Lewis gave up his opportunity to advance his rank within the militia.

-------- 5. It took 15 days for Jefferson's letter to reach Lewis in Pittsburgh.

-------- 6. Lewis was a humble servant.

EVALUATION (JUDGMENTS ABOUT THE VALUE OF IDEAS, OBJECTS, AND ACTIONS):

-------- 1. He profits most who serves best. (Arthur Sheldon—Rotary International)

-------- 2. Honor lies in honest toil. (Grover Cleveland)

-------- 3. Nothing endures but personal qualities—nothing. (Walt Whitman)

Source: Thanks to Jim Worthington, Ph.D., for the discussion statements.

Children as Historians

Historical research represents an attempt to put together the pieces of the past. Because such research deals with events that have already happened, it is often difficult to find precise and accurate reports. Historical researchers cannot control the events they wish to recapture; more often than not, they cannot even find enough information to document all the facts of an occurrence, much less all the inferences. Historical events such as the assassination of Martin Luther King Jr., the Watergate affair, the 9/11 attacks, and the events leading up to the invasion of Iraq illustrate the difficulties involved in attempting to reconstruct details of the past. The problems involved in even a relatively simple investigation, such as finding out about one's grandparents or reconstructing one's hairstyles, illustrate the difficult task of the historian!

Finding" history can be one of the most engaging activities young children ever undertake. Let's look at some ways in which your students can become historians. All the following examples of historical inquiry and discovery are meant to serve as models for the kind of active, hands-on, experiential teaching and learning I encourage you to do with your students. As you read the following sections, picture yourself and your class engaging in just such activities. I think that if you do, you will agree that history is intellectually and socially stimulating.

Oral Histories

Oral histories involve interviews with real people—older relatives or friends, perhaps, or the recorded voices of historical figures. This approach is particularly suited to young learners because it emphasizes interviews, rather than letters, documents, and other written records. Any number of oral history experiences can become part of your teaching: interviews with a town historian, with older members of the community, with members of certain ethnic or cultural groups, or simply with family members, fellow students, or older students in the same school.

One class studying family structures tried to reconstruct the daily life of a grandmother when she was the age of the class members. The teacher began by asking how many students knew one or both of their grandmothers and then where those grandmothers lived. About half the students knew a grandmother, and about half of them could say where she had been born or lived as a girl. The teacher then made lists on the board based on the students' guesses about what their grandmothers might have studied in school, what games they might have played, what they might have eaten, how they might have traveled, and so on.

Finally, the teacher said, "We've made lots of guesses about our grandmothers' lives. How do you think we could find out if we are right?" Immediately, the children responded, "We could ask our mothers. They might know" and "We could ask our grandmothers!"

As a result of this discussion (and in response to a note that the children drafted and the teacher sent home with each of them), two grandmothers visited the classroom. The students asked the grandmothers questions based on the categories they had established (School, Games, Food, Transportation, Clothes, Work), and the grandmothers' responses

A young historian and his good friend from another generation.

were recorded next to the students' guesses. In addition, each grandmother spent time teaching the class one game she had played as a child. When the interview was over, the students spent some time comparing their guesses with the answers their grandmothers had given. They were pleased to find that some of their guesses were right—and surprised that some were very wrong!

The next day, the teacher asked the students whether *all* grandmothers would have given the same answers to their questions. The students didn't think so. In order to find out, they decided to take home information sheets for their grandparents, parents, or guardians to fill out (see Figure 12.3).

Personal Histories

Every child has a history, and every child's history is interesting and worth studying. One way for students to learn about the structure and premises of historical documentation is for them to create histories of their own lives.

I suggest that from time to time, you have your students write autobiographical sketches (see Figure 12.4). In time, these sketches can be put together to form a comprehensive personal history. The data gathering, interviewing of parents, forming personal insights, and self-reflection that occur as a result of this process will make

> **Figure 12.3** *A Grandmother Information Sheet*
>
> | | |
> |---|---|
> | My Grandmother's Name | Wilma Pederson |
> | Her Place of Birth | Grand Rapids, Mich. |
> | Games She Played | Hopscotch, Tag, Run-Sheep-Run, Baseball |
> | Her Schoolwork | Reading, Numbers, Artwork, Writing |
> | Her Chores at Home | Set the Table, Watch Her Brother, Do Errands |
> | Food She Ate | Fruit, Vegetables, Meat, Cereal, Bread, Potatoes, Sweets |

historians out of all your students. Don't be surprised if they start the lifelong habit of keeping a personal journal. You never know what influence you might have!

Students can keep journals that document events across the year, or they can write about specific aspects of their lives. For example, Figure 12.5 shows Rhonda's chronological essay about her changing hairstyles, with photos to illustrate! Students can also take oral histories from one another, pretending to be television interviewers asking about the events of the past summer or the past week at school.

One interesting type of personal history has each student research the day he or she was born. In most cases, the local library will have copies (or microfilm) of daily newspapers, or students can use the Internet to find interesting events that took place on their special days. (Simply type in the date on a search engine—Google or Yahoo, for example.) Students of almost any age will enjoy reading the newspaper for the day they entered the world. Things to look for might include the following:

- Headlines and big events
- News makers and important people
- Sports stories
- Advertisements
- Want ads
- Movies and television shows
- Fashions
- Comics

Timelines

The concept of *chronology* is difficult for many children to acquire in a meaningful sense. Creating a timeline can provide a clear graphic aid that enables students to think of the passage of time in a more concrete way. One useful assignment is to ask each student to prepare a personal timeline, recording one or two significant events from each year of her or his life (see Figure 12.6). On a different scale, students can be asked

Figure 12.4 *An Autobiographical Sketch*

Bryan Abrahamson   Sept 7
        My Autobiography   3rd grade

My hole name is Bryan Miles
Abrahamson. im 9 years old
I'm a Diabetic.
    I half to watch what I'm eating

    Theres 4 in my failey.
and we have 4 pets to.
    My familys Names Brett Orice-
and Sivalry. I was Born Jan 10.

The best things i like in school is
Math Gym Art and lunch
    and i like Most of My
    theachers to Miss Beck and the
ohter nice Theachers.

The only club i belonged to was
a baseball club I played for the
yakees I would play sortstop third base
or outfield.

    My favorates pets are my
hermet crabs, threse manres are
Larry Crabby and Tom.

to create timelines that include people and events from historical eras. Topics like the following are suitable for historical timelines:

- Women in American history
- Voyages of discovery
- Great African Americans
- American presidents
- Scientists and inventors
- Authors and artists
- Events of the American Revolution or the Civil War

Figure 12.5 *Rhonda's Essay: "My Hair Styles"*

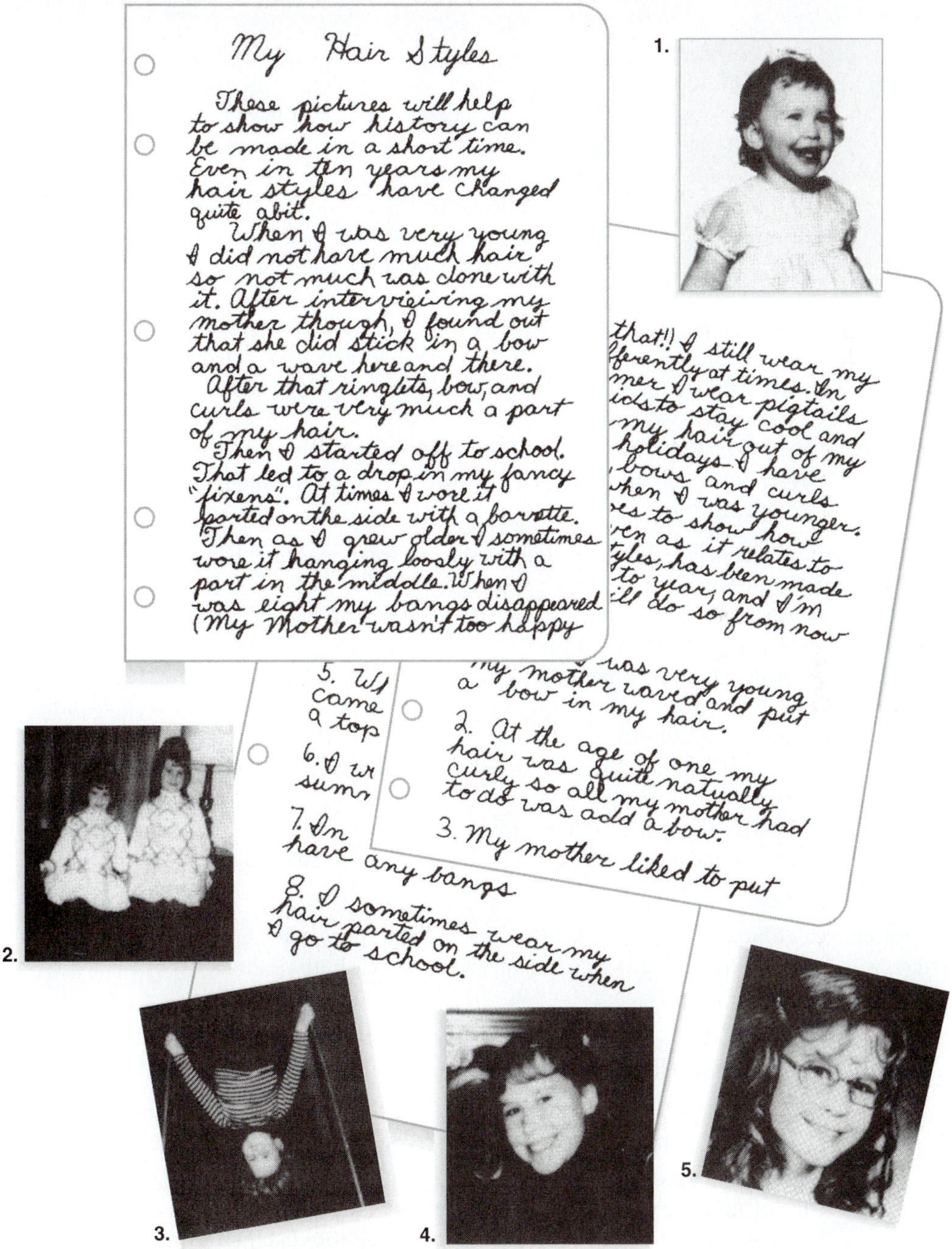

My   Hair Styles

These pictures will help to show how history can be made in a short time. Even in ten years my hair styles have changed quite abit.

When I was very young I did not have much hair so not much was done with it. After interviewing my mother though, I found out that she did stick in a bow and a wave here and there.

After that ringlets, bow, and curls were very much a part of my hair.

Then I started off to school. That led to a drop in my fancy "fixens". At times I wore it parted on the side with a barrette. Then as I grew older I sometimes wore it hanging loosly with a part in the middle. When I was eight my bangs disappeared (My Mother wasn't too happy

that!) I still wear my differently at times. In mer I wear pigtails ids to stay cool and my hair out of my holidays I have bows and curls when I was younger. es to show how ven as it relates to tyles, has been made to year and I'm ll do so from now

was very young a bow in my hair.

5. W/ came a top

6. I w sum

7. In have any bangs

8. I sometimes wear my hair parted on the side when I go to school.

2. At the age of one my hair was quite natually curly so all my mother had to do was add a bow.

3. My mother liked to put

Rhonda illustrated her essay with photos of herself at various ages.

CURRENT EVENTS
Focus on Historical Inquiry

It has often been said that the newspaper (and we could now add the Internet) is "the first rough draft of history." This is actually a very exciting thought. Newspapers and news Websites must meet daily and sometimes hourly deadlines. With the advent of the Internet, the flow of news changes by the minute. Twenty-four-hour-a-day cable news has also added to the speed with which the news is delivered. Take a few minutes to examine today's headlines and the stories behind them. Consider them as comprising the first rough draft of the history of our time. Eventually, scholars will sift through this information and revise it to form a second draft. But history is never final.

Here is one way to make historians out of your students: Have them examine history's first draft and evaluate it from the perspective of several years later, depending on their age. This activity is called "The Day You Were Born," and here is how it works.

Ask each student to go to the library (preferably, with a parent) and find a newspaper from the day he or she was born. Ask each student to write down answers to any or all of the following questions:

- What were the headlines and major stories on the day you were born? How do they differ from the headlines of today's papers?
- Which teams were winning in whatever sport was seasonal? Are they the same teams that usually win today?
- What comics were in the paper then? Are your favorites (if you have any) there?
- How much did a new car cost then? How much does a new car cost now?
- What movies were being advertised? Have you heard of any of them?
- In the want ads, what kinds of salaries were offered? What salaries are offered for comparable jobs today?
- How much did the newspaper cost then? How much does it cost now?
- What stories do you find most interesting in the paper from the day you were born? Why?

This project makes a wonderful way for a parent and child to spend a few hours together, working on a project that will almost inevitably engage both of them.

Experiential History Activities

Students can feel history come to life by replicating inquiries or testing possibilities from the past. For example, ancient Greek mathematician and philosopher Thales (sixth century B.C.) once journeyed to Egypt, where he was said to have used his knowledge of geometry to measure the height of the Great Pyramids and other structures. He is also said to have been able to calculate the distance from the shore to nearby ships at sea.

Figure 12.6 *A Student's Timeline*

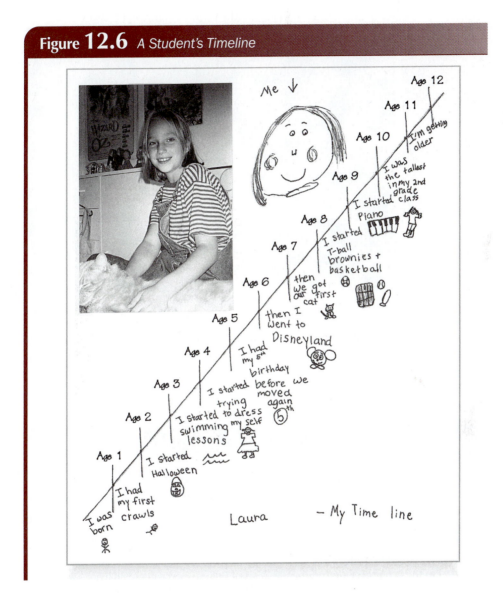

These kinds of measurements can be done easily today with technical instruments, but Thales had none available. All he needed was sunshine (to cast a shadow), knowledge of his own height, and a stick as long as he was tall. Ask your students: With just this much information, do you think you could calculate the height of the flagpole outside our school? Or the football goalposts? See if your students can figure out how Thales managed to make sophisticated calculations with only himself, a stick, and the sun as resources. Also see Sample Lesson 12.2 for an example of an experiential lesson.

Young historians replicate Thales' experiment by calculating the height of the flagpole on the school grounds.

Solving riddles of the past by interpreting stories and myths can be a fascinating experience for students. Try the following investigation with your students as an exercise in developing a hypothesis.

in the classroom   Did the Chinese Discover America?

Some historians believe that in 458 A.D., five men set sail from China and, following the Japan current, traveled 20,000 li eastward (20,000 li equals about 7,000 miles). They reached a land that they called *Fusang* and stayed there for about 40 years. They returned to China in 499 A.D., where one of them, Hwui Shan, reported to the emperor about their adventures. He also presented the emperor with a stone, almost transparent, about a foot in diameter and shaped like a mirror. A servant wrote down the story, and some scholars believe that it proves that Hwui Shan and his countrymen discovered the New World more than a thousand years before Columbus did.

As you read the following part of Hwui Shan's story, ask yourself if you agree with those scholars. Try to decide whether it was possible or probable that the Chinese reached the Americas before the Vikings or Columbus.

Hwui Shan's Story

Fusang is located twenty thousand li east of the country of Ta Han in China. The Land of Marked Bodies is seven thousand li northwest of Japan. Its people have marks or stripes on their bodies like wild animals. In front they have three marks. If the marks are large and straight, they belong to the upper class, but if the marks are small and crooked, they belong to the lower class.

The land of Fusang has many Fusang trees, which give it its name. The Fusang tree's leaves look like those of the T'ung tree in China. Its first sprouts are like bamboo shoots. The people of the country eat these sprouts. Their fruit is like a pear but reddish.

Hwui Shan's Claims	Archeological Evidence
1. Hwui Shan said he traveled east 20,000 li from China.	1,000 li = about 333 miles 20,000 li = about 7,000 miles Mexico via the Japan Current is about 7,000 miles from China.
2. The Land of Marked Bodies was 7,000 li from Japan.	Marked women lived at Point Barrow, Alaska, about 2,400 miles from Japan.
3. Fusang has copper but no iron. The people there also have a system of writing.	Archeologists have found that Mexican Indians used copper by 400 A.D. Spanish explorers discovered iron in Mexico after 1500 A.D. By 400 A.D., some Indians in Mexico had a system of writing.
4. The people of Fusang use large cattle horns as containers.	Scholars knew that Montezuma, the Aztec chief of Mexico, showed Cortez, the Spanish explorer, some large bison horns after 1500 A.D.
5. The Land of Women is 1,000 li beyond Fusang.	Central American monkeys live about 300 miles south of Mexico. These monkeys are shy, chattering, and hairy.
6. The Land of Fusang is named after the Fusang trees, which have reddish, pearlike fruit. Sprouts of the Fusang trees look like bamboo.	*Mexico* means land of the century plant. The century plant's sprouts look like bamboo. Some people call it a tree. The Mexican century plant grows to a height of about 30 feet. The plant does not have reddish, pearlike fruit. The prickly pear or cactus apple is reddish and grows on a cactus, which looks like a century plant.
7. Fusang people make thread and paper from Fusang trees.	Archeologists have found that Mexican Indians made thread from century plants, and a form of paper can also be made from them.
8. Fusang has no forts or armies.	Archeologists have found that around 400 A.D., the Mexican Indians were at peace.
9. Hwui Shan gave the emperor of China a mirrorlike object from Fusang.	Archeologists have found that some Mexican Indians used mirrors made of polished stone.
10. Fusang has carts pulled by horses, cattle, and reindeer.	Archeologists have found that the Mexican Indians put wheels on their toys. There is no evidence as yet to show that Indian adults made use of the wheel. Spaniards brought the first horses and cattle to the Americas after 1500 A.D. The reindeer nearest to Mexico are found in Norway and Siberia. Hwui Shan probably stopped over in Siberia.

Source: Adapted from Fielder, 1972, pp. 23–27.

The people also spin thread from the bark. They use the thread to make coarse cloth from which they make their clothing. They also make a finer fabric from this thread. The wood of the Fusang tree is used to build houses, and the bark is used to make paper.

Knowledge

1. Where were the explorers in the story from?

2. _____

3. _____

Comprehension

1. Give a brief summary of the story.

2. _____

3. _____

Application

1. Can you give the names and circumstances of other explorers who might have "discovered" America?

2. _____

3. _____

Analysis

1. Why don't all historians reach the same decision after they've seen the same evidence?

2. _____

3. _____

Synthesis

1. What are some reasons either for or against accepting this story?

2. _____

3. _____

The people of Fusang have a system of writing. But they have no forts or walled cities, no military weapons or soldiers. They do not wage war.

Their ground has no iron, but it has copper. They have large cattle horns which they use as containers. The largest horns hold about five gallons. They have carts drawn by horses, cattle, and deer.

The Land of Women is about one thousand li beyond the Land of Fusang. Its women are completely covered with hair. They walk standing up straight and chatter a lot among themselves. They are shy when they see ordinary people. Their babies are able to walk when they are one-hundred days old, and they are fully grown in three or four years. (Fielder, 1972)

After your students have all read this story, ask them to respond to this question: Did the Chinese really discover America? Encourage them to share their hypotheses with each other. Help them understand that even though they may have devoted a substantial amount of time and thought to answering the question, their conclusions must still be seen as hypotheses because so little information is presented for them to interpret.

Next, divide the students into small groups, and provide them with the chart on the previous page. Ask each group to build a database of information, based on the content of the chart, from which they can revise or refine their earlier hypotheses.

Older students might want to explore this issue further through Internet research. Younger ones might hone their map skills by studying the possible routes that the Chinese explorers might have taken. Students of all ages will learn about the hierarchy or taxonomy of interpreting information. The guide on the previous page shows how you might emphasize what kinds of knowledge students can gain from studying this kind of historical riddle.

Summary

Several issues are involved in bringing history to life for children. One matter of concern is for them to see themselves as part of history. The family is the key to this. Every family has a history, a heritage—one that children should feel good about. This means exploring their own pasts and the pasts of their parents, grandparents, and ancestors. Researching the newspaper from the day each child was born provides a sense of what was happening in the world when she or he arrived as a newborn baby. Timelines of significant events in children's own lives can provide a graphic sense of history, and once they have the idea of timelines, they can apply it to larger-scale events, such as the history of their community or state.

Another way to bring history to life is through the medium of storytelling. Finding out about the lives of parents and grandparents when they were children helps build continuity across generations, giving students a sense of what went before them. The good thing about such historical inquiry is that

it takes advantage of the stories already being told in families, with the added value of making the child a recorder of history. This is consciousness raising in action.

Your classroom itself is a good indicator of the level of interest you and your students have in history. If I could visit your class, I would look for timelines, bulletin boards, posters, photographs, maps, dioramas, drama, music, and art that speaks to a study of history. Fortunately, you don't have to do this by yourself. The children will be as helpful and creative as you allow them to be.

Finally, your task is to bring a sense of excitement and enthusiasm to the study of history. Enthusiasm, like the common cold, is catching. Just try it! If you talk to your students about books you're reading, read stories to them, recite stirring passages from inspirational moments in history, role-play historical characters, and generally extol the pleasures of historical inquiry, then magic will happen in your classroom.

Explorations

Reflect On . . .

1. Why should we study history? Write down three reasons that come to mind. Which of these do you think is most important? Why?
2. The National Council for the Social Studies (1994) says that "the primary purpose of social studies is to help young people develop the ability to make informed and reasoned decisions for the public good as citizens of a culturally diverse, democratic society in an interdependent world" (p. 2). How do you think the study of history fulfills this purpose?

In the Field

3. Celebrate a History Day in your classroom, either the class where you are student teaching or the class where this textbook is being used. Select a

time period, such as the American colonial era, and then develop an entire day's set of school lessons from that time—for example, colonial mathematics, history, geography, spelling, reading, games, and so on. Dress in period costume and role-play a colonial teacher. Ask your students to dress up, as well. Share a colonial meal and play colonial games. All this will take planning and research. A helpful Website to get you started is *www2.lhric.org/kat/wq/colonial.htm*.

4. Every town or city has one or more cemeteries. On your own or with other students, arrange to visit a nearby cemetery as a means of reconstructing some of the history of your local region. Record the birth and death dates from various tombstones and markers, with special attention to those that are the oldest. Write the first names

given to people of various eras to determine any trends. If you can, do a rubbing of an old tombstone with butcher paper and charcoal.

For Your Portfolio

5. Add some of your own history to your portfolio. Create a brief but creative résumé that shows your educational record, your work history, your travels, your hobbies and interests, samples of lessons, your motivation, a narrative that explains why you have chosen the teaching field, and a list of strengths.

Continuing The Journey: Suggested Readings

Hock, R., & Notess, G. R. (2007). *The Extreme Searcher's Internet Handbook.* Medford, NJ: Cyber-Age Books.

Hopping, L., & Hopping-Egan, L. (2003). *15 Primary Source Activities.* New York: Scholastic.

Nelson, K. (2007). *Teaching in the Digital Age.* Thousand Oaks, CA: Corwin.

Schlemmer, D., & Bratsch, M. (2008). *Teaching Beyond the Test.* Minneapolis, MN: Free Spirit.

Shoob, S., & Stoute, C. (2007). *Teaching Social Studies Today.* Huntington Beach, CA: Shell Education.

Stone, R. (2008). *Best Practices for Teaching Social Studies.* Thousand Oaks, CA: Corwin.

Thombs, M., Gillig, M., & Canestrari, A. (2008). *Using WebQuests in the Social Studies Classroom.* Thousand Oaks, CA: Corwin.

Veccia, S. H. (2004). *Uncovering History.* Chicago, IL: American Library Association.

Websites

Information and technology skills summarized into six steps. *www.big6.com/*

A Website dedicated to the use of the jigsaw cooperative method. *http://jigsaw.org/*

Directions on creating your own WebQuests for students. *www.webquest.org*

The center for teaching history with technology. *http://thwt.org/*

National center for history in the schools. *http://nchs.ucla.edu/*

National history education clearinghouse: teaching materials, best practices, and more. *http://teachinghistory.org/*

Related NCSS Standards and Principles of Powerful Social Studies

Curriculum Standards

Theme II, Time, Continuity, and Change

Learners in early grades gain experience with sequencing to establish a sense of order and time. The use of stories helps children learn historical concepts rooted in ethical and moral traditions. In addition, children begin to recognize that individuals may hold different views about events in the past. They begin to offer explanations for why views differ, and to develop the ability to defend interpretations based on evidence from multiple sources. They begin to understand the linkages between human decisions and consequences. The foundation is laid for the further development of historical knowledge, skills, and values in the middle grades (p. 13).

Early Grades

Purposes:

Knowledge of history enables students to see their lives as part of the larger story of humankind over time and to better understand their roles as contributing citizens of the community and nation, and members of an increasingly interdependent world.

Key Questions (Exemplars) for Exploration:

What happened in the past?
How do we learn about the past?
How was life in the past different from life today?
What caused certain events?
What are the consequences of past events for the present and future?" (p. 33).

Processes—The Learner Will Be Able to:

identify and use a variety of primary and secondary sources for reconstructing the past such as documents, letters, diaries, maps, textbooks, photos, and others. identify examples of both continuity and change as described in stories, photographs, documents . . . and to describe examples of cause-effect relationships. compare and contrast differing stories or accounts about past event, people, places, or situations, and offer possible reasons for the differences. use sources such as artifacts, documents, stories . . . to develop an understanding of the past and begin to see how knowledge of the past can inform decisions about actions on issues of importance today. use methods of inquiry of history and literacy skills to research and present findings (p. 33–34).

Possible Student Products—Learners Might Demonstrate Their Knowledge of Time, Continuity, and Change by:

drawing illustrations to show their interpretation of multiple accounts of the same event and offering ideas about why the accounts differ
using artifacts to offer guesses to reconstruct events and life of the past
participating in role-playing and reconstructing events
constructing timelines that indicate an understanding of a sequence of events (p. 34).

Source: National Task Force for Social Studies, *Expectations of Excellence: Curriculum Standards for Social Studies* (Silver Spring, MD: National Council for the Social Studies, draft 2008). The Council's website is www.socialstudies.org

---

SAMPLE LESSON 12.1   Role-Playing about the Civil War

GRADE LEVEL: Appropriate for grades 5–7.

NCSS STANDARD: Use various sources for studying the past, and compare different accounts of historical events

PURPOSE: To provide a frame for the students to use in evaluating both points of view in the Civil War.

OBJECTIVES: Students will be able to do the following:

1. Identify which states belonged to the Union and which states belonged to the Confederacy.
2. Identify three reasons articulated by the North and three reasons articulated by the South for the Civil War.

3. Identify and comprehend some of the feelings experienced by both Northern and Southern states.
4. Identify the qualities of exceptional leaders, regardless of their patriotic affiliation.
5. Feel compassion for participants in the Civil War, regardless of the side they fought on.

RESOURCES/MATERIALS NEEDED: Books on Civil War history; perhaps all or part of the PBS Ken Burns documentary on the Civil War; poster board and markers.

PROCEDURE:

1. Using an outline map on the board, remove the states from the map in the order they seceded from the Union.
2. Divide students into two groups: Union and Confederacy. From this point on, the two sides should not interact during the activity.
3. Have each side choose political and military leaders, draw their flags, and learn the background that supports their historical position. Students should, if possible, read primary source material—speeches by Abraham Lincoln, Robert E. Lee, Ulysses S. Grant, Jefferson Davis, and others; letters home from soldiers; and newspaper accounts of the war. Show students some of the photographs taken by Matthew Brady.

4. Have students create recruitment posters to encourage enlistment and support for their side.
5. Have each side make a presentation to the whole class, arguing their position in the war. Students might role-play Abraham Lincoln for the Union, Jefferson Davis for the Confederacy, or other leaders, or they may simply present a speech making their argument. Students from the opposing side may ask questions and discuss, but try to prevent anyone from arguing or haranguing without supporting his or her arguments.
6. Have students vote on which way they feel the Civil War should end, based on the arguments presented.

CLOSURE: Compare the results of your class vote with the real outcome of the Civil War. Are wars always decided based on rational argument?

EXTENSION: Let your class improve on history by having a reuniting ceremony, as Abraham Lincoln likely would have done had he lived. Have students research Lincoln's plans for Reconstruction, and note the differences between what he had hoped for and what actually happened. Why were his plans not implemented?

Source: Adapted from a lesson plan submitted by Carol Strickler (Grass Valley, Winnemucca, NM) to OFCN's Academy Curricular Exchange, Columbia Education Center, Social Studies.

SAMPLE LESSON 12.2 Nevada Trek

GRADE LEVEL: 6–7. Nevada history or U.S. history, westward expansion.

NCSS STANDARD: The study of people, places, and human–environment interactions leads to perspectives on the world.

PURPOSE: To give students a greater appreciation of what hardships the early emigrant parties were faced with in the movement westward and what accomplishments they achieved. To give students a better understanding of the geographical region of the Great Basin while gaining insights on what a trip like that might have been like.

OBJECTIVES: The learner will demonstrate the ability to make decisions that will benefit his or her party as they cross this country moving west, using skills including estimation, mapping, problem solving, and other appropriate social studies skills and strategies.

RESOURCES/MATERIALS: Pens, pencils, colored pencils, drawing paper, some basic information provided by the teacher, and a good imagination.

PROCEDURE:

1. Have students count off to create five teams or parties.
2. Provide each team with information sheets telling them the following: the dimensions of the wagon (4 feet by 10 feet), how much each wagon can hold (15,000 pounds), and the fact that the wagons have no brakes; what kind of animals are available (mules, which are the most reliable and sure footed but also are very expensive; horses, which pull the fastest and cost less than mules but more than oxen; and oxen, which are the slowest but also the cheapest to buy and feed); and how much each kind of animal eats per day.
3. Provide each team with a map of the terrain they must cover, with the start and end points and various routes marked.
4. Have each team create a list of what they will take as provisions for the long trip, including food, clothing, ammunition, spare wagon parts, and so on.
5. Have each team decide what route to take, choose a departure date, and use estimation to determine the length of time they will be on the trail. They should take into account the terrain, weather, and need to feed and water the animals.
5. Have each team draw and label a map showing the route that they intend to take from St. Louis to their destination arrival in the Sacramento Valley.

CLOSURE: Have each team share their route and provisions list with the rest of the class and explain why they made the decisions they did.

REFLECTION: Let students discuss the process they went through in making decisions. Demonstrate that sometimes different paths can accomplish the same goal.

Source: Adapted from a lesson submitted by Sandy Kellogg (Churchill County Junior High School, Fallon, NV) to OFCN's Academy Curricular Exchange, Columbia Education Center, Social Studies.

Social Studies and the Literacy Connection

One in seven adults lacks the literacy skills required to read anything more complex than a children's book, a staggering statistic that has not improved in more than 10 years. . . .

> —Jessica Calefati
> (quoted in *On Education*, June 22, 2009)

The first poems I knew were nursery rhymes, and before I could read them for myself, I had come to love just the words of them; the words alone. What the words stood for, or symbolized, or meant was of very secondary importance.

> —Dylan Thomas

"The ability to read and write is fundamental to full participation in American society. Our nation of farmers and mechanics has been transformed into one in which economic, civic, and social success depend on educational attainment for all, particularly in literacy. The rapid influx of technology into our daily lives and the internationalization of the economic marketplace have raised the demand for a literate society to the highest level ever." These words were written by A. P. Carnevale two decades ago. If anything, they are more true today than they were when he wrote them.

Citizenship in a democratic society is a major theme of social studies. Citizens govern a free society. They decide who will represent them in government, and they are expected to participate in all the rights and duties of free people. The idea of the participating citizen traces back more than 2,500 years to the time of Aristotle in ancient Greece. In the twenty-first century, participation involves understanding complex issues that affect all our lives. Literacy and democracy, therefore, are inseparable. A democratic society cannot function without a literate citizenry. The ability to read and write is not an option; it is a necessity. As John Jay, a citizen farmer and one of the founders of our nation, wrote, "Education is the soul of a republic."

Your position as a teacher of young citizens represents a sacred trust. You play a significant role in the lives of your students as you encourage them to read and write. Every worthwhile book that your students read will take them farther along the road to becoming informed citizens. Your school librarian and your local public library are your allies in this quest for literacy. You play a part in building a nation of readers, one student at a time.

Literacy can be defined as a person's ability to understand and use the communication tools of the time. Years ago, literacy was in the hands of a select few. Stories were told to ordinary people and handed down through the generations. This included poems, myths, histories, fables, and so on. Only a few could read and write. They held great power over those who could not. They made and interpreted the laws, for example. But by the seventeenth century, the printing press, which had been invented several centuries before that, had created an increasingly widespread phenomenon. Ordinary people began to learn to read and write. This, as much as anything else, made democracy possible. Literacy is power. In fact, the inhabitants of the New England towns of the seventeenth and eighteenth centuries were among the most literate in the world. This set the stage for democracy in the United States.

We live in an age when the communication tool kit has greatly expanded. Your students need not only to be able to read and write effectively but also to function within the context of electronic images and text. Of course, we will probably never reach the point where books and the print medium disappear (at least, I hope not, since I write books!). But in today's world, a whole new definition of literacy—one which must embrace the electronic world as well—has emerged.

The news about children and literacy is both good and bad. The good news is the sheer amount of good literature related to history, geography, economics, and the other social sciences has reached an all-time high. Each year, *Social Education,* the official journal of the National Council for the Social Studies, publishes lists of excellent books written for children and adolescents. The libraries are filled with outstanding trade books. Now the bad news. The National Assessment of Adult Literacy (2009) surveyed more than 18,500 Americans ages 16 and older and found that about 14 percent could not read or could comprehend only basic, simple text.

Functional illiteracy is a real threat to the lives of individuals and to society as a whole. The term *functional illiteracy* means that people cannot read the label on a medicine bottle or they cannot write a coherent paragraph describing even the most basic things. A related term, *aliteracy,* refers to someone who can read but chooses not to. Reading and writing are related pursuits. They support each other. They supply energy to each other. In this chapter, we will search for practical ways to increase both the amount and quality of students' efforts in these two very fundamental areas of learning.

Toward a Literate Society

One year, in the course of my career as an elementary teacher, I found myself wondering about two teaching and learning issues that I was sure were closely connected. The first issue was how to make real readers out of my students, and the second was how to improve my students' knowledge of social studies content, especially biography, history, and geography. See Figure 13.1 in this regard.

It was not that my students never read anything; each week during library period, many of them would check out several books to read, and, of course, I required the

Figure 13.1 *Related NCSS Standards and Principles of Powerful Social Studies*

Processes—The learner will be able to identify and use a variety of primary and secondary sources for reconstructing the past such as documents, letters, diaries, maps, textbooks, photos, and others. Identify examples of both continuity and change as described in stories, photographs, documents . . . and to describe examples of cause-effect relationships, compare and contrast differing stories or accounts about past events, people, places, or situations, and offer possible reasons for the differences, use sources such as artifacts, documents, stories . . . to develop an understanding of the past and begin to see how knowledge of the past can inform decisions about actions on issues of importance today, use methods of inquiry of history and literacy skills to research and present findings (p. 34).

Processes—The learner will be able to: formulate research questions to investigate topics in history, predict possible answers,

and use the historical method of inquiry to research and literacy skills to present findings. . . . (p. 40).

Literacy Skills: Emphasis must be placed on various types of literacy, from financial to technological, from media to mathematical, from content to cultural. Literacy may be defined as the ability to use information to function in society, to achieve one's goals, and to develop one's knowledge and potential. Teachers emphasize certain aspects of literacy over others depending on the nature of the content and skills they want students to learn. The table below provides links between literacy skills and the themes that form the basis for the social studies standards. These can be acquired by students at all grade levels using developmentally appropriate strategies. The following literacy skills are intended to be exemplary rather than definitive (p. 130).

Source: National Task Force for Social Studies, *Expectations of Excellence: Curriculum Standards for Social Studies* (Silver Spring, MD: National Council for the Social Studies, draft 2008). The Council's website is www.socialstudies.org

obligatory one-written-book-report-per-term from each student. Still, I wasn't satisfied with the way things were going, so I tried two ideas at once.

The first idea was to drop the written book-report requirement. That idea was received with great joy by students, some of whom mentioned that they didn't mind reading but that they disliked having to write book reports. Now, a teacher can't simply run a class just by asking the students their preference about whether to do something or not to do it. Still, it is important to listen to them and give them a feeling of some influence because it's their classroom. The reason their joy resonated with me was that I had bad memories of writing book reports myself. So, we agreed: no book reports.

The second idea I had was to develop a very simple (and that is the key) system of acknowledging and supporting students' reading habits. To kick off this phase of my plan, I gave every student in class a green bookmark made from construction paper. It was an inch wide and six inches long, with one end cut at an angle. That was it—no fancy designs or anything else. I told the students that when they had finished reading a book, they were to record the date, title, and author. They were to inform me when they had finished their first book, and I would then give them a red bookmark. After five books, they would be given a blue bookmark; after ten, a yellow bookmark; and so on, in increments of five.

The amount and quality of reading done by those students literally exploded. The growth was exponential. They liked keeping track of their reading, and they loved the paper bookmarks. Why, I asked myself, hadn't I come up with something like this sooner? Napoleon himself once noted that the greatest discovery of his life was that soldiers would die for ribbons. Maybe that was the beginning of behavior modification. At any rate, I learned that children would read for bookmarks. They loved to show me their growing lists, and it gave me a chance to listen to them tell me about their reading and to suggest biographies, historical fiction, histories, good fiction, and so on. Also, they were so proud of their bookmarks. It doesn't take much to make children happy if they know you care about them.

What happened that year was rather successful. I read more, the students read more, and even their parents started reading more. I got reports from parents who said their child used to watch television "all the time, but now he really wants to read." The nice thing about the bookmarks was that it gave every child her or his own measure of progress. It never became a competitive thing between students. Each child was able to compete against herself or himself and to improve the record. We had great class discussions about what it means to improve your own standards.

Through my individual discussions with students, I was able to get closer to them and, as a result, felt much more comfortable suggesting new books for them to read. It occurred to me that maybe I was really listening to them for the first time. The social

A child and his grandfather share a story. The home is a vital link to learning in a child's growth and development.

fabric of the classroom was changing for the better. We were reaching toward one of those transcendent moments in teaching and learning that can occur only when people feel empowered to chart their educational destiny and to talk about it comfortably with others.

Soon, something unforeseen occurred. The much-hated book reports had become a thing of the past, but the children were actually reporting on their reading more than ever. The difference was that it had an easygoing informality about it; in other words, it was a much more natural process, and that was fine because we were getting at *why* someone might read, rather than merely to comply with assignments. This is where the students' creativity emerged. They began to produce skits from books, do role-plays of famous characters, read brief excerpts from good books to the class, build model scenes depicting themes from books, draw elaborate posters advertising books they thought others should read, make bulletin-board displays, and a number of other things to share their knowledge.

These students had crossed a frontier that is seldom crossed in the annals of classroom life. Bringing me with them, they had crossed the frontier from teaching to learning. You think it was tough for the pioneers to cross the Rocky Mountains with their covered wagons? Yes, it was. But just try crossing the high barriers that separate true learning from teacher-centered instruction! Yet, once you've done it (and believe me, even most university students haven't done it), you won't want to go back to the low, swampy moral ground of just doing assignments that someone in charge wants you to carry out. True learning means freedom, and these children experienced it.

I am convinced that becoming a reader takes a lot of practice. A few children do it without any outside help, but most do not. In fact, many who could have become readers give up. I think that for most people, there is a threshhold that, once you cross it, you become a reader; no one has to tell you to read. I am also convinced that you and I and the textbook cannot "teach" students enough social studies to amount to very much. Jean Piaget made it clear that *telling* is not *teaching*. What we can do is support children's learning, which is a very different thing—as different as dependence is to independence.

A good book is the ultimate portable learning tool. It can be read in bed, in the bathtub, in a tree house, in the backseat of a car, and even in a chair. It can be set aside, picked up later, thrown in a backpack and carried to a park bench, and, best of all, it requires no batteries. The reader controls the pace. The great thing about it is that not only is it fun, but the reader can also learn about prehistoric times, pioneers, other cultures, other children, famous women and men, great adventures, and who knows what else along the way.

Literacy and Democracy

Returning to my earlier experience, the fact that my students were reading more was obvious to me, to them, and to others. The bookmarks seemed a small reward for all the energy and goodwill, and I was quite pleased with that result. Dropping the dreaded book reports had left me with a sense of ambivalence, because book reports are, and always have been, a part of reading—a kind of external obligation that proves you read the book. On the other hand, it seemed to have a liberating effect that was all to the good.

Keys to Early Literacy: Parents

For teachers of primary-age children, the challenge is especially fruitful. This is so because habits begin early in life, so it is easier to make reading, or anything else for that matter, a pattern if it is begun early.

The parents are the key here. Somehow, you are going to have to convince them to read to their children. In fact, research illustrates that parents reading to children is vital to their cognitive growth. This procedure is most effective when the parent does three things:

- *Elaborates on the text,* giving information and insight that might not be explicit
- *Refers to the child's own experiences,* drawing him or her into the reading by comparing and contrasting events in the story with things the child knows from experience
- *Pauses from time to time to ask questions* in order to actively involve the child, who may wish to guess what is going to happen next, compare this story with another one, or so on

I was getting to know the children better because we spent time talking about books they were reading, which would lead inevitably to discussions of their interests. It became easier and more natural for me to suggest good books to them, and they seemed always to welcome the suggestions. I was gradually coming to realize that they *were* reporting on the books they read; it was just that the reporting was casual and informal, much the same way members of a book club might share their reading with one another.

The important thing was that the students were reading, and they wanted to communicate their reading—witness the skits, role-playing, and model making discussed

A children's book club discussion.

earlier. We had somehow improved and expanded the whole theory of book reporting, at least for us, and the students had done much of it themselves. They had reached a stage of empowerment, and I began to understand what the term *facilitator* truly meant.

The level and quality of communication rose dramatically as the students shared their reading. The classroom was becoming one big book club that just happened to carry on some other business during the day as well—you know, stuff like spelling, math, science, and a few other subjects. But in time, those subjects followed social studies and were swallowed up by the book club as well. The psychological edge that we all enjoyed was based on the premise that we were reading, discussing, writing, and calculating, not because of a routine based on teacher-centered assignments but because of self-direction and a social fabric that had brought us together and made us a community of learners.

Reading and Writing

Writer John Gardner stated that the best way to learn to write well is to read good books. He's perfectly right, of course. Good writing, both its substance and its style, is the best model for anyone of any age who aspires to write. This is an important point for any teacher of children. In order to get them to read good literature and to want to express themselves clearly in writing, a teacher must develop positive relationships with them. The relationship aspect in teaching and learning is key.

Novelist John Fowles, author of *The French Lieutenant's Woman, Daniel Martin,* and many other wonderful books, makes a very interesting point about reading and its effect not only on one's writing but also on one's thinking. In *Daniel Martin,* Fowles suggests that reading frees the imagination, allowing it to roam creatively. This is so, he says, because the reader must supply his or her own images, thus creating an ongoing mental process of interaction with the written text. Older people who listened to radio adventures when they were children say much the same thing: They had to supply the images in their minds. Of course, if you read to the children from a good book for 15 minutes or so after lunch (the favorite part of the school day for many children), they will supply the images as they listen to you read. Fowles contrasts the image making of the reader with the captured imagination of the television viewer, who has both text and images supplied for her or him. There is little else to do in terms of mental construction.

Now, this is all very important when it comes to writing. The person who has read a great deal of good literature has been tutored in how to use words and craft sentences so that he or she becomes actively involved in image making. Reading and writing, then, are actually a seamless process, each one supporting the other. For the child who finds it difficult to write the words that convey exactly what she or he wants to say, a greater appreciation for good writing is possible.

Take a moment to read the few lines that follow from Ralph Waldo Emerson's poem "Concord Hymn," written to commemorate the beginning of the American Revolution. Allow yourself to create images of the scene.

By the rude bridge that arched the flood,
Their flag to April's breeze unfurled,
Here once the embattled farmers stood
And fired the shot heard round the world.

Figure 13.2 *An Eight-Year Old Child's Interpretation of the Poem, "Concord Hill."*

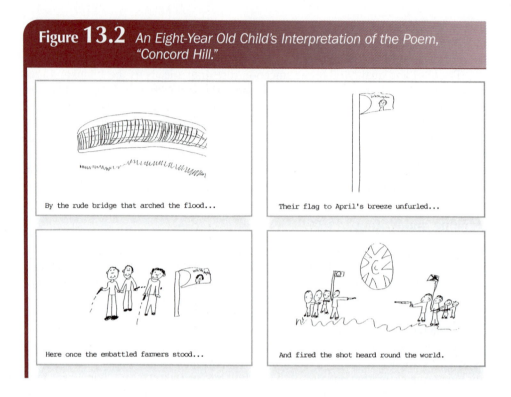

By the rude bridge that arched the flood...

Their flag to April's breeze unfurled...

Here once the embattled farmers stood...

And fired the shot heard round the world.

I suggest to you that any fifth-grade child who reads this poem, discusses it with a thoughtful teacher who supplies interesting historical information surrounding it, and draws pictures of the scene (see Figure 13.2) can probably write a description of the events that has more emotion and life in it than that found in the account in the social studies textbook.

Of course, the road to good writing and reading doesn't stop there. Children with whom you have a good relationship, who trust you and value your opinion, are ready and eager to take cues from you. So when you suggest to a fifth-grade child that he or she read *Johnny Tremain, Little Women,* or some other well-written, worthwhile book, you are suggesting more than a book title; you are bringing the wealth of your goodwill and trust to a child who wants your advice. Believe me, it's great to have wonderful authors such as Louisa May Alcott helping you teach a child to write well.

When considering writing and reading for children, it is important to relate it to modes of thought. The work of Benjamin Whorf illustrates rather well that the language people are exposed to (both written and oral) decides in great measure what thoughts are possible for them. They cannot escape from it into any other way of perceiving the world. Whorf's work was done with such culture groups as Inuits (Eskimos) and Native Americans, primarily Hopis. He showed that the rich vocabularies of these two groups in certain areas gave them an expressive ability that is indeed remarkable. For example, Inuits have an amazing number of words for snow, depending on the exact type of snow that might be falling at a given time. They can, therefore, think thoughts about snow that most English speakers cannot. The point of Whorf's research is that each individual can expand her or his vocabulary and, therefore, her or his range of thought and expression.

Keep in mind that what a person reads determines to a considerable extent what he or she becomes in life. Just recently, I talked with a teacher who told me that reading was her first love, and that was why she thought it was such an important subject in the school curriculum. When I asked her what she had read recently, she couldn't think of anything. I guess she meant it was important for children to read, but that she had already done that. This attitude simply will not work. If you want your students to read, you must model it. As you read, you will grow, and the students will sense the excitement and the growth.

Take a moment to consider the relationship between reading and writing as it is portrayed in the following example. A fourth-grade teacher read a descriptive paragraph from E. B. White's classic book *Charlotte's Web:*

> The barn was very large. It was very old. It smelled of hay and it smelled of manure. It smelled of perspiration of tired horses and the wonderful sweet breath of patient cows. It often had a sort of peaceful smell—as though nothing bad could happen ever again in the world. It smelled of axle grease and of rubber boots and of new rope. And whenever the cat was given a fish head to eat, the barn would smell of fish. But mostly it smelled of hay, for there was always hay in the great loft up overhead.

Then the teacher asked the students to write a group composition describing their own classroom. Notice the learning effect that a piece of well-written prose had on the children:

> The schoolroom was very large and old. It smelled of chalk dust and children's clothes. It often had a quiet smell—as if nothing bad could happen in school. It smelled of pencil lead, ink, ink paste, watercolor paints, and crayons. Whenever it rained or snowed, the wet coats and boots in the dressing room smelled like a skunk. When the children walked into the room, it smelled like potato chips, candy, nuts, and pumpkin seeds. Most of the time it smelled like smoke and dust. The dust came from the windows. The smoke came from the chimneys.

Experience and Discussion

In social studies, it is vital that children have direct experiences and vicarious experiences. Direct experiences build perceptions and ideas about reality. For example, a direct experience is taking primary-age children outside on a fall day to gather evidence of fall or allowing intermediate-level children to make a Native American meal with the guidance of a tribal member.

Vicarious experiences about human behavior and environments are often best supplied through print, film, or pictures. Of course, it would be fantastic to take your class to visit Japan or to travel backward through time to visit a colonial village, but in the absence of such possibilities, a teacher learns to use print and film strategically to build experience. Sample Lesson 13.1 allows students to combine emerging literacy skills with a lesson on cultural understanding.

Experience is necessary, but for it to become imbedded intellectually and emotionally, you must use your most characteristically human trait: *speech*. Schools will not improve until teachers are willing to give over vast amounts of time to both small-group and whole-class discussion. Too often, teachers fail to capitalize on the opportunity to really reflect and personalize experience. Talking about what they do, how they feel, how their perceptions change, and so on enables people to use their experiences as a springboard to deeper insight about themselves and others. Discussion also exposes people to the thinking of others who may have had the same experience yet whose perceptions of the experience are quite different. This adds a richness and a sense of quality possible only when people take the time to discuss things with others.

It sounds so simple, doesn't it? Unfortunately, research shows that student-initiated talk accounts for only about 7 minutes out of a typical 300-minute school day (Goodlad, 1984, 2008)

Social Studies and Language Development

The great Austrian philosopher Ludwig Wittgenstein offers a compelling argument linking language development to thinking and, therefore, to expression, both written and oral. Wittgenstein maintains that the limits of a person's language are the limits of that person's world. Thus, an individual's (or group's) world view is limited and determined by the language she or he commands.

The meaning of all this for classroom learning is that children need to read good material (unfortunately, the average elementary social studies textbook hardly qualifies), to write extensively, and to be given ample opportunity for oral discourse. The practice in recent years of journal writing is an excellent example of how children can be helped along the road to building up their talents for written expression.

In his book *Thought and Language,* Russian psychologist Lev Vygotsky (1986) examines the relationship between language and cognition. He comes to the conclusion that experience added to social interaction, or group sharing of written and oral language, is a key to language development. What is often overlooked or underestimated is that the expressive ability of children is an outcome of cognitive development, as well as an enhancer of cognitive development. In other words, you need to give your students as much practice as possible in reading, writing, and discussing.

Interpreting Text

A useful technique for combining reading and writing (and even oral discourse, for that matter) is called *interpreting text*. In a superficial sense, it looks like note taking as one reads, but it is far more than that.

Here's how it works: As a person reads a book, he or she actively interacts with the text. The interaction takes the form of responding to statements made by the author as well as adding the reader's knowledge, thoughts, feelings, impressions, questions, and insights. The purpose of interpreting text is to give the reader equal footing with the author, thereby giving the reader a participatory role. Thus, the role of the student is both reader and writer. Here is an example written by an 11-year-old student named Tony:

> I agree that the pioneers had to be tough and smart. Otherwise, they couldn't have made it with no roads and just covered wagons. So they are heroes for what they did. I never thought about it before, but maybe I get to live here because they settled our town. But I was just trying to think of how the Indians felt. Maybe they didn't know everything that happened. But they had lived there all their lives, and so had their grandparents back into history. It's hard for me to understand. Both the pioneers and the Indians had feelings. History is about the past, so when I read in this book everything I read about already happened. I still don't think the pioneers were wrong because they wanted to be farmers on different land. But I do think we should care about what happened to the Indians because they had a way of living that was good for them.

You can see in this child's writing a genuinely reflective viewpoint emerging. He is bringing something to the text. The child has feelings of ambivalence that transcend the reading of text merely for information. He is on the way to becoming an involved, critical reader.

Journal Writing

One of the more productive avenues toward improved thought and expression is journal writing. A journal encourages metacognition, or thinking reflectively about the

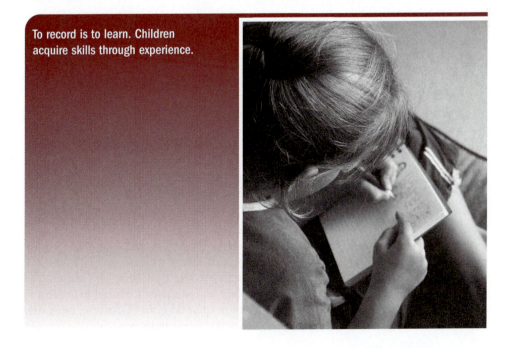

To record is to learn. Children acquire skills through experience.

experiences the writer has had. A good journal, like a good diary, includes thoughts, feel-ings, perspectives, insight, analyses, and other means of reflection. Some students like to imagine that their journals are ship's logs and that they are making entries each day as the ship sails from September to June.

In social studies, writing in a journal is useful as a way of reflecting on the ideas, skills, content, and values that are being considered. A journal should give a student a private avenue of expression for her or his personal growth. Take a moment to consider the journal entry written by a sixth-grade student:

February 17

I really enjoy sharing time when we get to tell about the biographies. Everybody tries to make it so interesting and it is so much fun that I never liked social studies as much as this year. Some days I look at the clock and wonder if it will ever turn two o'clock so we can get started, but today was the best of all when Maddie and Sean pretended they were Columbus and Chief Joseph who never really met but the way they did it made Columbus so surprised with the way things turned out. Now some of us are going to turn it into a play, I hope.

The Writing Process

In social studies, a useful place to begin the writing process is with descriptive writing. Remember that observing, recording, and explaining are three of the most basic social science processes. To make good descriptive writers of your students, you need to give them practice with the process itself. The writing process can be considered in four phases:

1. *Prewriting.* This is the initial, or warm-up, phase. In this phase, a young writer needs to consider the subject, think about whom he or she is writing for, and cre-ate images of what he or she would like to say.
2. *Drafting.* The writer is ready to take the first written approach to the subject. At this stage, it is important that the writer says what she or he needs to say in rough form.
3. *Revising.* This is a good time to discuss the work with someone else, to get teacher comments, and to consider not merely *what* to say but *how* to say it.
4. *Editing.* This is the phase where the finished product will emerge. Spelling, punc-tuation, elements of style, and so on are important because others will read the product.

Like anything else, it takes time and practice to become proficient as a writer. The earlier children begin the process, the more they will see it as a natural extension of their ability to communicate with others. They need to do a lot of writing, especially descriptive writing, and they need to read or listen to good writing.

in the classroom   Writing Descriptions

In a third-grade class, the teacher decided that she would give each child a chestnut and ask him or her to write a description of the chestnut. The children followed the four phases of the writing process, as follows.

In phase 1, the children looked up information on chestnuts, and the teacher read some background from a botany text she had obtained from the library. More important, the children drew several pictures of their chestnuts and chestnut trees. They worked with partners, telling them about their drawings and about their feelings as they drew their pictures.

In phase 2, each child began to write a description of her or his chestnut. These were rough drafts. The children shared their stories with their partners, and the teacher collected the rough drafts and made comments.

In phase 3, the children began helping each other with editing. They also considered the teacher's comments to help them with their expression.

In phase 4, each child wrote a finished paragraph about his or her chestnut and drew an accompanying illustration. The works were then displayed on the wall of the classroom.

Here is one child's finished paragraph:

> Let me tell you about my chestnut. It is a kind of chestnut called a horse chestnut. People don't eat them, but squirrels like them. I know, because I have seen the squirrels eat them and bury them. The chestnut is brown with a smooth, shiny shell. It is about an inch wide. If you cut it open, you will see it is white, about the color of a piano key. The chestnut came from a blossom on the tree, and when it grew it had a green spiked cover. The spikes are sharp. The best time to find chestnuts is in the fall when they drop off the trees. If you study my drawings you will see the chestnut from beginning to end, even what a cut-open chestnut looks like. Good-bye.

The writing process served this child well. She learned about sequencing her ideas, about defining an object using words and pictures, and about conveying both form and function, in this case about chestnuts.

The great civil rights leader, Dr. Martin Luther King Jr., speaks to his fellow Americans about equality, compassion, and dignity.

The Spoken Word

In the first century A.D., Roman orator Quintilian noted that speech is our most purely human attribute. Nothing, he said, separates humans from other creatures more clearly than the ability to speak words and to listen to the spoken word.

One could argue the point, citing other characteristics of the human condition as equally or more significant, but Quintilian's meaning is still well taken. Sadly, many educators seem to have forgotten just how important it is for children to be given the opportunity to develop their speaking and listening skills. It is all too easy to overlook this form of literacy.

In ancient times, people had little choice but to communicate using the spoken word. Many culture groups did not even have written language; others did, but had little means of storing the written word in an age before books. Today, the situation is quite the opposite. There are so many means of preserving the record that people tend to undervalue the spoken word.

The poor speaking abilities of most politicians today serve as a reminder that no progress has been made in this area. In fact, great speakers in American history—such as Patrick Henry, Daniel Webster, Abraham Lincoln, and, more recently, Martin Luther King Jr.—seem no longer to be found.

Primary teachers usually do a better job than others in teaching speaking and listening skills, mainly because their students cannot write or read as well as they can speak and listen. Show and tell, dictating stories, and other oral moments of the curriculum are extremely useful in this regard. This is simply not enough, however. As children grow older and more self-conscious, it becomes crucial to encourage and nurture opportunities for oral discourse.

To illustrate how significant this topic is, consider that certain surveys of adults have shown that their number-one fear is speaking in front of a group. Four distinctly different strategies, effectively employed, will go a long way toward remedying this situation.

Public Speaking

It takes courage and skill to talk to a group, and like any other skill, it can be improved only with practice. It is useful to bear in mind John Dewey's idea of the classroom as a learning laboratory, where children are encouraged to take risks, to experiment, and to practice the skills that are needed in everyday life.

Like any other complex task, speaking to groups needs to be approached using developmentally appropriate practice. A good place to begin is to have your students give brief 1- or 2-minute descriptive speeches, in which they hold a prop and describe something (e.g., a chestnut, a baseball, a doll, or whatever). As success builds, as it will in a nurturing environment, students can be given more complex tasks, such as describing a certain river system, telling how to catch a ball, or explaining how to sew a particular stitch.

Small-Group Speaking

In real life, people often find themselves in relatively small groups, engaged in conversation with others. The art of speaking and listening in such a forum is perhaps best facilitated in school settings by having children work in collaborative groups. As they engage in answering questions, solving problems, and developing ideas, they will benefit from acquiring certain skills, such as showing courtesy to others, speaking in turn, talking quietly, asking questions, agreeing and disagreeing civilly, participating actively, encouraging others, contributing their share, being open to different perspectives, and so on. These skills need to be pointed out by you and discussed reflectively by the class. *Circles of Learning,* by David and Roger Johnson (1994), is an excellent source of ideas and skills for promoting small-group learning.

Informal Talks

Contrary to the opinion of those who think classrooms should always be so quiet that one can hear a pin drop, they should, in fact, be places of conversation. Of course, there is a time for quiet, but students should be encouraged to talk with each other as they work together on projects. For one thing, it encourages both language development and social intelligence. For another, it is natural behavior for human beings. Children benefit greatly from expressing themselves to each other as they build a colonial village, draw a mural, rehearse a play, organize a game, prepare a meal, and so forth.

Ironically, there is far too little of this kind of shared activity in elementary school life, and your job is to make sure it happens. Social skills can be learned in such settings, especially if you and the class take the time to discuss appropriate behaviors for informal talk. In fact, the children will help you come up with rules governing their own behavior during these times.

A young speaker shares a book with the class. Public speaking is a cornerstone of a good education.

Group Presentations

You need to be sure that your students engage in presentations in which they are part of a group. Examples of this are panel discussions, demonstrations, pageants, dramatizations, musical productions, debates, and such video productions as "newscasts" and "feature shows." The spoken word is invoked doubly with this procedure. First is the informal talk that goes along with planning, getting prepared, attending to details, orchestrating, and otherwise making sure things are ready. Second is the presentation itself, in which an audience is addressed. Presenting involves deciding on roles, determining who speaks when and how much, fielding questions from the audience, and other problematic issues.

These four strategies will go a long way toward putting the *social* back in social studies. They are aimed directly at the development of thought and language, especially at its public expression.

Constructivist approaches take a clear view on the distinction between *information* and *knowledge* and the need for public expression of ideas. If a teacher employs only silent reading, worksheets, and paper-and-pencil tests, then *information* will serve the student well, at least until it's forgotten. But *knowledge,* which implies the construction of meaning by learners—an activity that uses information as a way to build more complex social and intellectual structures—depends heavily on interaction, exchange, articulation, sharing of thoughts, reflection, and public expression of ideas.

Media Literacy

The invention of the printing press and movable type by German inventor Johannes Gutenberg in the fifteenth century brought about the most profound revolution ever in the advancement of literacy. Everything changed as a result. Books became available to ordinary people, and stored knowledge became decentralized for the first time in history.

Now we are in the midst of another revolution in the annals of literacy. This revolution has been brought about by electronic technology, especially in the form of the Internet, which provides a means of communication that affords people access to databases and online information systems of an incredible range. In less than 15 years, the Internet has become an indispensable tool for everyone from stockbrokers to school children.

The kids you teach have grown up in an electronic age. Texting, Twittering, Facebook, YouTube, GPS devices, and other means of instant communication are all they have ever known. Whole libraries exist in virtual form. Access to information is overwhelming. Websites such as Google and Bing provide answers to almost any question imaginable. In fact, a curious phenomenon in teaching and learning has emerged for the first time in world history—that is, in many cases, the kids know more than the teachers. This has never been true of reading and writing, mathematics and science, the arts, and other areas of the curriculum. One time-honored attribute of a teacher is someone who knows more about the subject matter than her or his students. Well, the times are a-changing, to paraphrase the old Bob Dylan song. But this is actually good news. It means your students bring knowledge and skill to learning. Your task and mine is to capitalize on that.

Using the Internet in the form of the World Wide Web, children in remote sites of Alaska and in crowded urban centers can connect to classrooms in other countries, access the Library of Congress, and examine news reports from around the globe. For social studies teachers, the Internet can create a kind of global village, allowing them and their students to exchange pen-pal letters, stories, weather data, geography, history, and anything else of mutual interest. Useful Websites for school purposes include the following:

- *The Globe Program* at *www.globe.gov* is a wonderful interdisciplinary source for teachers who wish to combine social studies, science, and related environmental issues. Some 3,000 classes around the world are collecting and posting environmental data to the site. Research scientists actually use the student data and offer feedback.
- *C-Span* at *www.c-span.org* gives you and your students access to the U.S. House of Representatives, allowing you to watch the actual process of debate, voting, and so on in the halls of Congress. C-Span also covers other political events and serious items in the news.
- *NCSSonline* at *www.ncss.org* gives you access to the National Council for the Social Studies, the largest organization in the country devoted solely to social studies education. NCSS provides members with networks for all the social science disciplines and for special topics as well, including law education, moral education, multicultural education, and others.
- *Maps.com* at *www.maps.com* and its educational sibling, *maps101.com*, provide access to thousands of maps and mapping software, as well as lesson plans and activities.

These are but a few of the thousands of electronic addresses available, and the list grows every day. The educational challenge of the Internet and the World Wide Web is one of the most exciting events of our lifetimes. I hope you will take advantage of the possibilities.

Remember that Jean Piaget wrote that teaching is about possibilities, and the World Wide Web has created a new horizon of the possible. By the way, I'd love to hear from you. You can contact me at aellis@spu.com.

Summary

The key to this chapter is the interdependent relationship among reading, writing, and the spoken word as ways to communicate thoughts and feelings in social studies. Each of us constructs our own knowledge, but we do it best in social and intellectual contexts that provide access to productive ideas and that allow us, in turn, to build structures of meaning. Children who become avid readers, willing writers, and confident public speakers are on the way to lifelong learning.

Just imagine what a gift it is to a child to have a teacher who creates a learning landscape that offers nurture, support, and encouragement toward those ends. It is through the medium of language that people are able to define and express their hopes, fears, dreams, insights, and ambitions. Please make reading, writing, and the spoken word an integral part of your social studies curriculum.

Explorations

Reflect On . . .

1. Does *literacy* mean more than reading and writing competently? What other skills are needed to be truly literate?

2. What qualities does a teacher need to create an environment in which children feel they can express themselves openly?

In the Field

3. Create a webbing with a central theme. Then complete the webbing with some partners by brainstorming about what reading, writing, and speaking activities students could do. Try these activities with fellow students.

4. Observe a class where students are giving oral reports. Do the students seem comfortable speaking in front of the class? What does the teacher do—or not do—to make them more comfortable?

For Your Portfolio

5. Select a good primary level picture book with a social studies theme. Then develop a lesson around it—one that emphasizes discussion and reflection.

Continuing the Journey: Suggested Readings

Connelly, B., & Stern, S. (2007). *Let's Link Literature and Social Studies.* Lake Worth, FL: Humanics.

Cruz, B., & Thornton, S. (2008). *Teaching Social Studies to English Language Learners.* New York: Taylor & Francis.

Fredericks, A. D., & Grupp, J. (2007). *Much More Social Studies through Children's Literature.* Santa Barbara, CA: Libraries Unlimited.

Housel, D. (2007). *Leveled Texts for Social Studies.* Huntington Beach, CA: Teacher Created Materials.

Johnson, H., Freedman, L., & Thomas, K. (2007). *Building Reading Confidence in Adolescents.* Thousand Oaks, CA: Corwin Press.

Macceca, S. (2007). *Reading Strategies for Social Studies.* Huntington Beach, CA: Teacher Created Materials.

Ogle, D., Klemp, R. M., & McBride, B. (2007). *Building Literacy in Social Studies.* Alexandria, VA: Association for Supervision and Curriculum Development.

Websites

Literacy online resources and research in the United States and worldwide. *www.literacyonline.org*

National Institute for Literacy. *www.nifl.gov/*

An easy-to-use Website with a variety of resources including integrated lessons that build literacy skills and teach social studies content. *www.literacymatters.org*

SAMPLE LESSON 13.1   Comparing Cultures

GRADE LEVEL/SUBJECT: Appropriate for grades 1–5. Subject areas include language arts and social studies.

NCSS STANDARD: Human beings seek to understand their roots and to locate themselves in time.

PURPOSE: Using literature to encourage students to use higher-level thinking skills, to help them cooperate more sensitively with their peers, and to develop respect for cultures different from their own.

OBJECTIVE(S): As a result of this activity, the children will be able to:

1. Work with a partner to answer questions in a cooperative manner.
2. Compare two stories/cultures and point out how they are alike and different.
3. Share their own version of a well-known story and adapt it to another culture, elaborating on why they made certain adaptations.

RESOURCES/MATERIALS: A copy of Shirley Climo's *The Egyptian Cinderella.* (Any version of the Cinderella story from another culture may be used here. The idea is to help children find comparisons and contrasts between two versions from different cultures.)

PROCEDURE:

1. Review the Cinderella story with students. Write an outline on the board that reflects the agreed-upon storyline, characters, and important points.
2. Ask students to find partners (or assign partners), and explain that they should watch you for visual cues during the remainder of the lesson. Use any agreed-upon hand signals for cueing:

- Putting a finger to your head indicating "think time," when everyone should be silently thinking about the best answer to the question
- Holding up two fingers to indicate that students should whisper answers to their partners
- Holding up a hand to call for silence again

3. Once the strategy of hand signals has been explained, read the story *The Egyptian Cinderella* to the class. Pause to ask questions that will guide students to compare and contrast this story to the version of the story that you discussed earlier. Here are some examples of appropriate questions:

- How is the dress of Rhodopis (the Egyptian Cinderella) different from the one worn by the Cinderella you have previously read about? Why do you think they dress differently? Can anyone tell us how the climate of Egypt compares with the climate of the United States? (You may want to show the students Egypt and the United States on the globe and on a map to integrate geography into the lesson.)
- How are Kipa and the other two servant girls like or different from Cinderella's stepsisters? Do they treat Rhodopis fairly? Tell why you think they do or don't.
- Does this story have a happy ending? Compare the way this story ends with the ending of the Cinderella we know.

The questions should be varied and geared toward the age level of your class. Point out that similar stories often arise in different cultures, and identifying the differences and similarities between the versions can help us understand differences in cultures and values.

CLOSURE: Have students listen to or read a folktale from another culture that does not have a familiar equivalent in English. Then ask them to write an American version.

EXTENSION: As homework, ask students to have their parents or grandparents tell them or write down folktales or children's stories from their own cultures. If the students are all from a homogeneous background, ask them to find stories from other cultures in the library or on the Internet. Have students share these stories with the class, and talk about any themes that seem to keep recurring.

REFLECTION: Encourage students to see that different cultures often see things slightly differently and that we all need to be tolerant of one another's values.

Source: Adapted from a lesson plan submitted by Mychael Willon (Unified School District #259, Wichita, KS) to OFCN's Academy Curricular Exchange, Columbia Education Center, Social Studies.

Chapter 14

Epilogue: Keys to Where We've Been...

Our achievements of today are the sum total of our thoughts of yesterday. You are today where the thoughts of yesterday have brought you, and you will be tomorrow where the thoughts of today take you.
—Blaise Pascal

"We had the experience but missed the meaning" is a famous line from T.S. Eliot's wonderful poem, *The Four Quartets*. How often this is true! I've seen some pretty good lessons taught to students, lessons that could have been better if there had been some summing up, some looking back on where we'd been and forward to where it might lead. In this chapter, I want to share with you just a few thoughts that might make the difference between a pretty good teacher and a good teacher. So, you can think of these few pages as a reflective thinking session in which we try to find meaning in all the material that preceded this last chapter. Join me, please, in a session in which we try to capture the essence of social studies teaching and learning.

T he lessons learned from child development, cognitive psychology, brain science, and the constructivist movement have given us important knowledge of how children learn, how they view the world around them, and how they construct meaning. Put simply, we know that young people learn best in a

stimulating, supportive, active, engaging environment. They need adult direction, but they also need freedom to learn. Good teachers understand the balance and act accordingly. Constructive play is the work of childhood. The poet William Wordsworth wrote of "the glory and freshness of a dream" that is childhood.

We also know that human beings construct knowledge both individually and socially. Each child is a unique individual, and no two people learn alike. But each individual needs to be part of the social and moral fabric of life. We are social creatures. Good teachers create conditions that respect the individual and the group. Self-realization and team building are closely related. Identity and belonging are basic human needs that complement each other. Experience is the key. Experiences in self-expression and group belonging bring balance to a child's life. Finally, we know that active, engaging experience is crucial, but not complete without reflection. Socrates reminds us that the unexamined life is not worth living. Each day in your class should involve reflection on what was learned and its meaning.

We've been down a long road together. We've taken elementary social studies from theory to practice, from philosophy to application. Now, I'd like to ask you to reflect on what you've learned. How will you synthesize theory and practice into your own model of teaching and learning? What steps will you take to ensure that social studies is engaging, collaborative, enjoyable, and meaningful for you and your students? To help you in your thinking, I will devote some pages to the critical issues of experience, knowledge construction, and reflective thinking.

When you have read this concluding chapter, you should be able to call on the theoretical and practical dimensions covered previously to help you reach some conclusions of your own about how to be a good teacher, and about children as learners. Teaching and learning are practical pursuits, but for the professional, good practice is based on good theory.

It has been noted that "you can have experience without reflection, but you cannot have reflection without experience." After all, you have to have something to reflect about! This is a very important axiom of learning. We want the children we teach to become good citizens, capable scholars, and fulfilled persons. The dreams we have for our students (and our children) become reality as we nurture and support their inquiry and discovery, their teamwork and collaboration, and their growing sense of self and others.

The Importance of Experiential Learning

Teachers today have access to a variety of active teaching and learning strategies, including discovery, inquiry, cooperative learning, simulation, group investigation, and projects. These strategies have made it possible to create attractive, engaging, and potentially productive learning landscapes. Taken together and thoughtfully applied, they have the potential to remove textbooks and workbooks from their position of dominance in the social studies curriculum. These learning strategies have a common property in that they invite learners to share in active experiences, thereby creating a communal frame of reference that emanates from the investigation of an idea or problem.

For children, experience is the port of entry to reflective thinking. Without experience, students are relegated to a school life of verbal knowledge, which is, as Jean Piaget noted, not *real* knowledge. For example, read the following article:

England Fights Back in Tense Test

LONDON—Pace bowler Angus Fraser, not always the first choice of selectors' chairman Ray Illingworth, inspired an England fightback against West Indies in the second test at Lord's on Friday.

Fraser captured his 100th test wicket by removing Brian Lara for six and later produced a burst of two for one to cut short a recovery by Jimmy Adams (54) and captain Richie Richardson (49).

West Indies, replying to England's first innings of 283, were 209 for six at the close of a tense and absorbing second day watched by another capacity 28,000 crowd under cloudless skies.

Fraser, originally overlooked for the 1994–95 tour of Australia before being called up in an injury crisis, and left out of the team who lost the first test to West Indies by nine wickets, ended the day with three for 37 from 20 overs.

Playing on his Middlesex home ground, Fraser set the tone for a much-needed disciplined performance by England's pace bowlers on a dry pitch showing signs of disconcerting bounce.

But for four missed chances in the final session, three from Adams, England might have taken a firm grip.

After England's largely disappointing batting, the need for their bowlers to strike early was answered initially by Darren Gough and Fraser.

Gough struck with the fifth delivery off the West Indian innings, getting opener Sherwin Campbell caught behind for five by Alec Stewart with one that left the batsman a shade.

Now answer these questions:

- Did you have trouble pronouncing the words? Probably not.
- Did you understand what you read? Probably not.

When I read it, I found that I could barely figure out even the simplest sense of what took place, even which side won. Unless you have a background in the sport of cricket, you probably lack the schema necessary for an understanding of the story.

You and I need to remind ourselves that some children go down this road every day. We tend to confuse *ability* with *prior knowledge*. This is why experiential learning is so important in childhood. The words printed on the page are useful, but only if one's frame of reference can accommodate them.

How Reflective Thought Develops

John Dewey (1916) addressed the crucial nature of experience in learning when he wrote, "The fundamental fallacy in methods of instruction lies in supposing that experience on the part of pupils may be assumed." Dewey went on to say that "ready-made" subject matter and delivery systems in their variety of artificial forms (textbooks, workbooks, lesson plans, etc.) are a "waste of time." That's a pretty strong statement. He stated further that experience with ideas should begin in the most concrete forms and that it should be as "unscholastic" as possible. He advised teachers who wished to involve their students in experience "to call to mind the sort of situation that presents itself outside of school."

Dewey suggested that the most productive ways to engage students involve real problems and social issues. He said that students should begin their inquiry by poking around at a trial-and-error level. The important thing, he said, is the ultimate quality of a problem to be investigated because good problems "give the pupils something to do, not something to learn and the doing is of such a nature as to demand thinking, or the intentional noting of connections; learning naturally results."

Dewey (1916) was convinced that much of what comprises the official learning environment is hostile to reflective thinking. He decried the "great premium put upon listening, reading, and the reproduction of what is told and read." This statement is filled with irony when one considers the potential of social studies to create a sense of community. No wonder, Dewey claimed, that when children go to school, they might as well leave their minds at home, for they cannot use their minds in the abstract curriculum that prevails.

Dewey's observations separate the terms *abstract* and *intellect* with surprising clarity, given the criticism of his writing as conceptually dense and often obtuse. He offers no radical argument against reading or listening as avenues to understanding. Rather, his point is that when these processes are devoid of an experiential backcloth, the learner is left with emptiness, not insight.

Dewey (1916) wrote in the second decade of the twentieth century. One might suppose that learning environments have improved considerably since then. In fact, they have at the level of educational theory, in the realms of research in learning and teaching, and among a relatively small but growing number of informed teachers. Reference to systematic observation in schools, however, reveals less improvement than one might imagine.

The realities of school life changed very little in the twentieth century. John Goodlad (1984) notes that the most predictable event in secondary classrooms is the lecture and in elementary classrooms, seat work. Both are passive, abstract pursuits that offer little hope of intellectual or moral stimulation. Goodlad writes, "Three categories of student activity marked by passivity—written work, listening, and preparing for assignments—dominate in the likelihood of their occurring at any given time at all three levels of schooling. The chances are better than 50–50 that if you were to walk into any of the classrooms of our sample, you would see one of these three activities under way" (p. 105).

In a similar vein, William Glasser (1990) notes that "students in school . . . are asked to learn well enough to remember for important tests innumerable facts that both they and their teachers know are of no use except to pass the tests" (p. 7). Glasser calls this stuff "throwaway information" because it is unconnected to experience and, by inference, to the real lives of students. Even students who receive good grades will often remark that they do not remember much of anything about a particular subject or teacher. Glasser goes on to say that a majority of students, even good ones, believe that much of the present academic curriculum is not worth the effort it takes to learn it. No matter how well teachers manage them, he suggests, if students do not find *quality* in what they are asked to do, they will not work hard enough to learn the material.

Keys to Reflective Thinking

- Reflective thinking takes *time*.
- Reflective thinking requires *strategy*.
- Reflective thinking assumes *trust*.
- Reflective thinking requires *discipline*.

- Reflective thinking is *social and moral*.
- Reflective thinking assumes *experience*.

Source: Adapted from Ellis, 2001.

Constructivism and Social Studies

With the emergence of constructivist thought as a pervasive force in curriculum theory, it is once again becoming easier to find teaching and learning ideas that are based on meaningful experience and that offer the promise of quality. *Constructivism* is a theory of knowledge with roots in philosophy, art and architecture, psychology, and cybernetics. It asserts two main principles:

1. Knowledge is not passively received but actively built up by the cognizing subject.
2. The function of cognition is adaptive and serves the organization of the experiential world, not the discovery of ontological reality (i.e., having to do with the nature of being, existence).

The first principle represents trivial constructivism, a principle known since Socrates. The second principle suggests that knowledge cannot and need not be true in the sense that it matches ontological reality. It has to be viable only in the sense that it fits within the experiential constraints that limit the cognizing organism's possibilities of acting and thinking.

The greatest impact of constructivist theory to date has been in psychotherapy and in the empirical study of literature. In literature reading, meaning is supplied by the reader from his or her own store of experiential abstractions—thus, the subjective interpretation of text.

The teacher will realize that knowledge cannot be transferred to the student by linguistic communication but that language can be used as a tool in a process of guiding a student's construction. Students need experiences of high quality that are at once engaging and intellectually demanding. Reflective thinking, especially in regard to a search for meaning, and personal, social applications are crucial.

Thus, the basis of constructivity is that *experience precedes analysis.* The decade or more spent on such quests as time on task, behavioral objectives, and other teacher-centered instructional protocols proved to be a cul-de-sac along the road to inspiration in childhood learning, especially after the promise provided by the many learner-referenced social studies curriculum projects of a generation ago.

Constructivist thought, which invests learners in a search for their own sense of meaning based on many of the active teaching and learning strategies mentioned earlier, meets the conditions of what could be called an *experiential focus* in teaching and learning. Dewey (1916) himself foreshadowed the constructivist movement when he wrote that a person's ability to think about or apply reason to a given situation has a constructive function. He used the term *constructive* because a person constructs an idea or plan of action "which could not be produced otherwise." Social studies learning that is informal, exploratory, and interdisciplinary provides the needed conditions.

Yet engaging students *actively* is only half the battle. Active student engagement in a meaningful situation, problem, or issue makes it possible to create the conditions for reflective thinking because the students are bonded by a common experience. The experience becomes the focal point of reflective thought. Students reconstruct, evaluate, debrief, second-guess, and otherwise mentally reorganize what they did or what they are doing. It is from that concrete, common experience that students and teachers together can build the intellectual scaffolding necessary for the creation of ideas or concepts.

This is not easy to do. Goodlad (1984) said that in his seven-state study, he saw virtually no evidence of teachers teaching concepts. He concluded that either they felt concepts were unimportant or that they themselves did not think conceptually. However, concept teaching through reflective thinking is, in fact, the key to the saying "Less is more." This is because a few concepts carefully considered are worth far more as intellectual currency than the great amounts of information students are typically asked to cover. Teachers and learners must deliberately slow down, cover less, and think at length about what they are learning. Philosopher Jean-Jacques Rousseau knew this, and that is why he advised teachers to teach less and teach it well. In this same spirit, Alfred North Whitehead (1929) wrote, "What you teach, teach thoroughly" (p. 2).

Although it is imperative to include firsthand experience as an integral part of social studies learning, there should be no bias against abstract thought in constructivist classrooms. In fact, it is needed desperately. The abstract thought that one seeks, however, must be rooted in a meaningful frame of reference called experience. This was Francis Bacon's intent when he said that learning ought to be about facts—one's *own* facts and not someone else's. Bacon's Experience → Mind → Meaning model is much the same as that of Dewey:

Constructivist learning theory states that each of us must construct our own knowledge; others cannot give it to us. The role of experience and reflection in learning has been explored at length in the annals of cognitive research. Experience and reflection are, for example, the twin pillars of significance in constructivist learning theories. But one finds similar thinking in structuralist, developmental, and information-processing literature.

Robert Karplus, the director of the Science Curriculum Improvement Study (SCIS), developed a three-phase learning model consisting of preliminary exploration, invention, and discovery. Karplus notes that students need to start by exploring a concept using concrete materials. By starting an investigation in this manner, Karplus argues, a learner has a direct experience from which to begin processes of abstract thought. But to be meaningful, the learning cycle must continue beyond the direct experience.

Jerome Bruner (1963) makes a clear distinction between learning *by* experience and learning *from* experience, and the distinction lies not so much with the experience itself as with how one reflects back on the experience. Bruner notes that animals typically learn by experience. A dog that burns its paw on the stove will not repeat such a mistake. The dog is too intelligent for that. But the dog is incapable of reflecting on such ideas as heat transfer or thermodynamics as a result of its experience. So experience, as valuable as it is, is not enough. A search for meaning must accompany the experience.

These are the dual imperatives of constructivism. This is to say that in order for learners to think reflectively about important things, they must have direct experience. Equally important, they must also have opportunities to reconstruct their experience. The implication is that a given activity must be extended beyond the experiential phase into a time of reflection and knowledge construction.

To those who point out that there seems little new in these lines of argument, I advise a careful reading of the research-based policy guidelines that have appeared in leading educational journals and government publications over the last decade. The persuasive efforts aimed at school personnel to keep students focused on reductionist, teacher-centered, direct-instruction tasks have been legion.

Social Studies Strategies for Reflection

Attempts to redirect social studies toward a sense of greater activity and accompanying reflective thought inevitably bring up the element of time. Ask any teacher to name sources of frustration in her or his work, and the time factor invariably appears, usually in connection with having too little of it against too much material to cover.

John Carroll (1963) suggests that time is the most problematic variable in the curriculum. Most of what students are expected to learn in school settings is configured by class periods of an hour or less. This is obviously true at secondary levels, where separate subjects are assigned their own time slots, but it is more true at elementary levels than most care to admit. In addition, most social studies curricula are set on time vectors from the first day of the school year forward. Teachers feel the need to forge ahead in order to provide the coverage demanded by the textbook or the district guide. This is particularly true of basic subjects such as social studies. It is less true of so-called soft subjects such as art, physical education, and music.

Carroll implies that if educators would slow down the curriculum, most students would actually learn more. His proposition is that the curriculum favors only those who learn quickly. The problem, he believes, is that most students never have the opportunity to process or to reflect on what they are learning—in essence, what is taught never gets internalized or connected to other learning. This problem is especially vexing in social studies, where so much new content involving place names, dates, and events washes over learners daily.

It has been noted that average and below-average learners often leave out steps when they try to solve problems. Apparently, they go too fast in their efforts to keep up, taking mental shortcuts. An example of this would be a child playing, say, checkers who rather impulsively makes what seem on the surface to him or her to be reasonable moves. Often, the moves this young checker player makes are poorly thought out and could be vastly improved by talking through a move with another person, in which case certain lapses in logic might be confronted. To those who might think that such a procedure in checkers would be unfair, it is well to keep in mind that our teaching and learning objective is not to win against an opponent but to become better at what we do.

Thinking Strategies

Robert Sternberg (1986) and others suggest that students should be encouraged to think aloud with a partner in order to slow themselves down. Such a strategy allows the learner to find out how well developed her or his ideas really are. Thinking aloud brings the process of coming to thought to the surface, giving learners an opportunity to compare and contrast their ideas with those of others. In other words, it provides students with the opportunity to think reflectively.

Jean Piaget (1965) wrote about the social knowledge that develops from working and interacting with others. He was convinced that the linguistic compatibility found within the peer group enables students to teach each other quite effectively, perhaps more effectively than an adult teacher, whose language structure is quite different from that of students. Russian psychologist Lev Vygotsky (1986) wrote about the community of knowledge and insight that the members of a community must share in order for learning to come to life. These insights point to the need for major restructuring of social studies learning and teaching.

Problem-Solving Strategies

Here is a rather simple example of how we might develop strategies for slowing down and making our thoughts more explicit in order to make them more productive.

Imagine that there are 10 apples in a sack in a ratio of 3 red apples to 2 yellow apples. How many apples would you have to take out of the sack to be certain of having a matched pair either red or yellow?

This is a difficult problem for many children partly because it purposely contains some extraneous information. But is the problem inherently difficult or is it difficult because we expect students to solve it with paper and pencil after reading it from a page? Imagine two alternative methods of trying to solve the problem: (1) talking about it while drawing diagrams with a partner and (2) simply reaching into a container that held the apples several times and trying to construct with a partner why you got the results you did. Both of these methods take considerably more time than we generally allow for such problems, and both yield better results.

Some teachers, apparently satisfied with the results they are getting, simply do not see how we could possibly slow down the curriculum. They know they must cover a great deal of information to comply with the social studies agenda. One possible means of accommodation is for teachers to talk less. Research shows that teachers talk three times as much as their students (Goodlad, 1984, 2008). Since students outnumber teachers by about 27 to 1, it doesn't take a mathematics genius to figure out that students are allowed very little time to practice reflective thought.

A remedy for this situation, of course, is to use cooperative learning of some sort, where students are expected to share their thoughts and to listen to the thoughts of others. Cooperative learning not only changes the amount of student-to-student interaction so desperately needed for reflective thinking to occur, but it also changes the very social fabric of the classroom. Students are given far more control over their time, and teachers are able to shift from teaching as telling to allowing learning to take place.

Crossing the Frontier to Active Reflective Learning

Of course, much of this is already known by well-informed teachers. The problem lies with their many colleagues who are less informed about how to create the proper conditions for learning. Even among those who promote active learning, however, there is a reluctance to build in the extra time needed for genuine reflection by both students and teachers. Such a need is obviously not perceived by administrators as being necessary for teachers, who have little or no time to reflect alone or with fellow teachers. Therefore, it is little wonder that teachers often neglect reflective thinking with their students.

Economist Peter Drucker (1990) states in his provocative book *The New Realities* that schools will never improve until classrooms become places where people have crossed the frontier from teaching to learning. When the primary focus in a classroom is on *teaching,* a teacher-centered curriculum results. Teacher-centered instruction is the stuff of lesson plans, scripted activities, behavioral objectives, and predictable outcomes. When the focus in social studies is on *learning,* a constructivist curriculum emerges. Student-centered, constructivisit learning allows students the latitude to make choices, to play to their strengths, to work at length on projects, to develop ideas, to cooperate with other students, and to reflect on the quality and meaning of their work.

Instances of crossing the frontier from teaching to learning abound, but rarely in classrooms. Rather, they are found in the real world, where learners make their own connections, do their own investigations, and continuously process what they are learning.

Recently, I asked a colleague for some help with a problem I was having with a computer. He patiently walked me through a series of steps that got me on the right track. I asked him how he had learned so much about computers. He replied that he had learned what he knew by hanging around, using computers, and talking to other interested people. He explained that when he was in high school, there was a computer hooked up through a terminal to a mainframe and he used to go down to the little room where it was housed, close the door, and get online. He said he had never taken a computer class.

What my friend had done unwittingly was to follow John Dewey's prescription for learning: Make it experiential, make it as unscholastic as you can, and reflect on what you do with other interested people. This is how many children are learning on their own, outside school, when they play and discuss with friends the various video games, simulations, and so on. The success of Lego blocks in actually raising children's spatial intelligence is an example.

Perhaps you could cite similar examples of real learning from your own experience. In fact, you ought to write down and share with a friend a time when you were involved in *real* learning. The point is that such examples have significance because they have the power to redirect one's sense of teaching and learning away from formal, bookish procedures to the creation of learning environments that approximate real-world learning.

The Emotional/Intellectual Landscape

One other condition essential to creating classrooms where students and teachers think reflectively is that of a healthy emotional/intellectual landscape. Not long ago, I observed in a third-grade class where the teacher was doing an inquiry social studies lesson. The approach was inductive: Artifacts were available for the students to examine, the students were working in teams, and they were encouraged to make inferences from their observations and recordings. This was all to the good.

Unfortunately, the atmosphere was tense and rigid. The teacher kept interrupting the students to remind them to "stay on task," even though there was no evidence of misbehavior. Additionally, it became clear that the teacher was looking for right answers, and the students found themselves trying to please her or second-guess her wishes. None of the spontaneity that Piaget said must be present was there. Risk taking, outlandish ideas, a sense of humor, a relaxed and friendly pace—all were lacking.

In this case, what might have been a good formal curriculum was unraveled by a bad hidden curriculum. The possibility of one of those transcendent moments in teaching and learning that occur when a good experience is wedded to a good discussion was lost.

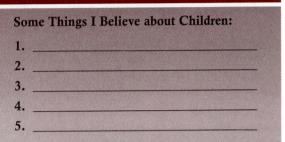

Keys to Teacher Beliefs

Following are a couple of simple but powerful tasks that involve writing statements of belief. First, write down several statements of belief about good teachers—in other words, some traits of good teachers. Then write down several things you believe about children. Create your own list of keys.

Some Things I Believe about Good Teachers:

1. _____
2. _____
3. _____
4. _____
5. _____

Some Things I Believe about Children:

1. _____
2. _____
3. _____
4. _____
5. _____

Take some time to share your thoughts with someone else. How are his or her statements similar to or different from yours?

Summary

The proper conditions for social studies derive from a complex set of strategies developed by teachers and students. Learning by doing is simply not sufficient in itself, and neither is direct experience—although both are important. You must be a guide, a fellow inquirer, an organizer of the environment, and a mediator of your students' thinking. You must establish a new set of priorities that run counter to the prevailing modes of instruction and classroom management. You must be committed to increasing the amount of student-to-student interaction, the number of decisions made by students, the amount of time given to reconstructing learning experiences, and the freedom given to your students to speak their minds and to take intellectual and emotional risks. When these conditions are met, the term *paradigm shift*—a term used so often to signal a basic transformation in what we do and what we expect to happen as a result—moves beyond the realm of cliché and into the realm of reality.

Explorations

Reflect On . . .

1. Discuss with a partner how you think classrooms would have to change in order for reflective thinking to become a reality.

2. Some people might argue that children are not capable of reflective thought. Do you agree? Why or why not?

In the Field

3. Many educators over the years have suggested that we teach less and teach it well. What are the implications for social studies of teaching less?
4. How can a teacher know if her or his students are thinking reflectively? What strategies are necessary to ensure that it will happen?

For Your Portfolio

5. Identify at least three differences you might expect to see between a constructivist classroom and a traditional classroom.

Continuing the Journey: Suggested Readings

Beyer, B. (2008). "What Research Tells Us about Thinking Skills." *Social Studies, 99* (5), 223–232.

> *Any teacher who is serious about teaching thinking should read this article.*

Dewey, J. (1938). *Experience and Education.* New York: Collier.

> *This very readable book sets the record straight on the balance between progressive and traditional teaching and learning.*

Ellis, A. (2010). *Teaching, Learning, & Assessment Together: The Reflective Classroom.* Larchmont, NY: Eye on Education, Inc.

> *Twenty practical strategies for promoting reflective thinking and raising achievement.*

Gredler, M. (2009). *Learning and Instruction: Theory into Practice.* Upper Saddle River, NJ: Pearson.

> *Excellent research-based overview of various forms of education.*

O'Mahoney, C., & Seigal, S. (2008). "Designing Classroom Spaces to Maximize Social Studies Learning." *Social Studies and the Young Learner, 21*(2), 25–27.

> *Authors show why the geography of the classroom is important and how to improve it.*

"10 New Ideas Using Inspiration for Social Studies, History, and Government." Retrieved July 3, 2009, from *www.inspiration.com/community/node/729*

Appendix

Standards Sampler

More and more, students must demonstrate mastery of standards set by national educational organizations or professional organizations in various disciplines, and the social studies is no exception. The following pages provide a brief overview of the standards created for both students and teachers by three groups: the National Council for the Social Studies, the National Center for History in the Schools, and the National Council for Geography Education.

National Council for the Social Studies
Thematic Standards*

Teachers of social studies at all school levels should provide developmentally appropriate experiences as they guide learners in the study of the following topics.

Culture and Cultural Diversity

Teachers should

- Enable learners to analyze and explain the ways groups, societies, and cultures address human needs and concerns.

- Guide learners as they predict how data and experiences may be interpreted by people from diverse cultural perspectives and frames of references.

- Assist learners to apply an understanding as an integrated whole that explains the functions and interactions of language, literature, the arts, traditions, beliefs and values, and behavior patterns.

*© National Council for the Social Studies. Reprinted by permission. Washington, D.C. NCSS.

• Encourage learners to compare and analyze societal patterns for preserving and transmitting culture while adapting to environmental and social change.

• Ask learners to give examples and describe the importance of cultural unity and diversity within and across groups.

• Have learners interpret patterns of behavior reflecting values and attitudes that contribute or pose obstacles to cross-cultural understanding.

• Guide learners as they construct reasoned judgments about specific cultural responses to persistent human issues.

• Have learners explain and apply ideas, theories, and modes of inquiry drawn from anthropology and sociology in the examination of persistent issues and social problems.

Time, Continuity, and Change

Teachers should

• Assist learners in understanding that historical knowledge and the concept of time are socially influenced constructions that lead historians to be selective in the questions they seek to answer and the evidence they use.

• Have learners apply key concepts from the study of history—such as time, chronology, causality, change, conflict, and complexity—to explain, analyze, and show connections among patterns of historical change and continuity.

• Ask learners to identify and describe significant historical periods and patterns of change within and across cultures, such as the development of ancient cultures and civilizations, the rise of nation-states, and social, economic, and political revolutions.

• Guide learners as they systematically employ processes of critical historical inquiry to reconstruct and reinterpret the past, such as using a variety of sources and checking their credibility, validating and weighing evidence for claims, and searching for causality.

• Provide learners with opportunities to investigate, interpret, and analyze multiple historical and contemporary viewpoints within and across cultures related to important events, recurring dilemmas, and persistent issues, while employing empathy, skepticism, and critical judgment.

• Enable learners to apply ideas, theories, and modes of historical inquiry to analyze historical and contemporary developments, and to inform and evaluate actions concerning public policy issues.

People, Places, and Environments

Teachers should

• Enable learners to construct, use, and refine mental maps of locales, regions, and the world that demonstrate their understanding of relative location, direction, size, and shape.

- Have learners create, interpret, use, and distinguish various representations of Earth, such as maps, globes, and photographs, and use appropriate geographic tools such as atlases, databases, systems, charts, graphs, and maps to generate, manipulate, and interpret information.

- Teach students to estimate and calculate distance, scale, area, and density, and to distinguish spatial distribution patterns.

- Help learners locate, distinguish, and describe the relationships among varying regional and global patterns of geographic phenomena such as landforms, climate, and natural resources.

- Challenge learners to speculate about and explain physical system changes, such as seasons, climate, and weather.

- Ask learners to describe how people create places that reflect culture, human needs, current values and ideals, and government policies.

- Challenge learners to examine, interpret, and analyze the interactions of human beings and their physical environments.

- Have learners explore the ways Earth's physical features have changed over time, and describe and assess the ways historical events have influenced and have been influenced by physical and human geographic features.

- Provide learners with opportunities to observe and analyze social and economic effects of environmental changes and crises.

- Challenge learners to consider, compare, and evaluate existing alternative uses of resources and land in communities, regions, nations, and the world.

Individual Human Development and Identity

Teachers should

- Assist learners in articulating personal connections to time, place, and social/cultural systems.

- Help learners identify, describe, and express appreciation for the influences of various historical and contemporary cultures on their daily lives.

- Assist learners in describing the ways family, religion, gender, ethnicity, nationality, socioeconomic status, and other group and cultural influences contribute to the development of a sense of self.

- Have learners apply concepts, methods, and theories about the study of human growth and development, such as physical endowment, learning, motivation, behavior, perception, and personality.

- Guide learners as they examine the interactions of ethnic, national, or cultural influences in specific situations or events.

- Enable learners to analyze the role of perceptions, attitudes, values, and beliefs in the development of personal identity.

- Have learners compare and evaluate the impact of stereotyping, conformity, acts of altruism, and other behaviors on individuals and groups.

- Assist learners as they work independently and cooperatively within groups and institutions to accomplish goals.

- Enable learners to examine factors that contribute to and damage one's mental health and analyze issues related to mental health and behavioral disorders in contemporary society.

Individuals, Groups, and Institutions

Teachers should

- Help learners understand the concepts of role, status, and social class and use them in describing the connections and interactions of individuals, groups, and institutions in society.

- Help learners analyze group and institutional influences on people, events, and elements of culture in both historical and contemporary settings.

- Explain to learners the various forms institutions take, and explain how they develop and change over time.

- Assist learners in identifying and analyzing examples of tensions between expressions of individuality and efforts used to promote social conformity by groups and institutions.

- Ask learners to describe and examine belief systems basic to specific traditions and laws in contemporary and historical movements.

- Challenge learners to evaluate the role of institutions in furthering both continuity and change.

- Guide learner analysis of the extent to which groups and institutions meet individual needs and promote the common good in contemporary and historical settings.

- Assist learners as they explain and apply ideas and modes of inquiry drawn from behavioral science and social theory in the examination of persistent issues and social problems.

Power, Authority, and Governance

Teachers should

- Enable learners to examine the rights and responsibilities of the individual in relation to his or her family, social groups, community, and nation.

• Help students to explain the purpose of government and how its powers are acquired, used, and justified.

• Provide opportunities for learners to examine issues involving the rights, roles, and status of individuals in relation to the general welfare.

• Ask learners to describe the way nations and organizations respond to forces of unity and diversity affecting order and security.

• Have learners explain conditions, actions, and motivations that contribute to conflict and cooperation within and among nations.

• Help learners identify and describe the basic features of the U.S. political system, and identify representative leaders from various levels and branches of government.

• Challenge learners to apply concepts such as power, role, status, justice, and influence to the examination of persistent issues and social problems.

• Guide learners to explain how governments attempt to achieve their stated ideals at home and abroad.

Production, Distribution, and Consumption of Goods and Services

Teachers should

• Enable learners to explain how the scarcity of productive resources (human, capital, technological, and natural) requires the development of economic systems to make decisions about how goods and services are to be produced and distributed.

• Help learners analyze the role that supply and demand, prices, incentives, and profits play in determining what is produced and distributed in a competitive market system.

• Help learners compare the costs and benefits to society of allocating goods and services through private and public sectors.

• Explain to learners the relationships among the various economic institutions that comprise economic systems such as households, businesses, banks, government agencies, labor unions, and corporations.

• Guide learner analysis of the role of specialization and exchange in economic processes.

• Provide opportunities for learners to assess how values and beliefs influence economic decisions in different societies.

• Have learners compare basic economic systems according to how rules and procedures deal with demand, supply, prices, the role of government, banks, labor and labor unions, savings and investments, and capital.

- Challenge learners to apply economic concepts and reasoning when evaluating historical and contemporary social developments and issues.

- Ask learners to distinguish between the domestic and global economic systems, and explain how the two interact.

- Guide learners in the application of knowledge of production, distribution, and consumption in the analysis of public issues such as the allocation of health care or the consumption of energy, and in devising economic plans for accomplishing socially desirable outcomes related to such issues.

- Help learners distinguish between economics as a field of inquiry and the economy.

Science and Technology

Teachers should

- Enable learners to identify, describe, and examine both current and historical examples of the interaction and interdependence of science, technology, and society in a variety of cultural settings.

- Provide opportunities for learners to make judgments about how science and technology have transformed the physical world and human society and our understanding of time, space, place, and human–environment interactions.

- Have learners analyze the way in which science and technology influence core societal values, beliefs, and attitudes and how societal attitudes shape scientific and technological change.

- Prompt learners to evaluate various policies proposed to deal with social changes resulting from new technologies.

- Help learners to identify and interpret various perspectives about human societies and the physical world using scientific knowledge, technologies, and ethical standards from diverse world cultures.

- Encourage learners to formulate strategies and develop policy proposals for influencing public discussions associated with science, technology, and society issues.

Global Connections and Interdependence

Teachers should

- Enable learners to explain how language, art, music, belief systems, and other cultural elements can facilitate global understanding or cause misunderstanding.

- Help learners explain conditions and motivations that contribute to conflict, cooperation, and interdependence among groups, societies, and nations.

- Provide opportunities for learners to analyze and evaluate the effects of changing technologies on the global community.

• Challenge learners to analyze the causes, consequences, and possible solutions to persistent, contemporary, and emerging global issues, such as health care, security, resource allocation, economic development, and environmental quality.

• Guide learner analysis of the relationships and tensions between national sovereignty and global interests in such matters as territorial disputes, economic development, nuclear and other weapons deployment, use of natural resources, and human rights concerns.

• Have learners analyze or formulate policy statements in such ways that they demonstrate an understanding of concerns, standards, issues, and conflicts related to universal human rights.

• Help learners to describe and evaluate the role of international and multinational organizations in the global arena.

• Have learners illustrate how individual behaviors and decisions connect with global systems.

Civic Ideals and Practices

Teachers should

• Assist learners to understand the origins and interpret the continuing influence of key ideals of the democratic form of government, such as individual human dignity, liberty, justice, equality, and the rule of law.

• Guide learner efforts to identify, analyze, interpret, and evaluate sources and examples of citizens' rights and responsibilities.

• Facilitate learner efforts to locate, access, analyze, organize, synthesize, evaluate, and apply information about selected public issues identifying, describing, and evaluating multiple points of view.

• Provide opportunities for learners to practice forms of civic discussion and participation consistent with the ideals of citizens in a democratic republic.

• Help learners analyze and evaluate the influence of various forms of citizen action on public policy.

• Prepare learners to analyze a variety of public policies and issues from the perspective of formal and informal political actors.

• Guide learners as they evaluate the effectiveness of public opinion in influencing and shaping public policy development and decision making.

• Encourage learner efforts to evaluate the degree to which public policies and citizen behaviors reflect or foster the stated ideals of a democratic form of government.

• Support learner efforts to construct policy statements and action plans to achieve goals related to issues of public concern.

• Create opportunities for learner participation in activities to strengthen the "common good," based on careful evaluation of possible options for citizen action.

The National Center for History in the Schools

Overview of K–4 Content Standards in History

Topic 1: Living and working together in families and communities, now and long ago

Standard 1: Family life now and in the recent past; family life in various places long ago

Standard 2: History of students' local community and how communities in North America varied long ago

Topic 2: The history of the students' own state or region

Standard 3: The people, events, problems, and ideas that created the history of their state

Topic 3: The history of the United States: Democratic principles and values and the peoples from many cultures who contributed to its cultural, economic, and political heritage

Standard 4: How democratic values came to be, and how they have been exemplified by people, events, and symbols

Standard 5: The causes and nature of various movements of large groups of people into and within the United States, now and long ago

Standard 6: Regional folklore and cultural contributions that helped to form our national heritage

Topic 4: The history of peoples of many cultures around the world

Standard 7: Selected attributes and historical developments of various societies in Africa, the Americas, Asia, and Europe

Standard 8: Major discoveries in science and technology, their social and economic effects, and the scientists and inventors responsible for them

National Council for Geography Education

The geographically informed person knows and understands the following.

The World in Spatial Terms

Standard 1: How to use maps and other geographic representations, tools, and technologies to acquire, process, and report information

Standard 2: How to use mental maps to organize information about people, places, and environments

Standard 3: How to analyze the spatial organization of people, places, and environments on the Earth's surface

Places and Regions

Standard 4: The physical and human characteristics of places

Standard 5: That people create regions to interpret the Earth's complexity

Standard 6: How culture and experience influence people's perception of places and regions

Physical Systems

Standard 7: The physical processes that shape the patterns of the Earth's surface

Standard 8: The characteristics and spatial distribution of ecosystems on the Earth's surface

Human Systems

Standard 9: The characteristics, distribution, and migration of human populations on the Earth's surface

Standard 10: The characteristics, distributions, and complexity of the Earth's cultural mosaics

Standard 11: The patterns and networks of economic interdependence on the Earth's surface

Standard 12: The process, patterns, and functions of human settlement

Standard 13: How forces of cooperation and conflict among people influence the division and control of the Earth's surface

Environment and Society

Standard 14: How human actions modify the physical environment

Standard 15: How physical systems affect human systems

Standard 16: The changes that occur in the meaning, use, distribution, and importance of resources

The Uses of Geography

Standard 17: How to apply geography to interpret the past

Standard 18: How to apply geography to interpret the present and plan for the future

References

Adler, M. (1982). *The Paideia Proposal.* New York: Macmillan.

Alter, G. (2009). "Challenging the Textbook," *Educational Leadership, 66* (8): 72–75.

American Anthropological Association (2009). "Anthropological Resources for Teaching Social Studies, Geography, Histroy, and Science." retrieved from world wide web www.aaanet.org, November 24, 2009 p.1.

American Economic Association (2009), retrieved from world wide web November 2009, www.vanderisit.edu/AEA/students.

American Political Science Association (2009) retrieved from world wide web www.aspanet.org, July 2009.

Anderson, C. (1993, April). "The Context of Civic Competence and Education," *Social Education:* 160–164.

Angell, A. (1991). "Democratic Climates in Elementary Classrooms: A Review of Theory and Research," *Theory and Research in Social Education:* 241–266.

Armstrong, T. (2009). *Multiple Intelligences in the Classroom.* Alexandria, VA: Association for Supervision and Curriculum Development.

Aronson, E. (2009). *Jigsaw Classroom Official Web Site.* www.jigsaw.org

Association of American Geographers (2009). "Geographic Education." retrieved from world wide web www.aag.org November, 2009.

Bales, R. (1957). *Effects of Size of Problem-Solving Groups on the System of Interaction.* Report to the
American Psychological Association. Washington, DC: APA.

Bandura, A. (1997). *Self-Efficacy: The Exercise of Control.* New York: W. H. Freeman.

Banks, J., & Banks, C. (2009). *Multicultural Education: Issues and Perspectives* (5th ed.). New York: John Wiley & Sons.

Berliner, D., & Biddle, B. (1997). *The Manufactured Crisis.* White Plains, NY: Longman.

Berman, S. (1990, November). "Educating for Social Responsibility," *Educational Leadership:* 75–80.

Beyer, B. (2008). "What Research Tells Us about Thinking Skills," *Social Studies, 99* (5): 223–232.

Biesta, G., Lawy, R., & Kelly, N. (2009). "Understanding Young People's Citizenship Learning in Everyday Life," *Education, Citizenship and Social Justice, 4* (4): 5–24.

Bloom, B. S. (1984). *Taxonomy of Educational Objectives.* Boston: Allyn & Bacon.

Bresman, D., Erdmann, A., & Olson, K. (2009). "A Learning Community Blossoms," *Educational Leadership, 66* (8): 68–71.

Brookhart, S. (2009). *Exploring Formative Assessment.* Alexandria, VA: Association for Supervision and Curriculum Development.

Bruner, J. (1963, 1994). *The Process of Education.* New York: Vintage Books.

Calderwoord, J., Lawrence, J., & Maher, J. (1970). *Economics in the Curriculum.* New York: John Wiley & Sons.

Campbell, L., & Campbell, B. (2008). *Mindful Learning.* Thousand Oaks, CA: Corwin Press.

Carnegie "Civic Education in Schools: The Right Time is Now." (2003) *Carnegie Reporter.* NY: Carnegie Corporations of New York, vol2; no.3.

Carroll, J. (1963). "A Model of School Learning," *Teachers College Record, 64:* 722–733.

Center for Information and Research on Civic Learning and Engagement. (2005). "Civics Education: What Students Are Learning." *Campaign for the Civic Mission of Schools: Educating for Democracy.* College Park: University of Maryland School of Public Policy.

Cheney, L. (2008). *We the People: The Story of Our Constitution.* New York: Simon & Schuster.

Collingwood, R. G. (1946). In T. M. Knox, ed., *The Idea of History.* London: Oxford University Press.

Cotton, K. (1996). *Educating for Citizenship.* Portland, OR: Northwest Regional Educational Laboratory.

Covey, S. (2008). *The 7 Habits of Happy Kids.* New York: Simon & Schuster.

Deutsch, M. (1949). "A Theory of Cooperation and Competition," *Human Relations, 2:* 129–152.

Devlin, S., & Freeney, A. (1973). *The Design of Surveys and Samples.* Newton, MA: Education Development Center.

Dewey, J. (1899). *The School and Society.* Boston: Houghton Mifflin.

Dewey, J. (1916). *Democracy and Education.* New York: Macmillan.

Diller, J., & Moule, J. (2005). *Cultural Competence: A Primer for Educators.* Belmont, CA: Wadsworth.

Drake, S. (2007). *Creating Standards-Based Integrated Curriculum.* Thousand Oaks, CA: Corwin Press.

Drucker, P. (1990). *The New Realities.* New York: Perennial Library.

Easton, D. (1966). *A Systems Approach to Political Life.* Boulder, CO: Social Science Education Consortium.

Ebel, R. (1971). *Measuring Educational Achievement.* Englewood Cliffs, NJ: Prentice-Hall.

Eggen, P., & Kauchak, O. (1996). *Strategies for Teachers: Teaching Content and Thinking Skills.* Boston: Allyn & Bacon.

Ellis, A. (2006). *Research on Educational Innovations.* Larchmont, NY: Eye on Education.

Ellis, A (2010). *Teaching, Learning, and Assessment Together: The Reflective Classroom* (2nd ed.). Larchmont, NY: Eye on Education.

Ellis, A., & Fouts, J. (1997). *Research on Educational Innovations* (2nd ed.). Princeton, NJ: Eye on Education.

"Ethnicity in 17th Century English in America." (2003). In R. Bayor (Ed.), *Race and Ethnicity in America.* New York: Columbia University Press.

Evans, L. (2009). *Reflective Assessment and Student Achievement.* Unpublished dissertation, Seattle Pacific University.

Fenton, E. (1967). *The New Social Studies.* New York: Holt, Rinehart, & Winston.

Fielder, W., ed. (1972). *Inquiring about American History.* New York: Holt, Rinehart, & Winston.

Fouts, J. (1989, Spring). "Classroom Environments and Student Views of Social Studies: A Replication Study," *Theory and Research in Social Education:* 136–147.

Fredericks, A. (2007). *More Social Studies through Children's Literature.* Englewood, CO: Teacher Ideas Press.

Gabriel, J. (2009). *How to Thrive as a Teacher Leader.* Alexandria, VA: Association for Supervision and Curriculum Development.

Gardner, H. (1983). *Frames of Mind: The Theory of Multiple Intelligences.* New York: Basic Books.

Gardner, H. (1991). *The Unschooled Mind.* New York: Basic Books.

Gilligan, C. (1982). *In a Different Voice: Psychological Theory and Women's Development.* Cambridge, MA: Harvard University Press.

Glasser, W. (1990). *The Quality School.* New York: Harper & Row.

Glover, R., & O'Donnel, B. (2003). "Understanding Human Rights: The Development of Perspective Taking and Empathy," *Social Studies and the Young Learner, 15* (3): 15–18.

Goodlad, J. (2004). *A Place Called School.* New York: McGraw-Hill.

Greco, P. (1966). *Geography.* Boulder, CO: Social Science Education Consortium.

Grosvenor, G. (2007). "The Excitement of Geography," *Social Studies and the Young Learner, 20* (2): 4.

Haberman, M. (1996). "Selecting and Preparing Culturally Competent Teachers for Urban Schools." In J. Sikula, T. Buttery, & H. Guyon, eds. *Handbook of Research on Teacher Education* (2nd ed.). New York: Macmillan.

Habermas, J. (1968). *Knowledge and Human Interest.* Cambridge, UK: Polity Press.

Halvorsen, L. (2009). "Back to the Future: The Expanding Communities Curriculum for Geography Education," *Social Studies, 100* (3): 115–119.

Hamilton, M. H. (2000). "Creating a Culturally Responsive Learning Environment for African American Students." In M. Magolda, ed., *Teaching to Promote Intellectual and Personal Maturity: Incorporating Students' Worldviews and Identities into the Learning Process.* San Francisco: Jossey-Bass, pp. 45–54.

Hamilton, M. H. (2004). *Meeting the Needs of African American Women: New Directions for Student Services.* San Francisco: Jossey-Bass.

Handbook of Research in Social Studies Education (2008)

Harper, R., & Schmudde, T. (1973). *Between Two Worlds: A New Introduction to Geography.* Boston: Houghton Miffiin.

Heidel, J., Lyman-Mersereau, M., & Janke, J. E. (Eds.). (1999). *Character Education: Grades K–6.* Nashville, TN: Incentive Publications.

Hirsch, E. D. (1987). *Cultural Literacy.* Boston: Houghton Miffiin.

Hirsch, E. D. (1991–2005). *The Core Knowledge Series K–8.* New York: Delta.

Jackson, P., Boostrom, R., & Hansen, D. (1993). *The Moral Life of Schools.* San Francisco: Jossey-Bass.

Johnson, D., & Johnson, R. (1974, April). "Instructional Goal Structure: Cooperative, Competitive, or Individualistic," *Review of Educational Research:* 213.

Johnson, D., & Johnson, R. (1988). *Cooperation and Competition: Theory and Research.* Edina, MN: Interaction Book Company.

Johnson, D., & Johnson, R. (2004). *Assessing Students in Groups: Promoting Group Responsibility and Individual Accountability.* Thousand Oaks, CA: Corwin.

Johnson, D., Johnson, R., & Holubec, E. (2002). *Circles of Learning.* Edina, MN: Interaction Book Company.

Johnston, J. H. (1995, November/December). "Climate: Building a Culture of Achievement." *Schools in the Middle:* 10–15.

Kaye, E. (1974). *The Family Guide to Children's Television.* New York: Random House.

Kinch, J. (1971). *Introductory Sociology: The Individual in Society.* San Rafael, CA: Individual Learning Systems.

Kirschenbaum, H. (1996). *100 Ways to Enhance Values and Morality in Schools and Youth Settings.* Boston: Allyn & Bacon.

Kohlberg, L. (1983). *The Psychology of Moral Development.* New York: Harper & Row.

Kohlberg, L., & Whitten, P. (1972, December). "Understanding the Hidden Curriculum." *Learning:* 14.

Kohn, A. (1999). *The Schools Our Children Deserve: Moving beyond Traditional Classrooms and "Tougher Standards."* Boston: Houghton Miffiin.

Krug, M. (1967). *History and the Social Sciences.* Waltham, MA: Blaisdell.

Lestvik., L., & Tyson, C. (2008). *The Handbook of Research in Social Studies Education.* New York: Routledge.

Lewis, C. S. (1947). *The Abolition of Man: How Education Develops Man's Sense of Morality.* New York: Collier Books.

Maher, J. E. (1969). *What Is Economics?* New York: John Wiley & Sons.

Marzano, R., & Arredondo, D. (1986). *Tactics for Thinking.* Aurora, CO: Mid-Continent Regional Laboratory.

McCombs, B., & Whisler, J. (1997). *The Learner-Centered Classroom and School.* San Francisco: Jossey-Bass.

Medina, J. (2003). "Brainchild: Stress and the Human Brain," *Brain Science and Human Learning, 26* (4): 24–26.

Medina, J. (2009). *Brain Rules.* Seattle, WA: Pear Press.

Meier, D. (2009). "Democracy at Risk," *Educational Leadership, 66* (8): 45–49.

Michigan Department of Education. (2001). *What Research Says about Parent Involvement in Children's Education.* Lansing: Author.

Morris, R. (2007). "Around the Blacksmith's Forge: Interdisciplinary Teaching and Learning," *Social Studies, 98* (3), 99–104.

National Adult Literacy Survey. (1993). Washington, DC: National Center for Education Statistics.

National Assessment Governing Board. (1994, 2001). *Geography Framework for the 1994 and 2001 National Assessment of Educational Progress.* Washington, DC: U.S. Department of Education.

National Assessment of Educational Progress (NAEP). (1998). *Report Card on Civics Education.*
Washington, DC: U.S. Department of Education.

National Center for Education Statistics (NCES). (1994, 2001). *National Assessment of Educational Progress: History Standards.* Washington, DC: U.S. Department of Education.

National Council for the Social Studies (NCSS). (1994). *Expectations of Excellence: Curriculum Standards for Social Studies.* Washington, DC: Author.

National Task Force for Social Studies (2006). *National Standards for Social Studies Teachers.* Waldorf, MD: National Council for the Social Studies.

National Task Force for Social Studies. (2008). *Expectations of Excellence: Curriculum Standards for*

Social Studies. Washington, DC: National Council for the Social Studies.

Nelson, P. (2005). "Preparing Students for Citizenship: Literature and Primary Documents," *Social Studies and the Young Learner, 17* (3): 21–29.

Oliver, D. (1964). *Invitation to Anthropology*. Garden City, NY: Natural History Press

O'Mahoney, C., & Seigal, S. (2008). "Designing Classroom Spaces to Maximize Social Studies Learning," *Social Studies and the Young Learner, 21*(2): 25–27.

Onosko, J., & Newmann, F. (1994). "Creating More Thoughtful Learning Environments. In J. Mangieri & C. Block, eds., *Creating Powerful Thinking in Teachers and Students*. Fort Worth, TX: Harcourt Brace.

Papert, S. (1984). *Mindstorms*. New York: Basic Books.

Perrucci, R. (1966). *Sociology*. Boulder, CO: Social Science Education Consortium.

Piaget, J. (1965). *The Moral Development of the Child*. New York: Free Press.

Rest, J., Narvaez, M., Bebeau, M. J., & Thoma, S. J. (1999). *Postconventional Moral Thinking: A Neo-Kohlbergian Approach*. New York: Erlbaum.

Rogers, C., & Frieberg, J. (1994). *Freedom to Learn* (3rd ed.). New York: Macmillan.

Rose, C. (1965). *Sociology: The Study of Man in Society*. Columbus, OH: Merrill.

Rowe, D. (1992). "A Conflict Model of Citizenship Education," *Curriculum*.

Rubin, B., & Giarelli, J. (2007). *Civic Education for Diverse Citizens in Global Times: Rethinking Theory and Practice*. New York: Lawrence Erlbaum Associates.

Scheuerman, R., & Ellis, A., eds. (2003). *North American Journeys of Discovery: The Expedition of Lewis & Clark*. Madison, WI: DEMCO.

Scheuerman, R., & Ellis, A. eds. (2004). *The Expeditions of Lewis and Clark and Zebulon Pike*. Madison, WI: DEMCO.

Schug, M., et al. (1984). "Why Don't Kids Like Social Studies?" *Social Studies Education, 48*: 382–387.

Schumacher, E. F. (1973). *Small Is Beautiful*. New York: Harper & Row.

Senn, P. (1971). *Social Science and Its Methods*. Boston: Holbrook Press.

Sharp, R., & Ellis, A. (1994). *Greenbelt Design*. Unpublished paper, Project 2061, American Association for the Advancement of Science.

Shearer, C. (2007). "Geographic Education Standards: An Overview for Teachers," *Social Studies and the Young Learner, 20* (2): 5–6.

Sheindlin, J. (2000). *Win or Lose by How You Choose*. New York: HarperCollins.

Simon, S., Kirschenbaum, H., & Howe, L. (1973). *Values Clarification*. New York: Hart.

Snyder, T., Dillow, S., Hoffman, C., & (ED), N. (2009). *Digest of Education Statistics, 2008. NCES 2009-020.* Washington, D.C.: National Center for Education Statistics.

Sommer, C. H. (2000). *The War against Boys: How Misguided Feminism Is Harming Our Young Men.* New York: Simon & Schuster.

Stearns, P. (1993). *Why Study History?* Washington, DC: The American Historical Society.

Stearns, P. (2006). *Childhood in World History.* New York: Routledge.

Sternberg, R. (1986). *Intelligence Applied: Understanding and Increasing Your Intellectual Skills.* San Diego: Harcourt Brace Jovanovich.

Strickland, C. (2009). *Exploring Differentiated Instruction.* Alexandria, VA: Association for Supervision and Curriculum Development.

"Teaching Social Responsibility." (2009). *Educational Leadership, 66* (8). Entire issue devoted to
social/civic theme.

Tomey-Purta, J. (1982). "Global Awareness Survey: Implications for Teacher Education," *Theory into Practice:* 200–205.

Tomey-Purta, J. (1983). "Psychological Perspectives on Enhancing Civic Education through the Education of Teachers," *Journal of Teacher Education:* 30–34.

Vogler, K., et. al. (2007, October). "Getting Off the Back Burner: The Impact of Testing Elementary Social Studies as Part of a State-Mandated Accountability Program," *Journal of Social Studies Research.*

Vygotsky, L. (1986). *Thought and Language,* A. Kozulin, trans. Cambridge, MA: MIT Press.

Wade, R. (2009). "A Pebble in a Pond." *Educational Leadership, 66* (8): 50–53.

Wadsworth, B. (2004). *Piaget's Theory of Cognitive and Affective Development* (5th ed.). Boston: Allyn & Bacon.

Ward, P. (1971). "The Awkward Social Science: History." In V. Morrissett & W Stevens, eds., *Social Science in the Schools.* New York: Holt, Rinehart, & Winston.

Watkins, F. (1960). In V. Van Dyke, ed., *Political Science: A Philosophical Analysis.* Stanford, CA: Stanford University Press.

Watson, G., & Johnson, D. (1972). *Social Psychology: Issues and Insights.* Philadelphia: Lippincott.

Wenmik, S. (2004). "Reporting on the Process of Legislation: A Civics WebQuest," *Social Studies and the Young Learner, 17* (1): 11–14.

West, M. (2007). "Problem Solving: A Sensible Approach to Children's Science and Social Studies Learning—and Beyond," *Young Children, 62* (5): 34–41.

Whitehead, A. (1929). *Aims of Education.* New York: Free Press.

Index

Credits